W9-ARA-238

Anglo-Saxon Saints and Heroes

The world of the hero-saints of the anglo-saxon golden age
iona
firth of forth
coldingham
lindisfarne
melrose
bamburgh
north sea
roman wall
jarrow
carlisle
monkwearmouth
hexham
ripon
whitby
northumbria
irish sea
york
humber r.
repton
wales
lichfield
crowland
burgh castle
mercia
east anglia
london
kent
weald
canterbury
wessex
sussex
exeter
nursling
selsey
english channel
quentavic
frisia
zuyder zee
utrecht
rhine r.
cologne
fulda
mainz
echternach
paris
meaux

ANGLO-SAXON SAINTS AND HEROES

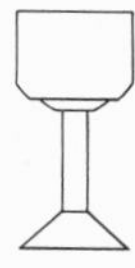

CLINTON ALBERTSON, S.J.

FORDHAM UNIVERSITY PRESS

Library of Congress Catalog Card Number; 67-16652

For My Mother and Father

CONTENTS

Northumbrian Golden Age (c. 670-730)

	Cuthbert	Wilfrid	B. Biscop	Ceolfrith	Willibrord	Guthlac	Boniface
			628 born				
633 *Edwin* †							
634 ⚔ Heavenfield	634? born	634 born					
635 Aidan to Lindisfarne							
642 *Oswald* †				642 born			
		648 Lindisfarne					
651 Aidan †	651 Melrose						
		652 Kent					
			653? Rome				
655 ⚔ Winwaed		655-8 Gaul					
					658 born		
	660? Ripon			660? Gilling			
		661? Ripon		661? Ripon			
664 Synod of Whitby	664 Lindisfarne	664 consecration in Gaul					
		666 expelled by *Oswy*	665? Rome & Lérins 668 Rome		665 Ripon		
669 Theodore arrives		669 restored					
670 *Oswy* †							
671 ff. *Ecgfrith's* early victories			671 Rome				
		672-8 Church at Ripon & Hexham			673? a monk		
			674 Monkwearmouth fd.	674 Monkwearmouth		674? born	675? born
	676 ff. Farne Is.						
		678 exiled by *Ecgfrith*	678 Rome 679? receives Bede	678 Rome B. Biscop	678 (-690) Ireland		
			681? Jarrow fd.	681? Jarrow			680? monastery at Exeter
			684? Rome				
685 ⚔ Nechtansmere	685-7 bishop						

688? Lindisfarne Gospels	687† on Farne	686 reconciliation	689? Biscop †	688? abbot of Monkwearmouth & Jarrow	690? Utrecht	689?(-698) warrior	then to Nursling
		691 exiled by *Aldfrith*			695 consecration in Rome	698 Repton 699 Crowland	
704 *Aldfrith* †		703? final trip to Rome 710 Wilfrid †					
714 Pippin II † 716 *Osred* †				716 Ceolfrith †		714 Guthlac†	716 Friesland 717 Nursling 718 Friesland 719 commissioned in Rome
718 *Cenred* † 719 Radbod †							722 consecration in Rome
729 *Osric* † 731 Bede's *History* 731? *Ceolwulf* deposed & restored 735 Bede † 737 *Eadbert* king: *Ceolwulf* becomes monk at Lindisfarne							732 Gregory III sends pallium
741 C. Martel † 751? Pippin III crowned					739 Willibrord †		738 Rome 3rd time 751? anoints Pippin III 754 Boniface †
757 Offa succeeds Aethelbald							

† = death of
⚔ = battle
italics = Northumbrian King

LIST OF PLATES

FRONTISPIECE: *The World of the Hero-Saints of the Anglo-Saxon Golden Age*

Plates I-VIII appear between pages 160-161

I. *The Lindisfarne Gospels* (fol. 27^r) (British Museum, Cotton Nero D IV)
This beautifully illuminated first page of St. Matthew's gospel reflects the whole rich amalgam of Northumbrian Golden Age culture. In the decorative pattern are Celtic spiral designs and Germanic interlaced beasts, while Coptic influence seems indicated by the broken border (at three of the four corners) of the page. The Roman Vulgate text with Northumbrian variants, written in Hiberno-Saxon script and glossed in Anglo-Saxon, is from a Gospel-codex written near Naples (from whence came Abbot Hadrian) in the sixth century. The whole is colored with finely graded shades of red, yellow, blue, green, purple, pink, brown, white and gold.
The Latin and Anglo-Saxon reads:
Ᵽ (= chi rho monogram) ihs (= Jesus) Xps (=Christus)
Matheus homo
onginneð godspelles cynreccenisse
incipit evangelii genelogia Mathei
bóc cneurise haelendes cristes
LIBER GENERATIONIS IHU (=Jesu)XPI (=Christi)
sunu davides sunu abrahames
FILII DAVID ΦILII ABRAHAM

II. *The Lindisfarne Gospels* (fol. 25^v)
This portrait page preceding St. Matthew's gospel contains almost no Celtic or Germanic ornament and reflects predominantly the Roman and Byzantine elements in Northumbria's Golden Age. Below the Latin "imago hominis", written in Anglo-Saxon script, stands the Greek "HAGIOS" and the Latin "MATTHEUS". The Matthew

some Germanic legend in which warriors are attacking a defended building.

X. *Franks Casket* (sinister portion of front panel)
British Museum. Photograph supplied by Mr. Geoffrey Ashburner, as above. Among the Franks Casket's scenes from Germanic and Roman heroic legend and history is introduced this Gospel scene of the Magi (so titled by the runic characters just above their heads) presenting gifts to Mary and the Christ Child. The larger Germanic runes around the outer edge explain that this is the bone of a whale which the sea had stranded on the rocky shore.

XI. *Ruthwell Cross*
The great cross in position inside the church of Ruthwell, Dumfriesshire, where it was moved in 1887. Another product of the Northumbrian Golden Age, the cross originally stood nearby in the open air.

XII. *Ruthwell Cross* (north face)
From a cast in the Victoria and Albert Museum. Photograph supplied by the Warburg Institute, University of London.

XIII. *Ruthwell Cross* (center panel of north face)
From a cast in the Victoria and Albert Museum. Photograph supplied by the Warburg Institute, University of London.

PREFACE

THE FOLLOWING HAGIOGRAPHIES, representing the earliest important surviving body of Old English literature, were written in Latin by Anglo-Saxons, probably all monks. (Two others belong in this group: the *Life of St. Gregory* by an anonymous monk of Whitby, soon to appear in a much-needed new edition and translation by Bertram Colgrave, and Bede's *Life of St. Cuthbert*, based on the earlier anonymous *Life of St. Cuthbert* which I have chosen to translate.) They serve to remind us that Old English culture grew up amid a late Roman context, and they make more evident how great a novelty the Anglo-Saxons' written vernacular literature is in the seventh- and eighth-century western world. The best introduction even to this Anglo-Saxon literature is probably a study of late imperial Latin rhetoric and early Christian Latin literature (see note 52 to Introduction), including patristic commentaries on the Scripture around which monastic life revolved. Aldhelm and Bede, respectively the first and the greatest scholars of the Anglo-Saxon Golden Age, have left us nothing written in the vernacular except for the few verses of Bede's "Death Song." They continued, each in his own way, the literary tradition of late Latin "mannerism" and rhetoric with increased emphasis on the early Christian substitution of the Bible for the pagan classics (see Curtius, *European Literature and the Latin Middle Ages*, pp. 46 ff., pp. 457 ff.; Laistner, *Intellectual Heritage of the Early Middle Ages*, p. 96).

Like a Germanic warrior wearing newly-captured Roman armor, the Anglo-Saxon monk handles Latin proudly but awkwardly, and with a boyish curiosity and enthusiasm. The early medieval Latin that he learned was not the best, by classical standards, and he studied it with a predominantly practical ecclesiastical purpose which usually resulted (always with the exception of Bede) in even less literary polish (see note 52 to Introduction). But his eager sincerity makes up for any lack of finesse. In my translations I have tried to retain as much of the fresh charm and vitality of this Latin as possible, even at the expense of transmitting some of the awkwardness. Its rhetorical parallelism, its epic formality, its alliteration (all often unsophisticatedly excessive, but often echoing a rich Germanic heritage of oral heroic poetry) are necessary ingredients of its own special flavor. The qualities of this prose preserve the spell of a never-to-be-recalled moment in the life of western man, when the heroic Germanic mind began deliberately and self-consciously to think and to write as a Christian Roman. The translator who tries to modernize here will very likely lose more than he gains. Of course I have broken up impossibly long sentences and rearranged rambling periods, and tried to make more specific whatever colorful possibilities seemed to be legitimately intended in somewhat general Latin expressions. For instance, *vir* ("man"), I very often translate as "hero." The context seems to make this interpretation obvious, especially in the many instances where their biographers apply it to Cuthbert and to Guthlac. Vergil's *arma virumque cano* would be precedent enough, but there are sufficient examples in Anglo-Saxon heroic poetry too. *Wer*, the Anglo-Saxon cognate of *vir*, seems clearly to mean "hero" in line 3172 (completed by Grein) of *Beowulf*, and in *Andreas* it often alternates with *haeleþ* ("hero"), depending upon the prosodic pattern of the particular line (for instance, see verses 144 and 1171).

Throughout the book I have taken pains to reproduce the original works as faithfully as possible, within the limits of readability. Whatever insertions I have made for clarity's sake, and all summaries of untranslated portions (space prohibited complete translation) are contained within square brackets. My intention, admittedly and perhaps overly optimistic, has been to produce a translation that would be of interest to the layman and not without value for the scholar.

For better or for worse, every bit of translation in this book, even that in the notes, is my own—except for Scripture quotations. Wherever I may have been able to improve on previous translations, the reason is very likely to be found in newer aids which have been available to me, such as J. F. Niermeyer's *Mediae Latinitatis Lexicon Minus* (Leiden, 1954 ff.).

On the exasperating question of the spelling of Anglo-Saxon names I have attempted to hold to the versions more commonly agreed upon among recent standard Anglo-Saxon studies. Each man who is the subject of a hagiography in this book is a saint in the Roman Calendar, even though the customary title of his Life may not so indicate. My principle on dates has been to follow Plummer for the most part, but Levison on disputed dates (see note 34 to *Life of Wilfrid*). In the notes only short titles are given for those items which are fully identified in the Bibliographical Note.

I am indebted to Loyola University of Los Angeles for granting me a sabbatical year, 1961-2, at Oxford University to begin the final research for this book and to travel north through the Golden Age land of Cuthbert and Wilfrid and Bede. Here at Loyola the University's clerical staff and the staff of the Von der Ahe Library gave me much gracious and expert assistance.

PREFACE

I am grateful to a number of scholars who kindly helped me with the book at Oxford in a variety of ways, direct and indirect, mostly by resolving questions for me and by proposing further questions in return: C. L. Wrenn (who also first opened the doors of Anglo-Saxon England for me over a decade ago), Norman Davis, J. A. W. Bennett, Ian Richmond, R. W. Southern, C. H. V. Sutherland, J. D. A. Thompson. Perhaps my greatest debt is to Bertram Colgrave, whose fine editions of three of these lives made my task so much easier and whose kindness in writing long answers to my questions was much appreciated. The shortcomings in the book, however, are my own responsibility.

For permission to make use of material previously published in a journal ("Anglo-Saxon Literature and Western Culture," *Thought*, Vol. 33 [1958] pp. 93-116), I wish to thank the editor, Joseph E. O'Neill, S. J.

For graciously providing me with photographs for some of the plates in this book and for granting or obtaining permission to reproduce them, I wish to thank Mr. G. S. Ashburner, of Colour Centre Slides, Ltd., Farnham Royal, Slough, Buckinghamshire; Mrs. Enriquetta Frankfort, of the Warburg Institute, University of London; the Librarian of the Bodleian Library, Oxford University; the Printer to the University of Oxford; Dr. W. O. Hassall, of the Department of Western Manuscripts at the Bodleian Library; the Royal Commission on Historical Monuments, The National Buildings Record, Fielden House, Westminster; the Ministry of Public Building and Works, London.

Collette Ecker and Fred Marx drew the Map of the World of the Hero-Saints of the Anglo-Saxon Golden Age. The Index owes much to the generous help of some of my students.

My thanks are also due to Vincent Blehl, S.J., of Fordham University, who first encouraged me to do this book, to Charles W. Kennedy, of Princeton University, who added encouragement along the way, and finally but by no means least, to my editor, Edwin A. Quain, S.J., whose expert care and great knowledge of things medieval have contributed much to the book.

Loyola University of Los Angeles CLINTON ALBERTSON, S.J.

INTRODUCTION

This is a book about heroes. More exactly, it is a book full of heroes, in which the heroes speak for themselves.

"Heroic Age" has long since become a sober, professional term, and there are any number of literary, historical, and sociological studies of the various Heroic Ages of the world—from Gilgamesh's Sumeria and Homeric Greece to the American Wild West.[1] But this is not another book *about* Heroic Ages. Instead, it is an attempt to swing open the great gates of one particular Heroic Age, one Camelot that went its golden way for a few years in the life of our planet, and to let you come inside and see it for itself. It lies in the Anglo-Saxon kingdom of Northumbria in Britain of the late-seventh and early-eighth centuries. Like that of all Heroic Ages it is a land of spaciousness of spirit. For a traveller from our Age of the Common Man, where "heroic" has become "neurotic," it is likely to be either exasperating or spellbinding—but hardly boring. It has the power to intoxicate with the perilous fascination of the gigantic, the larger-than-life-size. Its charm is not reserved for the scholar, whether in history or in literature, but awaits every reader interested in the spiritual odyssey of western man.

As a technical term, "Heroic Age" refers in our western world to two periods especially. The first centers about the Homeric warrior-kings and sea rovers of Mycenae who sacked Troy and probably Minoan Crete, and the second is the period, some 1600 years later, when the Germanic tribes moved west and south and "sacked" the Roman Empire. Both were times when a world was in the morning of things. Peoples were on the move, society was not resettled into

1. H. M. Chadwick's *The Heroic Age* (Cambridge, 1912) is the classic book on the subject. Jan de Vries' recent *Heroic Song and Heroic Legend* is a perceptive and wide-ranging introduction to the Heroic Age literature of many peoples, as is W. P. Ker's older *Epic and Romance* (London, 2nd edition, 1908). See also C. M. Bowra, *Heroic Poetry* (London, 1952), G. R. Levy, *The Sword from the Rock* (London, 1953), A. B. Lord, *The Singer of Tales* (Cambridge, Mass., 1960). See R. W. Chambers' essay, "*Beowulf* and the Heroic Age," in his *Man's Unconquerable Mind* (London, 1939), and Gilbert Murray's "The Heroic Age" in his *The Classical Tradition in Poetry* (Cambridge, Mass., 1927).

stable patterns, fortunes were waiting for the daring, and kingdoms could be won by personal courage. The virtues of the warrior and of the bold adventurer determined the ideal tone of life. Society revolved around the strong, enterprising chieftain and his courageous band of followers.[2] The essential cohesive elements were the personal loyalty of the retainers and the large-hearted liberality and bold strength of the leader.

> I remember well the times when we drank mead together. There in the feasting hall did we pledge ourselves to this lord of ours who showered treasures on us. We vowed if ever he should be in sore distress like this that we would make him good return for the gifts of war-gear—the helmets and the hard swords. And so he picked us freely from out the whole host for this exploit. He deemed us worthy of glorious deeds and gave us gifts, for he recked us good men with a spear, valiant warriors.... Now the day has come when our liege lord has need of the might of brave warriors. Let us take our stand at the side of our battle-chief as long as this grim and terrible flame threatens. As for me, God knows I would much rather that the fire swallowed me up along with my treasure-lord. I would deem it disgrace to return home again with our armor unless we first had felled the foe and protected the life of the lord of the Geats.[3]

An aristocracy of the brave evolved, whose ideals of life came in time to be summed up in the hero and sung by the poet. Jason, Achilles,

2. The personal retainers of the Homeric kings were the *hetairoi*, and the Germanic kings had their *comites* or "companions" (Cf. later Frankish "counts"). The *comites* constituted the *comitatus*, and Tacitus described for all time the relationship of the first-century Germanic chieftain and his *comitatus* (*Germania*, Chs. 13, 14). See note 24.

3. *Beowulf*, vv. 2633-2642; 2646-2656. Wiglaf, the loyal Geatish warrior, is attempting, without avail, to stir his comrades into coming to Beowulf's aid when the latter is hard pressed by a fire-breathing dragon.

In the same terms, loyal warriors exhort each other in the last of the Anglo-Saxon heroic poems, *The Battle of Maldon*, and vow to fight to the death around the body of their fallen lord (see Plate VIII). The symbol of utter woe in the Heroic Age was the lordless man. In that magnificent Anglo-Saxon poem, *The Wanderer*, such a lonely vagabond is tormented by memories of happier days when he greeted his lord in the hall with an embrace and a kiss, and knelt before him to pledge his loyalty and receive gifts of treasure (vv. 41-44). And in the doomed pass at Roncevaux, Roland exhorts the Frankish knights with almost the same Heroic Age appeal (*Song of Roland*, laisse 88, for example).

Odysseus, Ermanric, Attila, Siegfried, Theodric, all reached immortality by similar paths.

Obviously, however, the Greek and Germanic Heroic Ages are not the only ones, even in the western world, with a right to this title. There have been other ages of warriors and poets, where society was structured on a nobility of courage and daring. The Viking Age is one, and Romanesque France of the *chansons de geste* is another. We can speak of a Celtic Heroic Age, and the Anglo-Saxon Heroic Age. It is with this latter that the present book is concerned.

The Anglo-Saxon Heroic Age is of course but an extension of the Germanic Heroic Age to Romano-Celtic Britain. There, in the mid-fifth century, tradition tells us Hengest's and Horsa's adventurers poured across the Channel after the defending legions had been pulled south in a vain effort to save Rome.[4] It is mostly with the founding of the northernmost of the Anglo-Saxon kingdoms, Northumbria (i.e., north of the Humber River), that this book has to do. It was the first to achieve greatness, and much of its greatness, both military and cultural, was never equalled by the two which were to flourish later—Mercia in the midlands and Wessex in the south. And of course its reputation enjoys the enormous advantage of the fact that Anglo-Saxon England's greatest chronicler and the glory of her Golden Age, Bede, was a Northumbrian.

The beginnings of Northumbria are shrouded in the North Sea mist and it is not till the middle of the sixth century that with the aid of Bede and Nennius we can catch historical sight of anything.[5] This part of Britain was early divided into a southern kingdom, Deira, and a northern one, Bernicia, whose first Anglian king, Ida, reigned from 547. Bernicia and Deira are, in origin, Welsh names, and it was from the Welsh and Scots (i. e., Irish) and Picts that the invaders slowly wrested this northern land. The Angles seem originally to have come in small pirating expeditions like the Homeric Achaean freebooters who plundered through the archipelago and on the coast of Ionia. Some Germanic peoples had already been settled in Northumbria as mercenaries by the Romans. Now, in the latter half of the sixth cen-

4. Bede, *Ecclesiastical History*, Bk. I, ch. 15. And see following note.

5. For recent discussions of this early history of Northumbria, with references to what sources there are, see Chadwick, *Celt and Saxon*, pp. 323 ff., and Blair, *Roman Britain and Early England*, pp. 186 ff. Nennius is the supposed and much-disputed author or editor of a history of the Britons (*Historia Brittonum*) dating from about the eighth century (see Chadwick, *Studies in the Early British Church*, pp. 37-46). Bede is the eighth-century Northumbrian monk and scholar whose classic history of the Anglo-Saxon church will figure prominently in the whole of our book, and whose *Lives of the Abbots* we translate.

tury the sun was just setting on a Celtic Heroic Age in western and northern Britain.[6] Welsh kings bore Roman military titles and left inscriptions behind them couched in all the proud formality of the Imperial Byzantine court.[7] The heroic songs of their kingly families and the chronicles of Nennius tell of nameless battles with Germanic "robbers" perched on the rock fortress of Bamburgh that frowns over the North Sea some thirty miles down the east coast from the Firth of Forth.[8] Bamburgh was to become the Acropolis of the Bernician royal family which was to dominate the Northumbrian Golden Age. Celtic heroic songs and chronicles tell of prince after prince who fought the Saxons and gained renown in British poetry.[9] Most famous of them all was Arthur, whose legend was to follow a fortune almost as strange as the marvelous Welsh stories which surround its birth. From beleaguered Wales it fled across the Channel to Celtic Brittany, and then returned to England in Norman romance-garb to conquer the literary world of its Saxon conquerors.[10]

The Gododdin, a Welsh poem, good portions of which, at least, are by the British bard, Aneirin, of the late-sixth century, is starkly beau-

6. See Chadwick, *Celt and Saxon*, pp. 158 ff., 325 ff. Chadwick, *Studies in Early British History*, pp. 29-120. Lloyd, *A History of Wales*, I, chs. 5, 6.

7. See Nash-Williams, *Early Christian Monuments in Wales* (University of Wales Press, 1950), pp. 55 ff.

8. Nennius, *Historia Brittonum*, pp. 78-83. Translated also in Whitelock, *English Historical Documents*, pp. 236-38. See Plate V.

9. Nennius, *Historia Brittonum*, p. 80; I. Williams, *Lectures on Early Welsh Poetry*, pp. 50 ff., pp. 67 ff.; G. Williams, *An Introduction to Welsh Poetry*, pp. 18 ff.; Parry, *A History of Welsh Literature*, Ch. 1. The tragic old warrior, Llywarch, lost twenty-four sons one after another in battles against the Anglo-Saxons. Historically he was of the sixth century, a relative of the great Urien of Rheged, but the extant heroic poems about him seem to be of a later date (see I. Williams, *op. cit.*, pp. 34 ff.; G. Williams, *op. cit.*, pp. 32 ff.)

10. The possibility of an historical fifth-century British war-leader named Arthur has been adroitly sifted by Kenneth Jackson from the various Welsh sources (see pages 1 to 19 in Loomis, *Arthurian Literature in the Middle Ages*). Attempts to attribute late Roman cavalry tactics, however, to this Arthur (see, for instance, the fascinating conjectures of Collingwood in *Roman Britain and the English Settlements*, pp. 320-24), Jackson judges illusory. It is important to realize that the font of the Arthurian tradition was a mass of mostly unrecorded popular songs and stories of the pre-Latin British Heroic Age (Jackson, *op. cit.*, pp. 12 ff.; Loomis, *Wales and the Arthurian Legend*, pp. 20 ff.) shot through, however, with the borrowed glamor of Rome and her legions (Loomis, *op. cit.*, Ch. 1. David Jones, "Wales and the Crown," in *Selection II*, edited by C. Hastings and Nicholl [London, 1954] pp. 50-51).

tiful in the Heroic-Age way, combining the doomed courage of Nordic saga with Celtic color and verve. It tells how the lord of Dunedin (later Edinburgh) trained 300 picked British warriors for a year and feasted them on ale and mead. Then he sent them south to take the key Northumbrian stronghold at *Catraeth* (Catterick in Yorkshire), which the Romans had guarded with a fort and which the Celtic prince, Urien, had once held. Mounted on white horses and clad in Roman armor, bearing javelins and heavy spears, just as Arthur's British troops are often imagined (elsewhere in the poem, Aneirin actually mentions Arthur. See note 10), the war-band cantered down the level stretches of Watling Street, singing and bantering as they rode along. Charging furiously into battle against a vastly superior English force, they were finally cut down almost to a man.

About the year 580, four British kings (including the great Urien of Rheged whose kingdom was probably centered on old Roman Carlisle) swept the Bernician King Theodric from royal Bamburgh out to the off-shore island of Lindisfarne (to be made so famous by Aidan and by Cuthbert) where they besieged him three days and three nights.[11] But Ida's grandson, Aethelfrith, opened Northumbria's Heroic Age. He became king of all Northumbria by marrying the daughter of King Aella of Deira (whose name had occasioned the famous pun by Pope Gregory, recorded in the *Life of St. Gregory* by a monk of Whitby[12]) and exiling her brother Edwin. He crushed the Scots

11. Nennius, *Historia Brittonum*, p. 81. From what we can glean of him in Welsh song, legend and chronicle, Urien appears as lord of one of the most princely and Christian of sixth-century Heroic Age British families. Like Arthur, though to a lesser extent, he became a figure of later medieval romance, but we also possess some heroic poems composed about him by his own bard, Taliesin (G. Williams, *An Introduction to Welsh Poetry*, pp. 25 ff.; I. Williams, *Lectures on Early Welsh Poetry*, pp. 49 ff.; Parry, *A History of Welsh Literature*, pp. 1-3; Kenneth Jackson, "On the Northern British Section in Nennius," and Nora Chadwick, "The Celtic Background of Early Anglo-Saxon England"—both in Chadwick, *Celt and Saxon*). Welsh tradition has it that one of his sons, Rhun, became a monk and that he baptized the famous Edwin of Northumbria (see note 13), son of that King Aethelfrith who so harried the British (Nora Chadwick, "The Conversion of Northumbria," in Chadwick, *Celt and Saxon*). Carlisle may have been the center of Urien's kingdom (Chadwick, *op. cit.*, p. 159) and, in a further intertwining of the threads of this Heroic Age tapestry, tradition has it that Aethelfrith's grandson, King Ecgfrith, granted Carlisle to St. Cuthbert when the latter was made bishop (Chadwick, *Studies in Early British History*, p. 120).

12. See translation in Jones, *Saints' Lives and Chronicles in Early England*, pp. 103-04. And the same story is recorded by Bede (*Ecclesiastical History*,

of Dalriada in 603, and about 615 the Welsh at the Battle of Chester.[13] Before the latter battle Bede tells us he savagely slaughtered 1,200 monks from Bangor who had come out to pray for a British victory. But in 616 Edwin returned from exile (which may for a considerable part of the time have been among the Welsh. See note 13) and, with the help of King Raedwald of East Anglia, defeated and killed Aethelfrith in the Battle of the Idle. Aethelfrith's sons, Oswald and Oswy, fled into exile among the Picts and Scots, and Edwin ruled undisputedly over all of Northumbria. His power was felt as far south as Wessex, and west into Wales. In 627 he became Northumbria's first Christian king, baptized by Paulinus who was sent up from Kent, where England's first Roman missionary, Augustine, had established his see at Canterbury.[14]

Bk. II, ch. I). Bertram Colgrave is readying a new edition (and translation) of the Whitby *St. Gregory* to replace the old one by Cardinal Gasquet (Westminster, 1904).

13. The Irish king defeated here was Aedán mac Gabráin whom St. Columba had consecrated King of Dalriada in 574 at Iona (Adamnan, *Life of Columba*, Bk. III, ch. 5). Some hint of the crusading fervor with which the king campaigned against the Saxons may be seen in the fact that he named one of his sons Arthur (Jackson, "The Historicity of Arthur," in Loomis, *Arthurian Literature in the Middle Ages*. See pp. 3 and 4). And later kings, Henry II and Henry VII, were to bestow Arthur's magic name on their grandsons and sons, with a political eye to the Welsh.

A Welsh tradition, ignored by Bede, says that young Edwin of Deira spent the first years of his exile in Wales where he was raised by King Cadfan along with the latter's own son, Cadwallon, and that there he was baptized by the priestly son of King Urien (Plummer, *Baedae Opera Historica*, II, 114-5. Chadwick, *Celt and Saxon*, pp. 147 ff.). King Edwin's later attack on Cadwallon's kingdom would thus have been doubly hateful to the Welsh king and would help explain the ferocity with which the latter overwhelmed Edwin and his army in 633 and ravaged Northumbria (Bede, *Ecclesiastical History*, Bk. II, ch. 20). And the Battle of Chester, some fifteen years before the Battle of Hatfield, may have been occasioned by Aethelfrith's rage at the Welsh for harboring Edwin (Chadwick, *Celt and Saxon*, Ch. 5; Bede, *Ecclesiastical History*, Bk. II, ch. 2). The Anglian king's slaughter of the Celtic monks at Chester recalls the massacre of the Druids on Anglesey by the Roman legions of Suetonius Paulinus some five and a half centuries previously (Tacitus, *Annals*, Bk. IV, ch. 30).

14. In Bk. II, ch. 13 of the *Ecclesiastical History* Bede tells his unforgettable story of Edwin's debate with his counsellors and nobles about the feasibility of accepting the new religion. One of his nobles advised him thus: "My king, when I compare the span of life that a man knows on earth to all that rest of time which stretches beyond his ken, it seems to me like this. Suppose that

His reign was one of power and peace that laid the foundation for the brilliant Northumbrian Golden Age that was to come. As that Golden Age in turn was coming to an end, Bede was to look back wistfully at the veritable *pax Romana* which Edwin had established in his barbarian land. In an epic passage at the end of Chapter XVI of Book II in his *Ecclesiastical History*, Bede recalls how the peace was so strong in Edwin's day that a woman with a newborn baby could walk over all the island from sea to sea without being molested, and that, partly out of fear for their king but more out of love, no one even dared disturb the copper drinking cups which Edwin had provided along the highways wherever there was a spring. Such was Edwin's regal dignity that as he rode about his kingdom with his *comitatus* he was preceded, as he was in battle, by a standard-bearer displaying the royal banner, Roman fashion.

But still it was an unstable Heroic Age where peace was dependent on personal prowess and the chance of battle. Edwin, like the king before him, was killed in battle, in 633, by Cadwallon of Wales and Penda of Mercia. Back from their Celtic exile, during which they had accepted baptism, came the sons of Aethelfrith, and the very next year Oswald killed Cadwallon at the Battle of Heavenfield, near the Roman Wall not far from Hexham.[15]

Oswald soon became the subject of saga and legend, one of the first Englishmen to combine the hero and the saint. His memory took on that tone of martial Christianity so characteristic of the *chansons de geste* of crusading France. He provided the grand gesture, on which hero-cults grow, by erecting a wooden cross in the field just before the Battle of Heavenfield.[16] And in a dream-vision in his tent before the battle, St. Columba had appeared to him and promised him vic-

sometime when you and your princes and nobles are at table in wintertime, with a fire in the midst of the hall to warm you while storms of rain or snow rage around the world outside, suddenly a sparrow flits through the room. Darting in at one doorway it flashes right out again through another. For that one instant in the hall it is safe from the storm blast, but once this too brief moment of peace is spent the bird disappears from your sight back into the winter from which it came. Now just such a fleeting appearance is this life of man. And of what is to follow it or of what has gone before it we know nothing at all. So if this new teaching offers to push back that darkness any further I would say it is meet we accept it."

15. All the greatest Northumbrian kings were to be of Bernicia from now on, though Oswald's brother, Oswy, would unite the two houses by marrying Edwin's daughter, Eanfled, just as Oswald's father, Aethelfrith, had married Edwin's sister, daughter of King Aella of Deira.

16. Bede, *Ecclesiastical History*, Bk. III, ch. 2.

tory.[17] So Oswald's cross, as had Constantine's, became a victory symbol and played an incalculable psychological part in the Christianization of his pagan countrymen. His royal sway reached far. He was guest of honor at the baptism of King Cynegils of Wessex, and had no little say in that king's granting of Dorchester (in Oxfordshire) as the episcopal see for Birinus, the Apostle of Wessex.[18] Oswald carried on the construction of the church in York, which Paulinus had begun and Wilfrid was to finish.[19] But Oswald's heart was not in Roman York. The Roman Bishop Paulinus had fled south when Edwin was killed, so Oswald invited the Celtic monks to convert Northumbria. His exile had been spent among them, partly at the monastery of Iona, founded by the great Columba; he had been baptized by them, and spoke their language.[20] So at Oswald's request Aidan came from Iona and established a monastery on the island of Lindisfarne, in easy distance of royal Bamburgh, in the very heartland of Bernicia. And thus the full flood of that Celtic monastic contribution to Northumbria's Golden Age poured into a kingdom which had already long been subject to Celtic influences.[21]

17. Adamnan, *Life of Columba*, Bk. I, ch. 1.
18. Bede, *Ecclesiastical History*, Bk. III, ch. 7.
19. Eddius, *Life of Wilfrid*, Ch. 16.
20. Bede, *Ecclesiastical History*, Bk. III, ch. 3.
21. The proximity of royal Bamburgh and of the *villa regia* of Yeavering to Lindisfarne created a Hiberno-Saxon cultural heartland in Northumbria, especially during the reigns of the Celtic-exile kings, Oswald, Oswy, and Aldfrith, and it was here that "the main features of the Hiberno-Saxon style" of Golden Age art were put together (Bruce-Mitford, *Evangeliorum Quattuor Codex Lindisfarnensis*, II, 251-252). And though Aidan must have been reluctant to accept it, kingly patronage provided Lindisfarne with the wealth necessary to produce its Golden Age art. Hundreds of sheep or calves would have to have been provided, for instance, just to furnish the pages for the *Lindisfarne Gospels* (see note 29).

Then, besides the exile-kings of Bamburgh, another Celtic influence was the great number of young Anglo-Saxons who flocked to the Irish schools and who must have brought back much of Celtic culture with them (Bede, *Ecclesiastical History*, Bk. III, ch. 27). Ceolfrith's brother was one of these student-exiles (Anonymous *Life of Ceolfrith*, Ch. 3) and so was Willibrord (Alcuin, *Life of Willibrord*, Ch. 4).

Much of the Celtic influence was specifically Christian and religious, and extended into the liturgy. In a "Liturgical Note" to the Celtic *Book of Cerne*, Edmund Bishop remarked that "the prayers [whose compilation Bishop, in his *Liturgica Historica*, p. 581, attributed to Aethelwald, an eighth-century bishop of Lindisfarne] in this collection may safely be taken by the historian

One of the deepest channels of Celtic influence on Northumbrian culture was surely the royal exiles. Edwin, Oswald, Oswy, Aldfrith, all had spent much of their youth among the Celts. Aldfrith even obtained the reputation of a poet among the Irish. Perhaps, too, their own loneliness of exile had even rendered them all the more susceptible to the exile-theme of early Christian asceticism and the moody elegiac and pilgrimage motifs of Celtic poetry, and had transported an echo of the latter into the tone of Anglo-Saxon poetry. It was to the desperate loneliness of his earlier and probably Celtic exile that Edwin referred when he said, after learning that King Raedwald of East Anglia was planning to betray him, "Where on earth can I fly now, after having wandered through all the provinces of Britain these many long years, just managing in each place to slip out of the clutches of my enemies?" Bede reports it in the twelfth chapter of Book II of his *Ecclesiastical History*. And in the *Life of St. Guthlac* (Ch. 49), Felix tells how exiled Aethelbald of Mercia, heartsick and exhausted from his hunted life, would come in despair to seek comfort from Guthlac, who himself had been in exile and had learned the Celtic language (Ch. 34). Against such an emotional background *The Wanderer*, *The Seafarer*, and so many of the other Anglo-Saxon poems of the Exeter Book find a fitting harmony.

But the peace we saw Oswald establish in Bernicia did not last. This was still the dangerous Heroic Age, and in 642 at the Battle of Maserfelth Oswald fell to the sword of the same pagan King Penda of Mercia who had killed Edwin. Oswald's brother, Oswy, strove to hold Bernicia together while Penda raged as far north as the rock of Bamburgh, south into Wessex, and east into East Anglia where he slew the Christian King Anna. Finally in 655 Oswy managed to defeat and kill Penda at the Battle of the Winwaed (perhaps near Leeds) and the stage was fully set for Northumbria's Golden Age.

Oswy's undisputed rule over Northumbria was now extended to Mercia and hopefully consolidated by marriages between his family and Penda's. The security of his military conquests provided the wealth and freedom of life necessary for the flourishing of learning and art and the things of the spirit. Every Heroic Age bears within it the

as representing the type of devotional feeling prevalent in England in the youth of men like Willibrord, Boniface or Willibald" (*The Book of Cerne*, edited by Dom A. B. Kuypers [Cambridge University Press, 1902], p. 283). See the last part of note 15 to *Life of St. Cuthbert*. And see M.W. Pepperdene, *Irish Christianity and Beowulf: basis for a new interpretation of the Christian elements* [doctoral dissertation] University Microfilms, Ann Arbor, Mich. (5515). See also Ludwig Bieler's splendid book, *Ireland, Harbinger of the Middle Ages* (Oxford University Press, 1963).

seed of a Golden Age. Caedmon, the herdsman of Whitby Abbey, sang the epic of the Bible in the alliterative verse of Germanic heroic poetry. Most of those hero-saints whose biographies this book contains grew to manhood in Oswy's reign. Cuthbert probably served in Oswy's armies.[22] Wilfrid was received at his court,[23] Benedict Biscop served in Oswy's personal *comitatus* and was rewarded with an estate,[24] Ceolfrith's father had served in Oswy's *comitatus*, and young

22. Anonymous *Life of Cuthbert*, Bk. I, ch. 7, and my note 14.

23. Eddius, *Life of Wilfrid*, Ch. 2.

24. The various Anglo-Saxon and Latin terms of nobility in this age reflect the usual Heroic Age phenomenon of an aristocracy in process of formation through personal service (mostly military) of the king (Dawson pictures so well the similar rise of an adventurer-nobility in the later Heroic Age in France of the *chansons de geste. Medieval Essays* [New York, 1954], Ch. 10). The earliest ordinary Anglo-Saxon noble, accordingly, seems to have been a "companion" of the king (Latin: *comes*; Anglo-Saxon: *gesið*) a young man serving in the personal entourage (Latin: *comitatus*) of a king. As the young "companions" in time were rewarded with land for their service and became established nobles with high duties, such as serving the king in council, they became known as "thegns" (earlier in Wessex than in Northumbria), a word which literally meant "servant" *þegn*. In the eleventh century the typical thegn was thought of as possessing an estate valued at five hides of land (Stenton, *Anglo-Saxon England*, p. 480).

Then as the business of government in a settled kingdom began to assume more functions than fighting, the members of the *comitatus* took on various further titles, like *dux*, *princeps* (usually *ealdorman* in Anglo-Saxon and very frequently *eorl* ["earl"], after the Viking invasions) and *praefectus* (often *refa* in Anglo-Saxon; "reeve" in later English. See the Anonymous *Life of St. Cuthbert*, Bk. IV, ch. 8, for the reeve of Carlisle who gave Cuthbert a guided tour through the city's Roman ruins). *Comes* seems to have long remained as a general term for "noble"; though in Bede, and in Northumbrian writing generally, it is reserved for a *gesið*-with-property. *Minister* came to be even a more frequent equivalent of *comes*, though in the north both *minister* and *miles* are usually used for a young *gesið* before he has been granted land. In his famous letter to Egbert, Bede complains that in his day so much land is being given for the founding of monasteries that there will soon be none left to establish the young nobility on (Plummer, *Baedae Opera Historica*, I, 415; translated in Whitelock, *English Historical Documents*, p. 741).

In his *Life of St. Guthlac*, Felix twice uses *comes* for a man who has accompanied Aethelbald (king-to-be of Mercia) into exile (Felix, *Life of St. Guthlac*, Chs. 42, 45). The writer of the *Life of St. Cuthbert* speaks of a *comes* of King Aldfrith who possesses a household (Bk. IV, ch. 3), and of a *minister* (servant) in the service of another landed *comes* (Bk. IV, ch. 7). In his *Lives of the Ab-*

Ceolfrith himself entered a monastery founded by Oswy.[25] And in 664 Oswy presided over the Synod of Whitby with its momentous consequences for the cultural history of England.

By his decision at Whitby that in certain hotly contested ecclesiastical matters, such as the method of determining the date of Easter, the Church of Northumbria should follow the Roman rather than the Celtic custom, King Oswy brought Britain into the Latin West once for all. This proved to be a great step toward the unification of England and even—by means of the later Rome-oriented Anglo-Saxon missionaries, like Boniface—of Europe. But though it definitely tipped the scale for Rome in Britain, the Synod of Whitby by no means marked an end to all Celtic influence on Anglo-Saxon culture.[26] One of the foundation stones of the Anglo-Saxon Golden Age, Archbishop Theodore, who brought classical learning from Greece, and who put order and stability into the ecclesiastical organization of England, arrived a year before Oswy's death. One of the King's last important official acts was to grant saintly Chad to Theodore to be appointed as Bishop of Mercia for King Wulfhere.

bots, Bede tells us that Benedict Biscop was of "noble birth" (*nobili stirpe*), that he had been a *minister of* King Oswy, that this involved military service, and that he had been awarded land by the king (ch. 1). In the same book he tells us that Eastorwine was a "noble" (*nobilis*), and that as a *minister* of King Ecgfrith he had borne arms (ch. 8). The *Life of Ceolfrith* tells us that Ceolfrith was a noble (*nobilibus editus parentibus*), and that his father was master of a sizeable household and enjoyed a very honorable and responsible position in King Oswy's *comitatus* (ch. 34). Pope Leo III wrote of victorious King Offa's regarding St. Peter as his "standard bearer and comrade-in-arms." (*signiferum et comitem*) (Haddan and Stubbs, *Councils and Ecclesiastical Documents*, III, 524; Whitelock, *English Historical Documents*, p. 794).

But whatever may have been the changing fortune of their Latin titles, the Anglo-Saxon founders of noble Heroic Age houses seem ordinarily to have won their position by personal military service of a grateful king. The best study of all these terms is still Hector Chadwick's in his *Studies on Anglo-Saxon Institutions* (see especially pp. 105, 163-64, 326-27, 339-40, 343 ff., 349-50). There are good discussions of the Heroic Age Anglo-Saxon nobility in Girvan, *Beowulf and the Seventh Century*, pp. 43 ff. and in Blair, *Roman Britain and Early England*, pp. 247 ff. and in Stenton, *Anglo-Saxon England*, pp. 298 ff.

25. Anonymous *Life of Ceolfrith*, Chapters 34 and 2, respectively.

26. On the Synod of Whitby see Eddius, *Life of Wilfrid*, Ch. 10; note 32 to *Life of Wilfrid*; note 24 to *Life of St. Cuthbert*. On the Anglo-Saxon missionaries' influence on European unity see Levison, *England and the Continent*, chs. 4 and 5. On the continuation of Celtic influence in England after Whitby see Stenton, *Anglo-Saxon England*, pp. 124 ff.

The old warrior Oswy died in his bed in 670, but his son Ecgfrith died in a Heroic Age battle in 685 against the Picts,[27] losing a good deal of Northumbria's northern possessions after having previously lost the ascendancy over Mercia.[28] But his reign advanced the Golden Age. The wealth of his early conquests enabled Wilfrid to build the magnificent churches of Hexham and Ripon, and the king bestowed the monasteries of Monkwearmouth and Jarrow upon Benedict Biscop, who proceeded to stock their libraries with the great books of the Greco-Roman world.

Ecgfrith's successor, Aldfrith, who too had been exiled among the Celts, preserved the peace and saw the Golden Age fruition of Lindisfarne and Jarrow, centers of the Celtic and the Roman elements respectively in the brilliant Northumbrian cultural amalgam. Eadfrith produced the incomparable *Lindisfarne Gospels*, and at Jarrow Bede wrote his first works. About this time the marvelous stone crosses were carved at Ruthwell and Bewcastle. At last Bernicia's king need no longer be a warrior. Aldfrith was a scholar-king who provided thousands of sheep and calves for the vellum pages of the great books the monks copied, and he was not above spending a small fortune of a thousand or more acres of land to procure one fine book imported

27. The Pictish king, Brude mac Bile, who defeated and killed Ecgfrith in this Battle of Nechtansmere, was probably his cousin (Chadwick, *Studies in Early British History*, p. 160).

28. About 674, Ecgfrith had routed an invading Mercian army led by Penda's son, Wulfhere (Eddius, *Life of Wilfrid*, ch. 20), but in 678 the next king of Mercia, Wulfhere's brother, Aethelred, beat Ecgfrith decisively at the Battle of the Trent and put an end to Northumbrian sway over Mercia. During most of the eighth century the cultural and political center of gravity in Anglo-Saxon England shifted to Mercia. Under the successive rules of Aethelbald (dear friend of St. Guthlac) and especially of the great King Offa (respected friend of Charlemagne) Mercia enjoyed its own Golden Age. Many claim it was for Offa's court that *Beowulf* was written (see C. L. Wrenn's discussion of the theories in the Introduction to his edition of *Beowulf*, pp. 37 ff.), or that it was written in East Anglia during the latter's domination by Mercia (Wrenn, "Sutton Hoo and *Beowulf*," in *Mélanges de Linguistique et Philologie, Fernand Mossé in Memoriam* [Paris, 1959] pp. 505-06). The vexing question of the nature and extent of Mercian literary influence is much discussed (Vleeskruyer, *The Life of St. Chad*, Introduction: pp. 38 ff.). The poet Cynewulf most likely wrote in Mercia in the early ninth century (Sisam, *Studies in the History of Old English Literature*, pp. 1 ff., pp. 132 ff. Vleekskruyer, *op. cit.*, p. 46) and perhaps a great deal more of our extant Anglo-Saxon poetry was composed in Mercia, rather than in Northumbria as is usually assumed (Sisam, *op. cit.*, pp. 132 ff.).

from Rome.[29] It has been suggested that *Beowulf* may have been written at his court. "In art and religion, in scholarship and literature, the Anglo-Saxons of the eighth century were the leaders of their age."[30] During Aldfrith's reign the Northumbrian monk Willibrord inaugurated the Anglo-Saxon mission to the continent, the high-water mark of the Golden Age. Its glory had been miraculously sudden—as is the way with heroic things—and its decline as tragically and surprisingly swift.

After Aldfrith's death in 704 a rapid succession of indifferent, disappointing and disgraceful kings marked Northumbria's decline. Bede sensed it coming.[31] As he penned the last lines of his *Ecclesiastical History* in 731 Bede surveyed the great peace which had settled upon his Northumbria. Noting the vast numbers of nobles and commonfolk putting aside the arms of the Heroic Age and flocking into monasteries, he remarked: "What the outcome of all this will be, the next age will discover." His "ill-divining soul" proved sadly right.

Bede died in 735, only 101 years after Oswald's victory at Heavenfield, and the births of Cuthbert and Wilfrid. Now Boniface of Wessex in letter after letter from the German mission was pleading with the latter-day kings to preserve their glory.[32] At the end of the century, Alcuin,

29. Bede (*Lives of the Abbots*, Ch. 15) says that for a "marvelous cosmographical codex" which Benedict Biscop had brought from Rome, Aldfrith gave Ceolfrith (for his monastery of Jarrow) eight hides of land (i. e., possibly as much as 1000 or more acres). Bede considered a hide to be the amount of any given land that would be required to support one family (Plummer, *Baedae Opera Historica*, II, 40-1). And see note 27 to *Life of Wilfrid*. Ten hides seem to have constituted the standard holdings of a number of Northumbrian nobles (Brown and Bruce-Mitford, *Evangeliorum Quattuor Codex Lindisfarnensis*, II, 293). And for the more than 6000 pages of the three great Bibles which Ceolfrith caused to be copied (Bede, *Lives of the Abbots*, Ch. 15) at least 1500 sheep or calves would have to have been provided (Brown and Bruce-Mitford, *op.cit.*, p. 13). Again Aldfrith's royal bounty must have contributed. One of the greatest tributes to Aldfrith's love of learning was the lifelong affection shown him by Aldhelm of Wessex, one of the finest scholars in seventh-century Europe (Godfrey, *The Church in Anglo-Saxon England*, pp. 201 ff.; Duckett, *Anglo-Saxon Saints and Scholars*, Ch. 1; Curtius, *European Literature and the Latin Middle Ages*, pp. 45 ff., 457 ff.).

30. Dawson, *The Making of Europe*, p. 184.

31. Bede, *Ecclesiastical History*, Bk. V, ch. 23. Bede, *Letter to Egbert* (text in Plummer, *Baedae Opera Historica*, I, 405-423; translation in Whitelock, *English Historical Documents*, pp. 735 ff.).

32. See, for instance, the urgent plea for reform, co-signed by seven fellow-English bishops on the German mission, which Boniface sent to King Aethelbald

who had brought the final brilliant golden sparks from Northumbria to light the fires of Charlemagne's renaissance in France, could only pray brokenheartedly across the Channel while the Vikings ravaged among the ruins of Lindisfarne and Jarrow. A few years later, in 797, he wrote: "It seems in a way that the golden days of the English are almost at an end."[33]

of Mercia about 746 (translated in Whitelock, *English Historical Documents*, pp. 751 ff.). The effects of St. Guthlac's friendship seem to have rubbed off Aethelbald by this time, and Boniface rebukes him for the open scandal of his life, violation of convents, etc. And see notes 62 and 63 to Felix, *Life of St. Guthlac*.

33. *Alcuini Epistolae* 122, in Monumenta Germaniae Historica, *Epistolarum* vol. IV (*Epistolae Karolini Aevi*, vol. II, p. 179). In this letter to Osbert, a Mercian nobleman, Alcuin comments on widespread tribulation in England, a decline of truth and loyalty and sober decency. There is a translation of the letter in Whitelock, *English Historical Documents*, pp. 786 ff.

Lindisfarne and Jarrow, twin symbols of the Celtic-Roman fusion at the heart of the Anglo-Saxon Golden Age, were first sacked in 793-94. (And in the south, by some tragic appropriateness, the earlier years of the century saw the Saracens plundering the monastery of Lérins, to which the great Celtic and Anglo-Saxon monasteries had owed so much). But in all fairness to the Vikings it should be pointed out (as Sawyer does in *The Age of the Vikings*, pp. 136 ff.) that Anglo-Saxon monasticism had already begun to decay by some inner blight of the spirit before the first dragon-ships beached at Lindisfarne. Alcuin's rather grim letter of condolence to the harassed monks of Lindisfarne (Whitelock, *English Historical Documents*, pp. 778-79) is perhaps pointing in the direction of the truth when it suggests that the Vikings are but the scourge of Divine Justice. Many signs, such as Bede's letter to Egbert, and Alcuin's and Boniface's letters (see notes 31, 32), indicate overgrowth of the monasteries, laxness of life, worldliness, excessive lay control. In 747 a council held at Cloveshoe near Canterbury (and influenced by a Frankish synod held in the same year at the instigation of Boniface [Levison, *England and the Continent*, p. 86]) found it necessary to condemn many such abuses (Haddan and Stubbs, *Councils and Ecclesiastical Documents*, III, 362-76). It has been suggested that Boniface, paradoxically, may have unwittingly contributed to this sorry condition which he so inveighed against. His stirring appeals for volunteers to help him on the German mission may have drained the Anglo-Saxon monasteries of their best blood (Godfrey, *The Church in Anglo-Saxon England*, pp. 260 ff.). By the time of King Alfred monasticism was dead in England (Knowles, *The Monastic Order in England*, p. 24).

But its memory lived. Cuthbert's personality had won its way deeply into the heart of England. And there were the many precious manuscripts of Bede's *Ecclesiastical History* that recorded forever the "one brief shining moment" of the Anglo-Saxon "Camelot." This memory would help in the work of cultural

From Aethelfrith to Aldfrith it had been truly a Heroic Age. It was a warrior society and had its brutal side, but its best moments were brave, high-hearted and noble. When young Edwin had fled for his life and sought asylum with King Raedwald, Aethelfrith sent messengers to Raedwald promising him a treasure if he would murder the exiled prince. Unlike the kings who refused bribes offered for Wilfrid,[34] Raedwald at length gave way, either to the bribes or threats, and planned to do Aethelfrith's will. Meantime a loyal friend brought news of the plot to Edwin and urged him to flee. Edwin thanked him but refused to budge: "I cannot do this thing you suggest. How can I be the first to break this pact which I have sworn with so fine a king, seeing that he has done me no harm and has not threatened me in any way yet? And anyhow, if I should have to die I would rather be slain by him than by someone less noble."[35]

rebuilding under Dunstan's leadership in the tenth century (J. Robinson, *The Times of St. Dunstan* [London, 1923]; Duckett, *Saint Dunstan of Canterbury* [London, 1955]). But more important than the memory, was the living fruit of its spirit—in the persons of such as Willibrord, Boniface, Alcuin—which Anglo-Saxon England sent to the continent before the end. Charlemagne's renaissance could hardly have happened without Boniface and Alcuin, and without that host of Anglo-Saxon missionaries who filled important bishoprics and who produced in monasteries like Echternach and Fulda a wealth of scholarship and manuscripts (Levison, *England and the Continent*, Chs. 4, 5, 6). An Anglo-Saxon monk, Willibald (the famous Holy Land pilgrim, whom Boniface made bishop of Eichstätt), had a hand in reviving the spiritual life of Monte Cassino with such momentous consequence for all the West (*Life of Willibald* by Huneberc, pp. 172-73 in Talbot, *The Anglo-Saxon Missionaries in Germany*). As for Alcuin, it has been said that he became the spiritual ruler of Europe (Levison, *op. cit.*, p. 164; and see pp. 148-73. More recent studies are E. Duckett, *Alcuin, Friend of Charlemagne* [New York, 1951]; G. Ellard, *Master Alcuin, Liturgist* [Loyola, Chicago, 1956]; L. Wallach, *Alcuin and Charlemagne*, [Cornell, 1959]).

34. Eddius, *Life of Wilfrid*, Chs. 27, 28.

35. Bede, *Ecclesiastical History*, Bk. II, ch. 12. Of course there are two sides to this coin. Edwin's integrity reversed shows Raedwald's perfidy. Christian King Oswy was responsible for the murder of Christian King Oswine. King Sigbert of the East Saxons was murdered by his own kinsmen, and so on. There was the legendary cruelty of Queens Aelfthryth and Cynethryth, and of the princess Eadburh (Wright, *Cultivation of Saga in Anglo-Saxon England*, pp. 160, 103 ff., 92 ff.). Violent Heroic Age virtues are but a shade removed from violent vices. And in the mid-eighth-century twilight of the Golden Age, the vices began to get the upper hand—to judge from Boniface's and Alcuin's denunciations referred to in note 33. But here in the seventh-century morning we always have the impression that the highheartedness far outweighs the

But Raedwald's wife convinced her husband that no amount of gold could ever buy back his honor. Raedwald had a complete change of heart and helped Edwin raise an army and win his kingdom.

A king's followers, members of his *comitatus*, as Tacitus put it, were loyal to the death. To betray your lord was the crime of crimes. A monastery was founded in an attempt to wipe out the stain of Earl Hunwald's betrayal of noble and holy King Oswine, Aidan's dear friend.[36] When an assassin sent by the King of Wessex attempted to stab King Edwin, one of the king's men, named Lilla, leaped in front of the blade. He was killed by the thrust, which pierced him clean through and wounded the king. Then Edwin wreaked Heroic Age vengeance by marching against Wessex and slaying or capturing all who had had a part in the plot.[37]

And we see scenes too of high graciousness in this courtly world of heroes. It is hard to forget Bede's picture of noble, handsome King Oswine of Deira courteously insisting that holy Aidan accept the present of a royal steed to ride on his exhausting episcopal journeys, and of Aidan then impulsively offering the fine horse with all its trappings to the first poor beggar he met.[38] And we remember the kindly and beautiful eloquence with which formidable King Oswy spoke so persuasively of Christianity "in a brotherly way" to his pagan friend, King Sigbert (Sigeberht) of the East Saxons. Sigbert later accepted baptism, and received Cedd as the bishop of his East Saxons.[39]

These highminded nobles tended to regard Christianity in terms of their warrior code. When a king was baptized, Heroic Age loyalty demanded that the men of his personal *comitatus* follow their lord to the font. Bede pictures it for us in the cases, for instance, of Edwin and of Penda's son, Peada.[40] Penda of Mercia, fierce pagan to the

brutality and the ignobility, far more than in Gregory of Tours' violent picture of sixth-century Merovingian Gaul (though Gregory's reader should make allowances for the author's particular intentions in writing his history, as Wallace-Hadrill points out in Chapter 3 of his *The Long-Haired Kings*). After all, Raedwald's wife did plead with him to do the honorable thing, and he did listen and spare Edwin.

36. Bede, *Ecclesiastical History*, Bk. III, ch. 14. The greater stain was that of Hunwald's king, Oswy, who ordered the deed done. This monastery which the penitent king founded was Gilling, which Ceolfrith later entered. And Ceolfrith's father was a noble in Oswy's *comitatus* (anonymous *Life of Ceolfrith*, Chs. 2, 34).

37. Bede, *Ecclesiastical History*, Bk. II, ch. 9.

38. Bede, *op. cit.*, Bk. III, ch. 14.

39. Bede, *op. cit.*, Bk. III, ch. 22.

40. Bede, *op. cit.*, Bk. II, ch. 14; Bk. III, ch. 21. And in Gaul over 3000

last, had no objection to his numerous family's becoming Christian, nor to any of his people's being converted, providing that they were then sincere in the practice of their faith and in the service of the God they professed to believe in.[41] Occasionally the Heroic Age warrior-ethos balked at such things as Christian readiness to forgive enemies. Two of his kinsmen, for instance, murdered the Christian King Sigbert (mentioned above) simply because they could not stomach his leniency toward his enemies.[42] The transformation of Germanic warriors into medieval Europe's chivalric knights did not come about all in a day.

Family ties were sacred in this Heroic Age society. Genealogies had something of the power of a prayerful litany. The world that did the fighting and the ruling became an aristocratic world woven together by a web of widely crisscrossing family relationships. Penda's

of his Frankish warriors were baptized with Clovis (Gregory of Tours, *History of the Franks*, Bk. II, ch. 31).

41. Bede, *op. cit.*, Bk. III, ch. 21.

42. Bede, *op. cit.*, Bk. III, Ch. 22. The great old Germanic warrior, Clovis, long refused Christian baptism because he could not be convinced that a meek Christ could have possessed divine power (Gregory of Tours, *History of the Franks*, Bk. II, ch. 29).

It was no little achievement of later medieval society to have Christianized this Germanic warrior-ethos into chivalry. (Dawson traces the process clearly in chapter V of *Religion and the Rise of Western Culture* [N. Y., 1950]). There was a tenth-century prayer young German nobles said as they girded on their swords, in which they asked God to bless the weapon with which they intended to protect his servants against the cruelty of the pagans and to terrify all evil-doers (quoted by Daniel-Rops in *The Church in the Dark Ages* [London 1959], p. 570). Admittedly this military Christianity does not sit very well with our understanding of the New Testament, but they were not looking at things through our eyes. The same St. Bernard who helped launch the embattled Dark-Age Western spirit on the adventure of the love of God (Southern, *The Making of the Middle Ages* [London, 1953], Ch. 5: "From Epic to Romance"), whose tender devotion to the Blessed Virgin gained him the right to request of her the ultimate gift for Dante in the *Paradiso* (Cantos xxxi-xxxiii), was the same man who had a great deal to do with the founding of the Knights Templars and who gave them chilling (to us) exhortations to "kill for Christ," (*De laude novae militiae*. Migne, *PL* 182, 921 ff.). Being still in the Heroic Age, the world of the *Song of Roland* was quite consistent with itself (G. F. Jones, in *The Ethos of the Song of Roland* [Johns Hopkins, 1963] appraises it, I feel, less by its standards than by ours). And that, it seems to me, is the real import of St. Boniface's martyrdom. In one heroic gesture of non-violence he transcended his own Heroic Age and that of Archbishop Turpin who died at Roncevaux, sword in hand.

sister, for instance, was the wife of King Cenwalh of Wessex, while one of his daughters married King Alchfrith of Bernicia, and his son Peada married a daughter of King Oswy. When Wilfrid fled the wrath of King Ecgfrith in 681 he could find refuge neither in Mercia nor in Wessex, because the queen of the former kingdom was a sister of Ecgfrith, and the queen of the latter was sister to Ecgfrith's queen.[43] It reminds you for all the world of the interrelated Aegean aristocracy of the *Iliad*.

One of the most fascinating things of all is how this Anglo-Saxon heroic aristocracy seems almost to have transported itself en masse, ideals included, from the *villae regiae*[44] to the monasteries, once the age of conquest had reached a fair amount of stability about the middle of the seventh century. Both of the kings who refused Wilfrid asylum in 681 eventually abdicated their thrones and became monks—Aethelred of Mercia, and Centwine of Wessex. King Sebbi of the East Saxons entered a monastery at the end of the century. King Sigbert (Sigeberht) the Learned of East Anglia, who had been baptized in Gaul where he had been exiled by King Raedwald, and who founded a school in East Anglia with the help of Bishop Felix and teachers from Canterbury, exchanged his crown for a cowl in a monastery he founded himself. Tragically enough, however, his people forced the old warrior out of the monastery to help them fight off Penda. He refused to bear arms and was cut down in the course of the battle.[45] Many another king gave up his throne to follow the pilgrimage call to die in Rome—like Wilfrid's friend Caedwalla, famous Ine of Wessex, Cenred of Mercia, and Offa of the East Saxons.[46] Even Oswy

43. Eddius, *Life of Wilfrid*, Ch. 40.

44. The *villae regiae* were "royal palaces" scattered about the countryside. They were the real centers of the royal life. Births, baptisms, and marriages took place in them, and in them were kept the king's rents and treasures. Each seems to have had a great hall and a church. Bede mentions the *villa regia* of Yeavering and six others in Northumbria, and Rendlesham in East Anglia (consult the Index to Jones, *A Concordance to the Historia Ecclesiastica of Bede*). In Gaul, Wilfrid was consecrated bishop at the Merovingian *villa regia* of Compiègne (Eddius, *Life of Wilfrid*, Ch. 12. Bright, *Chapters of Early English Church History*, p. 242).

45. Bede, *Ecclesiastical History*, Bk. III, ch. 18. By this "absurd" act of Christian heroism Sigbert looks forward to Boniface's transcendence of the Heroic Age ethos (see note 42), and even to Dostoevsky's Father Zossima. See note 34 to *Life of St. Boniface*.

46. Bede, *op. cit.*, Bk. V, chs. 7, 19. This *peregrinatio* (pilgrimage) urge is another fascinating aspect of the Anglo-Saxon Golden Age, seemingly caught from the holy wanderlust of the Celtic Saints. Cf. L. Gougaud, *Christianity in*

of Northumbria, fiercely Celtic as he was, felt this spell of Rome at the last, but death intervened.

It has been estimated that from 613 to 829 about thirty Anglo-Saxon kings and queens left their thrones to enter monasteries.[47] The number of royal abbesses is astounding.[48] Oswy's Queen Eanfled, daughter of King Edwin, became Abbess of Whitby, as did her daughter, Aelffled. Ecgfrith's first wife, Aethilthryth, daughter of King Anna of the East Angles, became Abbess of Ely, and a saint. Ecgfrith's second wife, Iurminburg, became an abbess after her husband's death. And Ecgfrith's aunt, Aebbe, became abbess of Coldingham. All five of these high-born nuns figure in the life of Wilfrid.

All the biographies that follow in this book are a testimony to the astounding number of young Anglo-Saxon nobles, warriors even in the royal *comitatus*, who fairly flooded into the monasteries as the Heroic Age turned into the Golden Age.[49] By the end of the eighth cen-

Celtic Lands, (New York, 1932). But it is more than the spell of travel or adventure (though surely for the Irish, untamed by the Romans, this motive figures too); it is rather an ascetic longing to renounce one's loved homeland and die in self-inflicted exile in a foreign land to win the hundredfold of the Gospel promise (*e.g.*, see *Life of Ceolfrith*, Chs. 21, 27; and see Offa's reasons at beginning of ch. 19 in Bk. V of Bede, *Ecclesiastical History*). Wilfrid, Benedict Biscop, Willibrord, Boniface, Ceolfrith, Alcuin, all had felt its spell. And in Antony of Egypt's way it was followed by the anchorites, like Cuthbert and Guthlac. It has been suggested that it is this *peregrinatio* call which is tugging at the narrator in the beautiful Anglo-Saxon poem, *The Seafarer* (D. Whitelock, "The Interpretation of the Seafarer," in Fox, *The Early Cultures of North-west Europe*, pp. 261-72). See E. Duckett, *The Wandering Saints of the Early Middle Ages* (New York, 1959). See note 9 to *Life of Wilfrid*, and note 16 to *Life of St. Cuthbert.*

47. A. Plummer, *The Churches in Britain Before A. D. 1000* (London, 1911) 1, 228. Not a few royalty even of the Celtic Heroic Age had forsaken the throne for the monastery (Chadwick, *Celt and Saxon*, p. 332).

48. Howorth, *The Golden Days of the Early English Church*, III, 175 ff. Bede tells us that even in the early years of the seventh century, before there were many monasteries yet in England, numbers of young Anglo-Saxon noblewomen went to monasteries in Gaul to be educated and to become nuns, and that some were made abbesses there (*Ecclesiastical History*, Bk. III, ch. 8).

49. Benedict Biscop, noble warrior in King Oswy's service, became a monk at the age of twenty-five. Cuthbert, probably also a warrior of Oswy's and of noble birth (See Colgrave, *Two Lives of St. Cuthbert*, p. 344. An untrustworthy Celtic Life even has him descended from a high king of Ireland: see Grosjean, "Alleged Irish Origin of St. Cuthbert," in Battiscombe, *The Relics of St. Cuthbert*, pp. 144 ff.), entered Melrose at about seventeen. Eastorwine,

tury there were some forty major monasteries in existence. Not all their monks were nobles but superiors usually were. Ceolfrith ruled over more than 600 monks in Monkwearmouth and Jarrow. Many of the monks of course would be kinsmen and there was always the danger of a clan system and hereditary control, which Benedict Biscop explicitly legislated against.[50] Eastorwine, abbot of Monkwearmouth was a relative of his superior, Benedict Biscop. And when Ceolfrith entered the monastery of Gilling its previous abbot had been his own brother, and its present abbot was another relative. All these men just mentioned were nobles. Either the man himself or his father (as in Ceolfrith's case) had served in the personal *comitatus* of his king.

Perhaps the most interesting thing about this amazing Heroic Age of English monasticism is that, once realized for the widespread and special phenomenon it was, it makes the heroic cast of Anglo-Saxon literature so much more understandable. The latter is not due solely to the general influence of early Christian Latin literature and spirituality. These noble young monks brought with them into the cloister the heroic songs and sagas that the aristocratic families had been bred on.[51] As the epics of Homer's heroes had educated the Greek world,

relative of Benedict Biscop and warrior in King Ecgfrith's *comitatus*, was twenty-four when he entered Monkwearmouth. Ceolfrith, son of a thegn of King Oswy, entered Gilling at seventeen. Wilfrid, of noble birth, was only fourteen when he went to Lindisfarne as a kind of lay monk. Guthlac of the blood royal, exchanged arms for the cowl when he was twenty-four. In the ordinary Heroic-Age course of things these young unmarried nobles would have served in the king's wars till they received estates, founded families, and eventually became the *duces* and *principes* whose signatures we see on the royal charters. We think too of a later Heroic Age and of another troop of young noblemen, headed by Bernard, riding off to the Abbey of Cîteaux in Burgundy.

50. Bede, *Lives of the Abbots*, Ch. 11.

51. Their very names often descended from Teutonic heroes: Sigefrith, Theodric, Ingeld, Hyglac, Aethelric, etc. (See *Liber Vitae Ecclesiae Dunelmensis* in *Publications of the Surtees Society*, vol. 13). They brought with them of course into the cloister the old heroic songs and sagas they had learned from their childhood. These were the oral textbooks that taught the heroism they were to live. One of the reasons why heroic poems are found in monastic manuscripts may simply be that they were used in the education especially of noble lay-students living in the monasteries (Eddius, *Life of Wilfrid*, Ch. 21). See notes 6 and 29 to *Life of St. Cuthbert*. Though the monks, understandably, did not trouble to write many of them down, we can detect traces of more of them behind Bede's Latin prose and in some of the later chronicles. There seems to have been either a saga or a poem on the deeds of Hengest and Horsa (Wilson, *Lost*

so too did Germanic youth grow up on the pattern of its heroes. Aldhelm sang the old heroic songs even after he was a monk, Guthlac was inspired by them as a young man, Alfred was raised on them, Anglo-Saxon abbots had them sung to their communities, Dunstan was fond of them, King Edward is said to have read them regularly to his *comitatus*. Seeing *Beowulf* in the context of an Anglo-Saxon monastery should be no puzzle at all. Anglo-Saxon Christian poems like *Andreas* and *Elene* and *Guthlac*, cast in the mold of the old heroic poetry, seem quite in place, and so do the diction and alliteration from heroic poetry that seem almost by force of habit to have made their way into monastic Anglo-Saxon prose translations of Latin Lives, like that of St. Chad.[52] In that gem of Anglo-Saxon poems, *The Dream*

Literature of Medieval England, pp. 29-30). The chronicle of Henry of Huntingdon reveals traces of a lost poem or poems on the Heroic-Age battles of Aethelfrith, Edwin, Oswald, and Oswy (Wilson, *op. cit.*, pp. 32-33). Sometimes poetry got the upper hand. The Anglo-Saxon Council of Cloveshoe in 747 found it necessary to warn monks about being too taken up with "empty dreams of glory" (Canon 7). Preachers were ordered not to "declaim in the manner of secular poets" (Canon 12), and bishops were directed to see that monasteries did not become "resorts for poets and harpers and foolish tale-tellers" (Canon 20) (Haddan and Stubbs, *Councils and Ecclesiastical Documents*, III, 364-69).

But it is clear that, in less "reprehensible ways," the monks retained in the cloister this saga-fed heroic cast of mind. Wilfrid, as a venerable old monk and bishop, dispenses treasure among his brethren with all the aristocratic largesse of an Anglo-Saxon chieftain rewarding his *comitatus* (Eddius, *Life of Wilfrid*, Ch. 63). Aldhelm writes to Wilfrid's monks (on the occasion of Wilfrid's last banishment by the king) exhorting them to accompany their lord into exile the way any faithful "companion" must do (Whitelock, *English Historical Documents*, pp. 730-31). Alcuin wrote to Charlemagne recommending to him an ealdorman, Torhtmund, who had "faithfully avenged" his murdered lord, King Ethelred, by slaying the slayer (Whitelock, *English Historical Documents*, p. 795).

And the ordinary man too followed this heroic code of his nobles. A Wessex herdsman is recorded by the *Anglo-Saxon Chronicle* (for the year 755) for avenging the murder of his ealdorman. So it was that the ordinary men imitated their nobles also in this Golden-Age impulse for the monastic life. The ceorl followed the thegn into the cloister. All of Ceolfrith's 600 monks at Monkwearmouth and Jarrow were certainly not nobles (*Life of Ceolfrith*, Ch. 33). "It was the appeal to the imagination of the ordinary man which gave vitality to early English monasticism" (Stenton, *Anglo-Saxon England*, p. 158).

52. Vleekskruyer, *The Life of St. Chad*, pp. 19 ff. Traditional secular poetic techniques and oral-formulaic patterns (see F. P. Magoun, Jr., in *Speculum*, vol. 28 [1953] pp. 446-67) are used in the Anglo-Saxon metrical version of the Psalms (see R. E. Diamond, *The Diction of the Anglo-Saxon Metrical Psalms*

of the Rood, Christ strides to the Cross like a young Germanic "hero" (haeleth) going into battle.

> *Then the young hero, strong and stouthearted*
> *Very God of all power, threw aside his garments,*
> *And bravely in sight of all he mounted the tall cross,*
> *As he dared battle to win freedom for men.*
>
> (*Dream of the Rood*, vv. 39-41)

The Heroic Age ideal is most deeply involved in all these hagiographies that follow. All their subjects were Anglo-Saxon monks of this seventh-to-eighth century period, and all their Anglo-Saxon authors wrote the books in monasteries within the same period. Each of these writers treats his saint, in greater or lesser degree, as a hero. Felix fills Guthlac's story with the ring of Vergil's epic Latin. Even gentle Cuthbert is called "hero of God" and "warrior of the Lord," and the scene of Boniface's martyrdom has the heroic tone of a nobly-lost Germanic battlefield.

Of course the hero-saint is not a peculiarly Anglo-Saxon phenomenon. Throughout the whole early Christian world the saint steps into the hero's niche.[53] As Alexander had offered sacrifice at the shrine of Achilles in Ilion, so the faithful flocked to Cuthbert's tomb at Lindisfarne. Siegfried's grave was visited by emperors in a churchyard in Worms. A hero's relics were treasured, like Roland's horn in a church at Baye. Different parts of King Oswald's body were preserved in several different Anglo-Saxon churches. The shield of Aeneas could once be seen in Samothrace, and pieces of the True Cross were prized all over Christendom. It is still in terms of heroic combat that the medieval man thought of human greatness. St. Paul's vision of Chris-

[The Hague, 1963]). The alliteration and parallelism so common in our *Latin* lives is not so much due to the influence of these same qualities in Germanic verse as it is to their influence in late imperial Latin prose and early Christian Latin poetry and prose, both continental and Irish (see Baldwin, *Medieval Rhetoric and Poetic*, Chs. 4 and 5; Atkins, *English Literary Criticism: the Medieval Phase*, Ch. 3; Raby, *Christian Latin Poetry*, Ch. 5). Sometimes, however, in the more "heroic" parts of an Anglo-Saxon Latin life, one comes across a passage that almost echoes the binary movement of an Anglo-Saxon verse-line with its two halves bound together by functional alliteration (e. g., *vitiorum victor Benedictus et virtutum patrator egregius*, in Bede's *Lives of the Abbots*, Ch. 14 [Plummer, *Baedae Opera Historica*, I,377]). And see note 2 to Eddius, *Life of Wilfrid*; and note 4 to Life of St. Cuthbert, and my Preface to Felix, *Life of St. Guthlac.*

53. De Vries, *Heroic Song and Heroic Legend*, pp. 181 ff.; 236 ff.

tian life as a warfare is all pervasive. There was a halo of heroic glory about even the most ascetic anchorite living his saintly life in a quiet cave, and his story was sung in a manner fit for the halls of kings and noblemen. Guthlac in the lonely fenland is gloriously victorious over armies of demons. An early Syriac Mass prays for those of the fathers and brethren who are waging the battle on lonely mountainsides and in rocky caverns.[54] A Persian martyr-bishop prays before his "contest" and makes a typical heroic "boast" to die bravely like a hero so he can be an example for all the people of the East. In almost the same immortal words of Sarpedon in the *Iliad*,[55] he declares that since his has been the first place at table so he must now lead the way at dying.[56]

The hero's combat with dragons or with human foes is now preeminently the martyr's "contest," his battle with beasts or with soldier-executioners. Panegyrics of the martyrs succeed to the epics of the heroes. The Age of the Martyrs is often called the primitive Heroic Age of Christianity.[57] Boniface triumphs as a "hero-athlete." The martyr, like the hero of Germanic saga and, to a lesser extent, Greek epic, faces a last battle against overwhelming odds. Too late for the Age of Martyrs, the Egyptian and Celtic hermits turned to the bloodless martyrdom of asceticism.[58] A seventh-century eastern novel explains that monasticism grew out of the heroic desire to be "martyrs in intention."[59] St. Cuthbert is called a "martyr" by his biographer.[60] It is a warfare of the spirit which the Anglo-Saxon hero-saints wage, and their only overt foes are demons.

Much Roman army terminology finds its way naturally and unself-consciously into the early Christian vocabulary. The legions in their death-struggles with the barbarians were a paramount fact all through the West. So many of the first saints came from Roman military families: Pachomius, Martin, Victor, Januarius, etc. Clement calls on the new Christians of Corinth to preserve that discipline and order which marked the Roman army.[61] Christ wears the armor of

54. A. Hamman (ed.), *Early Christian Prayers* (London and Chicago, 1961), p. 214.

55. *Iliad*, Bk. XII, vv. 310 ff.

56. Hamman, *op. cit.*, p. 59.

57. J. Palanque, *The Church and the Dark Ages* (London, 1960), p. 7.

58. Ryan, *Irish Monasticism*, pp. 197 ff. See note 23 to Eddius' *Life of Wilfrid.*

59. *Barlaam and Joasaph*, formerly attributed to John of Damascus (quoted in *Acts of the Pagan Martyrs*, edited by Herbert Musurillo, S. J. [Oxford, 1954] p. 236, n. 1).

60. Anonymous *Life of St. Cuthbert*, Chs. 15, 16, 17.

61. Clement, *First Epistle to the Corinthians.* There was a widespread image of the heroic Roman legionary standard bearer (*signifer*). In Britain, legend

the legions in a mosaic in the Archbishop's Palace in Ravenna. And Bede, in Pauline terminology, verbally clothes Cuthbert in Roman armor.[62] A popular liturgical litany of the Frankish Church in the Age of Crusades seems to have developed from victory cheers of the Roman army.[63] St. Martin's funeral procession is compared to a Roman emperor's "triumph."[64] The Anglo-Saxon monks of Golden Age Northumbria lived in a land covered with stone memories of the legions. Ruined Roman forts along the Wall provided building material for the monasteries. Many a church or monastery was built inside the walls of a Roman fort—like Fursey's at Burgh Castle in East Anglia, and Willibrord's at Utrecht.[65] And there were more living military memories of Rome all about them in the heroic songs and traditions and names of the princely Celtic families of the "Men of the North."[66] The spirituality, the learning, the art, of neither of the two chief Celtic and Roman centers of the Northumbrian Golden Age—Lindisfarne and Jarrow—can ever be fully appreciated and understood except

might have even remembered the particular *signifer* of Caesar's tenth legion, who saved the day on the invasion beach when Rome first stormed Britain in 55 B. C. (Caesar, *The Conquest of Gaul*, Ch. V, 1). After Constantine's vision the Christian cross became pictorially and imaginatively associated with the Roman battle standard, as in Fortunatus' great hymn, *Vexilla Regis*, which was to become the marching song of the Crusaders. In a letter to Ethelheard, Archbishop of Canterbury, Alcuin exhorts him to his priestly responsibilities, telling him to bear the banner of the holy cross bravely in the forward battle line (Haddan and Stubbs, *Councils and Ecclesiastical Documents*, III, 476). And the Anglo-Saxon version of the *Ecclesiastical History* (Bk. IV, ch. 17) translates Bede's *symbolum* (creed) as *herebeacen* (battle standard).

62. Bede, prose *Life of St. Cuthbert*, Ch. 17.

63. E. Kantorowicz, *Laudes Regiae: A Study in Liturgical Acclamations and Mediaeval Ruler Worship* (Univ. of Calif., 1958) Ch. 2.

64. *Letters of Sulpicius Severus*, III (translation in Hoare, *The Western Fathers*, p. 60). And see note 61 to *Life of Guthlac.*

65. Verbist, *Saint Willibrord*, pp. 106 ff. Clarke, R. R., *East Anglia* (London, 1960), pp. 126 ff., 142. And see Colgrave, *Two Lives of St. Cuthbert*, p. 318. Even Columbanus' first religious house in Gaul, at Annegray, was an old Roman fort (Walker, *Sancti Columbani Opera*, p.xxiii). St. Antony made his hermitage in a deserted fort in the Egyptian desert (Athanasius, *Life of St. Antony*, in Migne, *Patrologia Graeca*, vol. 26, col. 862).

66. See notes 6, 9, 11, 13, *supra*. The famous fifth-century warrior-family of the British King Cunedda, who drove the Irish from North Wales, gloried in Roman military titles and names, and seems to have assisted in the defense of the Roman Wall (Lloyd, *A History of Wales*, I, 116 ff.). See note 8 to *Life of St. Cuthbert.*

against the rich and blended background of that Celtic-Roman world of the north.[67] Not all the Roman influences in the *Lindisfarne Gospels* or in Bede's mental world came from Canterbury. To see the complete mosaic one's glance must take in at the same time heroic, kindly, visionary Cuthbert of Lindisfarne, and Wilfrid of Ripon, masterfully Roman, with a touch of the Anglo-Saxon chieftain and even of Imperial Byzantium about him.

Lastly, I think it important to point out that against this whole Heroic Age background, the following hagiographies from that age should not seem disturbingly, naïvely exaggerated in their praises of their hero-saint's miracles and renown. Their authors are not modern historians or biographers, concerned about the careful handling of facts. The hagiographers freely manipulate facts and use them only as an excuse to praise God and to instruct and edify men. In the same way, no one expects the heroic-size statue erected to honor King Alfred in Wantage, the town of his birth, to be an exact likeness of the man. It expresses rather all the ideal royal qualities that any great king might be expected to possess in one degree or another. The hagiographers are writing about heroes and in a heroic literary tradition. Achilles and Beowulf do impossible things by ordinary human standards. Heroes are larger than life, they represent an eternal essence of virtue which mediocre everyman imitates them for, and prays to receive in some measure from them. The Greek hero was seen that way, and also the Christian hero-saint. Behind the hero is always a god.[68] The heroic

67. Though Celt and Roman clashed at Whitby in 664 on such Christian externals as the dating of Easter and the method of tonsure, still the Celt had deeper and more ancient ties with Rome. Patrick had brought Roman Christianity to Ireland two centuries before, and Ninian had brought it to a southern Scotland politically stabilized by the Roman peace of Stilicho (W. Simpson, *Saint Ninian and the Origins of the Christian Church in Scotland* [London, 1940], p. 21). It is very possible that the controversial Celtic customs of the seventh century were but the perpetuation of older Christian practices obsolete elsewhere, but which they, in partial isolation in the West, had preserved during the chaotic years of the Empire's dissolution. (Plummer, *Baedae Opera Historica*, II, 348-54 and Walker, *Sancti Columbani Opera*, p. xvi). The Celtic affection for Rome was deep-rooted. Even fiery Columbanus wrote of the greatness and glory Rome possessed in the eyes of "us Irish at the world's end." (Walker, *Sancti Columbani Opera*, pp. 48-49). And see note 60 to Eddius, *Life of Wilfrid*.

68. Douglas Hyde (*A Literary History of Ireland* [London, 1910]) points out in Irish epic cycles a historic sequence from gods to heroes, from heroes to men (and from men to fairies). The aristocratic heroes of Greek mythology and epic were a fusion of primitive, indeterminate gods and historic great men, a kind of "intermediate category" between the gods and ordinary men (Jameson,

is elevated to an eternal, universal plane where deeds and virtues are shared without any question of plagiarizing.[69] A deed of Hercules may be substituted at will for a deed of Achilles because in the heroic world all is in common. Felix feels no need even to explain when he uses another author's description of Cuthbert's death to depict Guthlac's death.[70] Felix's exaggerated, unnaturalistic style is surely due to

"Mythology of Ancient Greece," in Kramer, *Mythologies of the Ancient World*, p. 223. And see De Vries, *Heroic Song and Heroic Legend*, Ch. 9). The origins of epic seem surely to be religious (M. Eliade, "Recent Works on Shamanism," *History of Religions*, vol. I [1961], pp. 152-86; M. Eliade, *The Forge and the Crucible* [New York, 1962]; De Vries, *op. cit.*, Chs. 9, 10, 11, 12—especially). Even the form of epic seems to have "sacerdotal origins" (C. Autran, *Homère et les origines sacerdotales de l'épopée grecque* [Paris, 1938]). The hexameter of Greek epic seems to derive from hymns and oracles and to have been nurtured and refined by the priests (see the thesis of the whole first volume of Autran's work just mentioned, and see De Vries, *op. cit.*, p. 9).

69. The hagiographer as such is not trying to write history, or even biography, but his intent is to exalt an exceptional person, one who has attained a suprahuman dignity—a saint. With the saint as an individual he is not concerned, but with the moral ideal and example afforded by his deeds. He is not interested in the historicity of the facts but in their "myth"— their meaning and significance. The deeds of all saints exemplify the same spiritual and universal values and may be freely interchanged at the hagiographer's wish. Exaggeration naturally becomes involved in such glorification, especially if the recital of the Life is part of the Divine Office chanted in praise of God (Leclercq, *The Love of Learning and the Desire for God*, pp. 199 ff.). And in this light even the repetitions and parallelisms in the hagiographies (as in heroic epics) are seen to have a liturgical significance, with ancient roots in pagan incantation (De Vries, *op. cit.*, pp. 244 ff.). This whole process would obviously possess a continuity with the epic cult of pagan heroes, and even with myth and the reverence of the heroes' graves and relics (De Vries, *op. cit.*, pp. 230 ff.; Delehaye, *The Legends of the Saints*, pp. 126 ff.) and with the popular regard for the pagan Stoic martyrs (Musurillo, *Acts of the Pagan Martyrs*, pp. 236 ff.), and even with the literary "romance" which was to come (Jones, *Saints' Lives and Chronicles in Early England*, Ch. 4). Though the greatest and most appreciative authorities on hagiography find it necessary to make allowances for the primitive credulity displayed by the early saints' Lives (Colgrave, in Thompson, *Bede: His Life, Times, and Writings*, pp. 201-202; Delehaye, *The Legends of the Saints*, Ch. 2), it may well be, in the light of the foregoing, that in many cases no apology is really called for (Jones, *op. cit.*, p. 57).

70. Felix, *Life of Saint Guthlac*, Ch. 50, is modeled on Bede's prose *Life of St. Cuthbert*, Chs. 37-39. Bede may have caught the suggestion of a deathbed scene from the *Life of St. Antony*, but with the familiar "elegiac preoccupation

his desire to glorify his hero, to make Guthlac's cult in Mercia as famous perhaps as Cuthbert's in neighboring Northumbria.[71] The writer of Cuthbert's life is treating of a hero-saint about whom a cult has already sprung up and around whom a saga tradition has probably already arisen. Nevertheless in this *Life*, and in most of the others, it is remarkable how close a warm, homely English humanness comes to overbalancing the heroics. The sober, realistic, human tone of, for instance, Eddius' *Life of Wilfrid* and of Bede's *Lives of the Abbots* is partly due to their authors' close, personal relationship with their subjects. Deification needs a certain amount of distance.

Perhaps to see these *Lives* in their proper perspective it would be well to remember that culturally this Golden Age, Anglo-Saxon world is also Romanesque, and even largely Byzantine.[72] Its art shares

of the Anglo-Saxon mind" he developed the hint much further (Kurtz, "From St. Antony to St. Guthlac," p. 121). The touching magnificence of the death scenes in all these Anglo-Saxon Lives is remarkable and unforgettable. They add a new dimension of gentle grandeur to the heroically defiant death scenes of the pagan—and even Christian—martyrs, and they add a hopeful warmth to the heartbroken, quiet pathos of Greek funeral stele. A monk described Bede's death most movingly (see translation in Plummer, *Baedae Opera Historica*, I, lxxii-lxxviii). And see note 15 to *Life of St. Cuthbert.*

71. Colgrave, *Proceedings of the British Academy*, vol. 44, pp. 54-55. Tales of marvels from the East may also have indirectly contributed to the miraculous exaggerations in Anglo-Saxon hagiography, through the medium of the Lives of the saints of the desert (J. Lindsay, *Song of a Falling World* [London, 1948] pp. 224 ff.). And, more directly, there is the evidence of *The Wonders of the East* bound into the *Beowulf* manuscript (Sisam, *Studies in the History of Old English Literature*, p. 72 ff.), and of the Oriental version of an apocryphal story which is the ultimate source of *Andreas* (see K. R. Brook's edition of *Andreas* [Oxford, 1961] p. xv).

72. Godfrey, *The Church in Anglo-Saxon England*, pp. 176 ff., gives a good summary of the all-important Byzantine background of Anglo-Saxon culture. Signs of Byzantium are everywhere: in the Ruthwell Cross vine-scroll (Saxl, "The Ruthwell Cross," in *England and the Mediterranean Tradition*, pp. 1-19; Clapham, *English Romanesque Architecture*, pp. 63 ff.), in the illuminated manuscripts of Lindisfarne and Jarrow (Brown and Bruce-Mitford, *Evangeliorum Quattuor Codex Lindisfarnensis*, vol. II, pp. 292 ff.), in the Sutton Hoo treasure (Bruce-Mitford in Hodgkin, *A History of the Anglo-Saxons*, [3rd edition] II, 702; E. Salin, *La Civilisation Mérovingienne*, IV Partie [Paris, 1959], p. 330, traces the man-between-two-animals, on the Sutton Hoo purse lid, back through the Steppes to Gilgamesh in the "Sumerian Heroic Age" [S. N. Kramer, *History Begins at Sumer*, London, 1958, Ch. 24]), in the architecture of such churches as Brixworth (Clapham, *English Romanesque Architecture*, p. 31).

the same supranational stateliness; it is ceremonially, distortedly heroic. In Ravenna, from their gleaming mosaic that was fashioned while Heroic Age Northumbria was growing around the rock of Bamburgh, Justinian and his empress gaze down placidly, with large impersonal eyes and timeless, heroic unparticularity. They are neither primitive symbols of vague divinities, nor individual portraits of breathing persons. They belong to that aristocratic Heroic Age in between, where god and hero are still in the process of becoming man.

Heroic Ages are always located somewhere between myth and sophistication, between primitive terror and cultivated boredom, between the land of the jungle and cave troubled by strange gods, and the land of mass society whose most strange and troubling god is itself.[73]

And the channels for Byzantine influence were many. (See the suggestive article by R. S. Lopez in *Byzantion*, 18 [1946-8] 139-162). Pope Gregory, who launched the Anglo-Saxon mission, had been nuncio in Byzantium; Theodore came from the Byzantine world; and the Moslem invasion and the Iconoclast persecutions drove numbers of Byzantine scholars and artists to the West. There may have been an early traffic of Anglo-Saxon adventurers seeking service in Byzantium's armies—like the many Vikings who served in the Emperor's Varangian Guard. In his letter to Egbert, Bede complained that the inordinate appropriation of land for monasteries forced many young nobles to seek their fortune overseas (Plummer, *Baedae Opera Historica*, I, 415; translated in Whitelock, *English Historical Documents*, p. 741). Five hundred years later, Villehardouin's memoirs of the Fourth Crusade will remark on the presence in Constantinople of special forces of Englishmen and Danes, armed with their terrible axes (Villehardouin, *Memoirs of the Crusades*, [Everyman's Library, 1951], pp. 41, 46). Strangely enough, Anglo-Saxon coin-finds reveal little evidence of direct Byzantine contact (see P. D. Whitting, "The Byzantine Empire and the Coinage of the Anglo-Saxons," in Dolley, *Anglo-Saxon Coins*, pp. 23-38).

73. Heroes do not seem to exist in primitive societies where the communal preoccupation with placating the gods of nature is the paramount concern. Heroic ages only come later in more organized societies where war becomes an avenue to glory for individuals in an aristocratic class (C. M. Bowra, *Primitive Song*, [New York, 1962], pp. 133 ff.).

THE ANONYMOUS LIFE OF ST. CUTHBERT

Preface to the Anonymous Life of St. Cuthbert

Bertram Colgrave points out that this Life may well be the "earliest surviving piece of written literature" produced in England by the English ("The Earliest Saints' Lives Written in England," *Proceedings of the British Academy*, Vol. 44 [1958], p. 42). He dates its composition between the years 698 (eleven years after Cuthbert's death) and 705, by an unknown monk of Lindisfarne Abbey. In the light of this monk's constantly referring to Lindisfarne as "our island" and "our monastery" (e.g., in Bk. III, ch. 1; Bk. IV, ch. 7), it is hardly possible that Hwaetbert of Wearmouth is the author, as has been suggested (Dekkers and Gaar, *Clavis Patrum Latinorum*, p. 301). The fact that all seven extant manuscripts of this Life were written on the continent testifies to the popularity of Cuthbert (and to the thoroughness with which the Vikings and Henry VIII sacked the English monasteries) of whom it has been said that "no saint has left so deep an impression on the memory of the Anglo-Saxon nation" (quoted in Plummer, *Baedae Opera Historica*, II, 265). The cult of Cuthbert contributed even to the Golden Age of Anglo-Saxon art (see my note 2 to *Life of St. Cuthbert*; and Brown and Bruce-Mitford, *Evangeliorum Quattuor Codex Lindisfarnensis*, II, 14 ff.).

Bede's prose and verse *Lives of Cuthbert* were written not many years after the anonymous *Life*, and that he made use of the latter he admits in the Preface to his *Ecclesiastical History*. Bede's prose *Life* is fuller, and more rhetorically prolix, than the anonymous one. I have chosen to translate the latter because its greater brevity and particularity, and the fact that its author was a monk of the saint's own monastery, give it, I think, a greater charm.

The best edition, and the one I used for this translation, is Bertram Colgrave's in *Two Lives of St. Cuthbert* (Cambridge, 1940), pp. 60-139. The book includes also Bede's prose *Life of Cuthbert*, with translations of both, and copious notes. Another translation of Bede's prose *Life* is easily available in the Everyman's Library edition of Bede's *Ecclesiastical History*, and in a Penguin Classics book, *Lives of the Saints* (L 153). An invaluable recent source of information on St. Cuthbert is *The Relics of St. Cuthbert*, edited by Battiscombe (see my bibliographical note).

Bede's verse *Life of St. Cuthbert* was edited by Werner Jaeger (*Bedas metrische Vita Sancti Cuthberti* [Leipzig, 1935]), and some Middle English verse *Lives* are edited in *Publications of the Surtees Society*, Vol. 87.

THE LIFE OF ST. CUTHBERT

BOOK ONE

Chapter I: *Prologue*[1]

MY ONLY regret, holy Bishop Eadfrith,[2] is that I am not as capable of fulfilling the wishes of you and of the whole community in deed

1. In the fashion so common with medieval hagiography, the first two chapters are a remarkable tissue of literary borrowings from popular works. Our author helps himself freely to the fifth-century letter of Victor of Aquitaine on the Easter question (further interesting evidence of the interrelationship of chronology, Easter tables, chronicles, history and hagiography in seventh-century Anglo-Saxon England. See Jones, *Saints' Lives and Chronicles in Early England*), to the fourth-century Latin translation of Athanasius' *Life of Antony* by Evagrius of Antioch, and to the fourth-century *Life of St. Martin* by Sulpicius Severus. From the *Life of St. Cuthbert*, in turn, all this is borrowed almost word for word a few years later by Eddius Stephanus in the Preface to his *Life of Wilfrid*.

2. Eadfrith was the second bishop of Lindisfarne (from 698) after the death of Cuthbert, and to him Bede also dedicated his prose *Life of Cuthbert*, written a few years after the present anonymous one. Eadfrith is most famous for being named by a tenth-century note in the *Lindisfarne Gospels* as the one who wrote this marvelously illuminated copy of the Gospels in honor of St. Cuthbert—now one of the treasures of the British Museum. Scholars today maintain that Eadfrith must have done the illumination for this great book as well as the writing. See the volume of notes to the magnificent facsimile edition of the *Lindisfarne Gospels* (Brown and Bruce-Mitford, *Evangeliorum Quattuor Codex Lindisfarnensis*, II, 11). The steps in the creation of the great book are chronicled in a tenth-century inscription appended by the monk who glossed the manuscript. "Eadfrith, Bishop of the Church of Lindisfarne, originally wrote this book, for God and for St. Cuthbert and for all the saints together who are honored on this island. Ethelwald, Bishop of the Lindisfarne islanders, put the outside covering on it and tooled it in his expert fashion. Billfrith the anchorite fabricated the ornaments on the cover and decorated it with gold and gems and with pure gilded silver. Aldred, an unworthy and most lowly priest, glossed it in English with the help of God and of St. Cuthbert. . . ."

as I am in desire. For the task is a difficult one for me, and my powers of understanding are slight.[3] Yet, as far as I am concerned, even though I was overwhelmed by the amount of excellent material at hand, still I am satisfied that I have not failed in obedience to the command with which you taxed my powers. Although my ability was scarcely sufficient to perform perfectly the task enjoined me, it surely at least has made good my debt of duty to you. If anything has turned out other than as you wished I beg you to consider my inadequacy in exact relation to the demands imposed on it and to judge the labor of my imperfect enterprise more as a thing of duty than of merit. For the surest proof of my regard for you is that I devoted myself to your wishes far in excess of my powers.

Yet if I have produced anything worth your reading it is certainly attributable to divine grace. Moreover, your kindness is such as to stir even the indolent to achievement. There is no doubt the work has been carried through to completion by the faith of those very ones whose encouragement caused it to be undertaken, seeing that even I, the one on whom you so confidently place the injunction, become confident of accomplishing what you bid. Will anyone fail to understand how the task, which you believe even I am capable of fulfilling, was ventured upon only at your entreaties? Moreover, it was with great gladness that I received your gracious command, since this record of St. Cuthbert which I am making for you is also of no little profit and usefulness to myself. Just to know him for the person he was, is in itself a perfect way to virtue. To conclude in brief, even were you to believe everything that common report has circulated about Cuthbert, be assured that you would have heard only the smallest fraction of his whole great story. I am sure that no one could know all of it.[4]

3. All good medieval hagiographies begin with this protestation of the author's unworthiness for his high task. It reminds us of the opening invocation of the Muses in the classical epic, but more particularly it seems to be one of the traditional devices of ancient rhetoric passed down from late Roman literary "mannerism" to early Christian writers through the medium of authors like St. Jerome. Ernst R. Curtius calls it the rhetorical topos of "affected modesty" (*European Literature and the Latin Middle Ages*, p. 83 ff. and p. 411).

4. Here we have a tantalizing glimpse of what may well have been a vanished world of oral sagas and tales about Cuthbert that preceded his written Life. (see Wright, *The Cultivation of Saga in Anglo-Saxon England*, pp. 42 ff.). Bede

Chapter II : *Preface*

So I shall attempt to relate the life of St. Cuthbert, how he lived before his bishopric, for instance, and after he became bishop. However, I have not been able to find out about all of his miracles by any means. The ones, of course, which he alone was aware of are known to no one else. Having no need for human recognition, he wanted to keep all of his miracles hidden as far as he could. And even of those which we did know we have omitted many because we believed it would suffice to cite only the more outstanding ones. And there were our readers to be considered, lest crowding too much matter into the book should make it distasteful to them. So I beg my readers to have confidence in my story, and not to imagine that I have written down anything but what has been examined and approved. I would have chosen to keep silent rather than tell a lie.[5] But, granted that neither pen nor voice can really do justice to the great number of Cuthbert's works, let us proceed to these deeds.

refers to them too at the end of the Preface to his *Ecclesiastical History of the English People*. In so many ways the genesis of the saints' lives followed the birth-pattern traced by the secular epic and heroic poem. (See Wilson, *The Lost Literature of Medieval England*, pp. 104 ff.). First, in the case of poems, came the oral versions (see H. J. Chaytor, *From Script to Print* [Cambridge, 1945], p. 128, etc.; R. Girvan, "The Medieval Poet and His Public" in *English Studies Today*, edited by C. L. Wrenn and G. Bullough [Oxford, 1951] pp. 85-97) then from these lays were developed in the monasteries the Anglo-Saxon epic poems (Chaytor, *ibid*; Girvan, *ibid*; and Campbell, "The Old English Epic Style," in Davis, *English and Medieval Studies*, pp. 13-26). Latin verse seems to have exerted little direct influence on the latter (but see note 29). But when the vernacular stories of the saints were with some difficulty turned into the newly learned medium of Latin prose, Latin literary models were of necessity depended upon.

5. This avowal of historical trustworthiness is a stock feature of early hagiography. It is found—in practically the identical words—in all the models our author is following (see note 1). See note 69 of Introduction, and note 7 to *Life of Guthlac*.

Chapter III : *What a child foretold about him.*

At the start of the story we shall put an incident that happened early in his youth. We heard it from many, including the priest Elias, of our church, and Bishop Tumma, of holy memory, who learned it from St. Cuthbert himself—that is, the saint's divine predestination to the bishopric. They tell how when Cuthbert was eight he was the liveliest and most high-spirited of all the boys of his age. Often after the others had left the playground, worn out, he would remain, like a victor in the arena, waiting for someone else to come and play with him. One day when a crowd of boys, Cuthbert among them, were gathered on a playground, they started various kinds of vulgar horseplay. Some took off their clothes and stood unnaturally on their heads, with their legs stretched out and their feet sticking up in the air. Others, meanwhile, performed other tricks.

Now there was a certain little boy in the crowd, hardly three years old, who started pestering Cuthbert. "Be sensible," he kept telling him, "and give up these foolish pranks." When Cuthbert ignored him and his advice, the child began weeping and wailing so violently that they could hardly quiet him. Then, when asked what was the matter with him, he began to shout, "O holy bishop and priest, Cuthbert, these unseemly stunts to show off your athletic ability are not becoming to you or to the dignity of your office." Cuthbert could not quite grasp what all this was supposed to mean, but nevertheless he quit the silly games and began to comfort the child. Later he carried home with him the strange, prophetic words in his mind, as once blessed Mary had stored in her memory all the words foretold about Jesus.

Note well, brethren,[6] how by God's providence Cuthbert was revealed as one of the elect even before he was recognized by the fruits of his own labors, just as it was spoken of the patriarch by the prophet, "Jacob have I loved, but Esau have I hated" [Mal. 1:2-3]. Both Samuel and David were also chosen in infancy. And indeed Jeremiah the prophet and John the Baptist are said to have been sanctified from

6. Cf. *Heroes and Saints*, appendix I, *infra*, p. 78.

their mothers' wombs for the service of the Lord. This the teacher of the Gentiles confirmed when he said, "Whom He has predestined, these has He called," etc. [Rom. 8:30].

Chapter IV : *How an angel cured him.*

During this same period of his life, God exalted him by a second miracle, as one elected of the Lord. While still a boy living in the world he was afflicted with an ailment that tormented him terribly. A knee swelled up and the sinews so contracted that he limped badly, one foot barely able to touch the ground. One day when he had been carried outdoors and was lying alongside the house in the warm sun, he saw from afar off a man riding toward him. The man was noble in bearing and of a marvelous beauty, clothed in white garments and mounted on a splendidly caparisoned steed. Riding up to the boy, he set his wonder at rest with a courteous greeting and asked whether Cuthbert would be willing to receive him as a guest.[7] The lad, nothing daunted, disclosed his infirmity and answered, "If God so wished and had not bound me with the fetters of sickness on account of my sins, I would not be slow about ministering to guests in His honor." With that the stranger alighted from his mount and examined the boy's knee which, as Cuthbert explained to him, no doctors had yet looked at. The stranger advised him, "Cook up some wheat flour with milk, and while it is hot spread it on your knee." After the stranger had ridden on his way and Cuthbert had begun to put his prescription into effect, it suddenly dawned on him that this man was an angel of God. In a few days, in accord with his faith, he was cured. Then he gave thanks to the gracious God who had completely restored his health by means

7. In this gracious scene there is all the color and high courtesy of the great-souled ages of the epic and of the romance. We think of the host-and-guest scenes in the *Odyssey*, *Beowulf*, and *Sir Gawain and the Green Knight*—and in a later chapter of this same *Life of St. Cuthbert* (Bk. II, ch. 2). A twelfth-century illuminated manuscript containing Bede's *Life of St. Cuthbert* in the Bodleian Library, Oxford (MS. University Coll. 165, f. 12), depicts this episode of the angel horseman and Cuthbert. See Pl. VI.

of His healing angel, just as he had done for blinded Tobias. And from that time on, as he revealed to some most trustworthy men, he was never denied the help of angels whenever he appealed to God in his most desperate straits.[8]

Chapter V : *How he saw the soul of a bishop being taken up to heaven.*

On still another occasion during his youthful years in the world, he was with some other shepherds in the hills near the river Leader, grazing his master's flocks.[9] While he was following his custom of watching out the night with an endless litany of prayers, offered with simple faith from a loyal heart, he had a sudden vision granted him by the Lord. He seemed to gaze into the heavens which yawned open— not actually, by any unlocking of the elements, but to the eyes of his spirit. Like the blessed patriarch Jacob in Luz which was called Bethel, Cuthbert "saw angels ascending and descending," and bearing to heaven in their hands a holy soul, as it were, in a sphere of fire.[10] Waking the shepherds at once, he told them of the marvelous sight he had seen, and even foretold that the soul was that of a very holy bishop or of some other great person. And such, indeed, proved to be the fact, for a few days later they learned that the news had been carried far and wide of the death of our famous and holy bishop Aidan at the same hour of the night when Cuthbert had had his vision.[11]

8. Cf. *Rome and the Heroic Age*, appendix II, *infra*, p. 79.

9. And we think of another young man watching his master's flocks on Irish hills some 200 years before. He was a Romano-British captive and his name was Patrick.

10. In El Greco's "Burial of Count Orgaz," that controlled-explosion of sense and spirit, remarkable even for its Baroque Age, the soul of the Count is pictured as an unformed, wraith-like infant soaring from the arms of an angel heavenward in a white flamelike vortex.

11. Aidan was the godly and much-beloved Celtic monk and bishop whom King Oswald invited to Northumbria from Iona to found the monastery of Lindisfarne after the victory over Cadwallon at Heavenfield in 634. The Roman Bishop Paulinus had fled south after King Edwin was defeated and killed by

Chapter VI : *How the Lord sent him food on a journey.*

There is one more miracle from his youthful years which I cannot omit. Travelling once from the south and coming to the Wear River, at the place called Chester-le-Street,[12] he crossed over, but then was forced off the road by rain and wind and sought shelter in some shepherds' summer huts. Since it was now winter time, the huts were deserted and he could find no one to care for him and his horse, both worn out from travel and hunger. Unsaddling his horse and leading it inside he tied it to a wall, and settled down to wait out the storm. While he was praying to the Lord, he noticed the horse toss up its head to the roof of the hut, bite into some of the thatch and greedily pull it down towards him. All at once out of the straw tumbled some warm bread and meat carefully wrapped in a linen cloth. As soon as he had concluded his prayer[13] Cuthbert examined the package and decided

Cadwallon and Penda in 633. In Book III, especially chapters 5 and 17, of his *Ecclesiastical History*, Bede gives us a beautiful picture of Aidan and how he endeared himself to the Anglo-Saxons, kings and commonfolk alike, by his genuine and sturdy holiness and simplicity of life, his fearlessness in rebuking evil wherever he found it, his noble largeheartedness and a concern for the common people—so like that of Martin of Tours—which drew him into every corner of rugged Northumbria, usually afoot. (Characteristically, however, Bede cannot forbear gently rebuking Aidan for keeping the wrong Easter date—Cf. Plummer, *Baedae Opera Historica*, I,161.) It is therefore very appropriate that it should have been Aidan whom young Cuthbert in the Lammermuir Hills saw in this vision which was to set his life on so similar a path. Bede tells us (in Chapter IV of his prose *Life of St. Cuthbert*) that it was this vision which inspired Cuthbert to enter a monastery.

12. Here it was that many years later the Lindisfarne monks were to bring Cuthbert's holy body (and the *Lindisfarne Gospels*) for temporary refuge from the ravaging Danish Vikings. His remains were to find their final haven in Durham. (See Battiscombe, *The Relics of Saint Cuthbert*, pp. 37 ff.)

13. The humorous pointedness of this remark is lost on us unless we remember that these saints' Lives were read to monastic communities for their spiritual instruction (and usually during mealtime). Hungry young Cuthbert proceeded resolutely on to the conclusion of his prayer before examining the tantalizing food package.

that the food so timely provided for him was sent by God at the hands of the angel who had helped him through so many difficult situations. After he had given thanks to God, blessed the divine food, and eaten it, it immediately so refreshed and fortified him that in its strength he set off confidently on his way again, glorifying the Lord.

Chapter VII : *The omitted miracles.*

But, lest I should weary my reader, I shall be silent about all the other many deeds that flowered from Cuthbert's bountiful youth. I am more anxious to single out the quiet fruit of his mature years in God's service, full of the power of Christ. Thus I shall say nothing about the time when he was with the army encamped in the face of the enemy and, though he had only meager rations with him, managed to live royally the whole time.[14] He was nourished by divine means, just

14. Perhaps Cuthbert's soldiering (of which Bede tells us nothing) was in King Oswy's army which had to take the field more than once against Penda, the fierce pagan King of Mercia. In 642 the latter had defeated and killed Oswy's brother, the famous Christian King Oswald, victor of Heavenfield in 634. When Oswy succeeded to the throne of Bernicia, the northern section of his brother's Northumbrian kingdom, Penda gave him no rest, even though Oswy tried to placate him with treasures and with a son as son-in-law. (See Stenton, *Anglo-Saxon England*, p. 83.) At least twice Penda's army penetrated to the royal rock-citadel of Bamburgh, the ancient Bernician stronghold on the Northumbrian coast. On the second occasion they burned down the nearby royal country-residence in which Aidan had been given a chapel and living quarters, where he had died in 651. On the first occasion they had tried to fire the royal citadel itself, but Aidan was then still very much alive and enjoying a spiritual retreat on the jagged, lonely little island of Farne, just off the coast and within easy sight of towering Bamburgh. As soon as he spied Penda's flames he prayed to God, and winds blew the fire against the attackers and routed them (see Bede, *Ecclesiastical History*, Bk. III, chs. 16 and 17). Perhaps young Wilfrid watched the billowing smoke over Bamburgh from the off-shore island of Lindisfarne—several miles to the north—where Oswy's queen, in 648, had found him a place for a sort of noble-apprenticeship in monastic life. (See Eddius' *Life of Wilfrid*, Ch. II.) Penda was finally defeated and killed by Oswy in the Battle of the Winwaed, 654, three years after the death of Aidan and the entrance of Cuthbert into Melrose Abbey. By one of the paradoxes of this

as Daniel and the three children, after they had spurned the royal food, throve wondrously on even the smallest amounts of slaves' food. Nor shall I tell about his seeing the soul of a reeve carried up to heaven when he died. Lastly, I shall not recount how admirably he put demons to flight and cured the insane by his prayers.

BOOK II

Chapter I : *Concerning the beginning of his life in God's service.*

LEAVING his life as a layman, pious and sinless as it had been, he advanced to even better things after having arranged to bind himself to a stricter way of life in a monastery.[15] He bore up under the holy task with patience, because he had so long yearned for voluntary service in God's work that it had become a habit and part of his nature. Such fastings and watching did he undergo that his extraordinary strength alone convinced the incredulous.

Very often he spent whole nights in prayer, sometimes even continuing in it for two and three days at a time and not breaking his fast till the fourth day. He remembered well the saying of the Apostle Paul, "Now all chastisement for the present indeed seems not to bring with it joy, but sorrow: but afterwards it will yield, to them that are exercised by it, the most peaceable fruit of justice" [Heb. 12:11]. O my brothers, I do not presume to think I am worthy to tell his life. In fact, no one's words can describe it. He was of angelic aspect, of polished speech, holy in deed, spotless in body, noble in nature, weighty in counsel, orthodox in belief, most patient in hope,

Golden Age, all the children of this fierce pagan became Christians. The two daughters became nuns, and of the two kingly sons, Aethelred relinquished the throne to become a monk. Both sons figure in the life of Wilfrid.

15. Cf. *Cuthbert and St. John*, appendix III, *infra*, p. 81.

universal in charity. Nevertheless I shall attempt to unfold the story of his miracles.[16]

Chapter II: *How he ministered to an angel and was given three loaves of bread by God.*

Now there was another miracle in which this holy man of God, Cuthbert, was glorified for the first time after he had, with the Lord's help, taken upon himself the yoke of Christ's service and the tonsure of Peter, fashioned after the Crown of Thorns that circled the head of Christ.[17]

It happened in the monastery of Ripon, and we have the word of most reliable witnesses for it, witnesses who are still living. Cuthbert, the new novice, had been selected by the community to care for guests arriving at the monastery. One morning of a certain snowy, wintry day an angel of the Lord appeared to him in the guise of a visitor, a well-built man in the prime of life. In the same way angels had appeared in the form of men to the patriarch Abraham in the Valley of Mamre. And so Cuthbert, supposing all the while that the stranger

16. Cf. *Celtic Christianity and Egypt*, appendix IV, *infra*, p. 82.

17. Along with the date of Easter, the shape of the clerical tonsure was one of the main bones of contention between the Celtic and the Roman churches in Britain (see Eddius, *Life of Wilfrid*, Ch. 10). The Celtic monks shaved the front half of the head from ear to ear; and though they claimed the authority of St. John for this practice, Roman monks like Aldhelm charged that it was originated by Simon Magus, "the inventor of the art of magic" (Aldhelm in his famous letter to British King Geraint, of Devon and Cornwall, in Haddan and Stubbs, *Councils and Ecclesiastical Documents*, III, 270. And see Duckett's discussion of this letter in *Anglo-Saxon Saints and Scholars*, pp. 78 ff. See also Ceolfrith's letter to the Pictish King Nechtan in Bede's *Ecclesiastical History*, Bk. V, ch. 21).

But even though Cuthbert received the Roman tonsure at predominantly Celtic Melrose, he was among that group of Melrose monks who refused a few years later to conform to the Roman Easter date after they had been called to the newly-founded monastery of Ripon by King Alchfrith. The king sent them back to Melrose about 661 and handed the new monastery over to Wilfrid (see Bede, *Ecclesiastical History*, Bk. V, ch. 19. And see Eddius, *Life of Wilfrid*, Ch. 8).

was a man instead of an angel, received him kindly as was his wont, washing his hands and feet and drying them with towels. Because of the cold weather he even humbly rubbed the man's feet between his hands to warm them.

Cuthbert very earnestly invited him to wait till the third hour of the day when he could be served a meal, but the man, anxious to resume his journey, was unwilling and refused. Finally, however, after entreating him in the name of Our Lord Jesus Christ, Cuthbert overcame his resistance. Then, after the bell had sounded the third hour of the day and after prayer was over, he set out a table with what food he happened to have on hand. For it chanced that somehow there was no bread in the guest house except for fragments which he now collected for the "brotherly meal" and placed on the table. Then the man of God went back to the monastery to get a full loaf, but to no avail because they were still baking the bread in the oven. So he returned to his guest, whom he had just left eating, but the man had disappeared. Cuthbert could not even find his footprints in the snow that covered the ground outside. He realized then that the stranger was an angel of God, and in amazement took the table back to the storeroom. As soon as he entered, his nostrils were filled with the aroma of the most delicious bread, and he found three warm loaves there.

Then he gave thanks to God because in him had been fulfilled the saying of the Lord, "He that receiveth you, receiveth me. And he that receiveth me, receiveth him that sent me." And again, "He that receiveth a prophet in the name of a prophet, shall receive the reward of a prophet. And he that receiveth a just man in the name of a just man, shall receive the reward of a just man" [Mt. 10:40-41]. From this day on, God frequently fed him when he was hungry, as he confided to some sworn brethren, not boastingly but for the edification of many, just as Paul related many things about himself.

Chapter III: *How sea animals ministered to him, and how a brother who put him to the test was cured.*

Another story I must tell is the following one, passed on to me by many good men, among them Plecgils, who was a priest at the time in the monastery we call Melrose. Cuthbert was sent for by the nun, Aebbe, a widow and the mother of all in Christ. He came as he was bid to the monastery of Coldingham and remained there for some days.[18] Not relaxing his regular way of life he maintained his custom of singing and keeping vigil, and he took to walking along the seashore at night. A certain cleric in the community learned of this, and anxious to find out what Cuthbert did during the night, began to follow secretly at a distance and spy on him. But Cuthbert, the man of God, walked determinedly down to the sea and out into the waves up to his belt. Once even he was soaked all the way up to his armpits by the swelling, tumbling surf. Then when he came up out of the sea and knelt down on a sandy stretch of the shore to pray, two little sea animals followed right in his footsteps and stretching out humbly on the ground they licked his feet, and rolling on them they dried them with their furry skin and warmed them with their breath. After this service, as soon

18. Aebbe was the daughter of Aethelfrith, the last pagan king of Bernicia. After Edwin of Deira killed Aethelfrith in battle in 616, she may have accompanied her prince-brothers, Oswald, Oswy, etc., into exile among the Picts and Scots, and may have been baptized there (see Chadwick, *Studies in Early British History*, p. 160). She became one of the many royal Anglo-Saxon ladies who ruled as abbesses of monasteries. She is later to use her influence on her nephew, King Ecgfrith, to get Wilfrid released from prison (Eddius, *Life of Wilfrid*, Ch. 39). This phenomenon of the royal nuns is one of the fascinating parts in the picture of Anglo-Saxon England's "aristocratic" Golden Age (see H. Howorth, *The Golden Days of the Early English Church*, III, 175-237). Even more interesting is the fact that no small number of these monasteries, like Coldingham, were double houses, one for monks and one for nuns, all under the rule of the abbess. This practice seems to have been known early in the East and to have spread across Europe to Gaul and Ireland before the seventh century (see Ryan, *Irish Monasticism*, pp. 141 ff.). There was the famous one at Poitiers presided over by Frankish Queen Radegunda, immortalized in the poetry of Fortunatus. Aebbe's at Coldingham, on the Berwickshire coast (traditionally said to be founded by Aidan on the ancient site of a fortress) was the only one of the Anglo-Saxon double monasteries about which we learn of any scandals. Bede implies that its eventual destruction by fire was a sign of God's anger (*Ecclesiastical History*, Bk. IV, ch. 25). Perhaps Cuthbert's stay at Coldingham (Anonymous *Life of St. Cuthbert*, Bk. II, ch. 3) led to his prohibiting women to enter his church at Lindisfarne and to the subsequent exaggerated tradition of his anti-feminism. (See Symeon of Durham, *History of the Church of Durham*, Ch. 7 [Rolls Series, vol. 75, pt. 1, pp. 58 ff.])

as their ministrations were complete, they received Cuthbert's blessing and returned to their home in the waves. At cockcrow that man of God came home for formal prayer in the church of God with his brethren.

But the above-mentioned cleric from the community lay hidden among the rocks, trembling and terrified at what he saw. He passed such an anxious night that he came near to dying. Next day he threw himself at Cuthbert's feet and, weeping, begged pardon and absolution. The man of God answered him in prophetic words, "My brother, what is the matter? Have you tried to test me and spy on me more intimately than you should have done? Even so, since you confess it, this shall be forgiven you on one condition, that you will vow never to tell it as long as I am alive." And so the brother vowed (and kept the vow) and went away healed, with Cuthbert's blessing. But after the latter's death, he told many of the brethren how Cuthbert had been ministered to by animals, just as we read in the Old Testament that lions had served Daniel.

The brother told also how Cuthbert had, with the aid of spiritual sight, miraculously discovered the fact that he was lying hidden and observing him, just as Peter detected Ananias and Sapphira putting the Holy Spirit to the test.

Chapter IV : *Concerning the dolphin flesh which the Lord provided for him, and concerning his prophecy.*

On another occasion he set out from the same monastery of Melrose with two brothers and sailed to the country of the Picts where they arrived safely at what is called the region of the Niduari.[19] They re-

19. The sea here must have been the Firth of Forth, which is only about twenty-five miles above Melrose by the convenient old Roman road whose northern limits reached up from Corbridge (near Wilfrid's Hexham) at the Roman Wall (see Chadwick, *Studies in Early British History*, pp. 166-68). The road passed just to the west of Old Melrose by the ruined Roman fort of Trimontium on the Tweed. Route A 68 now parallels much of this section of the ancient highway of the legions. Trimontium (now Newstead) was one of the many Roman

mained there for some days in great want, afflicted with hunger, while a stormy sea prevented them from sailing on their way. Meanwhile that man of God, having prayed the whole night through on the shore, came to them on the morning of the feast of the Epiphany of the Lord (for they had begun their journey after the feast of the Nativity) and told them with great assurance, "Let us go look for food, begging of God in accord with what he promised when He said, 'Ask and it shall be given to you. Seek and you shall find. Knock and it shall be opened to you' [Mt. 7:7]. For I believe that the Lord will make us a present of something to celebrate this day on which the Magi paid Him homage with their gifts, and on which the Holy Spirit descended upon Him in the form of a dove after His baptism in the Jordan, and on which He turned water into wine in Cana of Galilee to strengthen His disciples' faith."

So the three of them rose and went searching. With Cuthbert in the lead, as though he were a guide, they went to the seashore and, looking about there, immediately discovered three portions of dolphin flesh that seemed to have been cut off with a knife by a human hand and washed with water. Thereupon the man of God threw himself upon his knees, giving thanks to the Lord, and said to his companions, "Take them up and bring them away, and let us bless the Lord. Three pieces, you see, will be sufficient for three men for three days and nights, and on the fourth day the sea will be calm for sailing." So they carried the food away and cooked it, and enjoyed the marvelous sweetness of the flesh. Remaining then three days through the storm, on the fourth day they sailed away in bright weather—as he had said they would—and happily arrived at a safe landing place. One of these two very brethren, named Tydi, who is still alive and a priest, gave us the story in the presence of many witnesses. He praised God for providing meat for Cuthbert on this occasion just as graciously as he once provided it for Elias in the desert. When he foretold the storm and the calm, Cuthbert was inspired by the same spirit with which the Apostle Paul prophesied to the voyagers in the Acts of the Apostles [Acts, 27].

sites associated with the Arthurian legend (Loomis, *Wales and the Arthurian Legend*, p. 16).

Chapter V: *How an eagle caught a fish in accord with Cuthbert's prophecy.*

The above-mentioned priest Tydi told us about yet another miracle which is known to many. One day Cuthbert was walking along near the River Teviot teaching and baptizing the countryfolk as he made his way southward among the mountains.[20] To a boy of his company who was walking by his side he said, "Do you suppose anyone has a meal ready for you today?" The boy replied that he knew of no relative along that route and that he hardly looked for any sort of kindness from foreigners and strangers. But the servant of the Lord spoke to him again, "Don't be discouraged, lad. The Lord who said, 'Seek ye therefore first the kingdom of God and His justice, and all these things shall be added unto you' [Mt. 6:33], will provide food for those who trust in Him. And He will provide also in order that the word of the prophet may be fulfilled, 'I have been young, and now am old; and I have not seen the just forsaken' [Ps. 36:25], and so forth. For 'the laborer is worthy of his hire'" [Luke 10:7].

Then, after these words, he looked up at the sky and saw an eagle flying. He said to his boy, "This is the eagle that the Lord has ordered to serve food to us today." A little later as they were walking on their way they saw the eagle sitting on the river bank. Running up to the eagle, as the servant of God bade him do, the boy found a large fish.[21] When

20. In Chapter IX of his prose *Life of Cuthbert*, Bede tells us that after Cuthbert took over Boisil's priorship of Melrose he frequently interrupted his busy life in the monastery to make long evangelical sallies without the walls. No village was too remote or inaccessible or poverty-stricken for him to visit, sometimes afoot and sometimes on horseback. He was known to have been away for as much as a month at a time. This monastic knight-errantry, bringing the Gospel from the cloister to the countryside, was the special note of Celtic monasticism which Bede had so ungrudgingly admired in Aidan. It descended less from Egypt than from Tours and St. Martin (see Appendix IV, p. 82).

21. These charming animal stories are another link between the monks of the Egyptian desert and the monks of Celtic Britain. One of the most famous episodes in Jerome's *Life of St. Paul the First Hermit* told how a crow's gift of a piece of bread enabled Paul to play the gracious host to his equally gracious

he brought it intact to Cuthbert, the latter asked, "Why didn't you give a piece of it to our hungry fisherman?" So the boy then gave a portion of the fish to the eagle as the man of God told him to do. Taking the rest of it with them to a group of people, they broiled it and all made a satisfying meal of it. Then, after praying to the Lord in thanksgiving, they set off in the will of God for the mountains, as we said above, "Teaching and baptizing them in the name of the Father and of the Son and of the Holy Spirit" [Mt. 28:19].

guest, St. Antony. It is revealing that this very incident is the only non-Biblical subject to find place among the ten principal panels that were carved on the great Ruthwell Cross in the course of our Northumbrian Golden Age (see Plates XI, XII, XIII). In fact, on the north face of this 18-feet-high cross four of the five panel-carvings pertain in one way or another to the early Christian preoccupation with the desert. In the top panel, along with the Lamb of God, is depicted St. John the Baptist, the desert saint *par excellence*. Below him Christ in glory stands on two beasts who suggest but differ from the traditional lion and dragon (as in the sixth-century mosaic in the Archbishop's Palace at Ravenna, where a beardless Christ wears the military garb of a Roman emperor), and Latin characters around the panel read, "Jesus Christ, judge of justice. Beasts and dragons acknowledged the Savior of the world in the desert." Next is the picture of Paul and Antony breaking bread in the desert, and the panel below that portrays the Flight into Egypt. Of further interest is the fact that all these panels contain animals, either real or symbolic. Even the fifth panel may have originally included the ox and the ass of Bethlehem, for the remaining traces of carving there suggest a Nativity Scene. Even the surviving top section of the original north face of the cross (it was broken off and later replaced backwards on the main stem of the cross) atop the shaft pictures St. John the Apostle and an eagle, in keeping with what appears to be St. Matthew and his angel on the lower of the four arms of the crosshead. The two missing arms probably included St. Luke with his ox, and St. Mark with his lion. (For detailed descriptions of the Ruthwell Cross see Brown, *The Arts in Early England*, vol. V, and J. K. Hewison, *The Runic Roods of Ruthwell and Bewcastle* [London, 1914] Ch. III. Clapham in Chapter III of his *English Romanesque Architecture* discusses the influence of Constantinople and Ravenna on the vine-scroll decorations of the Ruthwell Cross. Saxl, "The Ruthwell Cross," in *England and the Mediterranean Tradition*, pp. 1-19, discusses in detail the Eastern Mediterranean influences in the Ruthwell Cross, and provides good photographs).

Chapter VI : *Concerning the prophecy in which he foresaw the devil deceiving his hearers.*

At that time while he was there in the mountains, baptizing, as we said, he happened to be teaching the word of the Lord in a certain village in his usual earnest way. Suddenly, by the prophetic spirit of God, he foresaw the devil tempting his listeners and trying to hinder the hearing of the word of the Lord. So he forewarned them on the spot about the delusions of the great deceiver, saying among other things, "O my dear brethren, if any temptation should suddenly spring up outside, be steadfast and don't be deluded into running out, thus interrupting and even preventing the hearing of the word of God."

Then after he had taken up again the thread of his discourse and was expounding the words of the Gospel, they heard the crackling of flames from a burning house and the shouting of a crowd. Straightway his congregation, except for a few he held back by hand, rushed out excitedly and ran to the house which seemed to be on fire. In their frenzy to extinguish the flames they demolished the walls of the house, only to discover not the slightest trace of smoke which would have either preceded or followed a fire. Realizing then that they had been deceived by a devilish trick just as the servant of God had predicted, they returned to the building they had left and fell to their knees before the feet of the preacher. But he prayed for those who had been fooled by Satan's trickery and they won forgiveness after confessing that they realized it was one of the many cunning frauds perpetrated as supernatural apparitions. All of them therefore went home happy, much the wiser and sounder for Cuthbert's lesson.

Chapter VII : *How by a word of command he saved the home of his nurse from a raging fire.*

At this time the holy man of God was often invited to visit a saintly widow named Kenswith (who is still living today), who had raised him as a boy from the time he was eight years old till he came of age and took up the service of God. Therefore he called her "Mother," and was in the habit of visiting her. One day when he arrived at the village of Hruringaham, where she lived at the time, a house happened to be afire on the extreme east edge of town and a strong east wind was whipping up the blaze. His "mother," badly frightened, ran to the house he had stopped at and begged him to be good enough to implore God's help and save their homes from the raging flames that were threatening them. But Cuthbert very confidently reassured her, saying, "Fear not, for these flames will do you no harm." Then falling prone on the ground outside the door he prayed silently. And even as he was still praying a great wind rose from the west and drove the whole mass of flame harmlessly away from the houses. So, seeing the power of God was in him and that his protection had preserved them unharmed, they gave thanks and blessed the Lord.

Chapter VIII: *How he cured a woman who was tormented by a devil.*

There was a certain religious man, named Hildmer, who was especially dear to Cuthbert, and whose wife was terribly tormented by a devil. Grievously afflicted and tortured to the point of death, she gnashed her teeth and wept and groaned. When her husband saw that she was undoubtedly on the verge of a miserable death he set out for our monastery and asked for Saint Cuthbert, who happened to be prior of our community [of Lindisfarne] at that time.[22]

Hildmer explained to him that his wife was ill and at the point of death, but he did not reveal the fact that the affliction was madness. He was ashamed to let it be known that a woman once so religious was possessed by the devil. For he did not realize how frequent a thing it is for such a trial to happen to Christians. So he requested only that some priest be sent with him to administer the last rites. At once

22. Our author for some reason anticipates things in this chapter and narrates an event from Cuthbert's life at Lindisfarne, though it is not until the following chapter that he tells us how Cuthbert left Melrose for Lindisfarne.

the man of God went out to arrange for someone to be sent with him. But no sooner had he left than, touched by the spirit of God, he turned back again and recalled Hildmer, saying "Surely this office is mine. It would not be right for me to send anyone else to go with you in my place."

Then Cuthbert got ready and they all rode off together on horseback. Cuthbert saw tears on Hildmer's face and knew that he was grieving not only for his dying wife, soon to leave him desolate and his children motherless, but also for the shame of her terrible madness. Hildmer knew that the man of God would see her in her horribly degraded condition, shamefully abased, defiled with spittle, she who was once so modest and pure. So Cuthbert began to console him very gently and let him know that he already understood all about her infirmity which Hildmer had concealed from him. Then he added, speaking with the voice of a prophet, "Just as soon as we arrive at your home your wife, who you believe is already dead, will run out to meet me, and when she takes this horse's reins, which I now hold in my hands, the devil will be driven from her with God's help and she will be cured. Afterwards she will wait on us." So they arrived at the village, and the woman, as though rising from sleep, came to meet them. Then as soon as she touched the bridle the devil was completely driven out, her former health was restored, and she waited upon the visitors.

BOOK III

Chapter I: *How in his desire to live according to Scripture he finally took up the life of a solitary on an island and carved out a cell in the rock.*

St. Cuthbert therefore, as prior in the aforesaid monastery of Melrose, served the Lord well, and the Lord worked many miracles through him which I have endeavored to record for the sake of those whose faith is weak. At last, however, he fled worldly honor; he quietly and secretly left the monastery and sailed away.[23] Thereupon, being very persuasively invited by our venerable and holy Bishop Eata, he came with God's help to our island of Lindisfarne, where he cured the possessed and healed various other afflictions—sometimes even without his needing to be present.

23. Bede tells it differently in Chapter 16 of his prose *Life of St. Cuthbert.* With a concern for Roman discipline he states carefully that Cuthbert was transferred from Melrose to Lindisfarne by the direct order of his abbot, Eata. But the account of our earlier author rings more true to the nature of Cuthbert. He is Roman by grace, but by nature he "belongs to the world of ancient Irish saints" (Stenton, *Anglo-Saxon England*, p. 126). We can so readily picture him slipping away quietly from Melrose to follow the lonely call of pilgrimage-exile (*peregrinatio*) that stirred the Christian Heroic Age of Ireland and Anglo-Saxon England. Most of the manuscripts of our text say *enavigavit* here ("he sailed away"—Colgrave, *Two Lives of Saint Cuthbert*, p. 94) just as Adamnan wrote of Columba's leaving Ireland for Britain, *pro Christo peregrinari volens enavigavit* ("longing to be a pilgrim-exile for Christ, he sailed away"—Anderson, *Adomnan's Life of Columba*, p. 186). Earlier in the Life when our author described Cuthbert's short journey in the Firth of Forth (Bk. II, ch. 4) he simply used *navigans* ("sailing"—Colgrave's edition just referred to, p. 82). Guthlac was to follow the *peregrinatio*-call, in a more missionary sense, and Willibrord and Boniface, and a host of others. (For a recent discussion of the whole Celtic *peregrinatio* ideal see Chadwick, *The Age of the Saints in the Early Celtic Church*, pp. 82 ff.) Perhaps Cuthbert retraced the familiar path to the Firth of Forth and put to sea like the spellbound narrator of "The Seafarer" (see Dorothy Whitelock, "The Interpretation of *The Seafarer*," in *Early Cultures of North-West Europe*, edited by Fox and Dickins, pp. 261-272) to find some rugged island-hermitage. Or perhaps it was the North Sea that called him. At any rate, his abbot at Melrose, Eata, who had just been given the abbacy of Lindisfarne as well, after the Synod of Whitby (at which, in 664, King Oswy decided that the Northumbrian Church should henceforth follow the Roman Easter date in place of the Celtic) had demanded the abdication of the Celtic Bishop Colman, now forcibly invited (*invitatus coacte*) the wandering Cuthbert to be prior at Lindisfarne. Such Celtic monastic wandering as Cuthbert's was to be explicitly subordinated to Roman obedience some years later by the fourth, fifth, and sixth decrees of the new Archbishop Theodore's first synod in England (that Synod of Hertford, in 672, which "had a centralizing tendency which paved the way for the political union of the so-called Heptarchy." E. O. James, *A History of Christianity in England*, [London, 1963], p. 30. For the synod's decrees see Bede's *Ecclesiastical History*, Bk. IV, ch. 5). But twelve years later Cuthbert was to get his solitary hermitage after all.

And in his desire to live there in accord with Holy Scripture, he led a contemplative life within an active one and thus laid down for the first time the foundation of that way of life which we agreed upon and have observed up to the present day along with the rule of St. Benedict.[24] Then after many years his longing for a solitary life took

24. Gentle Cuthbert with his Celtic ways was the inspired choice to help bring the touchy, troubled monastic community at Lindisfarne into line with Roman practices after the Synod of Whitby. Their vanquished champion at that Synod, Bishop Colman, had gone back to Iona and with him had gone those of the brethren whose Celtic sympathies would not permit them to remain. But even those who chose to stay behind were in no mood to welcome an ardent Roman reformer. As it was, even Cuthbert had to bear no little abuse from some of them. They were most set against giving up their familiar way of life for the new discipline (see Bede's prose *Life of St. Cuthbert*, Ch. 16).

Our anonymous author makes it clear here that Cuthbert's "rule" was not just the Benedictine Rule. Perhaps, judging from his own rigorous mode of life, it was basically the stricter Columban rule, which even in monasteries in Gaul was followed for a long time along with the Rule of St. Benedict. In that case it was paradoxical that the new prior of Lindisfarne, sent there to bring the monastery more in line with Roman observance, also made it even more Celtic. And thus it must have been even more inevitable that he endear himself to the main body of the community because the natural inclination of Celtic monasticism was always toward the more ascetic, more Egyptian ideal. Thus we see in later centuries in Ireland it was the stricter Cistercian Order which was the most popular. The 12th-century Melrose, which rose near the ruins of Old Melrose of the Celtic Heroic Age of the Saints, was Cistercian. We can imagine what sort of reception Wilfrid, the victorious spokesman for the Roman rite at the Synod of Whitby (see Eddius, *Life of Wilfrid*, Ch. 10), would have received at Lindisfarne in 664—especially in light of the fact that as a young man he had himself received his first religious training there, while the holy Aidan, its Celtic founder, was still alive (Eddius, *Life of Wilfrid*, Ch. 2).

But it was defeated Colman himself who seems to have saved the situation by requesting King Oswy to have Eata of Melrose appointed to succeed him at Lindisfarne. Eata was one of the twelve English boys whom Aidan had taken into the monastery to educate right after King Oswald had first invited him from Iona in 635 (Bede, *Ecclesiastical History*, Bk. III, ch. 26). He was so Celtic in his ways, that, as we have seen, King Alchfrith had sent him and Cuthbert back to Melrose from the new monastery of Ripon for not following the Roman dating of Easter. But Alchfrith was only a sub-king (and a rebellious one at that, according to Bede, *Ecclesiastical History*, Book III, ch. 14) under his father, King Oswy, and the latter was probably no little annoyed at his son's zealous espousal of the Roman cause and of Rome's champion, Wilfrid

him to the island which we call Farne, amidst the waves, bound in by the sea on all sides. Before this hardly anyone had ever been able to stay there alone any length of time because of various devilish apparitions. But Cuthbert stoutheartedly routed them,[25] and then

(see Eddius, *Life of Wilfrid*, Ch. 7 ff.). Oswy himself had been converted and educated in exile by Celtic monks and had, tradition says, even had a Celtic princess (Rieinmelt—Queen of the Lightning) for wife before he later married the daughter (Eanfled) of the king (Edwin) who had exiled him (see Chadwick, *Celt and Saxon*, pp. 41 ff.). Oswy's brother, Oswald, had invited Aidan to Lindisfarne, and Colman, the second successor to Aidan's see (i. e., after Finan), was a dear friend of Oswy.

So even though at Whitby Oswy found himself obliged to decide for Rome by reasons of spiritual prudence (Eddius, *Life of Wilfrid*, Ch. 10) and of domestic harmony (his queen, raised in Kent, kept to the Roman Easter date, and was moreover annoyed at the confusion caused when part of the court celebrated the Easter feast while the rest were still keeping the Lenten fast. See Bede, *Ecclesiastical History*, Bk. III, ch. 25), still his heart was largely with the Celts. Hence it may well have been with no little satisfaction that after the Synod he deliberately placed in Colman's vacated office, Eata, the monk whom his son had ejected from the abbacy of Ripon in favor of Wilfrid, and who had been educated by Celtic Aidan. (Meantime, however, both Eata and Cuthbert had obviously agreed to keep the Roman Easter Calendar.) Shortly thereafter Oswy had another of Aidan's former pupils, Chad, appointed to Wilfrid's see of York during the latter's absence in Gaul (Eddius, *Life of Wilfrid*, Ch. 14. Ten years previously Oswy had sent Chad's brother, Cedd, also Aidan-trained, to convert the East Saxons under King Sigbert. See Bede, *Ecclesiastical History*, Bk. III, ch. 22). And about a year after the Synod of Whitby, Oswy refused to let Alchfrith make a trip to Rome, which the latter had planned to take with Benedict Biscop (see Bede, *Lives of the Abbots*, Ch. 2).

25. And so did Guthlac have to rout demonic haunters before he could take possession of his fenland retreat at Crowland (Felix, *Life of St. Guthlac*, Ch. 25). From remotest ages of myth, gods and heroes have fought dark powers to wrest some portion of the universe from their control. Apollo had to overcome the ancient python that possessed Delphi before he could found his shrine. Beowulf killed a dragon guardian and won a fated treasure for his people. And the serpents and dragons faced by gods and heroes merged into the demon foes of the saints. "And there was a great battle in heaven: Michael and his angels fought with the dragon . . . and that great dragon was cast out, that old serpent who is called the devil and Satan" [Apocalypse, 12:7-9]. Bede's account of Cuthbert's routing the evil spirits on Farne adorns the incident with all these timeless epic trappings of heroic combat. "But when the warrior of Christ advanced upon the island armed 'with the helmet of salvation, and the shield

by digging down almost a cubit into the stony ground and the very hard rock he made dwelling space. Another cubit above the ground he built a marvelous wall compounded of earth and of stones so huge as to defy the belief of all save those who knew that such strength of God was in him.[26] And he made little huts there from which he could see nothing except the sky above.[27]

of faith and the sword of the spirit, which is the word of God, all the fiery darts of the most wicked one were extinguished' [Eph. 6:16] and that foulest of foes was driven in headlong flight with the whole host of his allies. Then when this soldier of Christ had vanquished the army of the kings of terror and had become monarch of this land he had marched into, he founded a city worthy of his rule and erected dwellings within it that were fitting for such a city" (Bede's prose *Life of St. Cuthbert*, Ch. 17).

26. Cuthbert's stone hermitage is similar to those which the Celtic "saints" have left all over Ireland. See F. Henry's study of them in *Proceedings of the Royal Irish Academy*, vol. 58, Section C, no. 3 (1957), pp. 45-166, plus 49 plates. And as we watch Cuthbert handling the huge stones we think back to the Cyclopean stone walls of the Homeric Age fortress cities of the heroes. Wandering through the massive ruins of Mycenae and Tiryns today it is easy for the visitor to imagine forgotten giants wrestling these rocks into place. "Hector seized hold of a stone that was lying before the gate and carried it forward . . . . No two of a city's best men, the kind of mortals that we breed today, could lift such a stone from the ground onto a cart without difficulty. But he handled it lightly, and alone" (Homer, *Iliad*. XII, vv. 445-9). The circle of huge sarsen stones (each about as tall as the Ruthwell Cross—eighteen feet), which was set up at Stonehenge in Wiltshire during the Golden Age of Homeric Mycenae and the final years of Minoan Crete, displays technical signs of Mycenaean influence (see L. Cottrell, ed., *Concise Encyclopedia of Archaeology* [New York, 1960], p. 426). Graves of contemporary "Wessex warrior-princes" were rich with jewelry and armor reflecting eastern Mediterranean contacts (see J. and C. Hawkes, *Prehistoric Britain* [London, 1947], pp. 70 ff). Attempts have even been made to interpret the "megalithic" architecture of the Celtic Heroic Age as arguing a direct ethnic link with Mycenae and Crete and Egypt (see H. O'Brien, *The Round Towers of Ireland* [London, 1898] 2nd edition, pp. 85 ff.). Gordon Childe suggests that the megalith tombs of pre-historic Europe were the chapel-shrines of a wave of neolithic missionaries whom he calls "megalithic saints" and compares interestingly with the later Celtic saints (*The Prehistory of European Society*, [Penguin Books 1958] pp. 128 ff.).

27. Bede's description of Cuthbert's Farne hermitage in his prose *Life of St. Cuthbert* (Ch. 17) is ambiguous. It can mean either that the saint built for himself one building with two rooms, or two separate little buildings. Our anonymous author clearly explains that Cuthbert, in typical Celtic—and Egyp-

Chapter II : *Concerning the rock which four of the brethren could not budge but which he set into his wall all by himself.*

Once when four of the brethren visited him to help with his work, he bade them take his cart and bring him a certain rock which happened to be further back on the island. Obediently they went right off to the stone without delay, but they had to abandon it half way back so as not to destroy his cart or injure themselves. Then the brethren sailed away, but came back again on a visit not many days later. And there neatly fitted into Cuthbert's construction they recognized their stone which they had not been able to move. Then they fell to praising and glorifying the Lord, who works such great wonders in his servants, recalling the words of the psalmist, "God is wonderful in His saints," etc. [Ps. 67:36].

Chapter III : *How the Lord gave him a spring of water from the rock.*

It happened that again on another day some brethren came to visit him. As was his custom, Cuthbert first explained part of the Gospel to them, then after his instruction he said to them, "My dear brothers, you know that this place is practically uninhabitable because of lack of water. Therefore let us beg the Lord's help, and then will you dig

tian—fashion, built his two little buildings inside a surrounding wall or *cashel* (see Colgrave's note on p. 326 of his edition of *Two Lives of St. Cuthbert*). A good idea of Cuthbert's building-plan can be obtained from the sketch of a reconstructed eighth-century Irish monastic settlement appearing on p. 297 of Peter Bamm's fascinating illustrated book, *The Kingdoms of Christ. The Story of the Early Church* (London: Thames and Hudson, 1959). Dom Watkin ("Farne Island and St. Cuthbert," *The Downside Review*, 70 [1952], p. 297) interprets Bede's description to mean that Cuthbert's hermitage consisted of one building with two rooms.

into this rocky soil in the middle of the pavement-floor of my house, because God has the power to call up water from stony rock for him who asks. Once indeed he provided water from a rock for the thirsting people when Moses struck it with a twig. And when Samson thirsted He gave him to drink from the jawbone of an ass." So while Cuthbert prayed, the brethren dug into the ground as he had directed and suddenly they saw a stream of "living water" [Jn. 4:10,14] gush up from the rocky soil and flow forth in front of them. We ourselves have tested the pronounced savor of its sweetness and do continue to this present day to enjoy its taste. Even the servant of God himself, our anchorite, declared—as I have understood from the report of most trustworthy people—that for him this God-given water had the flavor of every kind of delightful drink.

Chapter IV : *How his servant, the sea, brought him wood.*

Another miracle which the Lord worked out of love for his soldier, and which I am not going to pass over in silence, is this one. He asked the brethren who came to visit him for some wood twelve feet in length which he wanted as the foundation of a certain small building. For there was a rock, hollowed out by the waves, which thrust up from the sea and bordered on the far edge of Cuthbert's hermitage. He planned to put the twelve-foot beam we spoke of over the edge of the rock and across to his living area, and then on top of it he intended to build a shed. But though he asked the monks for the beam he would not have obtained it (and may God not charge this against them) had he not prayed to our Lord Jesus Christ and received help from Him. For that very night the waves rose on the sea and brought a twelve-foot log floating in, especially in honor of the servant of God, and carried it to the hollow of the rock where it was to be put in position for the building. And so when they wakened in the morning the brethren saw it and gave thanks to God, astonished at how in honor of Christ the sea had shown itself to be more obedient to the hermit than had men. Still to this day the shed built on the crossbeam can be seen by seafarers.

Chapter V : *How Cuthbert drove away the birds, and then how he pardoned them when they returned with a little gift.*

Just as the sea made itself the servant of the man of God, in the manner which we related, so did the birds of the air obey him. Now at first for two or three years before he cloistered himself away behind closed doors, he labored and earned his daily bread from the work of his own hands, mindful of the saying, "If any man will not work, neither let him eat" [2 Thess. 3:10]. There on his island one day while he was digging up the earth in furrows he noticed that two crows, old residents of the place, were making a nest for themselves by tearing apart the roof of a shelter for sea travelers that had been built at the landing place. With a little wave of his hand he ordered the nest-builders to stop doing this harm to the monks. But as they paid no heed he finally became angry and drove them off the island with a stern command to depart in the name of Jesus Christ. Thereupon without any delay they abandoned their home in obedience to his order.

But after several days one of the two returned and perched on the edge of a furrow at the feet of the man of God, who was digging in the earth. Spreading its wings and bowing its head it began to croak loudly, grieving and begging humbly for forgiveness and pardon. Christ's servant acknowledged their penitence and granted them the privilege of returning. Then the crows, now that peace had been made, both returned to the island within the hour, bringing a little gift. For each carried in its beak an almost equal piece of hog's lard which it deposited at Cuthbert's feet. And after he forgave them this offence they have remained there to this day. These events were related to me for the glory of God by most trustworthy witnesses who visited him and throughout the course of an entire year greased their shoes with the lard.

Chapter VI : *Concerning his prophecy about the death of King Ecgfrith and about the heir, and about his own episcopate.*

A nun called Aelffled,[28] who was a virgin and a royal abbess, humbly entreated the holy hermit of God to sail to meet her in the Lord's name at Coquet Island. When he arrived the handmaid of God knelt down before him and proceeded to ask him many things. Finally, however, she boldly adjured him in the name of Our Lord Jesus Christ and the nine orders of angels and the persons of all the saints, and then she asked how long her brother, King Ecgfrith, would live. Thereupon the man of God, thus solemnly adjured, and fearing the Lord, began to speak in a roundabout way of the brevity of man's life, and concluded with these words: "O my handmaid of God, is it not but a short time even though a man were to live for twelve months?" Perceiving at once that he had spoken of the king, she wept bitterly. And after a year's time the overthrow of the royal power by the evil might of an enemy sword renewed for her and for many others the bitterness of those tears.[29]

28. Aelffled had, in her infancy, been consecreted to God by her father, King Oswy, in thanksgiving for his victory over Penda in the Battle of the Winwaed in 655. (And one recalls that when her mother, Eanfled, was a baby she too had been offered to God's service by her father, King Edwin, for help in a battle. She was the first Northumbrian baptized by Paulinus. See Bede, *Ecclesiastical History*, Bk. II, Ch. 9). Aelffled became abbess of Whitby after the famous Hild (in fact, for a time, Aelffled ruled Whitby in conjunction with her mother, Eanfled) and she was later to do a great service for Wilfrid (see Eddius, *Life of Wilfrid*, Ch. 59, 60), whom her abbess-aunt had previously assisted (*op. cit.*, Ch. 39), and whom her mother, as queen many years before that, had launched on his brilliant and stormy career (*op. cit.*, Ch. 2).

29. Cuthbert is foretelling the death of Ecgfrith at the Battle of Nechtansmere (685). In Book IV, ch. 8, the author of this Life tells how, on the occasion of the battle itself, Cuthbert, a bishop by then, has a vision of the tragic outcome which he imparts to Ecgfrith's queen.

It is interesting and typical that in the present passage our author uses a famous Vergilian word, "renewed" (*renovavit*), with its memory of quite other tears—Aeneas' for Troy, *Infandum, regina, iubes renovare dolorem . . .* ["You have asked me, your Majesty, to recall the unutterable sorrow. . . . "] (*Aeneid*, Bk.

But now she still persisted and put another question to Cuthbert. "By that same Unity and Trinity I adjure you to tell me whom he will have as an heir." He was silent for a moment, and then said: "You will find that he will be no less a brother to you than was the other." This seemed incredible indeed, but nevertheless she begged him earnestly to tell her where the heir-to-be was. He bore with her patiently and said, "O handmaid of God, why be astonished even if he should be on some island beyond this sea?" At once she understood that he had spoken of Aldfrith,[30] now peacefully reigning, who at that time was on the island called Iona.

II, verse 3). And in other Anglo-Saxon hagiographies too there are echoes of Vergil. Felix's *Life of Saint Guthlac* is full of them, and so, for example, is Alcuin's verse-chronicle "On the Bishops and Saints of the Church of York" (Rolls Series, Vol. 71, Part 1, pp. 349 ff.). Bede, and the Irish before him, knew Vergil (see Laistner, *Intellectual Heritage of the Early Middle Ages*, pp. 97, 123). Vergil has ever been an important link between the hero and the saint—not just in relating the classical hero and the Hellenistic saint, nor in just relating the classical hero and the Germanic saint, but even in the evolution of that Germanic hero concept itself which was to influence the Germanic saint-concept. A poem of such epic proportions as the Anglo-Saxon *Beowulf*, for instance, could hardly have developed so soon from the old heroic Germanic and Scandinavian short songs unless Latin epic had occupied a large space in the Anglo-Saxon monastic libraries. (See De Vries, *Heroic Song and Heroic Legend*, p. 58, and Campbell, "The Old English Epic Style" in Davis and Wrenn, *English and Medieval Studies*, pp. 13 ff.). And it was Vergil's epic which seems to have exerted the most influence (see T. B. Haber, *A Comparative Study of Beowulf and the Aeneid* [Princeton, 1931]). However, Campbell, for instance, argues that Latin verse had little demonstrable influence on the monastic origins of Anglo-Saxon poetic epic style (*op. cit.*). See note 4 *supra*.

30. Aldfrith was an older and illegitimate son of Oswy, whom Celtic tradition says was born of an Irish princess, daughter of one of the most learned men of seventh-century Ireland. (Most of the sources of our information about Aldfrith are referred to in Chadwick, *Celt and Saxon*, pp. 333 ff.). Bede says that Aldfrith was one of the many young Anglo-Saxon noblemen who became pilgrim-exiles in Ireland for the sake of the learning to be found there. But it is also probable that his exile among his books was no more voluntary than Prospero's was in Shakespeare's play. His brother Ecgfrith seems to have preferred this claimant to the throne out of the way, and wanted him tonsured as an added precaution. At any rate we know that he was at Iona around 684, and later that he was the respected friend of Abbot Adamnan of Iona, Columba's famous biographer. Among the Irish, Aldfrith was remembered as a poet, and in England this "philos-

And because she knew that the king wished to call Cuthbert to the episcopacy she went on to question him about himself, that is, whether the matter would turn out that way and how long he would be a bishop. In reply, after disclaiming any worthiness on his part for the dignity, he said that nevertheless he would not be able to hide himself from the honor of this office either at sea or on land. "And within the short space of two years," he said, "I shall find rest from my labors. But you now in your turn must receive an injunction from me in the name of Our Lord Jesus Christ, that as long as I live you will reveal this to no one." Finally, after voicing many more prophecies, all of which turned out exactly as he foretold, he sailed back to his hermitage.

Chapter VII : *Concerning the manner of his solitary life.*

And thus for several years did he persevere in this life of solitude, withdrawn from the gaze of men and enduring all manner of things with the same equanimity. His face always reflected the same spirit within.

opher-king" was the life-long friend of scholarly Aldhelm, and was praised for his learning by Eddius Stephanus, Bede, and Alcuin. Aldfrith's court has been suggested as the literary center which fostered the Golden Age poetry of Northumbria. Albert S. Cook even proposed the king himself as the author of *Beowulf* (*Transactions of the Connecticut Academy of Arts and Sciences*, 25 [1922], pp. 281-346).

Certainly Aldfrith was an important channel of those rich Celtic cultural influences which were so vital a part of the Northumbrian Golden Age. Roman Ripon and Wearmouth and Jarrow by themselves did not constitute a Golden Age. They needed Iona and Lindisfarne and Melrose. It is significant that during Aldfrith's reign Lindisfarne produced that glory of illuminated manuscripts, the *Lindisfarne Gospels*, and our anonymous *Life of St. Cuthbert*, perhaps the earliest piece of written literature in England, and that also at the same time Jarrow saw the composition of the first works of Bede. By restoring political stability to the kingdom after his father's shattering defeat at Nechtansmere, Aldfrith provided the climate of peace necessary for the things of the spirit to blossom at Lindisfarne and Jarrow. He may be called the "sunset king," last of Northumbria's great rulers, but like King Arthur in Sherriff's play who talks to his men with his back to the sunset, he looks bigger than life (see Sherriff's play [1955] about the end of Roman Britain, entitled "The Long Sunset").

Cheerful and happy always,[31] sadness never clouded his face with the memory of sin. But then neither was his happiness due to the lavish praises of those who marvelled at his manner of life. His conversation, seasoned with salt, consoled the sorrowing, instructed the ignorant, reconciled enemies, and persuaded all to put the love of Christ ahead of everything else. Before the eyes of all he opened the boundless vision of future happiness, and at the same time he disclosed the mercy of God and his blessings already graciously given. "Because God did not spare his own son, but delivered him up for the salvation of us all." [Rom. 8:32].

BOOK IV

Chapter I: *How he was forced by the synod to accept the bishopric.*

CONSEQUENTLY it was not long before he was appointed to the bishopric of our church of Lindisfarne by the wishes of King Ecgfrith and the Saxon bishops and the whole council. Then the king, and Bishop Tumma of holy memory, and chosen men from our community came to him within his hermitage and announced the decision of the council. On bended knees they adjured him by our Lord Jesus Christ to accept. Protesting and in tears, he was carried off to Archbishop Theodore[32] and the council who were still awaiting him.

31. This entire description of Cuthbert's virtues is borrowed verbatim from Evagrius' translation of Athanasius' *Life of St. Antony*, with one significant change. Where Athanasius had said that Antony never burst into laughter, the biographer of Cuthbert, writing in the Celtic atmosphere of Lindisfarne, substituted "cheerful and happy always." The irrepressible Celtic temperament tolerates no serious gloom. Its heroes laugh and its saints are cheery. From the beginning, Irish heroes laugh even at their own heroism (see V. Mercier, *The Irish Comic Tradition* [Oxford, 1962,], Ch. 2).

32. Theodore is one of the most important figures in Anglo-Saxon history. A monk educated in the Hellenistic world of Athens and Paul's Tarsus, he was

A short while later, therefore, he took up the bishopric; and though it is not in our power to relate how and in what degree he distinguished himself, we deem it better to say something about it than to be silent altogether.[33] He firmly refused to change from the kind of person he had been before, remaining just as humble at heart and keeping to the same style of dress. So he managed to fill the office of bishop with the utmost dignity and graciousness, but without renouncing the monastic life or eremitic perfection. In everything he followed the doctrine of Paul the Apostle, mindful of what he had said to Titus, "A bishop since he is the steward of God's house, must needs be beyond reproach. He must not be an obstinate or quarrelsome man, one who drinks deep, or comes to blows, or is grasping over money. He must be hospitable, kindly, discreet, upright, unwordly and continent. He must hold firmly to the truths which have tradition for their warrant; able there-

appointed to the primatial see of Canterbury in 668 by Pope Vitalian after King Oswy's candidate had died of the plague in Rome while waiting to be consecrated (Bede, *Lives of the Abbots*, Ch. 3). Arriving in England in 669, five years after the Synod of Whitby, Theodore proceeded to the task of complete ecclesiastical unification which Whitby had only falteringly begun. He set up an efficient Roman diocesan organization (which Boniface later was to reproduce in Germanic Europe) throughout the various Anglo-Saxon kingdoms, and his bringing the bishops together in general council was the first important step toward political unification of the country (see Stenton, *Anglo-Saxon England*, p. 133). Some of his finest bishops were Celts, but he would allow none of their holy idiosyncrasies to interfere with Roman discipline and practicality. (Paradoxically enough, he had the most trouble with the most "Roman" of his bishops—Wilfrid. See Eddius, *Life of Wilfrid.*) When saintly old Bishop Chad insisted on trying to make the visitations of his diocese on foot as Aidan had done, Theodore lovingly but quite firmly lifted him bodily into the saddle and sent him riding on his rounds (Bede, *Ecclesiastical History*, Bk. IV, ch. 3). And in Kent, Theodore, with the help of Abbot Hadrian of Byzantine Africa, who had fled from the Moslems to Grecian southern Italy, started schools which included Greek in their curriculum, and whose reputation for learning finally began to rival the Irish schools. Aldhelm, for instance, was attracted to Canterbury away from his Irish masters at Malmesbury. And Theodore must surely have been one of the channels for those Byzantine influences so evident in Golden-Age Anglo-Saxon art. (See Clapham, *English Romanesque Architecture*, Ch. 3.)

33. Much of this account of Cuthbert's episcopal virtues is borrowed from Sulpicius Severus' *Life of St. Martin.*

fore to encourage sound doctrine and to show the wayward their error" [Titus 1:7-9; 1 Tim. 3:3] Therefore, Cuthbert's speech was plain and frank, and at the same time full of nobility and dignity, sweetness and grace, whether he was treating of the ministry of the law or the teaching of the faith, or the virtue of chastity, or the practice of righteousness. He counselled everyone differently, so that, gauging his advice to each one's personality, he could determine in advance just what and when and how to speak. Above everything else he devoted himself especially to a life of fasting, watching, praying and the reading of Scripture. His memory served him in place of the books themselves when he went through the Bible.[34] Following the examples of the saints he kept peace with the brethren and preserved his humility and that greatest of graces, charity, without which no other virtue is of any account. He took care of the poor, fed the hungry, clothed the naked, received travellers into his house, ransomed captives, and protected widows and orphans, that he might merit the reward of eternal life amid the angel-choirs in the company of Our Lord Jesus Christ.

Chapter II : *About his manner of life as a bishop.*

As a bishop, therefore, Saint Cuthbert was so renowned for virtue that through him, by means of signs and marvels, the Lord fully and perfectly enhanced the dignity and the authority of his office. His priests and deacons who were with him have told us that in him was fulfilled both in a spiritual and a bodily sense what we read about the Apostles, "Whatsoever you shall loose upon earth, etc." and "Whatsoever you

34. Of course memorization would be a general necessity in the early medieval world of few books. And poorly lighted monastic churches would make the memorizing of the Psalter almost imperative. Wilfrid seems to have memorized two different versions of the Psalms (Eddius, *Life of Wilfrid*, Chs. 2, 3). The *Life of St. Antony* states that this saint knew large portions of the Scripture by heart, and such memorizing was part of the regular training in Celtic monasteries (Ryan, *Irish Monasticism*, p. 379 ff.). For the Celts this learned cultivation of the memory had its age-old roots in the practices of the Druids and the bards (Ryan, *ibid*, pp. 365 ff.).

shall bind upon earth" [Mt. 18:18]. For "there were many signs and miracles done before the people," as is said in the *Acts of the Apostles* [Acts 5:12].

Chapter III : *How he healed a noble's wife of a hopeless illness.*

One of these miracles concerned a certain noble[35] of King Aldfrith, named Hemma, who lived in the district of Kintis, and whose wife was confined with an illness that had brought her to the point of death. While our holy bishop was making his way about the countryside preaching the word of God to the people, he came to the village of this noble. Hemma at once went out to meet the bishop and, giving thanks to the Lord for his coming, graciously received him and his companions into his house and ministered to their wants. As soon as their hands and feet had been washed, he revealed to the bishop the thing which was the sorrow and pity of the whole household—the ebbing life of his wife who was already given up for dead. He asked the bishop if he would bless some water, trusting that if she were meant to die it would help her to die more easily, or if she were to be restored to life then it would cure her the more quickly.

Cuthbert thereupon sat down and, while all watched, blessed the water and handed it to his priest named Beta (still living) who then

35. "Noble" here has not the later meaning of an hereditary aristocrat living on land won by the exploits of some dimly remembered ancestor. The Latin word used by our author (and by Bede) is *comes* ("companion": usually translated into Anglo-Saxon by *gesið*). It takes us back to the heroic dawn of things when nobles were still daring young adventurers in the personal entourage of kings (*comitatus* is the Latin word Tacitus uses in the first century A.D. for the band of warrior-companions of a Germanic chieftain). By their own courage and loyalty they won rewards of land on which to found a family (see the many charters recording such Anglo-Saxon kingly grants in Finberg, *The Early Charters of the West Midlands*). Benedict Biscop was thus rewarded by King Oswy (Bede, *Lives of the Abbots*, Ch. 1). In the present instance, Hemma is one of King Aldfrith's "companions" who has already been given an estate. See note 24 to Introduction.

carried it into the bedchamber where the wife lay like a dead woman, drawing her last breath. He sprinkled the water over her and her bed, then he got her to open her mouth and swallow a little of the water. At once she regained the use of her senses and her understanding. Gratefully, she blessed God for dispatching such guests to restore her health; then without more ado she rose from her bed completely cured and, like St. Peter's mother-in-law, proceeded to wait on them. She was the first of all the household to offer the chalice of joy[36] to the bishop, who had just snatched from her the chalice of death as she lay dying.

Chapter IV : *Concerning the healing of a holy nun.*

From the priest Aethilwald, now prior of the monastery of Melrose, I learned of another cure, one which he himself witnessed. In his own words: "We came one day with the holy bishop to a village called Bedesfeld, where a certain nun who was a relative of mine lay ill. For almost an entire year she had been tormented with pain in her head and throughout one whole side of her body. No physician was able to cure her with any bodily salve. But when we told our bishop how she was afflicted with this ailment, and asked his help, he took pity on her and anointed her with the very chrism which he himself had consecrated. From that hour she began quickly to regain her strength. The pain diminished from day to day, and she was restored to her former health."

Chapter V : *Concerning the cure of a boy who was paralyzed.*

I learned of another similar miracle from the certain account of many reliable men who witnessed it. One among them, named Penna, gave

36. And we think of the many festive scenes in England's early literature where noble ladies offer this Germanic "chalice of joy" to royal guests. Geoffrey of Monmouth tells of Hengest's daughter presenting the chalice to King Vortigern (*History of the Kings of Britain*, Bk. VI, ch. 12), and in *Beowulf* (v. 625) Queen Wealhtheow offers the "hall-cup" to the hero of the Geats.

this account: "The holy bishop once had set out from Hexham on his way to the city of Carlisle. But in the middle of the journey a halt was made in the district called Ahse where he remained for two days, preaching the word to the crowds of people who came down from the mountains. He laid his hand on the head of each one of them, and anointed him with consecrated oil and blessed him. Meanwhile some women arrived carrying a boy stretched out on a litter. Bringing him to a wood not far from our tents where the holy bishop was, they sent a messenger to the bishop entreating him in the name of Our Lord Jesus Christ to bless the boy with his holy relics. They begged him also to pray to the Lord for the lad and beg God to pardon the sins that bound him and for which he suffered punishment. At the sight of this confident faith of theirs, the bishop thereupon dismissed us from his presence and prayed to the Lord. Then, blessing the boy, he drove out the disease and restored his health. Afterwards the bishop glorified the Lord Jesus Christ for aiding His servant who trusted in Him. For the boy got up that very hour and took something to eat, then departed with the women, thanking and glorifying the Lord for working such wonders in His servants."

Chapter VI : *How he cured a woman's child and prophesied about her whole family.*

The priest Tydi, whom I have mentioned before, related the following to me: "Once during that plague which wiped out so many districts, our holy bishop happened to be in a certain village called Medilwong, preaching the word of God to the survivors, when he turned to me and said with infinite compassion, 'Is there anyone in the village still suffering from this terrible plague, whom I may visit to instruct and bless?' I at once complied and pointed out to him a woman standing nearby who was sorrowfully weeping for a son who had just died, while she held in her arms another who was scarcely alive, swollen throughout his whole body, and struggling for his last breath. Without hesitating he went right up to the woman and kissed her child and blessed it and said to her, 'Dear lady, do not weep. Your son will be all right, and no one of your whole family who is still living will die from the plague.' That all this so happened, the mother and son are to this day living witnesses."

Chapter VII : *How a certain noble's servant was cured.*

Nor do I feel that I should neglect to mention an act of compassion related to me by one of our priests, Baldhelm, who is still among us. The incident took place in the very presence of Baldhelm, who at that time was a layman in the following of a certain noble. In his own words: "At the time when the holy bishop had set out to preach the word of God among the common people, my lord Sibba who was a noble of King Ecgfrith, and who lived near the Tweed River, invited him to visit his village. The bishop came, accompanied by some people piously singing psalms and hymns. After my lord had graciously welcomed the bishop, he showed him a servant of his whose life was pitilessly being choked out by a hopeless disease; in fact he was already breathing his last.

"Moved with compassion, the holy bishop blessed some water and bade me give it to the invalid. 'Give this water to your lord's servant, and with the Grace of God, in accordance with our saving faith, may the Lord so pardon him the sins for which he is afflicted that he will be granted an end to pain either in this life, in case he is meant to recover, or in the life to come, in case he is destined to die.' Immediately I did as he asked. Three times I gave the man to drink, and at once I beheld him brought back to life and restored to his former health with the aid of God's Spirit (for the Holy Spirit is not accustomed to work slowly). And the man is still alive, thanking the Lord and blessing the bishop, for whom he has never ceased to pray."

Chapter VIII : *Concerning his vision of the slaying of King Ecgfrith on the very day and hour that it happened.*

At the time when King Ecgfrith[37] was pillaging and ravaging in the land of the Picts (only at length to be overcome and slain, in accord

37. Ecgfrith, son of Oswy and Eanfled, was the last and perhaps most greatly

with the predestined judgment of God) our holy bishop journeyed to the city of Carlisle and visited the queen,[38] who was then awaiting

tragic of the warrior-kings of Northumbria. Except for Oswy, all of them died in battle, from Aethelfrith at the Battle of the Idle in 616 to Ecgfrith at Nechtansmere in 685. By early victories over the Picts in the north and over Mercia to the south Ecgfrith extended his sway so far that when Bishop Wilfrid fell out with him in 678 he could find security from the king's wrath only in the remote fastness of pagan Sussex (Eddius, *Life of Wilfrid*, Chs. 24-41). And though much of Ecgfrith's kingdom trickled away after the typically Germanic Heroic-Age defeat, the Götterdämmerung of Nechtansmere, still the golden years of his conquests had laid the foundations for the great cultural flowering that the reign of his scholarly half-brother, Aldfrith, was to see. Once the boundaries of the kingdom had been stretched to sufficient compass the Heroic Age of war and conquest was free to become the Golden Age of culture. As the business of battle slackened, more and more nobles became monks, like Eastorwine who had served in Ecgfrith's own *comitatus* (Bede, *Lives of the Abbots*, Ch. 18). During Ecgfrith's early victorious years Wilfrid's ecclesiastical possessions had been so extended by the king's conquests that the bishop was able to build and adorn at Ripon and Hexham two of the most splendid churches of their time (Eddius, *Life of Wilfrid*, Chs. 17, 22). During the same years Ecgfrith became the enthusiastic benefactor of one of the master builders of Northumbria's Golden Age, Benedict Biscop. The king gave him land and money for the founding of Monkwearmouth, and about 681 he most generously provided for the founding of Jarrow (see Bede's *History of the Abbots*, Chs. 1, 7)—perhaps the two most famous monasteries of the Golden Age, the monasteries which gave us Bede. Ecgfrith marked out the location for Jarrow's altar himself, and, tragically enough, the inscription stone still preserved at Jarrow indicates that the church was dedicated less than a month before his death (see the photograph and translation in Blair, *An Introduction to Anglo-Saxon England*, p. 156). Tragedies crowded upon him at the end. In 684 he became the first of many English kings to launch an ill-fated invasion of Ireland, against the pleading of the holy pilgrim-monk Egbert; and the following year, against the advice of Cuthbert himself, he invaded the land of the Picts and met his doom (Bede, *Ecclesiastical History*, Bk. IV, ch. 24). He died under the enemy swords, and around him his *comitatus* fell to a man, bound by the Heroic-Age Germanic warrior code (see Bede's prose *Life of St. Cuthbert*, Ch. 27). Some 300 years later another Anglo-Saxon warrior band was to die in a hopeless Viking-battle and hew their way to immortality in *The Battle of Maldon*, the last of the Anglo-Saxon heroic poems (see Plate VIII).

38. Queen Iurminburg, Ecgfrith's second wife, was the one who, by her jealousy of Wilfrid, made the king his bitter enemy. Eddius tells us that after the king's death she was transformed from a "she-wolf into a lamb of God" and, like so many Anglo-Saxon queens, became the abbess of a monastery

the outcome of Ecgfrith's expedition. Many priests and deacons still living testify that at three o'clock on the afternoon of the Saturday, the reeve of the city, named Waga, was showing them the city wall and a marvelously constructed fountain in it which, he explained, had been built long ago by the Romans.[39] The bishop was standing, leaning on his walking staff, with his head bent down toward the ground. Suddenly he raised his eyes heavenward, sighed and exclaimed: "Oh, I think that the war is over and that the decision has gone against our fighting men." Then everyone fell to questioning him anxiously,

(Eddius, *Life of Wilfrid*, Ch. 24). Here in Carlisle during the Battle of Nechtansmere she was visiting her sister's monastery (see Bede's prose *Life of St. Cuthbert*, Ch. 27). Eddius tells us that Iurminburg was sister of the queen of King Centwine of Wessex (Eddius, *Life of Wilfrid*, Ch. 40), so perhaps it is Centwine's queen (who had caused her husband to forbid Wilfrid asylum in his kingdom in 681), who now too has been transformed into a "lamb of God" and is abbess of the monastery in Carlisle. We have some evidence that Centwine abdicated his throne to enter a monastery shortly before his death in 685 (see Plummer, *Baedae Opera Historica*, II, 221), so perhaps husband and wife entered religion at the same time. It has even been suggested that the Abbess Eangyth who wrote a long letter to St. Boniface about 720 (Tangl, *S. Bonifatii et Lulli Epistolae*, pp. 21 ff.) and Centwine's former queen are the same person (Howorth, *The Golden Days of the Early English Church*, III, 233). But Smith and Wace, *Dictionary of Christian Biography*, II, 16, warn that the identification is hardly probable.

39. This guided tour around the ancient city inside the west end of Hadrian's Wall reveals fascinatingly how the Anglo-Saxons had fallen under the spell of Rome (and on Carlisle and Cuthbert see note 11 to Introduction). A haunting little Anglo-Saxon poem, *The Ruin*, speaks of Roman ruins (probably those of Bath in Somerset) as *enta geweorc*, "the handiwork of giants" (see the recent edition by R. F. Leslie in *Three Old English Elegies* [Manchester University Press, 1961]). It was in the neighborhood of the Wall and its ruined legionary forts and towns and chapels that so much of Northumbria's Golden Age lived out its span. In a real sense it even grew from the Roman ruins. Roman-dressed stones and columns went into Wilfrid's church at Hexham and into Benedict Biscop's Monkwearmouth and Jarrow. The dedication stone at Jarrow is cut in Roman characters that could have been copied from any of scores of tablets along the Wall. Classical elements in such Northumbrian art as the *Lindisfarne Gospels* may well be traceable to the local influence of provincial Roman art in these extensive ruins of the Wall (Bruce-Mitford, *Evangeliorum Quattuor Codex Lindisfarnensis*, II, 115 ff., and Saxl, "The Ruthwell Cross," in *England and the Mediterranean Tradition*, pp. 18-19).

wanting to know what had happened, but he would only answer enigmatically, "Oh my children, consider how wonderful the sky is, and recall how inscrutable are the judgments of God," and so forth. And then a few days later they heard everywhere the news of the sad and tragic battle which had taken place the very same day and hour that the vision of it had come to him.

Chapter IX : *About the hermit who died on the same hour that the holy bishop had prophesied for his own demise.*

A certain worthy hermit named Herbert, from an island of the western lake,[40] made a habit of coming to speak with St. Cuthbert when the latter was in Carlisle. On one of these occasions they were conversing about spiritual things, as was always the hermit's wish, and saying their many prayers together. Suddenly, after having given the hermit much spiritual instruction, the holy bishop uttered a prophecy—one which he had spoken to many. "Oh my dearest brother, be sure that you say and ask about all those things that are most important to you, for after this hour we will never again see each other in this world—just as Paul predicted to the Ephesians."

Then the hermit fell on his knees at the bishop's feet and entreated him with tears: "I beg you in the name of Jesus Christ, the Son of God, to ask the Holy Trinity not to leave me behind in this world after your death, but to admit me into the joy of the eternal kingdom with you." So while the hermit lay prostrate, the bishop prayed at once to the Lord. Then he said, "Rise and rejoice, for this is actually going to be granted you by the Lord Jesus Christ just as you asked." Therefore why not come right to the conclusion of the story without delaying through a long circumlocution? The bishop and the hermit both later

40. This was Derwentwater, and the island on which Herbert the hermit lived is still known as St. Herbert's Isle. Bishop Cuthbert was paying a second later visit to Carlisle on this occasion for the purpose of bestowing the veil on Iurminburg, and of ordaining priests (see Bede's prose *Life of St. Cuthbert*, Ch. 28).

died on the same night and at the same hour, in accord with the bishop's promise; and they reign together with Christ forever and ever.

Chapter X: *How a brother fell from a tree and how Cuthbert saw his soul being carried to heaven.*

The Abbess Aelffled, a most trustworthy witness, told me about another miracle of supernatural knowledge involving the holy bishop. It happened that one day when they were sitting together among a company at table, in his diocese of Ovington, she was amazed to see the man of God become so rapt in a trance that he dropped the knife he was holding and let it fall onto the table. Then in a low voice, unheard by the others, she asked him what it was that had been revealed to him. His answer was: "I saw the soul of a servant of God from your household carried to heaven in the hands of angels and placed in the choir of angels and holy martyrs."[41] When she asked him the man's name, he responded, "You will give his name to me tomorrow while I am celebrating Mass."

So that very hour the abbess sent a messenger to her monastery to ask which of the brothers had died recently. But he found everyone there alive. However, after inquiring carefully they learned that one of the brethren living out in the shepherds' huts had fallen down from the very top of a tree and was killed, his whole body shattered. Next day the messenger returned to the abbess and reported what had happened, and the abbess ran at once to the bishop. He was dedicating the church there that day and was singing Mass. Coming breathless into the church at that point in the Mass when the *Memento Domine famulorum* was being said, she indicated to the bishop that the name of the brother was Hadwald. Thereupon not only in this affair did she realize Cuthbert's spirit of prophecy, but in all things she recognized

41. Bede's account of this incident includes a humorous touch so typical of "Celtic" Cuthbert. When Aelffled turned to Cuthbert at the table and anxiously inquired why he had gone limp and dropped his knife, he replied: "Do you think I am able to eat all day long? I have to rest sometime" (Bede's prose *Life of St. Cuthbert*, Ch. 34).

his apostolic foreknowledge, a foreknowledge which clearly predicted in many ways even his own death.

Chapter XI : *How of his own volition he gave up the bishopric to return to his former way of life.*

And so after two years, of his own accord, he relinquished the worldly honor of his bishopric. Filled with the prophetic spirit of God and foreseeing his own death, and drawn by the love of his former solitary life, he went back again to the island whence he had once been forcibly removed. There he remained alone, content with the society of angels and with their service, full of hope and placing his trust wholly in God, while his now ailing body was afflicted with some sickness.

Chapter XII : *How a brother was cured of dysentery.*

During the last stages of his illness he asked a certain faithful and experienced brother named Walhstod (who is still living) to come as a special assignment and look after him in his cell. Now this monk, though ill himself with dysentery, gladly consented, and the first time he touched the bishop he felt his own sickness leave him completely. With grateful tears he often recalled the story for his brethren and pointed out that before he was restored to health he had been so ill as to be practically given up for dead.

Chapter XIII : *How he peacefully passed to the Lord and was buried with honor in our church.*

After he had received Communion, Bishop Cuthbert of holy memory raised his eyes and hands to heaven, commended his soul to the Lord, and, while still sitting up, breathed his last and departed without a sign in the path of his fathers.[42] They brought his body by boat over to our island of Lindisfarne, where we first washed the whole body, then wrapped a cloth about his head and placed a host on his holy breast. He was wrapped in a waxed shroud, then clothed in his priestly vestments, and had his shoes on in readiness to meet Christ. While his soul made merry with Christ, and his incorruptible body rested as though asleep in his stone coffin, we buried him with all honor in our church.

Chapter XIV : *How his body was found incorrupt after eleven years.*

Now by the prompting of the Holy Spirit, after eleven years it happened that the foremost men of the entire community decided after a council was held by the elders, and after permission had been granted by Bishop Ealdberht, to raise the remains of holy Bishop Cuthbert's bones from the sepulchre. But when they first opened the tomb they found a marvel—the entire body was as intact as when they had laid it there eleven years before. The skin had not withered and wasted away, and the sinews had not dried up; nor was the body stretched stiff and rigid, but the limbs were moveable at the joints, and in their repose they looked fully alive. His neck and knees were like those of a living man, and as they lifted him from the coffin they were able to bend his body as they wished. No part of the vestments or shoes which had been next to his skin had worn away. When they unwound the wrappings about his head they found that the cloth still retained its first shiny whiteness. Both this cloth and the new shoes he had on are preserved for a testimony to this day near the remains in our church.

42. Bede's fuller account of Cuthbert's death on the little island of Farne, about seven miles below Lindisfarne, is very moving. Felix copies it in great part for his account of Guthlac's death (Felix, *Life of Saint Guthlac*, Ch. 50).

Chapter XV : *How a father's only son, who was tormented by a devil, was healed in the presence of Cuthbert's remains.*

And in honor of His holy martyr[43] after his death, the Lord granted health to many men in accordance with their faith. Thus one time a father of a family came to our island bringing, in a wagon,[44] his son who was plagued by a demon and was screaming and weeping and tearing his body. He brought the boy to the relics of the holy apostles and martyrs of God, as he had been privately instructed to do by the priest Tydi[45] (often mentioned by me), who had himself not been able to heal the boy and drive out the demon. And so the demoniac shouted and screamed, as we have said, and the many who heard him were struck with horror. Many even lost hope that any remedy would be able to restore health to the poor boy. But one good man of strong faith who was moved to pity put his trust in God and implored the help of St. Cuthbert. Then he blessed some water and sprinkled in it a little of the earth from that trench in which the water that washed our holy bishop's dead body had been poured out. The boy took a sip. of the blessed water, and that very night he stopped his mad babbling. The next day he came with his father, and in the presence of our community, offered his prayers of thanksgiving before the relics of the

43. Referring to a confessor as "martyr" is another link between Celtic and Eastern Christianity. The early monks of the Egyptian desert embraced heroic asceticism as a substitute for the bloody martyrdom that was denied them. Irish monks too, with no opportunities for martyrdom till the Viking invasions of the ninth century, looked on a life of strict renunciation as a martyrdom. The seventh-century *Cambrai Homily* lists three kinds of martyrdom—white, green, and red. The first two refer to ascetical mortification, the third to shedding of blood (Chadwick, *The Age of the Saints in the Early Celtic Church*, pp. 93-95).

44. The traveller to Holy Island (Lindisfarne) even today can drive there at low tide across the wet sand.

45. Again a humorously human touch. The priest Tydi, reluctant to broadcast the fact that he himself has failed to cure the boy, but anxious that the lad be healed, went to the father secretly and urged him to take the sufferer to the shrines on Lindisfarne.

saints for whose love he believed God had heard him. Then glorifying the Lord "in his saints" he returned, cured, to the home from whence he had come.

Chapter XVI : *How a brother was freed, in honor of the Martyr, from an infirmity.*

God wishes to fulfill in Cuthbert what Christ Jesus foretold about John the Evangelist when he said, just before leaving the world, "It is my will that he should wait till I come" [Jn. 21:22]. For every day many miracles are worked among us by the power of the Lord in honor of the holy confessor of God and of his incorruptible body. We recall one of these which happened only recently.

A brother of the household of Bishop Willibrord[46] came to us from across the sea and was hospitably received, but while he was staying in the guesthouse he came down with a serious illness. After a long affliction he was almost wasted away and had so little hope of life that he fell into despair. One Sunday he said to a servant of our monastery, "After the celebration of Mass today take me, if you possibly can, to the place where the body of God's confessor rests. For I believe if I put my hope in God with a pure and constant faith that in honor of His servant either he will bless my ailing and wasted limbs with the wholeness of health from the whole and incorruptible body of the saint, or he will set me free from the bonds of misery and grant me some share of the heavenly glory which Cuthbert's soul possesses."

To conclude the story without more ado, the brother was brought there by the servant with difficulty, then he stretched out in front of

46. Perhaps this visit is a key to one of the many mysteries attendant upon the great works of Anglo-Saxon Golden Age art. It is now thought that the beautifully illuminated *Echternach Gospels* were executed at Lindisfarne, as another product of the same school of artists who produced the *Lindisfarne Gospels* (Brown and Bruce-Mitford, *Evangeliorum Quattuor Codex Lindisfarnensis*, II, 16, 89 ff.). Could the monk from Willibrord's monastery who visited Lindisfarne on this occasion be the one who conveyed the Golden Gospels with him to Echternach when he returned home after his cure?

the relics with his face to the ground, and prayed. As soon as his prayer was ended he rose up, cured, and gave thanks to the Lord. He walked away by himself, without anyone's help, and returned to the guest-house. Then, after a few days, he set out again on his way in God's will, a sound man.

Chapter XVII : *How a boy was freed there of a palsy which afflicted his whole body.*

There is another similar miracle I would like to mention which happened this very year. A young lad who was a paralytic was brought in a wagon from another monastery to the skilled physicians of our monastery. They tried with every possible cure to relieve him as he lay there helplessly with almost all his limbs powerless. But they accomplished nothing after long effort and, despairing of ever curing him, they gave him up altogether. When the boy, therefore, saw that he was deserted by earthly physicians, he broke into tears and said to his servant, "This terrible powerlessness and deadening first began in my feet and from there spread through all my members. So I shall beg the abbot for the shoes which were on the feet of the holy and incorruptible martyr of God." The servant acted on his idea and brought the shoes that same night and put them on the boy; then the lad rested. Wonderful to tell, the next morning he got up and stood on his feet to sing the praises of the Lord. Before this he could barely move any part of his body except his tongue. On the following day he went round to all the shrines of the holy martyrs and thanked the Lord for having restored him to his former health in response to his faith and by the merits of the holy bishop.

Chapter XVIII : *Concerning various miracles that have been omitted.*

And so, my brothers, I have written down a few things, and have left out innumerably more lest anyone should be so overwhelmed and bored that he would read none of the book at all. For example, I have said nothing of the many afflicted demoniacs in many localities who have attested that for his sake alone the demons left them and never possessed them again, and further that he healed others by his presence and a mere word. Nor have I said anything of the brethren who resolved in their hearts, no one else knowing, to ask him for something they needed, and how with his prophetic spirit he anticipated their requests and provided them with their heart's desires before any of them could ask him. Of this prophetic spirit Paul has said, "To us, then, he has made a revelation through his Spirit" [1 Cor. 2:10]. Nor do I tell of the many great miracles worked in two places by blessed bread; nor of the cup of blessed water, and how to one who drank after him it appeared to have all the sweetness of wine. Nor do I tell how a deacon of the holy bishop Winfrith was twice cured of an illness by the relics of our confessor of God.

This work is ended. Fare you well ever in Christ.

Appendix I

Heroes and Saints
(p. 36, *supra*)

The pointed address reminds us that this Life, like most, was composed to be read by and to the monks of the saint's own monastery. Our word *legend* comes from Latin *legenda*, referring to the portions of saints' Lives appointed to be read in the monastic Office, or even at mealtime, on the saints' feastdays. Alcuin, for instance, explicitly reveals this intent in the Preface to his own *Life of St. Willibrord* addressed to the abbot of Willibrord's Echternach (Alcuin, *Life of St. Willibrord*, note 1). There is a fundamental continuity of development from such pious *legend* to the romance (see Jones, *Saints' Lives and Chronicles*, pp. 51 ff.). And we recall the suggestion of the French scholar, Bédier, that the practice of monasteries' extolling their hero-saints in song and story had much to do with the eventual origin of the *chansons de geste*. (Jan de Vries, in chapter two of *Heroic Song and Heroic Legend*, explains how modern scholarship sees Bédier's theory as only part of the answer).

These warriors of the spirit (Bede often refers to monastic life as *militia spiritalis*; for instance in *Lives of the Abbots*, Ch. 8) were nurtured on a diet of great deeds done by the saints, just as the king's warriors and nobles were trained to greatness by the songs and sagas of the heroes (see note 51 to Introduction).

The *Iliad*, along with its sister epics, was the textbook of heroic virtues for most of the aristocracy of the ancient Grecian West (see the splendid first chapter in H. I. Marrou, *A History of Education in Antiquity* [New York, 1956]). Then, after the Germanic Heroic Age, northern heroes become the models. Heroic tales led Guthlac to seek martial glory (Felix, *Life of St. Guthlac*, Ch. 16). Alfred read the Anglo-Saxon heroic poems in his boyhood, and Charlemagne had stories of the great deeds of old read to him at table. He even caused a written collection (now lost) to be made of Germanic songs of kings and warriors (see Einhard, *Life of Charlemagne*, Chs. 24, 29). The *Longer Saga of Olaf Tryggvason* tells how King Edward the Confessor at Easter time used to read the Saga of King Olaf to his chief nobles and his *comitatus* (quoted by Wright, *The Cultivation of Saga in Anglo-Saxon England*, p. 67). Even Anglo-Saxon abbots, most of whom—like Wilfrid, Benedict Biscop, Ceolfrith, Eastorwine—were nobles, had the great heroic tales read to their communities. Alcuin once wrote to an abbot of Lindisfarne to rebuke him for having harpers sing of the ancient heroes in the monastic refectory. There should be more reading about Christ than singing about Ingeld (see *Alcuini Epistolae*, 124, in Monumenta Germaniae Historica, *Epistolarum*, vol. IV, *Epistolae Karolini Aevi*, vol. II). To so many of the Anglo-Saxon abbots, the traditional heroic songs had been a vital part of their aristocratic breeding. To them instinctively there was something deeply the same in the hero's ideal of nobility and in the saint's. Hence, I think, there is really no incongruity about *Beowulf's* being a monastic manuscript as De Vries, for instance, convincingly suggests (*Heroic Song and Heroic Legend*, pp. 58 ff.). In this connection it is interesting to note how the noble Gallo-Roman, Sulpicius Severus, explicitly attacks this whole attitude of mind (thus attesting to its prevalence) in the Preface to his late-fourth-century *Life of St. Martin*: "What does posterity gain by reading about Hector fighting or about Socrates philosophizing? Not only is it folly to imitate them, but it is madness not to oppose vehemently what they stand for. Those who judge the value of man's life only by the deeds of this world have abandoned their hopes to the tellers of tales and their souls to the tomb. . . . When this delusion of man's is perpetuated by literature it has the full power to bewitch many with the sterile dream of philosophy or of that foolishness called valor" (Migne, *Patrologia Latina*, 20, 159-160. And there is a translation by Hoare, *The Western Fathers*, p. 10). But even Sulpicius Severus admits to something valid in the "delusion" when, later in the Life (Ch. 26), he refers to Martin's acts of self-discipline in terms of heroic Homeric deeds.

Appendix II

ROME AND THE HEROIC AGE

(p. 38, *supra*)

After recounting this incident of the gracious angel, Bede, in his prose *Life of St. Cuthbert* adds in the following chapter (III) an episode that reveals the sullen hostility the pagan Anglo-Saxon countryfolk felt toward the Christian monks. It seems that a party of monks was bringing in a supply of wood on rafts to a monastery on a river in the north. Suddenly a violent wind began to blow them toward the mouth of the river and the open sea beyond. An attempt by those in the monastery to come to their aid in boats was thwarted by the storm. Thereupon the monks on land could only kneel helplessly on the bank and pray for their brethren. Meantime on the opposite bank a jeering crowd of people had gathered from the countryside. They shouted that the hapless monks were reaping their just deserts "for despising man's ordinary rights and proposing strange and unheard-of ways of living." Young Cuthbert, who was standing among them, rebuked them for their inhumanity and told them they would do much better to pray for the monks' safety. "But they turned on him in a boorish rage and *unpacked their hearts with words.* 'Let no man pray for them,' they said, 'and may God have no mercy on any of them. They have robbed men of their ancient ways of worship and nobody knows how the new worship is supposed to be followed.'" But Cuthbert knelt down to join his prayers to those of the anxious monks, and soon the rafts were blown safely back to land.

The antipathy of the Anglo-Saxon country people here is much the same as that of the continental Saxon countryfolk whom Boniface was to face in his trial-of-faith at Geismar (see p. 309). Chaucer's Wife of Bath will later express in a lighter vein this age-old hostility of the rural pagan for the Christian desecrators of his shrines. She laments that all the fairies and elves have been driven from the woods and fields by the prayers of the friars.

It is interesting in this passage of Bede's that his vocabulary reveals the aristocratic cast of the Christian Anglo-Saxon mind of the Golden Age. The mocking pagans on the river bank were "a crowd of commoners" whose "boorish jeers proceeded from boorish minds." The monastery, however, was peopled with "a noble band of men." This but reflects that "aristocratic" mentality of all Heroic Ages—even of those like the early Icelandic before its farmer adventurers had had time to become landed nobility. But about this particular Anglo-Saxon Heroic-Age *noblesse* there is also another special tone. The Anglo-Saxon monk fell heir to a Germanic Heroic Age which was drawn with instinctive admiration toward the ideals of Rome and the spiritual heritage of the Greek Heroic Age. The first historic Frankish chieftain proudly bore a Roman title and sent his son to be reared at the Court of Ravenna (see H. Daniel-Rops, *The Church in the Dark Ages* [London, 1959], p. 184.) The Romano-Britons too had worn the mantle. Patrick was born to it in Roman Britain. Read the fiery letter he sent from Ireland in the mid-fifth century to the soldiers of a British chieftain, Coroticus, who by molesting Christian converts in Strathclyde had lost their right to be named "fellow citizens of the Romans." (See *The Works of St. Patrick*, trans. Ludwig Bieler [Newman Press, 1953], p. 41.) Royal Celtic families in Wales proudly preserved Roman names and titles and adopted the legionary standard, the dragon, as their own banner. (See Margaret Deanesly, "Roman Traditional Influence Among the Anglo-Saxons," *English Historical*

Review, 58 [1943] pp. 129-46; esp. 135 ff.) Up to the early seventh century a Celtic Heroic-Age society of princes and warriors and poets, "The Men of the North," heirs of a long process of Romanization, ruled the critical Roman-Pict borderland north of Wales (see Chadwick, *Celt and Saxon*, Ch. 10; and see note 66 to my Introduction). Some hundred years before our *Life of St. Cuthbert* the British monk, Gildas, had excoriated his countrymen for failing to defend their proud Roman heritage against the invading Anglo-Saxons. And the Anglo-Saxons too fell under the spell of Rome. They used Roman official titles, borrowed Roman formulae in their charters and other documents, inserted Roman emperors in their royal genealogies (see Margaret Deanesly, *op. cit.*). Anglo-Saxon kings had standards borne before them in battle, Roman fashion (Bede in his *Ecclesiastical History*, Bk. II, ch. 16, tells us how Edwin made use of one even on peacetime journeys), and minted their first coins after hoarded Roman models (see J. P. C. Kent, "From Roman Britain to Saxon England," in Dolley, *Anglo-Saxon Coins*, pp. 13 ff.). Many Anglo-Saxon churches and monasteries were built of the stonework from nearby Roman ruins, fortresses and villas (see note 39; and see note 65 to Introduction, and note 64 to Eddius, *Life of Wilfrid*).

Appendix III

CUTHBERT AND ST. JOHN

(p. 41, *supra*)

Cuthbert entered the Celtic monastery of Old Melrose in 651. Tradition says that it was one of the daughter-houses of Columba's great Iona. It was not far from the spot along the Tweed where now stand the romantic Gothic ruins of the later Cistercian monastery sacked by Edward II, Richard II, and Henry VIII, and immortalized by Sir Walter Scott whose home at Abbotsford is close by. Somewhere in the broken shadows cast by the delicate stone tracery of the great empty windows is buried the heart of Robert the Bruce. See Plate IV. The hero was the abbey's greatest benefactor. Aidan, whose death had figured as we have seen, in Cuthbert's decision to become a monk, had come to Lindisfarne from that same Iona from which Old Melrose was founded.

In his prose *Life of St. Cuthbert* (Chapter VI) Bede tells us that noble young Cuthbert rode armed into the monastery grounds, jumped to the ground, and committed his spear and his steed to an attendant while he went into the church to pray. Boisil, the prior, was standing close by and was overheard to remark prophetically, "Behold the servant of God." In the second chapter after this Bede tells us touchingly how Boisil lay dying of the plague some ten years later and how when he knew by foreknowledge that only a week of life remained to him he arranged to expound St. John's Gospel to the young monk, Cuthbert, who had just recovered from an attack of the plague. The old man possessed a manuscript-copy of St. John bound in seven gatherings, and the dying master and his intent pupil went through it according to plan, one gathering each day. (A copy of St. John's Gospel in a seventh-century red goatskin binding, found inside the coffin of St. Cuthbert in 1104, put there perhaps at Cuthbert's burial in 687, and now preserved at Stonyhurst College in Lancashire, was long thought to be this very book of Boisil's. Scholars now maintain that it was written at Wearmouth or Jarrow, and hence after Boisil's death. See Mynors and Powell, "The Stonyhurst Gospel," in Battiscombe, *The Relics of St. Cuthbert*, pp. 356 ff., and Brown, *Evangeliorum Quattuor Codex Lindisfarnensis*, Vol. II, p. 57.) This Celtic monk's fondness for St. John is specially interesting in view of the fact that a Johannine influence is often detected in Celtic Christianity (for instances at the Synod of Whitby the Celtic party cites St. John as the Apostolic authority for their position—see Eddius, *Life of Wilfrid*, Ch. X) and proposed as one element of an early contact between the Celtic Church and the Eastern Church through the intermediary of the church in Gaul (for example, see *The Antiphonary of Bangor* [ed. F. E. Warren], Part Two, [Henry Bradshaw Society, vol. X, London, 1895], pp. xxii ff.; pp. 54 ff.). And it is often pointed out, for instance, that the great second-century bishop of Lyons, Irenaeus, had been a pupil of Polycarp in Smyrna, and that Polycarp had known St. John. At least there seems certainly to have been a pronounced Eastern strain in Celtic Christianity. (Liturgical scholars, like Edmund Bishop, have traced out a fascinating odyssey of certain prayer-forms from early Christian Syria to southern Gaul and to Mozarabic Spain and from there to Ireland and on to Anglo-Saxon England [quite possibly by the ancient sea routes of the "grave Tyrian traders" in Arnold's "Scholar Gypsy," coasting the Iberian peninsula, touching at Celtic Galicia, then up across the Bay of Biscay to Celtic Brittany and on to western Ireland, a route still followed by fishing fleets today].) (See Chadwick, *The Age of the Saints in the Early Celtic Church*, pp. 49 ff., and Bishop, *Liturgica Historica*, esp. chs., VII, VIII.)

Appendix IV

CELTIC CHRISTIANITY AND EGYPT

(p. 42, *supra*)

Most of this chapter's description of Cuthbert's ascetical practices is copied from Evagrius' translation of Athanasius' *Life of St. Anthony*. The striking affinity between the heroic asceticism of the early saints of the Egyptian desert and those of Ireland and Celtic Britain has long been puzzled over. Direct influence seems unnecessary to explain it. All early western monasticism, even Italian, drew heavily on the East. The similarity in any event touches in other ways upon something too deep to be sufficiently explained by the accident of direct physical contact between Egypt and Ireland. The Heroic-Age Celtic spirit, like that of the princely north British family of Urien of Rheged (whose warrior-son, Rhun, is supposed to have become a monk and to have baptized Northumbria's King Edwin even before the baptism by Paulinus that Bede records. See note 11 to Introduction), seems rather to have been naturally predisposed to the same great-souled simplicity and the same high gallantry of total conquest of the flesh which inspired the saints of the desert, especially the early more eremetical saints of North Egypt. And it was Celtic monasticism that determined the tone of so much of Anglo-Saxon monasticism of the Northumbrian Golden Age. Monkwearmouth and Jarrow, and Wilfrid's Ripon and Hexham were conspicuous Roman islands in this Celtic sea. But even Wilfrid had received his first training in Lindisfarne. Nobility of blood or breeding seems somehow to have sensitized such as Antony and Paul, Columba and Cuthbert and Guthlac, to that stirring of the spirit which breathed indiscriminately across the Heroic Ages of the world. By some mysterious alchemy of the soul, the hero and the hermit became kin. When Alexander dreamed on the deeds of Achilles, when an Emperor's official was stirred to imitate the life of St. Antony (St. Augustine's *Confessions*, VIII, 6), when Willibrord longed to follow in the footsteps of the fabled holy men of Ireland (Alcuin's *Life of Willibrord*, Ch. IV), they were all answering to much the same spell of heroic excellence. Tales of Germanic heroes fired Guthlac to a warrior's life (Felix, *Life of St. Guthlac*, Ch. XVI), and the stories of the monks of the desert drew him to the holy wilds of Crowland (*op. cit.*, Ch. XXIV).

But that this correspondence of spirit between Christians of the North and of the East was also fostered by direct contact is hardly to be denied. Even before the Saracens drove numbers of them west in the seventh century, many Eastern Christians made their way to Gaul, and some even to Ireland, like the seven Egyptian monks who were recorded as being buried in one place there (see Meissner, *The Celtic Church in England*, p. 206). And there are any number of indirect evidences of contact. Copies of the early Lives of the desert saints must surely have made their way to Ireland and Britain before Benedict Biscop began his continental book hunting. Many signs of Coptic influence traced in the *Book of Kells*, for instance, argue strongly that "there must have been a direct connection between early Irish Christianity and the monasteries of Egypt and the highly orientalized Greek Christianity of the southeastern Mediterranean." (P. Meyer in *Evangeliorum Quattuor Codex Cenannensis. The Book of Kells* [Berne, 1951] III, 48). And this "connection" must largely have been by means of books. The possible routes taken by that contact have also been much discussed. The more traditional theories see it as coming via the Christian communities of southern Gaul, especially from the influence of John Cassian at Lérins, where St. Patrick is supposed to have passed some of the preparatory years for his mission. (See G. T. Stokes, *Ireland and the Celtic Church*, 3rd edition [London, 1842], Chs. 9 to 11. Chadwick, *Poetry and Letters in Early Christian Gaul*, p. 169, 205 ff. Mrs. Chadwick suggests that Greek monasticism, not Egyptian or Syrian, had the earliest influence on Lérins, pp. 146 ff.).

Others see St. Martin of Tours playing a more important role than St. Patrick in the transmission (Owen Chadwick, *John Cassian: A Study in Primitive Monasticism* [Cambridge, 1950] p. 203). Others emphasize the sixth-century British monasteries in Wales as important avenues of contact (Ryan, *Irish Monasticism*, pp. 107 ff.).

Other hallmarks of Celtic monasticism, such as a preoccupation with learning and a devotion to pastoral activity, are not especially Egyptian (though Mrs. Chadwick would qualify the former of these two statements. See *Age of the Saints in the Early Celtic Church*, pp. 36 ff.). The former is partly an inheritance from Druidic tradition, reinforced by learned practices from the Christian monasteries of southern Gaul, and the latter stems largely from the influence of St. Martin of Tours (Ryan *op. cit.*, pp. 365 ff., 404 ff.). The Celtic pilgrimage-urge is not Egyptian. In an exhortation to monks of the Egyptian desert St. Antony might almost seem to be criticizing the wanderlust of the Celtic monks: "The Greeks wander through strange lands beyond the sea in quest of learning. But for us there is no need to be a pilgrim in order to find the kingdom of heaven. For long ago the Lord told us that 'the Kingdom of God is within you'" (Athanasius, *Vita S. Antonii*, in *Patrologia Graeca*, 26, 873). Brendan is thus more akin to Odysseus than to Antony.

THE LIFE OF BISHOP WILFRID

---

by Eddius Stephanus

Preface to the LIFE OF ST. WILFRID

Written sometime between 710 (the year of Wilfrid's death) and 720, very shortly after the anonymous *Life of St. Cuthbert*, this biography of Wilfrid was "almost the earliest considerable piece of literature" written in England (Colgrave, *The Life of Bishop Wilfrid by Eddius Stephanus*, p. ix). Wilfrid was one of the most colorful personalities in early English history. His life was a "grand gesture" molded to heroic proportions and it touched significantly on almost every aspect of the Anglo-Saxon Golden Age. His biographer, probably the Eddius of Chapter 14, rose to the occasion and gave us a fascinating epic in very tolerable Latin. It possesses drama, excitement, and even humor. Bede's facts on Wilfrid in his *Ecclesiastical History* are often more exact, but Eddius' account of his hero is much fuller and far more appealing. First-person references scatttered throughout the biography suggest that Eddius was a monk of Ripon (chs. 17, 45, 67, 68) and that he accompanied his lord on at least two (chs. 27, 52, 53) of those exiles which consumed over half of Wilfrid's episcopal career and drove him through Britain, Gaul, Frisia and Italy.

To make this new translation I have used the best text, that edited by Colgrave (*The Life of Bishop Wilfrid by Eddius Stephanus*, Cambridge, 1927). Two earlier editions are still available: a good one by W. Levison in the Monumenta Germaniae Historica (*Scriptores Rerum Merovingicarum*, VI [Hanover and Leipzig, 1913] pp. 163-263), and one by J. Raine in the Rolls Series (Vol. 71, Pt. 1 [London, 1879]).

Colgrave's edition contains a translation and there is a new translation in the Penguin Classics (*Lives of the Saints*, L 153). A few extracts are translated in Whitelock, *English Historical Documents*, pp. 691-97. There is a fine chapter (2) on Wilfrid in Duckett, *Anglo-Saxon Saints and Scholars.*

THE LIFE OF ST. WILFRID

Preface

IN THE NAME of our Lord Jesus Christ. Here begins the humble apology of Stephen the priest, who writes about the life of St. Wilfrid, a bishop worthy before God.

[Addressing his "revered lords," Bishop Acca and Abbot Tatberht,[1] who have set him this task, Eddius goes on to copy word-for-word the Preface to the popular *Anonymous Life of St. Cuthbert* which had been written a few years previously.]

Chapter I: *Here begins the matter of the birth of St. Wilfrid the bishop, and of a miraculous portent attending it.*

[His future sanctity, and the light he was going to be "to almost all the churches of Britain," was announced to his startled neighbors by an apparition of towering flames that seemed to consume the house in which he was being born.]

1. This is the Acca who was Wilfrid's dear friend, and who was present at his miraculous recovery in Meaux, and succeeded him as Bishop of Hexham (Chs. 56, 65). Bede addressed many of his works to Acca. A. S. Cook attempted to show that Acca wrote the Old English poem, *Andreas*, to glorify Wilfrid (*Transactions of the Connecticut Academy of Arts and Sciences*, 26 [1924] 245-332). Tatberht is Wilfrid's kinsman who succeeded him as Abbot of Ripon (Ch.63).

Chapter II : *Here begins the story of how in his boyhood he chose God.*

During his boyish years he was obedient to his parents and endeared himself to all who knew him; he was quite handsome and was of a pleasant disposition, gentle, modest, and dependable, and he did not succumb to the usual silly crazes common to boyhood. To all who called at his father's home he exemplified the saying of the Apostle James, "quick to listen, slow to speak" [James, 1:19] and whether they were nobles of the king's own company or were their servants he waited upon them with trained ease, in accordance with the words of the prophet, "they all shall be taught of God" [John, 6:45, quoting Isaias, 54:13].

Finally, however, when he was fourteen [A.D. 648] he made up his mind to leave his father's estate and set out somehow in the service of heaven,[2] for his mother had died and he could not get along with his stepmother who took a dislike to him.[3] So he was given a company of men suitably armed and mounted, as he was, and he had them so

2. Eddius' Latin plays here on the words *rura* and *iura* (*paterna rura*: paternal estate; *iura celestia*: laws of heaven). The musical balance of the two phrases (*paterna rura deserere, iura celestia quaerere*) is a common feature in early medieval rhythmic Latin prose, and here it almost seems like an echo of some Latin Christian poem. There are many such puns and jingles in other Dark-Age Latin. In his work on the rhetorical figures in Scripture, Bede points to the device of balancing off phrases by similar endings and of playing on words (Migne, *Patrologia Latina*, 90, 178). Even turning prose into verse, and vice versa, became fashionable practice. Aldhelm was well known for it. Bede wrote both a prose and verse version of his *Life of St. Cuthbert.* See Curtius' discussion in *European Literature and the Latin Middle Ages*, pp. 147ff. See note 52 to Introduction.

3. This intriguing touch of realistic biography suggests that the writer is too near his subject to give him the romanesque greater-than-life-size stature of the usual hagiography. The immediate motivation which Eddius adduces here for Wilfrid's (and Cudda's) religious vocation has more of the earthy plausibility of the normal Christian economy of providence than does the miraculous vision that Cuthbert's more heroic biographer presents as the occasion of the latter's vocation (Bede's prose *Life of St. Cuthbert*, Ch. 4).

fitted out with fine apparel that with them at his back he had the right to stand in the presence of kings.[4] After his father had blessed him, the way Isaac had blessed Jacob, and Jacob his sons, that they might increase and multiply into a mighty people, Wilfrid set forth. He made his way to Oswy's queen, Eanfled,[5] and, thanks to the kind offices of some nobles he had once served in his father's home,[6] he was highly spoken of to the queen and presented to her. Almost at once, with God's help "he found favor in her eyes" [Esth. 2:9] for he was indeed a fine looking young man and possessed a most brilliant wit. Consequently, when he requested that he be allowed to serve God with her counsel and under her patronage, she granted it.

Now at that time there happened to be a nobleman, named Cudda, serving in the personal *comitatus* of the king, very dear to him and most loyal, who was planning to give over his worldly career because of a paralytic infirmity, and take up the monastic life under regular discipline on the island of Lindisfarne. So the queen earnestly recommended to him the young man who had just come to her, as someone who might attend him and thus serve God. Wilfrid at once eagerly under-

4. Here we might almost seem, anachronistically, to be in some later chivalric age. Yet this is the world of seventh- and eighth-century Anglo-Saxon nobility, as mirrored in *Beowulf.* There exists a definite continuity of courtliness in which Hrothgar's kingly hall claims kinship with the castle of the Green Knight. Beowulf, "for all that he moves in the world of the primitive heathen Heroic Age of the Germans, nevertheless is almost a Christian knight" (R. W. Chambers, *Man's Unconquerable Mind* [London, 1939] p. 66).

5. Eanfled is the first of those noble women who were to play such important parts in Wilfrid's life (see note 121). Daughter of the great King Edwin, and the first Northumbrian to be baptized by Paulinus (see note 28 to *Life of St. Cuthbert*), she was educated in the monasteries of Kent with their strong Roman traditions (Bede tells how some oil that had been blessed by St. Aidan calmed a storm for the young princess as she was sailing home from Kent to be married to King Oswy—*Ecclesiastical History*, Bk. III, ch. 15). Perhaps it was from Queen Eanfled that young Wilfrid first caught that admiration for Rome which was soon to become so important in his life.

6. We wonder whether Ceolfrith's father (see *Life of Ceolfrith*, Ch. 34) may have been among those thegns of King Oswy who were waited upon by young Wilfrid, and who introduced him to the queen. If so, Wilfrid returned the kindness of the father some years later when he ordained his son, Ceolfrith, at Ripon (*Life of Ceolfrith*, Ch. 3).

took the service[7] suggested by the queen and soon became loved as a son by his lord and all the older monks in the monastery and as a brother by those who were more his own age. They loved him for the wholehearted humility and obedience with which he tried to follow every rule of their way of life, even to the point of learning by heart the whole Psalter and several books of the Bible.[8] As a layman his head was still untonsured, but all evil habits were cut from the heart with which he served God and merited to share in the blessing of Samuel who attended the priest Eli.

Chapter III : *How he longed to see the Church of St. Peter, the Prince of the Apostles.*

Then after the space of a year the Holy Spirit incited the young man to venture on a road as yet untrod by any of our race and to make a pilgrimage to the see of the Apostle Peter,[9] leader of the Apostles,

7. Wilfrid's position at Lindisfarne suggests the monastic counterpart of an Heroic Age squire. It is paradoxical that the man who was to become such a determined Roman opponent of the Celtic "party" in the Northumbrian church, should have spent his first year in the religious life at Celtic Lindisfarne. And the great Aidan was still bishop and abbot of Lindisfarne at that time (648). He did not die until 651, a few days after the treacherous murder of his dear friend, King Oswine (see note 36 to Introduction).

8. See note 34 to *Life of St. Cuthbert.*

9. But the road to Rome was soon to know many an Anglo-Saxon foot. Wilfrid, Benedict Biscop, Ceolfrith, Willibrord, Boniface, all made the journey—and all (except for Ceolfrith) more than once. Some eighty years later Bede remarked that it was a common thing to see Englishmen—nobles and commoners, laymen and clerics, men and women—making their way eagerly to Rome to visit the shrines of the saints, in the hope of winning from the saints all the more gracious a reception into the kingdom of heaven (*Ecclesiastical History*, Bk. V, ch. 7). So many Anglo-Saxon pilgrims flocked to the center of Christendom that a special district in Rome was set apart for them, called the *Schola Saxonum* (Levison, *England and the Continent in the Eighth Century*, pp. 36 ff.; G. B. Parks, *The English Traveler to Italy*. I, *The Middle Ages to 1525* [Rome, 1954], Ch. 1; Duckett, *The Wandering Saints of the Middle Ages*, Ch. 13; Chadwick, *Poetry and Letters in Early Christian Gaul*, pp. 16 ff.). And see note 46 to Introduction.

in the belief that there every knot of his sins would be loosed and that he might receive the happiness of a papal blessing. This resolve he made known to his master who, being wise, recognized at once that it was of God and gave his very dear son his consent to possess himself of this source of all good. Thereupon, at Cudda's advice, Queen Eanfled sent the young man in due state to her own kinsman, King Erconberht of Kent.[10] She dispatched messengers ahead to commend him most earnestly to the king and to request that Wilfrid might stay with him until he could find dependable travel companions bound for the Apostolic See. Then when the king observed that this young man who thus came to him had established a regular routine of prayer, fasting, reading and nightly vigils, he came to love him exceedingly. Wilfrid now committed to memory the Roman version of the psalms, in the fifth edition, whereas he had previously known them in Jerome's revision.[11]

10. King Erconberht was the first English king to order the destruction of idols. His aunt, Ethelberg, was Eanfled's mother. His wife, Sexburg, a daughter of the famous King Anna of East Anglia (killed by Penda, and proposed by some as the king commemorated in the Sutton Hoo ship burial), later became Abbess of Ely. There she succeeded her saintly sister, Aethilthryth, whom we will see earlier in life as King Ecgfrith's first queen and one of Wilfrid's greatest benefactors (see Chs. 19, 22).

11. The rememorizing of the 150 Psalms in another version would be no mean feat. The assumption would have been that here in "Roman" Kent this second version would have been St. Jerome's, while at Lindisfarne he would have read the older, or Old Latin version. But something like the opposite seems to have been the case. The puzzling *quintam editionem* ("fifth edition") seems to be a scribal error for *antiquam editionem* ("ancient edition") according to Colgrave (*Life of Wilfrid by Eddius*, p. 152). Perhaps "Jerome's revision" Wilfrid used at Lindisfarne was the so-called Gallican Psalter (Jerome's second revision of the Old Latin Psalter). Since this version was not used at services in Rome, though it did become incorporated in the Vulgate Bible, Wilfrid's new Roman loyalties may have led him in Kent to switch to the so-called Roman Psalter (substantially, it now seems, the same as the Old Latin version. See Van den Born and Hartman, *Encyclopedic Dictionary of the Bible*, cols. 1956-57, 2555-56). During his sojourn in Kent he must surely have studied under Archbishop Honorius of Canterbury, who in turn had been a disciple of the leader of the Roman mission to Britain, Augustine. Interestingly enough too, Honorius had been a good friend of Aidan, despite the latter's Celtic views on the Easter date (Bede, *Ecclesiastical History*, Bk. III, ch. 25).

But day followed day, and a year went by before the king could fulfill the queen's request and find a guide for the now bored and weary young man. He prevailed upon a certain remarkably gifted and highborn man named Biscop Baducing,[12] who was hurrying to Rome, to take Wilfrid in his company. So the servant of God set forth on his pilgrimage [probably some time in 653] like Jacob, with the blessing of his parents—a blessing which eventually was to stand him in good stead. He was affable with everyone, keen of mind and strong in body, quick of foot, ready for any good deed, and sadness never clouded his face. In high spirits and enjoying every minute of the journey, he arrived safely at Lyons, a city of Gaul. There he tarried for some time with his companions while his more serious-minded guide went on without him, just as Barnabas left Paul on account of John (surnamed Mark).

Chapter IV: *How Wilfrid was kindly received by Bishop Dalfinus.*

Blessed be God who defends and protects his servants with the assistance of good men! For in the city just mentioned it happened that the man who was archbishop, Dalfinus[13] of holy memory, was favorably impressed by this servant of God with such pleasant manners, and he opened his home to him and his companions with gracious hospitality. In the young man's bright and cheery face he saw mirrored a blessed conscience. So he furnished Wilfrid and his company with an abundance of everything needed for their comfort as though they were his own kin, and he even expressed the desire to adopt Wilfrid as his own son. "If you will remain here," he told him, "and put your

12. See Bede's *Lives of the Abbots*, Ch. 2.

13. Throughout this account Eddius seems to have confused two different men. Dalfinus was the Count of Lyons and it must have been his daughter who was offered in marriage. It was his brother, Aunemund, who was the archbishop (Colgrave, *Life of Wilfrid by Eddius*, p. 153). Both seem to have been conquered by the charm of this extraordinary young man, as had been Queen Eanfled, Cudda, King Erconberht, and the community at Lindisfarne.

trust in me, I shall make you ruler *in perpetuum* over a good part of Gaul. I shall give you a maiden as your wife, my brother's daughter; and you yourself I shall adopt as my son, while you shall have me as a father to assist you faithfully in everything."

The answer of the saintly servant of God was wise, as befitted his training. "I have made vows to the Lord and must carry them out, leaving my kin and the home of my father,[14] as Abraham did, to visit the Apostolic See and learn the regulations of Church discipline so that I may help my people to grow in the service of God. Thus I hope to receive from God what he promised to those who love him. 'Every man that has forsaken father or mother,' and so forth, 'shall receive his reward a hundredfold, and obtain everlasting life' [Mt. 19:29]. But if death has not claimed me on the journey and I am still alive, I shall come back and look upon your face again." As the holy bishop listened to such words as these he realized that Wilfrid was a genuine servant of God filled with the Holy Spirit. So he supplied him with everything necessary for the journey, including guides and money, and sent him on his way in the peace of Christ to the Apostolic See.

Chapter V: *How he happily arrived at the See of St. Peter the Apostle.*

So Wilfrid[15] and his companions arrived safely, in joy and thankfulness, at the long-desired See of the Apostle Peter, chief of the Apostles. Just as the most excellent teacher of the Gentiles journeyed to Jerusalem to the disciples of the Lord "lest perhaps he should run, or had run

14. Eddius has given Wilfrid's answer the epic cast of the traditional heroic "boast." The hero must be about his destiny. We recall Aeneas' words to Queen Dido as he rejects her plea to linger at Carthage (*Aeneid*, Bk. IV, vv. 331 ff.) and we remember Beowulf's avowal that he has left his homeland to fight Hrothgar's monster for sake of glory and gratitude (*Beowulf*, vv. 407 ff.).

15. At the risk of inadequately transmitting the epic feel of Eddius' treatment of Wilfrid, I have in the course of this Life omitted many of the constantly repeated "Homeric" epithets that accompany Wilfrid's name: "servant of God," "hero of God," etc.

in vain" [cf. Gal. 2:1,2], so did that most lowly little spark of our race, kindled into flame by God, come to Rome "from the ends of the earth to hear the wisdom" [Mt. 12:42] of the rulers of the world. In the oratory dedicated to St. Andrew the Apostle,[16] he knelt humbly before the altar above which four gospels had been placed. There he implored the Apostle, in the name of the Lord God for whom he suffered, that he would intercede with the Lord to grant him the ability to learn the eloquence of the gospels and teach it among the heathen.

And so did it come about, as the testimony of many bears witness. For in the course of the many months he spent going round to the shrines of the saints every day to pray, he found a teacher who became his faithful friend, through the help of God and of the Apostle. His name was Boniface; he was an archdeacon, one of the wisest of the counselors. From him Wilfrid learned the four gospels of Christ perfectly and the method of calculating Easter, which the schismatics of Britain and Ireland had no knowledge of.[17] And many other rules of ecclesiastical discipline Boniface the archdeacon very carefully taught to Wilfrid as to his own son. Then finally he presented him to the pope of blessed memory and explained the whole marvelous story of the young servant of God's journey. Placing his blessed hand on Wilfrid's head, the pope prayed over him and blessed him. Then God's

16. This may have been the very monastery of St. Gregory and of England's St. Augustine, and hence a most sacred pilgrimage-spot for any Anglo-Saxon (Colgrave, *Life of Wilfrid by Eddius*, p. 153).

17. Eddius is too harsh on the Celts here. Their method of calculating the date of Easter was neither schismatical nor heretical, and it did trace back to the Eastern practice of St. John and St. Polycarp (see Chapter 10). This Asiatic quartodeciman ("fourteenth") custom dated Easter on the fourteenth Nisan, no matter what the day of the week; but sometime after the end of the second century it gave way to the Roman custom of commemorating Easter always on Sunday (J. Lebreton and J. Zeiller, *History of the Primitive Church* [London, 1946] III, 586 ff.). The only dispute remaining had to do with several different systems of calculating which Sunday should be selected. See note 67 to Introduction, and note 15 to *Life of St. Cuthbert.* Wilfrid's dislike for the Celtic custom would also have been nourished by his stay in Gaul, for the bishops there had been violently opposed to Columbanus and other Celtic missionaries because of their stand on this Easter controversy—among other things. Some very interesting letters by Columbanus allow us to see behind the scenes in this quarrel (Walker, *Sancti Columbani Opera*, pp. 2 ff.—text and translation).

servant set forth on his way in the peace of Christ, taking with him a supply of the holy relics which he found in Rome. He returned safely to his fatherly patron, the archbishop of Lyons (a city of Gaul).[18]

Chapter VI : *How he received from Bishop Dalfinus the Apostle Peter's form of tonsure, and how the same Dalfinus was martyred.*

Wilfrid found that Bishop Dalfinus was safe and well, so as a dutiful son he went to pay his respects to his "father," and told him the whole happy story of his journey. The bishop, on his part, gave thanks to God that the Lord had preserved his son from harm as he traveled to Rome and back. Then Wilfrid stayed on with him for three years and acquired much learning from very well-educated masters,[19] while the bond of affection between the old man and the young man grew ever stronger.[20] Having an ardent desire for the form of tonsure of

18. Eddius has already (in Ch. III) told us that Lyons is a city in Gaul. He may have repeated it for somewhat the same reason that the epic poet repeats his identifying epithets. Part of the reason stems surely from the very nature of all "oral" literature intended to be read in installments over an extended period of time. In this too, heroic poetry and hagiography agree (see note 6 to *Life of St. Cuthbert* and note 69 to the Introduction).

19. The Romans had developed an admirable educational system in Gaul (Chadwick, *Poetry and Letters in Early Christian Gaul*, pp. 21 ff.).

20. It is very probable that much in Wilfrid's later career is explainable by these three years he spent in ancient, imperial Lyons. The great focal city had its memories of Roman emperors, and of bishops, like Irenaeus, who were a power in shaping the new Roman world. Perhaps Roman Wilfrid's later opposition to Roman Theodore's attempts to limit his authority will puzzle us less if we remember these three impressionable years the young man basked in the paternal affection of Archbishop Aunemund. These princely Gallo-Roman bishops perpetuated the spell of the *old* Rome (fixed in the letters of Sidonius Apollinaris like a moth in amber) with its traditional reverence of splendor and dignity and authority. In the fifth century they had had their Heroic Age when the mantle of Roman civil authority fell to them as barbarian hordes battered at the gates of their cities. They became Roman governors and generals, and bishops all in one (Chadwick, *Poetry and Letters in Early Christian Gaul*, Chs. 9, 10, 11). The great Germanus of Auxerre even directed Britons in a

the apostle Peter, fashioned in the shape of the crown of thorns encircling the head of Christ, Wilfrid was only too glad to receive it at the hands of the holy Archbishop Dalfinus. As the old man placed his holy hands on Wilfrid's head his mind was full of fond plans for making him his heir, if God should so will. But God had in mind something else, better for our race.

Now at that time a hateful queen named Balthild[21] was persecuting the Church of God. Just as of old the most wicked Queen Jezebel slew God's prophets, so this queen ordered nine bishops to be killed—having passed over the priests and deacons. Among the condemned was this Bishop Dalfinus; so the state officials ordered him, in a most peremptory manner, to appear before them. Knowing full well what was going to happen to him, yet with his spirit undaunted, the bishop went to the place of the contest.[22] Wilfrid went along with him,

victorious battle against Picts and Saxons when he was in Britain on a papal mission to investigate the Pelagian heresy (Bede, *Ecclesiastical History*, Bk. I, ch. 20.). The same priestly son of British Urien who, tradition says, baptized King Edwin (note 13 to Introduction) may also have written a Life of St. Germanus (see Chadwick, *Studies in the Early British Church*, pp. 110 ff.; Chadwick, *Celt and Saxon*, pp. 161 ff.). And Eddius (in a chapter that reads like the scenario for an epic film) will tell us of Wilfrid too directing a battle against Saxons (Ch. 13). And though we shall see Wilfrid's devoted pastoral leadership (Chs. 26, 41), we will also see the wealth, magnificence, and munificence of his household outshining that of his king's (Ch. 24), and we will see him fighting strenuously during most of his episcopal life against what he considered an unjust curtailment of his authority. The image of the lordly Gallo-Roman bishops was to weigh far more in the shaping of his own stormy episcopal career than was the earlier simpler memory of Aidan.

21. Balthild had a storybook life. She was an Anglo-Saxon slave sold in Gaul who became consort to a Merovingian king (Clovis II) and figured strongly in those dark struggles between the Merovingian aristocracy and the Frankish Mayors of the Palace. It was probably Ebroin, the Mayor of the Palace (and see note 85), who was responsible for the murder of Archbishop Aunemund (Colgrave, *Life of Wilfrid by Eddius*, p. 154). Paradoxically enough, Wilfrid's friend, Bishop Agilbert, seems to have supported some of Ebroin's evil schemes (Plummer, *Baedae Opera Historica*, II, 203). Balthild founded the monasteries of Chelles and Corbie and eventually ended her life as abbess of the former, with a reputation for sanctity (Levison, *England and the Continent* p. 9 ff.). It was very likely because of the English queen that English Wilfrid's life was spared on this occasion.

22. Eddius' Latin for "to the place of the contest" is *ad locum agonis*. The

despite the bishop's protests, and joyfully proclaimed: "Nothing finer could happen to us, than that father and son should die together and be with Christ."

So the holy bishop was crowned with martyrdom. But when St. Wilfrid took off his outer garments and stood there fearlessly, all ready for the palm of martyrdom, the officials wanted to know who he was. "Who is that fine looking young man who is so ready for death?" They were told that he was "a man from across the sea, of the race of the Angles in Britain." Then they ordered, "Spare him; do not touch him." And so you see how our Saint Wilfrid now became a confessor,[23] like John the Apostle and Evangelist who sat unscathed in a caldron of boiling oil, and drank deadly poison which did not harm him. It was of him and his brother James the Apostle that Jesus said, "Can you drink the chalice which I shall drink?" [Mt. 20:22] and so forth.

Chapter VII : *How he was welcomed by King Alchfrith.*

Then after his father the bishop had been buried with due honor, St. Wilfrid the confessor boarded a ship, accompanied by the blessings of many and a store of holy relics, and with a wind that blew in the direction of the sailors' wishes they reached their own kingdom without incident and put safely into port. Now when Alchfrith, who was

latter word (from the Greek, ἀγών) was originally used for athletic contests, and in early Christian times was applied to the struggles of the martyrs (and hence our "agony." Milton's *Samson Agonistes* reflects the changing meanings). The word is another bridge between the hero and the saint. Martyred Boniface was referred to as an "athlete" who had been "triumphant" in the "contest" (Willibald, *Life of Boniface*, note 36). And St. Antony had been called an "athlete" in Athanasius' *Life of St. Antony* (Migne, *Patrologia Graeca*, 26, 862).

23. See Introduction, p. 23. St. Antony too had unsuccessfully presented himself for martyrdom at Alexandria during the Maximinian persecution and, bitterly disappointed, had returned to his spiritual martyrdom in the desert (Athanasius, *Vita Sancti Antonii* [*Patrologia Graeca*, 26: 910, 911]. And King Theuderic accused fiercely intransigent Columbanus of trying to force him to martyr him (Wallace-Hadrill, J. (ed. and tr.) *The Fourth Book of the Chronicle of Fredegar*, [London and N. Y., 1960] Ch. 36).

ruling with his father Oswy, heard that such a worthy servant of God had come from the Apostolic See with his companions and was preaching the true Easter and had mastered the complicated discipline of the Church of St. Peter the Apostle, which the king loved very dearly,[24] then, at the urging of his faithful friend, King Cenwalh[25] of the West Saxons, he bade the saint pay him a visit.

Wilfrid therefore came at the king's invitation and saluted him with a greeting of peace: "Jesus Christ the Son of God, thus instructed his disciples and their leader, the Apostle Peter: 'In whatsoever house you shall enter, say: "Peace be to this house"' [Mt. 10:12]. First we ought to lay the foundation for this peace within ourselves between body and soul, as the teacher of the Gentiles preached, 'May the peace of Christ rejoice in your hearts' [Col. 3:15]. Next, we must have peace between ourselves and our neighbours, as Christ commanded, 'Have salt within yourselves and have peace among you'" [Mk. 9:49].

As soon as Wilfrid had finished his address the king bowed down at the feet of this chosen servant of God and asked for his blessing, for it seemed to him as though an angel of God were speaking.[26] So Wilfrid blessed him, and they entered into conversation. The king

24. Perhaps Alchfrith imbibed his passionate love for Rome from his mother, Eanfled (see note 6). His father, Oswy, ruled Northumbria from Bernicia and appointed Alchfrith as sub-king in Deira. King Oswy, smarting perhaps over his son's role in promoting the Synod of Whitby (see note 24 to *Life of St. Cuthbert*), vetoed Alchfrith's proposal to accompany Benedict Biscop to Rome shortly after the synod (see Bede, *Lives of the Abbots*, Ch. 2). It has been affirmed (Brown, *Arts in Early England*, V, 201-02; Willett, F., "The Ruthwell and Newcastle Crosses," *Memoirs of the Proceedings of the Manchester Literary and Philosophical Society*, 98 [1956-7] pp. 115-16) and denied (Page, R., "The Bewcastle Cross," *Nottingham Medieval Studies*, IV [1960] pp. 35-57) that the Bewcastle Cross was erected in memory of Alchfrith—probably by Wilfrid.

25. Cenwalh had rejected the Christianity which Bishop Birinus had brought to Wessex in the reign of his father, King Cynegils. Driven into exile later by Penda, Cenwalh was converted by King Anna of East Anglia. To succeed Birinus, Cenwahl invited to the See of Wessex that Bishop Agilbert who was soon to become a great friend of Wilfrid (Ch. 9). Benedict Biscop was a good friend of Cenwalh (Bede, *Lives of the Abbots*, Ch. 4).

26. We cannot resist a smile at Eddius' earnestness. His version of Wilfrid's words of greeting strikes us as far too much on the stuffy side to be so easily mistaken for angelic eloquence. But we must not forget that this is heroic talk, larger than life-size, more formal, like salutations in the *Iliad*.

asked him discerning questions, being an intelligent man, about the diversities of discipline in the Roman Church and in its formation. And the other, being well informed, gave a clear and intelligent response to all his questions. Afterwards the king implored him by the Lord and by St. Peter the Apostle to remain with him so that he could preach God's Word to himself and all his people, since the voice of the Spirit fairly sang out through him. And as Wilfrid could perceive the king's affection for him, he consented to stay. At that moment the soul of each of them was inseparably linked to the other, just as we read that the souls of David and Jonathan were intertwined one with the other.

Chapter VIII : *How Alchfrith made him a present of the monastery at Ripon.*

After a time, as the affection between them grew from day to day, Alchfrith first gave Wilfrid ten hides[27] of land at Stanforda, and a little later [probably about 661], for the good of his own soul, presented him with the monastery at Ripon, along with thirty hides of land; and Wilfrid was made the abbot.[28] But now in proportion as the door of this world was being opened wide to him by the Lord and by St. Peter the Apostle, even so much the wider did he open the bountiful door of his almsgiving in the Name of the Lord to the poor, to orphans and widows, and to those afflicted with every variety of infirmity. Thus he revealed clearly what his heart had wanted to do in the days of his poverty. Look now, brethren, behold and wonder at how great a boon God granted the king who "found a fine pearl and immediately bought it without delay" [cf. Mt. 13:46]. And not only did King Alchfrith love the Abbot Wilfrid, but all the people,

27. A "hide" seems to have meant about 120 acres, at least in the east of England (Stenton, *Anglo-Saxon England*, p. 276). And see note 29 to Introduction.

28. Cuthbert and Eata had just been expelled from Ripon for being too Celtic to suit Alchfrith (note 17 to *Life of St. Cuthbert*). Wilfrid, as the new abbot, invited Ceolfrith and companions from Gilling to take Eata's and Cuthbert's places (*Life of Ceolfrith*, Ch. 3).

nobles and commoners, looked on him as a prophet of God, which he was.

Chapter IX : *How he was ordained priest by Bishop Agilbert.*

It was at that time that Bishop Agilbert[29] came from across the sea to visit King Oswy and his son, Alchfrith. King Alchfrith told him about the holy abbot, Wilfrid, who had come from the Apostolic See, and repeated what he had heard of him from those who knew him, namely, that he was a humble and peaceful man, given to fasting and prayer, kind, sensible, unassuming, compassionate, full of the power of God's grace, modest, prudent, temperate with drink, willing to learn and well able to teach, straightforward and frank in his speech.[30]

"Therefore I ask you to confer on him the order of the priesthood," the king said, "so that he can be my personal chaplain."[31] "Such a man ought in fact to be a bishop," answered Bishop Agilbert, in a spirit of prophecy. So at the request of the king he ordained Wilfrid as a priest at Ripon. And just as David was chosen as a boy by the Lord and anointed by Samuel, and after many testings merited to receive the gifts of prophecy, so did St. Wilfrid the priest, after many blessings by God's saints, receive so many gifts in the sight of God

29. Bishop Agilbert, a Gaul who had studied in Ireland, had fallen out with King Cenwalh in the meantime (see note 25) and had left Wessex (Bede, *Ecclesiastical History*, Bk. III, ch. 7). The king was irritated by his foreign speech, and Agilbert was annoyed at the king's decision to divide his diocese—as Oswy was to do to Wilfrid's diocese (Ch. 24). Agilbert must have had no little influence on his friend, Wilfrid, and it is very likely that Wilfrid, like Agilbert, would have been a happier bishop in Gaul than in England.

30. This is a stock formula of episcopal virtues and appears in a number of hagiographies, just as set verse phrases and patterns keep reappearing in the heroic poems (see, for instance, the *Life of Cuthbert*, Bk. IV, ch. 1).

31. Bede's explanation of the same incident makes use of the consecrated Heroic Age terms (*Ecclesiastical History*, Bk. V, ch. 19). He says that King Alchfrith wished to have Wilfrid for his *individuo comitatu* ("personal *comitatus*"). See notes 2 and 24 to Introduction.

and men that nobody can count them. Not only did God grant the gifts, but he also watched over him in his difficulties.

Chapter X : *About the debate between St. Wilfrid the priest and Bishop Colman on the calculation of Easter.*[32]

Once during the episcopacy of Colman,[33] metropolitan of the city of York, while Oswy and his son Alchfrith were reigning, abbots and priests and persons of all ranks of ecclesiastical government gathered together in a monastery called Whitby [in the year 664].[34] In the presence of the most devout and saintly Abbess Hild,[35] and in the

32. Bede's longer account of this Synod of Whitby (*Ecclesiastical History*, Bk. III, chs. 25, 26) is much harder on the Celts than Eddius' version here. The later Anglo-Saxon translation of Bede's *Ecclesiastical History* omitted these two chapters entirely, along with other matter that was likewise not of such immediate English interest (see discussion by D. Whitelock in *Proceedings of the British Academy*, 48 [1962] 62-64). On the Easter controversy see note 17, *supra*, and on the Synod see notes 26 and 67 to the Introduction. On Oswy's and Alchfrith's roles in the Synod see note 24 to *Life of St. Cuthbert*. It may well be too that, Queen Eanfled's sympathies being with Rome (see note 6), she helped force her pro-Celtic husband's hand at Whitby. It would not be the first time an Anglo-Saxon queen advanced the cause of Rome with her husband. Christian Queen Bertha, for example, surely had something to do with the favorable reception King Ethelbert gave Augustine's band of Roman missionaries when they landed in Kent in 597.

33. Colman was an Irish monk from the monastery of Iona who was made bishop of Northumbria in 661. But his see was at Lindisfarne—certainly not at Roman York! And he was not a metropolitan (Colgrave, *Life of Wilfrid by Eddius*, pp. 156-57).

34. Today on the headland at Whitby the ruins of the later Norman abbey stare over the North Sea and keep the memory of the great synod, and of Caedmon's first poetry. Depending on whether they believe Bede reckoned his years from September to September or from December to December, scholars date the Synod of Whitby respectively in 663 (Stenton, *Anglo-Saxon England*, p. 129) or in 664 (Levison, *England and the Continent*, p. 265, p. 272). The late Paul Grosjean suggested new reasons for electing 664 (see *Analecta Bollandiana*, 78 [1960] 233- 274).

35. Another of the highborn Anglo-Saxon nuns, Hild, a relative of King Edwin, had first decided to enter Balthild's monastery of Chelles in Gaul, but

presence also of the two kings and of two bishops, Colman and Agilbert, they attempted to find out which was the most correct opinion about the dating of Easter—i. e., whether Easter should be observed on the Sunday between the fourteenth day of the moon and the twenty-second, in the manner of the Britons and the Irish and of the whole northern part of the country, or whether it would be better to celebrate Easter Sunday by the calculation of the Apostolic See between the fifteenth day of the moon and the twenty-first. Time was accorded first of all to Bishop Colman, as was proper, to present his position, while all listened. He spoke his mind boldly:

"Our fathers and their predecessors, clearly inspired by the Holy Spirit, as Columba was, established the celebration of Easter on the Sunday after the fourteenth day of the moon, following the example of John the Apostle and Evangelist who leaned on the Lord's breast at the Last Supper and was called the one who loved the Lord. He celebrated Easter on the fourteenth day of the moon and we, just as did his disciples Polycarp and others, celebrate on that assurance. For our fathers' sake we dare not nor do we wish to change. I have presented the opinion of our party; you state yours."

Agilbert, the bishop from across the sea, and Agatho his priest, bade St. Wilfrid explain the position of the Roman Church and Apostolic See in his winning and eloquent way and in his own tongue.[36] So Wilfrid gave the response, modestly as always, to Colman's argument:

"Long ago at Nicaea, a city of Bithynia, three hundred and eighteen of our fathers, most holy and most learned, met together and made an admirable investigation into this question. Among other decisions they reached, was the settling upon a complete lunar cycle of nineteen years which never contained any indication that Easter was to be kept on the fourteenth day of the moon. This is the rule in effect

was persuaded by Aidan to remain in Britain. Strongly Celtic in her sympathies she opposed Wilfrid to the day of her death as a holy old woman at Whitby (see Ch. 54). See Bede, *Ecclesiastical History*, Bk. IV, ch. 23.

36. Bede (*Ecclesiastical History*, Bk. III, ch. 25) says that Oswy asked Agilbert to present the Roman postion, and that the latter in turn proposed Wilfrid since he would be able to explain it in English. From this it has even been improbably suggested that Agilbert had been deputed by Rome to call the synod, and that "his priest Agatho" was the future pope of that name (Howorth, *Golden Days of the Early English Church*, III, 194, 358, 365).

with the Apostolic See and with almost the entire world, and hence our fathers concluded their series of decrees with this statement: 'Let him be anathema who shall speak against any one of these.'"

Then when St. Wilfrid finished speaking, King Oswy with a smile put a question to the whole assembly: "Tell me, who is the greater in the kingdom of heaven, Columba or the Apostle Peter?" The entire synod responded with one voice and in common agreement: "The Lord decided this when he said, 'Thou art Peter and upon this rock I will build my church and the gates of hell shall not prevail against it. And to thee I will give the keys of the kingdom of heaven, and whatsoever thou shalt bind upon earth shall be bound also in heaven and whatsoever thou shalt loose upon earth shall be loosed also in heaven'" [Mt. 16:18-19].

Wisely the king replied: "So, he is the porter and the keeper of the keys; therefore he is a man with whom I am not going to have any argument,[37] nor will I have any part with those who do quarrel with him, and I shall never oppose any of his decrees as long as I live."

Then Bishop Colman was informed as to what must be done, as long as he disdained the tonsure and the Easter rule out of human respect for his fellow-countrymen, namely, that he must step down from office and relinquish his see to another and better occupant. And so he did.

Chapter XI : *About Wilfrid's election to the bishopric.*

[Shortly after the Synod of Whitby, Wilfrid is selected by the kings and their counsellors as the one most fit to succeed to Colman's vacant see, and the selection is approved by all the populace. Then follows a formulaic catalogue of the ideal episcopal virtues possessed by Wilfrid.][38]

37. And Ceolfrith's letter on the Easter question to King Nechtan of the Picts concludes with the same argument (Bede, *Ecclesiastical History*, Bk. V, ch. 21).

38. The list is borrowed, verbatim in great part, from the anonymous *Life of St. Cuthbert* (Bk. IV, ch. 1) which in turn seems to have borrowed it from Isidore of Seville (Migne, *Patrologia Latina*, 83, 785-86).

Chapter XII : *How Wilfrid was consecrated in Gaul.*

On his election to the episcopacy, St. Wilfrid made the following address: "My lords and revered kings, it is by all means imperative that we providently take thought as to just how, after your election, I may be able with God's help to accede to the episcopal office without criticism on the part of catholic men. For there are here in Britain many bishops, whom it is not my place to criticize, though I know for a fact that they are Quartodecimans just like the Britons and the Irish.[39] Men ordained by them are not received into the Christian communion by the Apostolic See, and neither are those received who even agree with the schismatics. Therefore, in all humility I earnestly request you to send me under your protection overseas to the land of the Gauls,[40] where many catholic bishops are to be found, so that, though unworthy, I may be enabled to receive the rank of bishop without any objection by the Apostolic See."

The kings heartily approved of this plan and provided him with a ship, a force of men, and a generous sum of money, so that he should make his entrance into Gaul in imposing state.[41] Immediately upon his arrival [in 664] a large gathering of not less than twelve catholic

39. Eddius seems partisanly to be putting words in his hero's mouth. The Celts were not Quartodecimans (see note 17) and Wilfrid certainly knew they were not.

40. "For everything in the civilized world of the Roman Empire, Gaul was the threshold of Britain" (Scott Holmes, *The Origin and Development of the Christian Church in Gaul During the First Six Centuries of the Christian Era* [London, 1911] p. v.).

41. Perhaps among the princely presents Wilfrid brought for the consecrating bishops was the so-called Franks Casket (named after the Englishman who purchased it from a Paris antique dealer). This exquisite little whalebone box now in the British Museum—except for one panel—with its carvings of scenes from the Bible, Teutonic mythology, and Roman history, most likely came from the same Golden Age Northumbria that produced the *Lindisfarne Gospels* and the Ruthwell Cross (Brown, *The Arts in Early England*, Vol. VI, Part I, Ch. 2). The fusion of several worlds in the art of the Casket and of the *Gospels* is typical of the fascinating amalgam that Anglo-Saxon culture was (see Plates IX, X).

bishops was summoned, of whom one was Bishop Agilbert. When they had heard the account of his public testimonial of faith, the whole body of bishops consecrated him publicly before all the people with great rejoicing and ceremony.[42] Then, in a customary ritual of theirs, they raised him aloft seated in a golden chair, and the bishops alone, no one else assisting, carried him with their own hands into the church while they chanted hymns and psalms in chorus. And so, some time later, they let him take his leave to go back to the episcopal see of the city of York[43] with a parting admonition in the Name of the Lord to remain ever in the catholic faith, just as the Apostle Paul bade his son Timothy guard the high purpose that he had undertaken at the laying on of his hands.

Chapter XIII : *How the Lord rescued our bishop and his company from the sea and from the hands of the pagans.*

Then as they were sailing across the British sea from Gaul with Bishop Wilfrid,[44] and the clerics were singing and chanting psalms in chorus to praise God and to keep time for the oarsmen,[45] suddenly in mid-ocean a violent tempest blew up and the wind shifted against them, just as it had against the disciples of Jesus on the Sea of Galilee.[46] As

42. Bede tells us Wilfrid was about thirty years old at the time (*Ecclesiastical History*, Bk. V, ch. 19). By our standards he would be very young for a bishop, but this was the Heroic Age.

43. Naturally Wilfrid would be expected to move the see from Celtic Lindisfarne back to Roman York where Paulinus had established it—York, with its memories of Constantine, and of the Legio VI Victrix.

44. This was probably in 666 (Plummer, *Baedae Opera Historica*, II, 317), and Wilfrid had left England right after the Synod of Whitby in 664. For the second time now Wilfrid had obviously found Gaul much to his liking.

45. And we think of King Canute's boat song, composed to the chant of the monks as he rowed by Ely (Wright, *Cultivation of Saga in Anglo-Saxon England*, pp. 36-37), and even of Marvell's "Bermudas," with its boat song by other English Christians in a new world.

46. Christ's boat on the stormy Sea of Galilee is the subject of some of the most fascinating Anglo-Saxon and Germanic Dark Age manuscript illuminations

the gale swept furiously along from the southeast, white-foaming mountains of waves drove them deeply ashore in a kingdom they had not yet seen, that of the South Saxons. There the waves loosed their hold on ship and men, sped back across the land, slipped off the beaches, and sank back into the womb of the sea.

Straightway a great host of pagans swarmed round, clearly bent on seizing the ship to divide its valuable booty among themselves and to overcome the men and take them captive, or to kill them on the spot if they resisted. Then our holy bishop spoke to them calmly in an attempt to pacify them and buy off the lives of his people with the offer of a great sum of money. But they were furious and stone deaf to all pleas. They refused, like Pharaoh, to let the people of God go, and arrogantly maintained that everything cast upon land by the sea belonged to them as their own personal property.

Meanwhile the high priest of their idolatry stood like Balaam, on a high grave-mound[47] in full view of the pagans and strove with all his strength to curse the people of God and bind their hands with the spell of his magic.[48] But one of our bishop's men took a stone that had been blessed by all the people of God and hurled it from a sling, the way David did. It struck the forehead of the sorcerer as he stood cursing and pierced him to the brain. Death, never to be trusted,

(See Plates IV and XVI in A. Grabar and C. Nordenfalk, *Early Medieval Painting* [New York, 1957]).

47. These age-old tumuli, long since despoiled of their funeral treasures, still dot the landscape of Sussex and of other English counties. Their spell of sad mortality haunts Thomas Hardy's stories of Old Wessex. It was in such a tumulus (either a prehistoric barrow, or more likely a Roman chambered tomb) in the fenland of Lincolnshire that St. Guthlac built his hermit's cell (Felix, *Life of St. Guthlac*, Ch. 28; and Colgrave's note, pp. 282-84). In 1939 a tumulus at Sutton Hoo in Suffolk yielded to excavators the fabulous burial treasure of a seventh-century Anglo-Saxon king (Bruce-Mitford, "The Sutton-Hoo Ship Burial" in Hodgkin, *History of the Anglo-Saxons*, [3rd. ed.] Vol. II, Appendix; Green, *Sutton Hoo*). *Beowulf* concludes with the erection of its hero's funeral mound, and the *Iliad* ends with the building of Hector's barrow.

48. For other interesting instances of such spellbinding in this Celtic and Anglo-Saxon world see Colgrave, *Life of Wilfrid by Eddius*, p. 160; Plummer, *Baedae Opera Historica*, II, 260; Wright, *Cultivation of Saga in Anglo-Saxon England*, pp. 124 ff.

snatched him all unawares, as it did Goliath, and his lifeless corpse toppled backwards down onto the sand.

Thereupon the pagans rushed into position for battle, but they launched their host against the people of God in vain. For the Lord fought on the side of the few. Just as Gideon, at the command of the Lord, with 300 men slew 120,000 Midianite warriors in one attack,[49] so these men of our holy bishop's retinue, although few in number (they were 120 men, the same number as the years in Moses' age), were well armed and courageous. Holding a council of war among themselves they made a pact that no one would turn his back on anybody and drop out of the fight, but that all would act so as to win either death with honor or life with victory.[50] Then St. Wilfrid the bishop and his clergy knelt down and raised their hands to heaven, and again brought down the help of the Lord.[51]

Thus one time when Joshua, the son of Nun, and the people of God were fighting against Amalek, Moses gained the victory by continually imploring the Lord's protection while Hur and Aaron held up his hands. In the same way here these few Christians overpowered the wild, fierce pagans three times and put them to flight with no little slaughter, and at the cost of only five men killed on their own side—which is a marvel. Then the great bishop prayed to the Lord his God, who thereupon commanded the tide to flow back in before its regular time had come round. The pagans, whose king had come up, were just getting ready for a fourth assault with all their might when the sea came flooding in and covered the whole shore. The ship was

49. The Old Testament images add heroic scope to the narrative, just as allusions to earlier heroes of epic and saga do to the *Iliad* and to *Beowulf*. Early Christian Biblical epic poetry grew naturally from the classical tradition of epic poetry (Curtius, *European Literature and the Latin Middle Ages*, notice the "sequence" of explanation through pages 241, 240, 237, 236, 183, 184, 397 ff., 46, 457 ff.).

50. Typical Heroic Age *comitatus*-loyalty again, and a "battle boast" as in the *Battle of Maldon*.

51. With his prayers Wilfrid brings the fighting courage that in other northern battles was often incited by the scop's heroic songs. Wright gives an especially intriguing example in *Cultivation of Saga in Anglo-Saxon England*, p. 64. And tradition has it that William's minstrel, Taillefer, sang a *Song of Roland* as he led the Norman knights into battle at Hastings.

floated and made its way back out to sea. While the men gave thanks to the God who had so gloriously honored them, a favoring wind blew from the southwest and they reached a safe haven at Sandwich.

Chapter XIV : *How Chad meanwhile had been consecrated for Wilfrid's See.*

After a time, when St. Wilfrid the bishop had still not come back from across the sea, King Oswy consented to another's irregularly preempting his bishopric. The king was impelled by envy and urged on by the ancient enemy of mankind and influenced by those who took sides with the Quartodecimans against the rule of the Apostolic See.[52] Though they acted in ignorant violation of canon law, the man they appointed—without Wilfrid's knowing anything about it—to the episcopal see of the city of York, a man from Ireland named Chad, was a most sincerely religious servant of God and an admirable teacher.[53] But as soon as St. Wilfrid the bishop arrived it became only too apparent how wrong the action had been.

Wilfrid, however, went back humbly to his post as abbot of the monastery at Ripon and stayed there for three years, except for frequent invitations to perform various episcopal functions in the kingdom of his sincerely devoted friend, Wulfhere, king of the Mercians.[54]

52. For a possible explanation of Oswy's action see note 24 to *Life of Cuthbert.* Oswy did repent of his treatment of Wilfrid, for Bede tells us how a few years later, after Wilfrid's reinstatement at York, the old king, now sick and dying, wished to end his days in Rome "at the holy shrines," and offered Wilfrid a generous sum of money to come with him as his guide (*Ecclesiastical History*, Bk. IV, ch. 5). But death intervened, just as Oswy himself had intervened when his son Alchfrith had wanted to go to Rome with Benedict Biscop.

53. Chad was one of the most lovable of those Anglo-Saxon monks raised, like Cuthbert, in the Celtic tradition. Bede gives a touching account of his holy death (*Ecclesiastical History*, Bk. IV, ch. 3).

54. Wulfhere was one of the amazingly Christian children of pagan King Penda (see note 14 to *Life of St. Cuthbert*). His wife was St. Ermingild. He may be the Wulfhere whose name has been conjecturally read in the runes of the Bewcastle Cross (Brown, *The Arts in Early England*, V, 262-63).

God had fostered this most gentle king as a man after his own heart. Among other good deeds he made gifts to our bishop of many tracts of land in various districts, for his soul's salvation, and Wilfrid straightway established monasteries on them for the servants of God. Egbert[55] too, the devout king of Kent, invited our bishop to visit him; and there he ordained many priests (of whom Putta was one, who afterwards became bishop) and not a few deacons. For Deusdedit, who succeeded Archbishop Honorius[56] as bishop, had died.

And so Wilfrid lived respected and loved by all and exercising his episcopal functions in various localities. Then he returned to his own realm bringing with him the singers Aedde[57] and Aeona, and masons, and instructors in almost all the crafts; and he greatly improved the ordinances of the churches of God with the Rule of St. Benedict. At that time, therefore, with God's help, the great gateway of faith swung open in those districts to the saintly bishop, as it had to the Apostle Paul.

Chapter XV : *How he was reappointed to his see.*

[In 669, after Wilfrid's three years in retirement at Ripon, Archbishop Theodore arrived from Rome as the new Archbishop of Canterbury and ordered Chad to relinquish the See of York to its rightful occupant.[58] Chad obediently stepped down and Wilfrid "returning good for evil," had him appointed as bishop at Lichfield and gave him the land there that King Wulfhere of Mercia had previously presented

55. Egbert succeeded his father, Erconberht, whom we saw in Ch. 3. Egbert consulted with Oswy to send Wighard to Rome to be consecrated as Archbishop of Canterbury. And Theodore was sent back in his stead after Wighard died of the plague (Bede, *Lives of the Abbots*, Ch. 3).

56. See note 11.

57. Aedde is most likely the Eddius who wrote this very *Life of Wilfrid*. And see Bede, *Ecclesiastical History*, Bk. IV, ch. 2.

58. En route from Rome, Theodore stayed in Gaul for a time with Wilfrid's good friend, Bishop Agilbert, and this may help explain why Theodore moved so soon after his arrival to restore Wilfrid to his see.

to himself. So Chad was reconsecrated in the Roman rite and lived out a holy life as bishop.]

Chapter XVI : *How the metropolitan*[59] *church in the city of York was restored.*

During the reign of King Oswy after Wilfrid had been installed as metropolitan bishop of the city of York, attention was called to the ruinous state of the stone buildings[60] of that city's church of God, first built and dedicated by the holy Bishop Paulinus long ago in the days of the most Christian King Edwin. The roof was too worn with age to keep out the rain, birds flew in and out through the uncovered windows and built nests inside the building, and the neglected walls were revoltingly filthy as a result of the rain and the birds. When our holy bishop looked at all this it struck him to the soul, like Daniel, to see that the "house of God" and "of prayer" had become "like a den of thieves,"[61] and he straightway set about planning its repair in accordance with God's will.

59. York did not strictly become a metropolitan see till 735 (Colgrave, *Life of Wilfrid by Eddius*, pp. 156-57).

60. Eddius calls them *officia*, for which Du Cange (*Glossarium Mediae et Infimae Latinitatis*) gives "buildings connected with a church" as one meaning. Brown (*Arts in Early England*, I, 186 ff.) points out that early Anglo-Saxon churches seem to have had small buildings attached, and that this practice was more Celtic (and Eastern) than Roman. But he adds that this had once been common in Rome and Gaul too, and had simply been retained longer by the Celts after having fallen out of vogue elsewhere. And see note 67 to Introduction.

61. These texts are really from Isaias (56:7) and Jeremias (7:11). Eddius seems to have confused them with Chapter 5 in Daniel which describes Baltasar's profaning of the sacred vessels which his father, Nabuchodonosor, had looted from the Temple of Jerusalem. This frequent inaccuracy in Scriptural reference is merely a sign (when it is not a clear case of quoting a variant version) that the Anglo-Saxon scribes are not bothering to check the texts but are relying on the stock of Scripture selections left in their memory from their daily reading of the Office, Mass, and spiritual books.

First of all he renovated the decayed roof, covering it skillfully with pure lead, and he covered the windows with glass[62] which kept out birds and rain but allowed light to shine through inside. He also washed the walls so that they shone, in the words of the prophet, "whiter than snow" [Ps. 50:9]. And besides adorning the interior of God's house and the altar with various furnishings and vessels, he also richly endowed it outside with many estates he had acquired for God and thus did away with its poverty by presenting it a wealth of land. The saying of God about Samuel and all the saints was fulfilled in Wilfrid: "Whosoever will glorify me," he said, "him will I glorify" [1 Kings (=Samuel), 2:30]. He was beloved and honored by God and by all the people.

Chapter XVII : *Concerning the building of the Church at Ripon and its dedication.*

Along with this God-given worldly prosperity there grew in our bishop, friend of the eternal Bridegroom, an ever more burning love for the virgin Bride espoused "to one man" [2 Cor. 11:2][63] and born of charity, the mother of all good. This Bride so pure and modest, so chaste, gentle, and meek, he dressed beautifully "in many-splendored gowns" [Ps., 44:10], and graced her with the seemly customs and manners of the Church as with the very flower of loveliness. As the prophet says, "All the beauty of the king's daughter is within" [Ps., 44:14]. For as Moses constructed of many different colors an earthly tabernacle built with hands, after the pattern shown him by God on the

62. See Bede, *Lives of the Abbots*, Ch. 5. Wilfrid's windows at York seem, contrary to Bede, to have been a few years earlier than Benedict Biscop's. And for other instances of glass in early Anglo-Saxon churches see Levison, *England and the Continent*, p. 171, note 2.

63. This phrase from St. Paul, and the following snatches of verses from Psalm 44, appeared frequently in the recitation of the Divine Office, and Eddius' memory would have them ready at hand for the right occasions. *The York Breviary* (*Publications of the Surtees Society*, Vols. 71, 75) contains the Pauline verse, for instance, in the Capitulum for None in the Common of a Virgin (II, 68); and the verses from Psalm 44 occur in the sixth lesson of the Common of the Blessed Virgin (I, 681), and in Matins for Tuesday in the Psalter (I, 782) etc.

Mount, for the purpose of quickening the devotion of the people of Israel to the worship of God, so did the most blessed Bishop Wilfrid adorn in a splendid manner with gold and silver and many brilliant colors the bridal chamber of the true Bridegroom and Bride for the eyes of all those who believe in their heart and loyally profess the faith.

He built and completed a church at Ripon constructed all of dressed stone, from its foundations in the ground[64] to its summit, and supported on high by various columns and side-chambers.[65] At last when the church was completed, on the day of dedication he invited the two most Christian kings and brothers, Ecgfrith[66] and Aelfwini, and along with them was a great gathering of abbots and reeves and of other high-ranking noblemen and dignitaries of every kind. Like Solomon the Wise they consecrated the church, dedicating it to the Lord in honor of St. Peter the Prince of the Apostles for offering up the prayers of the people. They dedicated to the Lord the altar too, and its bases, and draped it in cloth of purple and gold. In these ceremonies the people had their part, and all the prescriptions of canon law were exactly performed.

Then St. Wilfrid the bishop, standing at the altar, turned to face the congregation and there in the presence of the kings read off a list

64. All that certainly remains of Wilfrid's work today is the small crypt to which the visitor descends from inside the nave of the present cathedral. It was intended for preserving relics on display, like the *confessio* sunk in the floor of St. Peter's in Rome. The "dressed stones" and "columns" Eddius mentions probably came from ruined Roman buildings so plentiful in this neighborhood of Hadrian's Wall. Bede tells how Abbess Sexburg of Ely used beautifully dressed stones from an abandoned Roman town to make a tomb for her sister, Aethilthryth, Wilfrid's great friend (*Ecclesiastical History*, Bk. IV, ch. 19). Charlemagne brought columns from buildings in Ravenna and in Rome itself for his basilica at Aix-la-Chapelle (Einhard, *Life of Charlemagne*, Ch. 26).

65. Eddius' word, *porticus*, seems best translated as "side-chambers," or "side-chapels." Many an early Anglo-Saxon church seems to have had numbers of such small columned side-chapels, often flanking the nave outside and opening into the body of the church through narrow doorways (see Taylor, "Some Aspects of English Pre-Conquest Churches," in Clemoes, *The Anglo-Saxons*, pp. 142-43; Clapham, *English Romanesque Architecture*, p. 31; Brown, *The Arts in Early England*, II, 129).

66. Oswy had died in the meantime (670). Ecgfrith seemed at first to have inherited his mother's attitude toward Wilfrid rather than his father's.

of lands which kings previously and on that very day had granted him for their souls' sake, along with the assent and signature of the bishops and all the high-ranking noblemen. He also clearly enumerated the churches which the British clergy had abandoned in various districts as they fled the hateful sword's edge in the hand of our nation.[67] It was indeed a gift most pleasing to God, this signing over of so many lands by devout kings to our bishop for the service of God. They were in these areas: in the neighborhood of Ribble and Yeadon and the district of Dent and Catlow, and so forth.

Then, with the conclusion of the sermon, the kings began a great banquet lasting three days and three nights. They made merry along with all their people, and were magnanimous to their enemies and humble with the servants of God.

But among all the other splendid things that went into the adornment of this house of God,[68] our holy bishop added yet another marvel-

67. Eddius here allows us a tantalizing glance into the Celtic Christian substratum of Northumbria's culture and into the fierce and fabled hostility between the two races. The savage campaigns of King Aethelfrith had fanned hatred in the north to a high pitch seventy years before this (see Introduction, p. 5). The ensuing see-saw years of battle had a ferocity suggestive of a war of extermination (Chadwick, "The Battle of Chester," in *Celt and Saxon*, pp. 184-85; Meissner, *The Celtic Church in England*, Ch. 5). Almost a hundred years later the young warrior, Guthlac, is fighting fiercely against the Celts (Felix, *Life of Guthlac*, Chs. 16-18). We caught a glimpse of smoldering resentment in the northeastern borderland even in the *Life of St. Cuthbert* (Bk. II, ch. 5) and Aldhelm in the southwest told of Celtic priests refusing to use the same church with Saxon priests or to eat off plates that Saxons had used (Haddan and Stubbs, *Councils and Ecclesiastical Documents*, III, 271; and Duckett, *Anglo-Saxon Saints and Scholars*, pp. 78 ff.).

68. The booty and tribute from Ecgfrith's early military victories must have contributed to Wilfrid's building program. The marvelous works of jewelry found, for example, in the Sutton Hoo ship-burial and in St. Cuthbert's coffin have convinced us that many of the treasures with which Wilfrid adorned Ripon and Hexham were surely of local manufacture. (Green, *Sutton Hoo*, Ch. 5; and Bruce-Mitford, "The Pectoral Cross,"in Battiscombe, *The Relics of St. Cuthbert*, pp. 308 ff.). But we know too, from these finds and from others, that precious goods from the rest of the known world made their way to Dark-Age Britain—*lapis lazuli* from India, silverware from Byzantium, garnets from Ceylon, fine fabrics and glassware from Egypt (Bruce-Mitford, *ibid.*; R. Jessup, *Anglo-Saxon Jewellery* [London, 1950]; C. Radford, "Imported Pottery Found at Tintagel," and D. Harden, "Glass Vessels in Britain and Ireland A. D. 400-

ous gift, something unheard of before our day. For the salvation of his soul he had the four gospels inscribed in letters of purest gold on leaves of empurpled vellum, and illuminated.

And he instructed the jewelers to contrive a case for the books, all of the purest gold and the most precious gems.[69] As a testimonial to his blessed memory all these treasures and a goodly number of others are preserved to this day in our church where his remains lie at rest and where his name is remembered in prayer every day without fail.

Chapter XVIII : *How he restored a child to life.*

[One day in the town of Ontiddanufri, where Bishop Wilfrid had ridden to baptize and confirm, he was prevailed upon by a distraught mother to raise her dead first-born child to life and baptize it, and thus free it "from the mouth of the lion" [Ps. 21:22]. "Do not doubt the power of Christ," she pleaded . . . .]

The holy bishop had no doubt of the power of Christ, and as the woman spoke it seemed to him that he could hear the faith of the Syro-Phoenician woman[70] in her voice, so he uttered a prayer and

1000," in Harden, *Dark-Age Britain*; Aileen Fox, *South West England*, Ancient Peoples and Places [Thames and Hudson, London, 1964]). Bede (*Lives of the Abbots*, Chs. 4, 6, 9) and Eddius (*Life of Wilfrid*, Ch. 33) tell us how Benedict Biscop and Wilfrid imported rich cargoes of treasure from Rome and Gaul to adorn Northumbria's churches. And Aldhelm imported similar treasures for the churches of Wessex (Duckett, *Anglo-Saxon Saints and Scholars*, pp. 67-68, 71-72).

69. Eddius' Latin word, *bibliotheca*, can mean either the covering for a book or a separate case to contain the book. Sheeted with gold and silver and encrusted with gems they unfortunately proved irresistibly tempting to the Vikings, and few have survived (see the indescribably beautiful Anglo-Saxon, French, and German Gospel covers, especially those from the eighth to eleventh centuries, in the Pierpont Morgan Library, New York). We know that the *Lindisfarne Gospels* once possessed such a jewelled cover (Brown, *Arts in Early England*, V, 334). One of the Anglo-Saxon riddles describes the binding of such a splendid book (R. Gordon translates it in his *Anglo-Saxon Poetry*, [Everyman's Library] revised edition, 1954, pp. 297-98).

70. See St. Mark, 7, 25-30.

then placed his hand on the dead body of the boy. Straightway it began to breathe again and received back the spirit of life. Then after Wilfrid had baptized the revived infant he handed him back again to his mother, and enjoined her in the Lord's name that when her son reached the age of seven she give him back to him for the service of God.

But later as the mother watched her baby become a fine-looking boy she succumbed to the evil urging of her husband, and, spurning their pact with the bishop, fled the country. However, the bishop's reeve, named Hocca, made a search for the boy and found him hidden away in the care of some Britons, so he took him away by force and brought him back to the bishop. The boy, whose Christian name was Eodwald and his given name, Bishop's Son, lived in the service of God at Ripon until he met his death in the great plague.[71] O how great and marvelous is the mercy of God! who by means of his honored servant called a non-baptized infant back into this life from death so that he could be baptized and live for an everlasting life of happiness to come.

Chapter XIX : *Concerning the king's victory over the fierce Picts* [A.D. 671-673].

Now during those days the devout King Ecgfrith and his most blessed Queen Aethilthryth[72] (whose incorrupt body still gives witness that it was unstained during life) were of one mind with Bishop Wilfrid in all things, and there ensued peace and happiness among the people and, with God's help, a succession of bountiful years and of victories over their enemies.[73] It was like the case of Joash, the young King

71. Perhaps he died in the same visitation of the plague which in 685 swept off all the monks at Jarrow except for Abbot Ceolfrith and one young boy—probably Bede (*Life of Ceolfrith*, Ch. 14). Wilfrid's determination to hold the woman to her word is but another example of the importance of an oath in Heroic Age society. Personal loyalty was the paramount cohesive force.

72. Aethilthryth ("noble strength") was the daughter of King Anna and later abbess and saint of Ely. She was known as St. Audrey, and the celebration of St. Audrey's Fair gave us "tawdry."

73. During these halycon years Queen Aethilthryth gave Wilfrid the land for Hexham monastery (See Ch. 22).

of Judah, who took care to keep in God's good favor and thus triumphed over his enemies, as long as the great high priest Jehoiada was alive, but who fell from God's friendship after the death of the high priest and lost a good part of his kingdom. Just so did King Ecgfrith—and there are many witnesses to bear it out—extend the boundaries of his kingdom in every direction by a succession of celebrated victories; but once the harmony between him and the bishop was destroyed and the queen had left him to dedicate herself to God,[74] then the king's days of victory came to an end.

For in the first years of his rule, while the kingdom was still weak, the savage Picts in their raging pride began to loathe being subject to the Saxons and they threatened to throw off their yoke of servitude. Collecting a numberless host from every nook and cranny of the north, like swarms of ants sweeping down from their hills in the summer, they threw up an earthen fortification to protect their threatened land.[75] As soon as he learned of this, King Ecgfrith, who was meek among his own people but courageous in the face of his enemies, hurriedly readied a troop of mounted men[76] for he was not a man who was slow

74. One can hardly help sympathizing with the exasperated king who saw Wilfrid encouraging his wife to leave him and become a nun. The bishop presided over the ceremony of her veiling in the monastery of Coldingham in 672.

75. As far as I know, this sentence (Colgrave, *Life of Wilfrid by Eddius*, p. 40) has always been understood as though the erecting of the mound was part of the simile referring to the ants. But the logical structure of Eddius' Latin sentence seems to demand that *muniebant aggerem* ("they threw up an earthen fortification") be taken in parallel with *despiciebant* ("they began to loathe being subject") and *minabant* ("they threatened") and hence be referred to the Picts. The Roman terms are the proper military ones for a mound-and-ditch construction. For a discussion of Pictish earthen fortifications see R. W. Feachem, "Fortifications," pp. 66-86 in *The Problem of the Picts*, edited by F. T. Wainwright (New York, 1956). If this proposed translation is correct then the "concealed host" of Picts in the following sentence (*supra invisibilem hostem*) can simply mean that they were "intrenched." In correspondence with me about this suggested translation, Dr. Colgrave raises further interesting points: "Does it imply that Eddius thought that the Antonine Wall was in fact a Pictish construction? It would also be better to translate *supra* as 'from above.' They dug themselves in and so were invisible from above. Of course it might be a reference to Pictish underground dwellings or merely trenches."

76. It has been remarked that this is the first mention of English cavalry in history (Colgrave, *Life of Wilfrid by Eddius*, p. 165). Though it seems they

to take action. Trusting in God like Judas Maccabeus, he and a brave sub-king, Beornhaeth, led the small force of God's people in against a host that not only vastly outnumbered them but was also intrenched. He made an enormous slaughter of them, filling two rivers so full of their corpses that—marvelous to tell—he and his men were able to walk across on them dry-shod and pursue and slay a multitude of fugitives. The Picts were then reduced to slavery and were quiet under the yoke of captivity to the day of the king's death.

Chapter XX : *Of his victory over the King of the Mercians* [A.D. 673–75].

Then after this victory Ecgfrith, together with the bishop, ruled the people as a just and holy king. Like David he was strong in crushing his enemies but humble in the eyes of God. From God he received the courage to break the necks of rebellious peoples and insolent kings, and for all things he always gave thanks to God. Wulfhere, for instance, King of the Mercians, who was proud of heart and insatiably ambitious,[77] stirred up all the southern peoples against us. He was not bent

fought on foot, for Eddius says they walked (*ambulantes*) across the corpse-choked rivers in pursuit of the fugitives. Over 700 years earlier there had been Roman cavalry forces in the first invasion fleet which Caesar led against Britain, but a hitch in the operation prevented their being landed to go into action with the infantry legions. The latter had a bad time of it when horsemen and a strange army of Celtic war chariots out of the Homeric past clattered down on them from the chalk downs (Caesar, *Conquest of Gaul*, Ch. 5, 1). There were Roman cavalry units on duty in Britain during the subsequent years of occupation (for instance, we know that a cavalry force from Holland was once stationed at the Roman fort of Burgh Castle—D. A. White, *Litus Saxonicum* [Madison, Wis., 1961] p. 52). Later, in Roman fashion, the Britons may have sent mounted troops against the invading Anglo-Saxons (see notes 9 and 10 to Introduction). Then the Bayeux Tapestry shows us William of Normandy transporting his cavalry across the Channel in 1066 and attacking at Hastings. It is now even thought possible that Harold might normally have opposed him with an equal cavalry force had he had time to assemble his army properly (C. W. Hollister discusses new opinions in *Anglo-Saxon Military Institutions* [Oxford, 1962] pp. 136 ff.).

77. Wilfrid's "heroic" goodness is *so absolute* for Eddius, as Eve's loveliness

so much on merely warring as he was on humiliating us and forcing us to pay tribute. But God was not guiding him. Ecgfrith, King of Deira and Bernicia, with unwavering courage and a heart full of faith, followed the advice of his counsellors and the teaching of the bishop to trust in God, as Barak and Deborah did, to protect his country and guard the churches of God. With a force as small as theirs had been he attacked the proud enemy host and, with God helping his little army, he destroyed them. A countless number of them were slain, their king was put to flight, and Ecgfrith imposed a scale of tribute on the kingdom. And when Wulfhere died later through some cause or other, then Ecgfrith ruled a wider realm for some time in peace.

Chapter XXI : *Of the goodness of our bishop.*

[As Ecgfrith's political kingdom grew, so did Wilfrid's ecclesiastical one, over the Saxons in the south, and the British, the Scots, and the Picts in the north. In all these places he ordained priests and deacons to help him. But in the midst of plenty he lived temperately, and even ascetically. Among other things, his sense of moral and physical cleanliness led him to bathe every night, winter and summer, until Pope John advised him to desist out of consideration for his age] . . . And so it came about that the abbots and abbesses of almost every monastery bound over their property to him by vow, either continuing to administer it in his name or else arranging for him to inherit it after their death. And secular officials too, noblemen of the realm, gave him their sons to educate either for the service of God if they should so choose, or, if they preferred, to be intrusted to the king's charge as warriors when they came of age. But all these favors kindled the flames of envy and hate in many hearts,[78] and the devil was quick to blow the fires

was for Milton's Adam, that his evaluation of other people sometimes varies according to their attitude to Wilfrid. Back in Chapter 14 this fearsome Wulfhere was a "most gentle" king showering gifts of property on Wilfrid. But, on the other hand, Eddius never really turns Archbishop Theodore into a villain, even before that prelate was reconciled with Wilfrid.

78. We think of the brilliant "court" of Thomas Becket, that dangerously outshone King Henry's.

higher. Our holy bishop, however, in the words of the illustrious doctor, patiently "armed himself right and left" [2 Cor. 6:7] and weathered prosperity and adversity with equal composure. Always he continued to bestow gifts on clergy and laity alike with such largesse as to have no equal.

Chapter XXII : *Concerning the building of the Church at Hexham* [A.D. 672-678].

Accordingly Wilfrid clung unfailingly to the Lord, putting his trust in Him and offering his dearest vows to Him who had given him everything. So it was that when the holy Queen Aethilthryth gave him an estate at Hexham, he dedicated it to God and built a church on it in honor of St. Andrew the Apostle.[79] It is not in my poor power to describe how its foundations were set deeply in the earth with crypt-chambers of wonderfully dressed stone,[80] and how above the ground rose a church of many parts supported on various columns and many side aisles and chapels, and furnished with walls of astounding length and height, surrounded by various winding passageways with spiral stairs leading up and down. Our holy bishop was indeed taught by the Spirit of God when he thought out the construction of these buildings, for we have not heard of any other church built so splendidly this side of the Alps.[81] Moreover who has the power to tell how Bishop

79. The 12th-century *History of the Church of Hexham* by Prior Richard says that Wilfrid dedicated the Church to St. Andrew in gratitude for a favor the saint had granted him (see Eddius, Ch. 5) on his first visit to Rome (*Publications of the Surtees Society*, 44, 10).

80. The pilgrim today in the later church of Hexham can still walk down ancient stone steps into this barrel-vaulted crypt of Wilfrid's. Many of its cut stones were brought from the Roman camp at Corbridge.

81. And Wilfrid built a further splendid church at Hexham in the centrally-planned manner (radiating out from one central dome) of Justinian's great Byzantine Santa Sophia in Constantinople and San Vitale in Ravenna. Prior Richard (*op. cit.*, Ch. 4; see note 79) describes it as being in the form of a tower or dome, almost circular, with four transepts and porches. He says that it was dedicated to Mary, and that it and a church to St. Michael were begun by Wil-

Acca of blessed memory, by the grace of God still living, enriched this multichambered building with magnificent ornamentation in gold and silver and precious stones, and how he clothed the altars in cloth of purple and silk? Let us now return to our story.

Chapter XXIII : *How a boy on the verge of death was restored to health.*

[While the masons were working on the highest part of the church walls a young man named Bothelm fell from a pinnacle at a great height and was shattered on the stone pavement. He was carried outside for dead, but after the bishop and the brethren had prayed over him and the bishop had blessed him, he revived. Physicians bandaged his broken limbs and he improved from day to day, and is still living and giving thanks to God.]

Chapter XXIV: *How envy was stirred up against our bishop and how he was expelled from his see* [A.D. 678].

The Treacherous One prowled around the sheepfold of God "like a roaring lion" [1 Pet., 5:8], in the words of Peter the Apostle, ever on the watch, day and night, for a way to get inside. He desired first of all to overcome the bravest soldier, so that the timid might be the more easily overcome. Taking up his usual weapons, therefore, he sought out the weak vessel—woman—by whom he has so often defiled the whole world.

So it was that at this time, by the devil's insinuation, King Ecgfrith's queen, named Iurminburg, was racked with envy—though after the death of the king she was to be transformed from a she-wolf into a lamb

frid in response to his vision at Meaux (Eddius, Ch. 56) and were completed by Bishop Acca.

of God and perfect abbess and most admirable mother of her community.[82] But now this sorceress straightway shot the poisoned arrows of words from her quiver into the king's heart, as did the most wicked Jezebel who slew the prophets of God and persecuted Elias. With eloquence Iurminburg reckoned up for the king's ear all Wilfrid's display of secular magnificence, his riches and the vast array of his monasteries and the imposing size of his buildings, as well as his formidable host of armed retainers decked out in all the finery of royalty.

Such missiles as these pierced the king to the heart, and so the pair of them contrived cunningly to humiliate the head of the Church—to their own ruin—and boldly to defraud him of the gifts given him by kings for the service of God. In defiance of the will of God they summoned Archbishop Theodore to be an ally in their madness, as Balak did Balaam, with the offer of presents, which blind the eyes even of the wise. When the archbishop came to them they revealed what they intended to do to humiliate Wilfrid, and he—may God forgive him—consented unjustly to condemn Wilfrid though he was guiltless of any offence. So, while Wilfrid was absent, three bishops were brought in from elsewhere, not subjects of this diocese; and Theodore by himself, irregularly and without precedent, consecrated them over their own separate parts of the diocese of our bishop.

As soon as he learned of it our holy bishop went to the king and the archbishop and demanded to know for what reason they had, like robbers, defrauded him of possessions bestowed on him by kings—and this even though he was guilty of no crime. Before all the populace they made our bishop an infamous reply: "We charge you with no criminal guilt of any offence, but the judgment we have passed on you we shall not alter."

Our bishop, however, was ill-content with such a fraudulent judgment and, on the advice of his fellow-bishops, he decided instead to seek the judgment of the Apostolic See, just as the Apostle Paul appealed to Caesar when he had been condemned without cause by the Jews. Thereupon as the holy bishop turned from the royal tribunal he said to the king's flatterers who were laughing with glee, "On the anniversary of this day, you who are now laughing spitefully at my

82. Cuthbert himself conferred the veil upon her in her sister's monastery at Carlisle (Bede's prose *Life of St. Cuthbert*, Ch. 28).

condemnation shall then weep bitterly in your consternation." And so it came to pass in accord with the prophecy of the saint. One year later, to the day, the corpse of the slain King Aelfwini was borne into York, and all the people wept bitterly and tore their garments and their hair.[83] His brother survived him but reigned without any victories to the day of his death.

Chapter XXV: *How Bishop Winfrid was robbed.*

As Bishop Wilfrid prepared to board ship with his band of retainers and his clergy, he left behind him in the hands of the newly-consecrated bishops many thousands of his monks, mourning and weeping and begging God unceasingly to direct Wilfrid's journey in accordance with His will. But the enemies of our prelate would not let their evil designs rest. Assuming that Wilfrid would proceed by the most direct route to Rome and hence would sail south to Quentavic,[84] they sent messengers on ahead with presents for Theodoric, King of the Franks, and for the wicked Duke Ebroin,[85] requesting either that they doom Wilfrid to a greater exile, or that they slay his retinue and rob him of everything he had with him. But the Lord saved him from the hands of his enemies as from the hands of Herod. For at that time the

83. Aelfwini, younger brother of King Ecgfrith (Eddius, Ch. 17), was probably sub-king of Deira, as Alchfrith had been under Oswy. He was killed by the Mercians in the Battle of the Trent in 679 (see note 28 to Introduction) and only the mediation of Archbishop Theodore prevented an ensuing blood-feud between King Aethelred and King Ecgfrith (Bede, *Ecclesiastical History*, Bk. IV, ch. 21).

84. On the French coast near modern Étaples.

85. Ebroin was the same scheming Mayor of the Palace who was most likely responsible for the death of Archbishop Aunemund (Eddius, Ch. 6). He is also the one who in 668 detained Abbot Hadrian (on his way to England with Theodore) because he suspected him of carrying on secret negotiations between the Byzantine Emperor and the Anglo-Saxon kings (Levison, *England and the Continent*, p. 13). Ebroin's figurehead king, Theodoric, is nominal ruler in Neustria, while King Dagobert (in Ch. 28) is ruler of Austrasia—the western and eastern portions, respectively, of the Frankish kingdom.

holy Bishop Winfrid[86] had been driven out of Lichfield and while he was traveling along that very route he fell into the hands of Wilfrid's enemies as into the jaws of a lion. He was seized at once and robbed of all his money, many of his company were killed, and the holy bishop was left in a desperate condition despoiled of even the clothes on his back. For they had mistakenly supposed him to be the holy Bishop Wilfrid, misled by the fortunate error of one syllable.

Chapter XXVI : *How his voyage brought him to Friesland.*

Our holy bishop, on the other hand, had turned the prows of his ships to the east, and the gentle wind he wanted carried him and his company happily to Friesland [A.D. 678]. There he found vast multitudes of heathen, whose king, Aldgisl, received him with honor. Straightway our saintly bishop obtained the king's leave to preach the word of God everyday. So he announced to them the true God, Almighty Father, and Jesus Christ his only Son, and the Holy Spirit coeternal with them, and he taught them convincingly about the one baptism for the remission of sin and about everlasting life in the resurrection after death.

Moreover, he backed up all his teaching very effectively in their eyes, for at the very time of his arrival there had been a much greater catch of fish than usual, and in all ways the year had been a bountiful one. Now they attributed this to the power of the Lord whom the holy man of God preached. Hence in that year of fortune they accepted his preaching; and all the nobles, save for a few, and many thousands of the common folk, were baptized in the name of the Lord. So he first planted in that region the foundation of faith, to use the Apostle's words, and his son who was raised at Ripon, Willibrord, bishop by the grace of God, is still building on it, toiling most laboriously. His reward awaits him in eternity.

86. He had succeeded Chad in the see of Lichfield (see Ch. 15).

Chapter XXVII : *How the king refused a bribe offered for Wilfrid.*

Now at this same time Ebroin, duke of King Theodoric of the Franks, sent his messengers to King Aldgisl of the Frisians. They brought letters in which he saluted the king in words of peace and promised on oath to pay him a full bushel of gold solidi[87]—truly a damnable bribe—if he would either apprehend Bishop Wilfrid and send him to him alive, or kill him and send his head. At once the king ordered the letter read for all to hear while we and the messengers were feasting there in the palace in the presence of his people. As soon as it was read he took the letter in his hands and tore it into pieces, and then while everybody stared he threw it into the blazing fire in front of him. To those who had brought it he said: "Report to your master what I say to you now: 'May the Creator of all things so tear to pieces and consume to ashes the kingdom and the life of him who perjures himself before his God and fails to keep a pact that he has made!'" With that the messengers retired in confusion from the presence of this king who would not consent to a crime, and went back whence they had come, to their master.

Chapter XXVIII : *How the kings, Dagobert and Perctarit, received him* [A.D. 679].

After our bishop, dear to God, had spent the winter among the Frisians and had won many people for the Lord, with the coming of spring he and his company resumed with God's help their journey to the Apostolic See. He came to the King of the Franks named Dagobert and was most courteously received with every mark of respect in

87. A bushel was a measure of about twenty pounds in Roman times. A Merovingian gold solidus was equivalent to about forty silver denarii (Chadwick, *Studies in Anglo-Saxon Institutions*, pp. 64 ff.).

gratitude for the kindness Wilfrid had once shown him. For in his youth this king had been driven into permanent exile by his enemies who had taken over the rule of the kingdom.[88] So he had taken ship and reached Ireland with God's help. Then as the years passed by, his friends and kinsmen heard of reports from travellers that he was still alive and flourishing in the prime of life. Whereupon they sent messengers privately to Bishop Wilfrid asking if he would invite Dagobert over from Ireland and then send him on to them to be their king. This our holy bishop did. After receiving him on his arrival from Ireland and fitting him out in magnificent state with arms and an imposing force of retainers, he sent him on his way to his own land. Now, therefore, the king was very mindful of these acts of kindness and with evident sincerity he implored Wilfrid to accept the most important bishopric in his kingdom, the one attached to the city of Strassburg. And when Wilfrid declined the offer, then the king sent him on to the Apostolic See laden with a wealth of splendid gifts and with his own bishop, Deodatus, for a guide.

The two bishops then proceeded on their way and with God directing them came to Perctarit, King of Campania,[89] a humble, gentle man who lived in awe of the Word of God. Receiving the pilgrims with kindness according to the command of the Lord, he told our holy bishop: "Your enemies have sent messengers to me from Britain with their best wishes and with promises of the most wonderful gifts if I will restrain you by force from continuing on to the Apostolic See. They say you are a bishop in secret flight. I refused to do anything so heinously wicked, and sent back this answer: 'I was an exile once when I was a young man. I was driven out of my fatherland and found asylum with a pagan King of the Huns, who made a pact with me, in the presence of the idol which was his god, that he would never betray me or hand me over to my enemies. Then after some time messengers came to the pagan king with word from my enemies. They promised under oath to give him a full bushel of gold solidi if he would hand me over to them for execution. He would not consent to it, and returned this answer: "The gods would most assuredly

88. On King Dagobert (II) see Levison, *England and the Continent*, p. 49.

89. Our travellers are now in the plains of (hence: Campania) Northern Italy. Perctarit was King of the Lombards (Levison, *op. cit.* p. 14).

cut off my life if I did this impious thing and broke the pact I made before them." And I who know the true God, how much more firmly will I refuse to give my soul to perdition for the wealth of the whole world.'"

So he graciously provided our holy bishop and his retinue with guides and sent them on their way with all due honor to the Apostolic See that they had so long desired to reach. And thus did the Lord honor Wilfrid with his protection everywhere he travelled.

Chapter XXIX : *How Agatho, the most blessed Pope of the Apostolic See, together with his holy synod, received the letters of our bishop.*

[In Rome, in 679, Wilfrid found his case was already known, for a monk named Coenwald had arrived with letters from Theodore. Wilfrid was called courteously to a synod of over fifty bishops and priests held in the Constantinian Basilica and presided over by Pope Agatho. In a preliminary address, the deacon and sub-deacon of the Sacred College of Cardinals (Andrew, Bishop of Ostia, and John, Bishop of Porto) stated that, from their reading of the letters thus far presented on both sides of the controversy, they found no sufficient canonical grounds for Wilfrid's deposition. Then Pope Agatho called for the secretary to read out the petition which Wilfrid had brought with him.]

Chapter XXX : *This is Bishop Wilfrid's petition.*

[Wilfrid, styling himself "a lowly and unworthy bishop of Saxony," stated his assurance that his case would be given a fair hearing by the Roman See. He declared that, though he hesitated to accuse Archbishop Theodore, the latter had removed him from his see for no uncanonical act and, solely on his own authority, had placed three bishops in his stead. Wilfrid pointed out that instead of attacking those who have despoiled him "like robbers," he has appealed to the judgment of the Holy See. He asked that if Rome should agree to Theodore's partition of the diocese then that they at least give him bishops with whom he could work in unanimity and who were not strangers or outsiders.]

Chapter XXXI : *Of Pope Agatho's answer.*

[The Pope commended Wilfrid's action in appealing his case to Rome and in expressing his willingness to abide by the latter's decision.]

Chapter XXXII : *Of the synod's answer.*

[The synod, together with Pope Agatho, declared that Wilfrid should be given back his former see and that he should consecrate fellow-bishops of his own choosing. Anathemas were then pronounced against any who should withstand this decree, and blessings were bestowed on all who should assist in its execution.]

Chapter XXXIII : *Concerning our bishop's return* [A.D. 680].

So after Bishop Wilfrid, dear to God, had spent many days there[90] he was directed, in accord with the papal order and the command of the entire holy synod, to take with him the written decision of the Apostolic See and to show it to King Ecgfrith. And our holy bishop, firm in his loyalty, was humbly obedient in every detail to the injunction of the Apostolic See as he had promised to be. First he spent several

90. During this time he attended the Sixth Ecumenical Council, against Monothelitism, and made a profession of faith in the name of the Church of northern Britain and Ireland—a profession that was to stand him in good stead in a critical moment in Rome some twenty-four years later (see Ch. 53).

days going around to the shrines of the saints to pray, and for the consolation of the churches of Britain he obtained a great number of saints' relics from reliable men he could trust.[91] And he made a written record of each relic, what it was, and of which saint it was. Then, as he always did, he bought many other fine things—which would take too long to enumerate here—for the adornment of the house of God. And with the blessing of the Apostolic See and of the entire holy synod, and with the help of God, he set out on the return journey to his land, light at heart and rejoicing at the way everything had gone.

He proceeded on his way through Campania with the victorious verdict of the Apostolic See, crossed the mountains, and arrived in the territory of the Franks. There his faithful friend Dagobert had recently been treacherously killed by the perfidy of the dukes and with the consent of the bishops—a horrible thing to have to say! Now one of these bishops intercepted Wilfrid with a huge army. In his evil heart he had every intention, if God had not withstood him, of robbing all of Wilfrid's retainers and either reducing them to serfdom or selling them as slaves, or killing them if they resisted. Our holy bishop he intended to hold confined under guard to await the judgment of Duke Ebroin. He demanded to know by what boldness Wilfrid traveled so rashly through the land of the Franks: "You who are worthy of death for sending back to us from exile one who was made king through your help,[92] one who was a destroyer of cities, who despised the advice of his counsellors, who beggared the people with his demands for tribute like Roboam the son of Solomon, and who despised the churches of God and their prelates. For these evil deeds he has paid the penalty of death and his corpse lies buried in the ground."

Our holy prelate returned the bishop a humble answer: "In Christ Jesus and by St. Peter the Apostle I tell the truth and lie not [cf. 1 Tim. 2:7] when I say that I was merely following God's command to the Israelite people, who were dwellers in a strange land, when I took care of this man and helped him while he was living in exile as a stranger.

91. Interesting reference to the growing traffic in bogus relics, and Wilfrid's awareness of it.

92. And in *Beowulf* the Swedish King Onela killed the Geatish King Heardred for harboring exiled Swedish royalty (vv. 2379 ff.).

It was for your good, not your harm, that I gave him a place in the sun. It was so that he could be a builder of cities, a comfort to the citizens, a consultant of the elders, a defender of the churches of God, in accordance with his own promise in the name of the Lord. My most righteous bishop, what else would you yourself feel obliged to do other than what I did in the Lord, if an exile of royal blood should come to your holiness from our nation?"

The bishop replied, "May the Lord watch over your homecoming" [Ps. 120:8], and so forth; and "Woe to me, a sinner. Forgive me, for like the patriarch Judah, I see that you are much more just than I. May the Lord be with you and may St. Peter the Apostle assist you."

Chapter XXXIV : *How the king spurned the decisions of the Apostolic See.*

[When the Pope's judgment of the case was read to a synod of the chief nobles and prelates convened by the king, Wilfrid was immediately accused of having purchased the favorable decision for a price.]

. . . Then at the command of the king and his counsellors and with the consent of the bishops who occupied Wilfrid's see, it was decided that he should be held in prison for nine months, shorn of all the dignities of his state. For, as we said, no sooner had the documents of the Apostolic See been opened and read out, than the king—sad to say—flew into a rage, with his flatterers urging him on, and defied the decision of Peter, Chief of the Apostles, who has received from God the power of binding and loosing. Then, swearing by his soul's salvation, he gave strict orders that our holy bishop be despoiled of everything save the clothes on his back and be kept in solitary confinement, and that his followers be scattered to the four winds and none of his friends be permitted to visit him.

The queen, whom we have mentioned before, made use of the occasion to take away from the man of God his necklace-reliquary filled with holy relics—it horrifies me to tell it—and she wore it as jewelry at home in her private apartments and when she was traveling abroad in her chariot.[93] But this brought great misfortune upon the queen, as happened to the Philistines when they put the Israelite people to flight and paraded the captured Ark of God through their cities.

Chapter XXXV : *How he encouraged his followers.*

[He exhorted them to take consolation in the memory of the persecution of God's people in the Old Testament and of Christ and his disciples in the New.]

Chapter XXXVI : *How a house was illumined by God.*

When he had finished his words of consolation, the officers of the king took hold of our holy bishop and led him, "as a sheep to the slaughter" [Is. 53:7] that opens not its mouth, to the reeve named Osfrith who ruled the royal borough of Broninis. They stood Wilfrid before him and ordered the man in the king's name to guard the holy bishop closely—he who then could well have been called the light of Britain because of the great merits of his faith—in some secret dungeons dark with foul vapors, and without the knowledge of any of his friends. The thegn was faithful to the king, so by the latter's pressing command he held the holy bishop under guard in hidden cells that were rarely reached by sunlight during the day and not lit by lamps at night.

[Wilfrid spent much of the time singing psalms, and his guards were terrified by the light that often filled his dungeon during the night. The king offered him part of his former bishopric back if he would deny that the apostolic decree was genuine, but Wilfrid replied that he would rather have his head cut off than do such a thing.]

93. St. Jerome had remarked on the "superstitious women" of Rome who ostentatiously wore reliquaries of the true Cross (*Patrologia Latina*, 26, 175).

Chapter XXXVII : *How a woman was healed.*

[Osfrith's wife became stricken with a mortal palsy, and at the reeve's frantic request Wilfrid cured her by sprinkling holy water over her and praying, after the man had brought him to her bedside. She is now living as an abbess, named Aebbe.]

Chapter XXXVIII : *How the chains fell from him.*

Now the reeve did not dare, out of fear of the king, to continue to show respect to our holy bishop, and yet because of Wilfrid's holiness he feared the wrath of God and had no wish to mistreat the man. So he sent messengers to say to the king: "I implore you by my life and your salvation not to force me to my own perdition by punishing this holy and innocent bishop any longer. For I choose rather to die than to torture such a blameless man."

At this news the king was furious and ordered Wilfrid taken to his town of Dunbar to the reeve named Tydlin, who was supposed to be a harder man. Him he commanded to keep this great man and great bishop in solitary confinement, fettered hand and foot. Thus compelled by the king's order, the reeve directed the smiths to make iron chains, and they diligently set about the inexcusable operation by first taking the measurements of our holy confessor's limbs. But God was against them. For always the chains were either too tight and narrow to fit around his limbs, or else they were too wide and loose so that they fell free from the feet that had journeyed for the Gospel and from the hands that had baptized. The smiths became so frightened that they left the man of God unchained, while he continued singing psalms and giving thanks to God—as the Apostle said to the Hebrews, "Bearing up under a great struggle against afflictions, made into a spectacle by disgraceful treatment, suffering the robbery of all his goods" [cf. Heb. 10:32, 33]—and all these things had been inflicted by his own countrymen. So, against their will, they kept him in isolated confinement until the time set by God.

Chapter XXXIX : *How the queen was afflicted and then cured.*

Meanwhile the king and his queen had been making their royal progress through cities and fortified towns and villages, feasting and making merry every day. On one occasion they came to the monastery called Coldingham, presided over by a most holy and sensible abbess named Aebbe,[94] sister of King Oswy. Here during the night the queen was possessed by a devil and, like Pilate's wife, she was so afflicted and tormented that she scarcely expected to live till day. As soon as the first light of morning appeared the abbess went to the queen and saw that her limbs were all contracted and tightly entwined in a knot, and that clearly she was dying.

So she went to the king in tears and pointed out to him why, as far as she knew, this tragic misfortune had happened to him. She told him boldly: "I know—and know for a fact—that you have deposed Bishop Wilfrid, dear to God, from his episcopal see without his being guilty of any crime at all, and that when he was driven into exile he went to the Apostolic See and returned with documents from that See which shares with the Apostle St. Peter the power of binding and loosing, and that you foolishly ignored the documents and plundered his possessions, and finally that you have added evil to evil by shutting the saint up in prison.

"But now, my son, do what your mother bids you. Break his chains and send a trustworthy messenger to him with the holy relics which the queen took off his neck when he was robbed and which she carried around from town to town like the Ark of God—to her own destruction. If you are unwilling to do the best thing, which would be to have him back in the bishopric, then set him free and let him leave your kingdom with his friends and go wherever he pleases. In that case I believe that you will remain alive and the queen will not die. But if you should refuse this, neither of you will go unpunished, as

94. She is not the Aebbe of Ch. 37, but the aunt of Ecgfrith. See note 18 to *Life of St. Cuthbert.* St. Cuthbert visited her at Coldingham (*Life of St. Cuthbert,* Bk. II, ch. 3).

God is my witness." The king straightway obeyed the virtuous abbess and released our most holy bishop. He gave him leave to depart freely with his relics and with all his assembled companions—and the queen was healed.

Chapter XL : *How Berhtwald received the holy bishop.*

So Bishop Wilfrid with his companions left his homeland and set forth into exile. He turned his steps towards the [Anglo-Saxon] kingdoms of the south, and God who stays by his saints in their trials, sent to meet him a reeve named Berhtwald. Of noble blood, this man was a nephew to King Aethelred of the Mercians and was most kindhearted. As soon as he saw such respectable men and heard from our holy teacher the reasons for their wandering, then he implored them in the Lord's name to remain with him, and in all kindly solicitude he offered the servants of God a portion of his land to live in. Our holy bishop thanked God for thus providing him some comfort by this sanctuary of rest, and accordingly lost no time in founding a small monastery on this property which had been given him for God's sake. It is still there in the possession of the monks to this day.

But the grudging envy of man's ancient enemy, the devil, never sleeps. As soon as King Aethelred and his queen,[95] who was the sister of King Ecgfrith, heard that the man of God had been expelled from his country and was staying on their reeve's land and enjoying a moment of rest, they forbade Berhtwald, under threat of serious punishment, to let him stay with him for so much as the space of one day. This they did to curry favor with King Ecgfrith. Driven hence by hate, though the monks remained there, our bishop then made his way to the king of the West Saxons named Centwine. But here too he stayed only a short while, on account of the persecution that dogged his steps. For the queen there was the sister of Queen Iurminburg

95. Queen Osthryth was to be mysteriously murdered in 697 (Bede, *Ecclesiastical History*, Bk. V, ch. 24; and see Finberg's conjecture in *The Early Charters of the West Midlands*, pp. 176–77).

and hated him bitterly. Because of the friendship between these three kings, therefore, Wilfrid was driven away from there.[96]

Chapter XLI : *How he converted the pagans in Selsey to God* [A.D. 681-6].

But there seems little point in delaying over more of these instances. The fact is that he had been released from prison and expelled from his own country in such a manner that no asylum was to be permitted him on either side of the sea in any other land where the power of Ecgfrith prevailed. Relentlessly Ecgfrith continued to stir up persecution and direct it against him in whatever land he had a mind to settle down.

But in those days there happened to be a certain portion of our nation which had persistently clung to its pagan ways up to that very time. Their rugged hills and dense forests had made them impregnable to attack by other peoples. And so, with God directing him after human help had failed him, our holy bishop fled to those pagans of Sussex.[97] He sought out their king, whose name was Aethilwalh, and told him the whole bitter tale of his exile. At once the king gave his solemn promise to so strong a compact of peace and friendship between them that he swore none of the bishop's enemies would succeed in terrifying him by threats of the sword of some bellicose foe, nor in getting him to break this ratified pact by any offer of rewards and presents, however great.

The holy man of God rejoiced at these consoling words and thereupon, after giving thanks to God, began to preach the Gospel. On

96. We see the predominance of Northumbria even beginning this last quarter of the seventh century. The kings of both Mercia and Wessex refrain from crossing Ecgfrith in this matter of Wilfrid—even though Aethelred had beaten Ecgfrith in the Battle of the Trent about a year earlier. But both these inhospitable kings, Aethelred and Centwine, later abdicated their thrones and entered monasteries—Centwine not long before his death (Plummer, *Baedae Opera Historica*, II, 221), and Aethelred in 704. During the last years of his kingship, Aethelred became one of Wilfrid's most faithful friends (Chs. 43, 45, etc.).

97. He had narrowly escaped death at the hands of the South Saxons fifteen years before (Ch. 13).

the king and queen first of all he gently urged the word of God and the splendor and extent of his kingdom, giving as it were milk without guile. Then with the consent of the king, God permitting, the pagan people were assembled at the insistence of our holy bishop, people who had never yet been preached to and had yet to hear the word of God. Taking his stand then in their midst, our holy bishop spoke after the manner of Our Lord Jesus Christ and of his Precursor: "Do penance, for the kingdom of heaven is at hand" [Mt. 3:2] and, "Be baptized every one of you in the name of God the Father, and the Son, and the Holy Spirit" [Acts, 2:38], and so forth.

For many months the evengelical preacher preached with a mellifluous eloquence. The long sweep of his polished words covered in marvelous order everything Almighty God did to put idolatry to shame, from the beginning of the world to that day of judgment when eternal pain will be readied for sinners, and eternal life for those chosen by God. Then indeed did our holy bishop find grace in the sight of the king, and a great gateway of faith [cf. Acts, 14:26; 1 Cor., 16:9] as the Apostle says, swung open for him. On one day he baptized many thousands of pagans (as Peter the Apostle did) of both sexes, who forsook idolatry and professed faith in Almighty God, some indeed willingly, others forced by command of the king.[98] By God's grace the king became gentle and devout, and to this saintly new evangelist and baptist who had thrown open the way to eternal life for him and all his people, he made a present of his own royal country estate in which he was living. He granted it for an episcopal see, and later added to it 87 hides of land in Selsey. There Wilfrid gathered his brethren about him and founded a monastery as a haven of rest and retreat, and his successors possess it to this day.[99]

98. Such conversion by command was a frequent occurrence in the early medieval world. Charlemagne forced baptism on conquered Saxons, and Alfred on defeated Vikings. But in the Heroic Age the swearing of allegiance to the Lord could be considered quite as normal a matter for compulsion as was swearing allegiance to a temporal lord. And see Introduction, p. 16. But there were many gentler conversions too among the Anglo-Saxons (see Bede, *Ecclesiastical History*, Bk. III, ch. 22; Bright, *Chapters of Early English Church History*, p. 482).

99. Eddius omits the charming story Bede tells about Wilfrid's winning

Chapter XLII : *How Caedwalla became king.*

As time wore on, the people of God's Church were growing more numerous from day to day by our bishop's efforts, and the glory of His name shone out splendidly. Then one day there appeared, out of the wild forest land of Chiltern and the Weald, a certain nobly-born exile named Caedwalla. Eagerly he sought the friendship of our holy bishop, praying him to teach him and to help him as a faithful father, while he in turn swore on oath to be an obedient son.[100] They sealed this compact with God as their witness, and they fulfilled it faithfully. For Christ's saintly bishop often encouraged the distressed exile and aided him with no little assistance and support till the day came when he was strong enough to humiliate his enemies and at last gain possession of his kingdom.[101]

Then once Caedwalla had overcome and slain his enemies and was ruling as king over the entire land of the West Saxons, he humbly invited our bishop, St. Wilfrid, to come to him.[102] For Wilfrid, who

the people over during a time of famine by teaching them how to fish with nets (*Ecclesiastical History*, Bk. IV, ch. 13).

100. This royal exile from Wessex reminds us of exiled Aethelbald of Mercia coming to seek solace from St. Guthlac (see Felix, *Life of St. Guthlac*, Ch. 49).

101. This was in 685. Perhaps out of embarrassment for his hero's sake, Eddius is silent about the fact that in the meantime Caedwalla, like Fortinbras, "shocked up a list of lawless resolutes," outlaws from the forests of Chiltern and Andredeslea, and murdered Wilfrid's friend Aethilwalh. He was soon driven from the throne of Sussex by the slain king's ealdormen, but after he gained the throne of Wessex he led an avenging army back into Sussex and killed one of the ealdormen who had deposed him (Bede, *Ecclesiastical History*, Bk. IV, ch. 15).

102. Caedwalla is a Celtic name, and it has even been suggested that he was a son of the Cadwallon who killed King Edwin and ravaged Northumbria (and see note 13 to Introduction), and that his real intention in attacking Sussex and in striking for the throne of Wessex was to continue his father's crusade to drive the Saxons from Britain (Meissner, *The Celtic Church in England*, Ch. 5. But similar names in the sources have led to much confusion in this matter. See Plummer, *Baedae Opera Historica*, II, 122; and Chadwick, *Celt and Saxon*, p. 35). Had Caedwalla any such plans it is hard to see how Wilfrid could have been unaware of them, and harder yet to see how he could have given Caedwalla assistance if he had been aware of them. Though, admittedly, Wilfrid

was having such success converting the people of Sussex to God and was giving such grand glory to the name of the Lord, was his respected father and dear to him beyond all others. Our revered father came at once, and King Caedwalla immediately installed him as the supreme counsellor of all his kingdom. Just as the King of Egypt, when Joseph had been brought to him from prison, "made him master of his house . . . that he might teach wisdom," as the prophet says [Ps. 104:21, 22].

Then indeed was our saintly bishop exalted by God, for the victorious King Caedwalla honored his father most splendidly out of the pure love of his heart and showered upon him innumerable gifts of land and a wealth of other gifts, for God's sake. With a bold heart he held his kingdom safe either by the victorious edge of the sword or an indulgent treaty of peace.

Chapter XLIII : *How peace was made between our bishop and Archbishop Theodore* [A.D. 686-7].

[When he felt the end of his life was near, Archbishop Theodore's conscience began to trouble him for having sided with the kings who had wished Wilfrid deposed. He called the latter to a meeting in London and offered to appoint him as the successor in his own see. Wilfrid asked rather that he write to his former enemies and ask them to restore all that they had taken from him; Theodore's successor should be determined by a council. So Theodore wrote to King Aldfrith of Northumbria, to Aelffled, Abbess of Whitby, and to King Aethelred of Mercia, begging them to be reconciled with Wilfrid. Aethelred received the returning bishop gracefully, gave back to him many monasteries that were his, and remained his friend for the rest of his life.]

might well have been sympathetic with any movement to depose Centwine of Wessex, because of the shabby treatment he himself had received from that king (Eddius, Ch. 40). Dying of a battle wound, Caedwalla made his way to Rome to be baptized by Pope Sergius on Holy Saturday, 689, and expired ten days later (Stenton, *Anglo-Saxon England*, pp. 69-70; Bede, *Ecclesiastical History*, Bk. V, ch. 7).

Chapter XLIV : *How King Aldfrith received our bishop.*

[After King Ecgfrith and the flower of his army fell in battle against the Picts, King Aldfrith had succeeded to the throne of Northumbria. In the second year (686-87) of his reign he acted on Archbishop Theodore's request to make peace with the exiled Wilfrid. The latter was restored to the episcopal see at York and given back the monasteries of Hexham and Ripon.][103]

Chapter XLV : *Of the rancor that was kindled between them.*

Then those who had stirred up the old quarrel roused themselves as from a sleep, and loosing a storm blast of hate from their bag of winds, they made a mariner's nightmare out of the sea of life which had been basking of late in happy serenity. The firebrand of strife, but lately quenched, they kindled into flame again. For indeed there were times when peace and good-will reigned between the wise king and the holy hero, and they shared the joy of all manner of good things. Then at other times the brew of evil would come to a boil and spoil everything. And so for many years they lived in this see-saw way, now in agreement, now at odds with each other. But at length an intolerable blaze of hatred flared up and King Aldfrith drove the holy man of God out of Northumbria.

Now the chief cause of their quarreling was the same as it had been from the beginning, namely the unlawful confiscation of lands and revenues belonging to the Church dedicated to St. Peter the Apostle

103. Bede tells us that Wilfrid administered the bishopric of Lindisfarne for a year (687-688) after the death of St. Cuthbert (*Ecclesiastical History*, Bk. IV, ch. 29). In his prose *Life of St. Cuthbert* (Ch. 40) Bede seems to hint at trouble on Lindisfarne during this year, caused perhaps by repressive measures of Wilfrid against the community's Celtic customs (Colgrave, *Two Lives of St. Cuthbert*, p. 357).

[at Ripon]. The second cause was the abolition of this monastery's liberty by making it into an episcopal see. For it had been granted to us under privilege of exemption [from episcopal control] which St. Agatho and five kings had firmly and unalterably established in our possession. The third cause was that he kept forcing us to obey the orders and decrees of Archbishop Theodore who had been sent from Rome—not, however, those canonical regulations which he had laid down when he first came to us as bishop, nor the ones he laid down in the last years of his life when he brought all our churches together in a harmony of law and love, but rather those laws which he had passed in the middle period of his life when discord had broken out among us here in Britain. So our holy bishop refused to submit to this and went to his faithful friend Aethelred, King of the Mercians who, out of respect for the Apostolic See, received him with great honor. Under the protection, therefore, of God and of this king, Wilfrid took possession of the substantial dignity of that bishopric which the most reverend Bishop Sexwulf had governed before his recent death.

Chapter XLVI : *Concerning the Atswinapathe Council* [A.D. 703].

[During Aldfrith's reign Wilfrid was invited to a council of nearly all the bishops of Britain held at Austerfield. There, "at the instigation of King Aldfrith and certain abbots," the bishops demanded that Wilfrid be judged by the decrees of Archbishop Theodore. Wilfrid agreed to abide by any decision made in accord with canon law, but then he rebuked them for ignoring the Apostolic decrees in his regard for the past 22 years.]

Chapter XLVII : *How plots against him were laid bare.*

Meantime, while no method of procedure for the assembly had yet been formally agreed upon, a certain one of the king's men who was deeply devoted to our bishop for having raised him from his very cradle days, stole out of the king's tent in disguise and, losing himself as a stranger amidst the crowds of bystanders, made his way to our bishop. To him he revealed the real reason behind their decision and explained the whole thing.

"They definitely intend to deceive you with this trick. They will get you ahead of time to sign an agreement to accept whatever decision they alone shall make, so that afterwards you will be helplessly bound by this chain and quite unable from then on to alter anything. Indeed the outcome of their decision will be that everything you were ever known to possess in Northumbria, whether it be a matter of the bishopric or of monasteries or of anything whatsoever, all this you will lose. And if you gained possession of anything in the kingdom of the Mercians by grace of King Aethelred, all this you will be forced to hand over to the archbishop who may bestow it on whomever he wishes. And finally by thus condemning yourself with your own signature you will have disqualified yourself for your office of honor." With this the man departed, careful not to be noticed.

Then when the saintly man heard this and understood the method of their trickery, he became more cautious about his signature which they now demanded again and again—and he was a man of the greatest bravery and firmness. They demanded that he return them answers on the spot, and finally with open threats they made it clear to him that if he did not at once acknowledge his submission to their judgment he would straightway find himself under sentence of condemnation. He answered them: "As soon as I hear the decision of the archbishop and find that it concurs with the regulations established by the holy fathers, then I will accept it with all my heart and will submit."

Eventually, however, they were forced to give up any attempt to conceal their plan, seeing that many people had known all about it for some time. At first they declared that they wished to despoil our holy bishop so thoroughly of all his possessions that in all Northumbria and Mercia he would not own even the tiniest part of a shed. But the ruthlessness of this judgment, pronounced by both the archbishop and the king, shocked even Wilfrid's enemies. It was wicked, they said, to deprive so widely famous a man of everything he owned, and this even though he was guilty of no serious crime. So the bishops thought the matter over again a little more humanely and finally announced that they would give him back a monastery, but only that one which he had built at Ripon. This he had long ago consecrated, along with all that belonged to it, as a gift to St. Peter, and to it he had given the privilege he obtained from Pope St. Agatho for every abbot and community that should ever live there. However, they added the condition that he would have to take an inviolable oath, signed by his own hand, that he would reside there quietly and not go beyond the bounds of the monastery without the king's leave, and that he would not exercise any episcopal function. In fact (horrible to relate!) they even exerted the utmost pressure to compel him to forswear, of his own accord, his right to his honored office.

To this our holy bishop spoke out fearlessly and firmly: "Why do you force me to sign my own condemnation and to turn the miserable sword of suicidal ruin against myself? Must I, without any suspicion of guilt, make the speaking of my name a scandal to those who hear it, now after I have been called—though unworthy—by the name of bishop for almost forty years? Was I not the first, after the death of the pioneer fathers sent over by St. Gregory, to root up the poisonous weeds planted by the Scots? Was I not the first to convert the entire nation of Northumbria in accord with the mind of the Apostolic See, to the true Easter and to the tonsure in the form of a crown, which previously had been shaved from the top of the head down the back? Did I not teach the manner of singing according to the practice of the primitive church with two choirs singing in harmony and alternating the responsories and antiphons? And did I not establish the monastic way of life according to the rule of St. Benedict the Abbot which no one had yet introduced here?[104] And now how shall I pass a sudden sentence of condemnation on myself without being conscious of any wrong-doing?

"No, with regard to this issue most recently raised and with which you are trying to violate my sacred office, I appeal in all confidence to the Apostolic See. Whichever one of you presumes to set aside the dignity of my office, I challenge him today to come with me to Rome to obtain a judgment. For before I shall consent to being tried

104. And see Ch. 14. St. Augustine had brought the Benedictine rule to Kent from Rome in 597. In Northumbria, however, the Celtic monastic rules were the more general fashion until Wilfrid brought the Roman Benedictine rule to Ripon.

on these matters by you alone, the wise men of Rome must be accurately informed on exactly what charge you wish to despose me."

To this the archbishop and the king replied: "Just now surely he has become guilty. Let us charge him and condemn him for preferring Rome's judgment over ours." And to the archbishop's proposal the king added: "If you wish, I shall have my army force him in no time at all to confess himself prepared to submit to our decision this time." But the rest of the bishops in council said: "We must not forget that he came here under our promise of safe conduct. He would not have dared come otherwise. In the same safety let us all return peacefully home."

Chapter XLVIII : *How he returned to King Aethelred.*

So after this discussion the fruitless council was dissolved with the consent of both parties and everyone left for home. By the intervention of God, therefore, his servant was delivered from the hands of his enemies, and thus unscathed made his way back to faithful King Aethelred. Our holy bishop presented himself before the king and gave a report of the whole bitter attack by the assembly, which had been directed against him contrary to the king's order. Then he also inquired of Aethelred what he had officially decided about the properties and personal possessions he had bestowed upon him. The king replied: "I will not add to your troubles by destroying the means of livelihood of these monks who have dedicated themselves to the Church of Blessed Peter the Apostle. But while I live I shall, with God's help, keep everything in the same situation in which I have always preserved it, until I have first sent my messengers or letters to Rome with you to inquire about these charges that are being pressed. By my desire to do what is right I hope to find salvation."[105] After this answer they parted with happy expressions of friendship, and each returned home.

105. Throughout this whole incident poor Aethelred's concern for his soul's salvation seems somewhat reluctantly impelling him to help Wilfrid at the probable cost of antagonizing Aldfrith, just as he had previously been reluctant to offend King Ecgfrith by aiding Wilfrid (Ch. 40).

Chapter XLIX : *Concerning our excommunication.*

But Wilfrid's enemies who had expropriated his goods for themselves announced that we and all who associated with us were debarred from the company of the faithful. So utterly did they denounce all communion with us as to decree that if any of our abbots or priests should be invited to the home of one of the Christian layfolk and should bless the meal set before him with the Sign of God's Cross, then that food was to be taken outdoors and thrown on the ground as if it were food offered to idols. And they ordered that the dishes from which any of ours had eaten should be washed before anyone else touched them—as though they were polluted with filth.[106]

Chapter L : *Concerning his voyage on the way to Rome* [*ca.* A.D. 703].

[Wilfrid and his party sailed to the continent and after a long overland journey on foot arrived in Rome to be greeted kindly by Pope John.[107] The latter called a council of his bishops and clergy, and invited Wilfrid and the messengers from Archbishop Berhtwald[108] who had arrived

106. And see note 67 for Aldhelm's charge that Celtic priests treated Saxon priests this same way.

107. An incredible thing it is indeed that an old man of seventy should have made such a journey on foot. Yet Eddius, who was with him, implies that he did not ride horseback until he became ill in Gaul on the return trip (Ch. 56). It was perhaps this journey which occasioned Aldhelm's famous letter to Wilfrid's clergy (note 51 to Introduction) and it seems to have had its effect, for Acca and Eddius and others did accompany their persecuted lord. On this trip he passed through Frisia, where he had brought the Gospel on a similar journey twenty-five years before. Here he enjoyed now a last glad reunion with his former pupil of Ripon, Willibrord, who was reaping such fruit on the mission (Bede, *Ecclesiastical History*, Bk. III, ch. 13).

108. This is the same Archbishop Berhtwald of Canterbury before whom Boniface first gained notice several years later, and who sent Boniface off to Germany with his blessing (Willibald, *Life of Boniface*, Ch. 4).

with the written accusation from Britain, to present their cases. Wilfrid's petition was read out first to the assembly.]

Chapter LI : *Concerning the written petition.*

[Wilfrid states that this, his third visit to the Apostolic See, is occasioned by attacks in Britain on his possessions and privileges that are protected by decrees of Popes Agatho, Benedict, and Sergius. He promises to abide by the present pope's decision after the case is heard, and asks His Holiness to send King Aetheldred of Mercia a confirmation of the papal immunity attached to the monasteries and lands conferred on Wilfrid by Aethelred and his brother Wulfhere. He asks too that Alafrith of Northumbria be urged to fulfill all the decrees of Pope Agatho, and that in case it should seem more prudent not to return the bishopric of York and the other monasteries to him, then at least that the monasteries of Ripon and Hexham be restored to him.]

Chapter LII : *How Pope John declared that the writings of his predecessors would have to be re-examined.*

[After Wilfrid's petition was heard, he and his party were given leave to return to their quarters, and Archbishop Berhtwald's accusation against Wilfrid was heard by the synod. Then his party too was given leave to retire, and it was announced that the whole matter would in due course be closely examined in the presence of both parties. Then Pope John announced to the bishops of the synod that they must in the meantime carefully reread all the previous papal correspondence on the question so that, with God's help, they might more readily arrive at the truth.]

Chapter LIII

[When (in 704) the synod reconvened, the accusers of Wilfrid were asked to begin the presentation of their points.]

They said: "The first item of our accusation is that the Bishop Wilfrid here present did contumaciously spurn and ignore the judgments that were passed in synod by Berhtwald, the saintly archbishop of the church of Canterbury and of all Britain, a man sent by this very Apostolic See. We have presented the opinion of our side, now let us hear your defence."

And so our holy Bishop Wilfrid rose to his feet, a man burdened with the honor of many years, and, his revered brethren about him, spoke in the presence of the whole assembly: "As a humble suppliant I implore your supreme Holiness to do me the honor, unworthy as I am, of listening to my account of the truth of this matter. While I was in attendance at the council, along with my abbots and priests and deacons, one of the bishops in session there was sent to ask me, in the name of the king no less than that of the archbishop, whether I would be willing to accept the decision of the archbishop alone and whether or not I would be prepared to carry out with all good will whatever judgment he should decide upon.

"To such a question I replied, 'Before we declare whether or not we can commit ourselves to carrying it out, we must know what the sentence is.' But he maintained that he did not know, and said that the archbishop did not wish the content of the decision revealed in any way to any of our party until we had first, in the presence of the council, affixed our signature to an attestation that we had elected to abide in all things by his sole decision, and that we would not veer from it one bit one way or the other.

"I said, 'Never before have I heard of any man's being compelled by such a narrow and tight constraint as this that he should admit to being wholly bound by oath to carry out prescriptions, however impossible, even before he knows the nature of the decree.'[109] However, there in the presence of the assembly I did promise that they would find us wholeheartedly prepared to submit to the judgment of the archbishop on every item which should be found consonant with the regulations and canons set down by the holy fathers and not at odds in any way with the synodal pronouncements of St. Agatho and of

109. This injunction laid on Wilfrid reminds us of the trick that Olaf Tryggvason's Christian missionaries put over on the unhappy pagan Icelanders (*Njal's Saga*, Chs. 104, 105).

all his orthodox successors." Such was the defence offered by our holy bishop, after which he took his seat in silence.

Whereupon the holy synod replied: "Bishop Wilfrid, beloved of God, has presented in canonical wise the grounds which constitute his defence." Then they began to smile and talk Greek among themselves and say many things which they kept from us. Finally they addressed the accusers: "You are not unaware, dearest brethren, of the regulation we have amongst our canons: 'Whenever many offences are charged against clerics by their accusers, and the first one brought up cannot be proved, then they are not allowed to proceed to the rest of the charges.' Nevertheless, out of respect for the holy archbishop who was sent to his post by the authority of this very Apostolic See, and out of regard for this most blessed Bishop Wilfrid who has for so long been fraudulently—it is asserted—dispossessed, we desire to bring the matter to an end once and for all. Therefore, with the assistance and guidance of God and of St. Peter, Prince of the Apostles, we shall devote ourselves diligently for as many days or even months as are necessary to the task of investigating thoroughly every point in the case."

After these words our bishop and his companions felt the first flush of the joy of victory and with the synod's leave they returned to their dwellings to make ready for the conflict yet to come. The other party, however, retired to their quarters not a little disconcerted at the way the proceedings had commenced. Then in the course of many days that grew into many months, as the clouds of lies were dispersed by the sweeping winds of wisdom, and as the sun of truth shone through with the help of God and St. Peter, our holy bishop was seen to be telling the truth and was absolutely exonerated from any charge that warranted deposition. For, to put it briefly, after being tested for four months in the fiery furnace of seventy sessions of the papal synod he emerged purified. And in this the apostolic power lent him assistance in a way that I shall now explain.

During the reign of the thrice-blessed Agatho, in the holy paschal time, on the third day of the feast, a synod had been called in session to combat heretical perversities. One hundred and twenty-five orthodox bishops were present, each one of whom made a profession of the true faith in the name of his province and city and confirmed it with his signature. Now on this later occasion it happened that the proceedings of that earlier synod were read out before all the people in a loud voice, in the Roman fashion. Among all the other things in the document, occurred the following: "Wilfrid, beloved of God, Bishop of the City of York, who has appealed his case to the Apostolic See and by that See has been absolved from all charges whatever, definite and indefinite, and who is met in synod at the seat of judgment with 125 brother bishops, has confirmed with his signature a profession of the true and catholic faith which he has made in behalf of all the northern part of Britain and Ireland and of the islands inhabited by the peoples of the Angles and the Britons and of the Scots and the Picts."[110]

And so when they heard this all the wise citizens of Rome were amazed. Boniface and Sizentius and some others, who had known him in the days of Agatho of blessed memory, declared: "That man whom the most blessed Agatho long ago sent home cleared and freed by Apostolic authority from the charges against him, that man is this Bishop Wilfrid here present and beloved of God, whom now once more—for shame!—the machinations of enemies have forced into exile from his own see. So respected an old man who has held the office of bishop for forty years and more has been brazenly and boldly accused in an assembly before the Apostolic See by—it must be noted—one who is a mere deacon and others who have no ecclesiastical rank at all. These lying accusers have even made use of forged documents against this most eminent person and his revered brethren. Therefore they deserve to suffer punishment and to waste away in the lowest dungeon of prison until they die." Thereupon did the men of Rome declare that this had been truly spoken.

The most blessed Pope John of the Apostolic See then spoke: "Let the blessed Wilfrid, a bishop, beloved of God, in whom we have found no blame of guilt after examining the case so carefully in so many sessions of our council, let him know that he is released from the charges by the authority of the blessed Apostle Peter, Prince of the Apostles, who has the power of binding and of loosing even from secret sins. Let him know also that what was decreed about him by the blessed Agatho and the illustrious Benedict and St. Sergius, bishops of the Apostolic See, this our poor unworthiness too, with the consent of the entire synod, has decided to confirm—those decisions which were

110. See Chapter 33 and note 90.

sent in writing to kings and archbishops at the hands of the blessed Bishop Wilfrid. This we confirm by the following [letter]."

Chapter LIV

[In his letter to Kings Aethelred of Mercia, and Aldfrith of Deira and Bernicia, Pope John reminded them that Archbishop Theodore's and Abbess Hild's charges against Wilfrid were pronounced upon by Pope Agatho after a synodal examination and that his decision was confirmed by his successors, and that Archbishop Theodore complied with it. Now this most recent renewal of the dissension had been carefully examined in Rome but since all the principal parties to the dispute were not present, a council should be called in Britain by Archbishop Berhtwald at which Bishops Wilfrid, Bosa,[111] and John should present all the issues of the dispute. Then if the archbishop still felt unable to conclude the entire matter let him send these men to Rome for the case to be settled in a fuller council.]

Chapter LV : *How he was bid to return home, and how he brought holy relics with him.*

And so at long last after the many months of almost daily examination and debate, Wilfrid tasted the victory of a complete exoneration. Now more than ever he longed to spend these last years of his life in the city of the Apostles and to await death there, "crucified to the world." But the Apostolic Father and the synod both bade him do otherwise, this man who long ago had humbly pledged his obedience.[112]

111. Bosa had been educated in Hild's monastery of Whitby and was given the see of York after Wilfrid's first expulsion by Ecgfrith. Acca was trained under him at York (Bede, *Ecclesiastical History*, Bk. V, ch. 20).

112. Here in Wilfrid's heart the old Celtic-Roman battle is fought out for the last time. As we always knew he would, he leaves Rome to be more a Roman, in disciplined obedience to command. Solitary pilgrimage-exile was

In the Lord's name they enjoined him, now that he was freed at last from the charges and aspersions that had tormented him, to return home bearing their written decisions to the kings and the archbishop, and there to ease the sorrow of his subjects and renew the joy of his friends. So our holy bishop, with his life-time's mastery of obedience, departed for home with the blessing of the saints. First however he went round to the shrines of the saints with his companions and collected, as he always did, authenticated holy relics from certain trusted men, and purchased vestments of purple and silk for the adornment of his churches. Then he set out on the long journey across the level stretches of the plains and over the rugged mountain trails and at length reached the land of Gaul.

Chapter LVI : *How our master fell ill and how Michael came to him.*

But there as they were travelling along our holy bishop was seized with a grievous bodily illness. At first they put him on horseback but finally they had to carry him in a litter by hand while they grieved for him and called tearfully on God. He was borne into the city of Meaux scarce alive, and his companions had no doubt that he was dying. Indeed, for four days and four nights he had not tasted any food or drink at all, and as he lay there unconscious only his breathing and the warmth of his limbs gave evidence that he was alive.

At length on the fifth day, as the morning light was breaking, an angel of the Lord in dazzling white raiment appeared to our bishop and said: "I am Michael the herald of the Most High God, who has sent me to tell you that years have been added to your life because holy Mary, God's Mother ever virgin, has interceded for you, and the tearful prayers of your subjects have reached the ears of the Lord. This will be a sign for you that from this hour your health will grow

not to be his. His lot was to serve in the legion, not to fight Homeric single-handed combats on the adventurous margin of the world at Troy, or Heorot, or Farne, or Crowland. (Young Benedict Biscop too gave up a pilgrimage-exile in Rome at a Roman call of command—Bede, *Lives of the Abbots*, Ch. 3)

better day by day and you will reach your homeland. And all those things that were most dear to you shall be yours again, and you shall finish out your life in peace. But you must also be ready, for after the space of four years I shall visit you again. And now call to mind how you have erected churches in honor of the Apostles St. Peter and St. Andrew, but for holy Mary ever virgin who is interceding for you you have built nothing. You must put this right and dedicate a church in her honor." After these words the angel of the Lord was taken up out of his sight and disappeared.

Thereupon our holy bishop, as though he were just wakened from sleep, raised himself and sat up in the midst of his group of clergy who were tearfully chanting [the prayers for the dying]. "Where is Acca our priest?"[113] he asked. The latter was called and came at once, full of joy.[114] He joined in the thanksgiving that the brethren offered to the Lord as soon as they saw Wilfrid sitting up and speaking. Then when the others had been asked to leave the room, Wilfrid related to his faithful Acca alone (who now by the favor of God graces our times as a bishop) a detailed account of the entire vision just as I have described it above. The holy priest was keen of mind and understood

113. Bede tells us that after studying under Bosa at York, Acca had attached himself to Wilfrid and his following "in the hope of a better plan of life" (*Ecclesiastical History*, Bk. V, ch. 20). Wilfrid calls him "my priest," and the *Anglo-Saxon Chronicle* (for the year 710) calls him "Wilfrid's priest." The relationship suggests the ecclesiastical counterpart of that devoted personal loyalty of the "companion" or thegn for the king. And King Alchfrith had wanted to make Wilfrid his priest (*comes individuus*: Ch. 19). See note 24 to Introduction.

114. One manuscript has an amusing variation on this passage. It has Acca hurrying to the bedside not *cum gaudio* ("with joy") but *cum gladio* ("with a sword"). [For texts see Colgrave, *Life of Wilfrid by Eddius*, p. 122, note 4]. Drowsy inattention most likely occasioned this copyist's slip of the quill, but I like to imagine a young monk with a puckish and gently iconoclastic Celtic sense of humor giving in to a hint from the imp of the absurd. "Behind the bards and the hagiographers, who endlessly strive to outdo each other in their accounts of heroic deeds and saintly miracles, there lurks the figure of the sceptic and/or parodist" (V. Mercier, *Irish Comic Tradition* [Oxford, 1962] p. 12). There is already a hint of comic relief in the supposedly dying Wilfrid's suddenly sitting up and calling for Acca, to the probable consternation of the lamenting brethren clustered about his bed. Then upon the scene bursts the summoned Acca, sword in hand.

at once (and gave thanks to the Lord) that in this manner years had been added to the life of our bishop by the intercession of holy Mary, Mother of the Lord, and by the prayers of his subjects. He remembered that in the same way fifteen years had been added to Hezekiah, king of Judah: five of which were added because of the election of David his father, another five because of the intercession of the prophet Isaias in the temple of God, and the remaining five years of life because of the goodness of the king himself and because he had turned to the wall and wept.

Chapter LVII : *How he returned back across the sea.*

[A few days later Wilfrid had recovered sufficiently to sail across to Kent where Archbishop Berhtwald was reconciled with him, after which they went on to London attended by a great crowd. Later he was joyfully greeted by his old friend Aethelred, who promised to be ever faithful to the decrees Wilfrid brought with him from Rome. Aethelred then summoned Cenred, the man whom he had meantime appointed to be king of Mercia in his place,[115] and got him to promise the same.]

Chapter LVIII : *How King Aldfrith perished for despising Wilfrid.*[116]

[On Aethelred's advice, Wilfrid sent Badwini the priest and Alfrith the teacher to request an audience with King Aldfrith of Northumbria. Aldfrith put them off to a later date, and at this second meeting gave his answer:]

115. While Wilfrid was in Rome, Aethelred had left his throne for the monastery of Bardney, where he later became abbot. And four years later (in 709) Cenred too was to relinquish his crown, and to become a monk in Rome along with King Offa of Essex (Bede, *Ecclesiastical History*, Bk. V, ch. 19).

116. Levison would date Wilfrid's illness at Meaux, his return to England, and King Aldfrith's death, all in 704 (*England and the Continent*, p. 279, note 7).

"O my brothers, I respect you both. Ask of me anything that you need for yourselves and I will grant it to you out of my respect for you. But from this day forward bother me no more about the case of Wilfrid your lord. What the kings before me decided together with the archbishop and their counselors, and what we ourselves later decided in company with the archbishop sent from the Apostolic See and almost all the bishops of our people of Britain, that is something which I tell you I shall never change, as long as I live, on account of any documents that you tell me are from the Apostolic See." But he later changed this opinion completely, and sincerely repented.

Chapter LIX

[Growing gravely ill not long afterwards, the king expressed the wish that Wilfrid might come to him before he died so that he could make amends to the bishop. He vowed that if he recovered he would put everything right between himself and Wilfrid, and he prayed that in case he should die his successor would make peace with the bishop "for the salvation of my soul and his own."]

These words were reported to us by most trustworthy witnesses who actually heard them. One of them is the Abbess Aelffled,[117] "a most prudent virgin" [cf. Mt. 25:1ff.] who is in fact the daughter of a king; another is the Abbess Aethilberg.[118] And many other witnesses have confirmed the words. But the king's sickness destroyed him. For many days he was without the power of speech, and at last he died.

After him Eadwulf reigned for a short time. Accompanied by the king's own son, Wilfrid came back from exile and sent messengers from Ripon to the king as to a friend. But because of the ancient grudge, his counselors persuaded the king to answer severely and

117. See note 28 to *Life of Cuthbert*. Her reporting of the king's dying words saves Wilfrid at the Synod in the next chapter.

118. The abbess is possibly the same Aethilberg who was a daughter of King Anna and sister of Wilfrid's friend, Aethilthryth (Colgrave, *Life of Wilfrid by Eddius*, p. 184).

harshly, in this fashion: "By my salvation I swear that if he has not left my kingdom within the space of six days, then any of his companions whom I find will be put to death." After these bitter words a group of men took oaths against him and drove him from the kingdom which he had ruled for two months. In his place reigned a boy of royal birth, named Osred. He was a son of King Aldfrith and became the adopted son of our holy bishop.[119]

Chapter LX

[In the first year of Osred's reign (706) Archbishop Berhtwald called the synod which Pope John had sent instructions for two years previously, and which was to try and reach a decision on Wilfrid's case. The king and his chief nobles with his abbots and three of his bishops and the Abbess Aelfled, "who was always a comfort to the whole province and by far its best counselor," met with Archbishop Berhtwald and Bishop Wilfrid in a place near the river Nidd. The archbishop opened the synod by having the letters read out which he and Wilfrid had received from Rome.]

After the reading all were silent, till Berhtfrith, the ealdorman who was next in rank to the king, said to the archbishop, "Those of us who need a translation would like to hear what the apostolic document says." The archbishop replied, "These decisions of the Apostolic See are expressed at great length and in an indirect and roundabout manner of writing, but the meaning of both documents comes to the same thing and I shall explain just this essential meaning in a few words."

[Berhtwald then explains that the synod has a choice either of making a complete peace with Wilfrid and restoring as much of his former possessions as Berhtwald and his counselors shall decide, or of going to Rome and having the matter judged in council there. But the bishops

119. Osred grew up to be a terrible contrast to his father, Aldfrith. Before he was slain at nineteen, the vicious tyranny of his reign had marked the end of royal greatness in Northumbria. Boniface wrote that the rights of the Church in England had never been violated till the days of King Ceolred of Mercia and Osred of Northumbria (Whitelock, *English Historical Documents*, p. 755).

object to reversing their former decisions, especially those made with Berhtwald himself and King Aldfrith at Austerfield.[120]]

But before any more opinions were aired the most blessed Abbess Aelffled spoke up, and her words truly had the blessing of heaven: "Let me tell you King Aldfrith's last wish. As he lay ill and dying he made this vow to God and St. Peter: 'If I live I shall comply with all those judgments of the Apostolic See concerning the blessed Bishop Wilfrid which hitherto I have refused to obey. But if I die then tell my son, my heir, that for the salvation of my soul he must carry out the apostolic decision concerning Bishop Wilfrid.'"[121]

When she had finished, Berhtfrith, the aforesaid ealdorman of the king, spoke up in agreement: "Indeed, this is the will of the king and of his ealdormen, that in every detail we should obey the injunction of the Apostolic See and the orders of King Aldfrith. For once when we were besieged in the city called Bamburgh[122] and surrounded on all sides by an enemy force, we took shelter inside a narrow cramped place on the rocky hill and talked over what we should do. We all swore to God that if He would bestow on our royal child his father's kingdom[123] we would fulfil whatever the apostolic mandate had stip-

120. See Ch. 46.

121. As Aelffled speaks the words that are to bring about the salvation of Wilfrid we recall how her mother, Queen Eanfled, had been the first patron of the gallant young man setting out to make his mark in the world (Ch. 2). In fact, looking back now from the final act of Wilfrid's dramatic life, we note how many other women there were too who played important roles in it, either as heroines or villainesses. There was his stepmother at the very start, whose cruelty caused him to leave home (Ch. 2). Then there was the English slave-girl and Merovingian queen, Balthild, who seems at least unknowingly to have been the cause of saving his life in Gaul (Ch. 6). King Ecgfrith's first wife, Aethilthryth, gave him the land for Hexham monastery (Ch. 22); and Ecgfrith's aunt, Abbess Aebbe, won his release from prison (Ch. 39). Queen Iurminburg persecuted him bitterly (Chs. 24 ff.), and her sister, Queen of Wessex, had him driven from King Centwine's realm (Ch. 40), while Queen Osthryth had him expelled from Mercia (*Ibid.*). Saintly Abbess Hild of Whitby opposed him for his Roman sympathies (Chs. 10, 54).

122. See Introduction, pp. 4 ff., and Index.

123. It was seemingly a fight with the supporters of some other aspirant to Aldfrith's vacant throne. In Chapter 59 Eddius tells of Eadwulf's reigning for two months and then being driven out.

ulated concerning Bishop Wilfrid. And no sooner had we made our vow than the enemy changed their minds and practically fell over themselves in their haste to pledge friendship with us. The gates were opened, we were freed from the spot we had been penned in, the enemy was put to flight, and the kingdom was ours."

[After this the bishops took counsel among themselves, sometimes with the archbishop, sometimes with Aelffled, and the upshot was that a complete and permanent peace was made with Wilfrid, and Ripon and Hexham with their belongings were restored to him.][124]

Chapter LXI

[The peace of soul thus ensuing was the greatest blessing gained by both parties, and not the least by:] . . . us who had been scattered across many lands of exile serving with sad hearts under strange lords,[125] but who now live in peace with all men who have everywhere been reconciled with our lord. We live a life to which hope has returned and we rejoice and exult in the blessing of it.

Chapter LXII

[But joy was tempered with grief, for within about two years Wilfrid fell desperately ill again, in the course of a journey to Hexham. The brethren "seized their accustomed weapons of prayer" and implored God to allow Wilfrid at least to make the proper disposal of his possessions and to appoint abbots for his various monasteries before he died. He did arrange all things in order, and then regained his health.]

Chapter LXIII

And so our holy bishop lived on in a rich autumnal peace amid the happiness of his own. Those of his affairs which some had previously

124. He never did recover the bishopric of York.

125. The Anglo-Saxon lordless man again, the man of *The Wanderer*, evocative symbol of utter sorrow. See note 21 to Introduction.

considered to be poorly taken care of he now set in perfect order during the year and a half after his illness. For not long before his blessed and memorable death he had the treasurer open up his treasure-chest at Ripon in the presence of two abbots and some very faithful brethren, eight in number all told,[126] whom he had asked to come to him. He directed the treasurer to put out before them all of the gold and silver and precious stones and to divide them into four piles which he specified.[127] Without delay the man did everything just as our holy father bade. Then to the faithful witnesses our holy bishop said: "Dearest brethren, I want you to know this plan of mine which I have had in mind for a long time now, namely, to make my way to the see of St. Peter the Apostle and to look upon it once again and, *Deo volente*, to finish my life there where I so often won freedom from the charges of my enemies. My purpose was to carry with me the richest of the four shares of this treasure as gifts for the churches of the saints, and for the church of holy Mary the Mother of the Lord, and to offer presents to St. Paul the Apostle for the salvation of my soul. But if God has provided otherwise, as is so often the case with the plans of old men, and if the day of my death has really come upon me, then in the name of Jesus Christ I bid you, my faithful friends, to send these gifts by messengers to the churches I have mentioned.

126. Eddius gives us the names of five of them in the next chapter.

127. Dispensing gold to his followers as his life approaches its grand close, Wilfrid might for all the world be living out a scene from the typical heroic poetry of his people. Even in the Anglo-Saxon biblical poems the Old Testament patriarchs are transformed into Germanic heroes, noble "earls," distributing treasure to their *comitatus* (e.g., *Genesis*, vv. 1181 ff.). And there is a deeper, darker level of similarity that neither Wilfrid nor Eddius is aware of. Gold hoards in Teutonic literature are won by blood and they bring tragedy in their wake. The Nibelung hoard was fated (see discussion by De Vries, *Heroic Song and Heroic Legend*, pp. 54 ff., 66 ff.). The treasure that dying Beowulf won for his people brought them no rescue from their fate (see Quirk's discussion of the fatal-gold theme in *Beowulf*, in *Early English and Norse Studies*, edited by A. Brown and P. Foote [London, 1963], pp. 165 ff.). Gold hoards were always guarded symbolically by the evil dragon, and even though the Christian Cross may have driven him away for a time, the ancient curse still bided its time. Such wealth as Wilfrid's surely helped bring on the malady which was soon to destroy Anglo-Saxon monasticism (see note 33 to Introduction). The Golden Age nourished its own seed of doom.

"Of the three remaining portions divide one among the poor of my people for the salvation of my soul. Let the superiors of these two monasteries so dear to my heart [i. e., Ripon and Hexham] divide the second remaining share among themselves so that with presents they can win the friendship of kings and bishops.[128] Distribute the third portion of the treasure, to each according to his due, among those who have toiled and suffered with me through the long exiles and to whom I have not given gifts of land, so that they will have the means to maintain themselves after I am gone."

Again after a little while he said to his faithful witnesses: "Remember, my brethren, that I am placing in charge of this monastery of Ripon the priest Tatberht here, my kinsman, and my close companion all these years.[129] He shall share the rule with me as long as I live, and after my death he is to have complete charge without any question. I am making these decisions now in order that when the Archangel Michael[130] pays me his visit he will find me ready. For many signs of my death are gathering round me."

Chapter LXIV

After giving these directions he asked for a bell to be rung to call the whole community of Ripon together in chapter. Then our holy bishop

128. Bede tells us (*Ecclesiastical History*, Bk. III, ch. 5) that Aidan of Lindisfarne had deliberately refused to court the favor of Bamburgh's kings this way. Here again in Aidan and Wilfrid we see the confrontation of two worlds: the holy asceticism of heroic Celtic intransigence, and the holy practicality of the Roman mind trained to the diplomacy and government of Empire.

129. Benedict Biscop spoke out against abbots' appointing of kinsmen to succeed them in office (Bede, *Lives of the Abbots*, Ch. 11). He explained, however, that it was the *abuse* of the practice that he condemned, the selecting of the abbot *solely* by reason of birth. He himself had appointed two of his relatives as abbots, Ceolfrith and Eastorwine.

130. The warrior archangel, noble leader of the heavenly *comitatus*, was peculiarly the Heroic Age's own. Henry Adams explains so well how he was adopted by the Norman Heroic Age (*Mont Saint-Michel and Chartres*, Ch. 1). But yet it is interesting and significant that in the Anglo-Saxon Heroic Age far more churches were dedicated to "Roman" St. Peter than to any other saint (Levison, *England and the Continent*, pp. 259 ff.).

went in, took his seat, and addressed them: "Our most reverend brother Caelin, who for a good length of time has had some charge over the proper observance of our rule of life and has worked hard for the Lord, now has a longing to go back to his former way of life and the solitude of the wilderness, and to live his life for God alone as he did before. This I no longer wish to refuse him.[131]

"But for the rest of you, my will is that you adhere in all worthiness to our regular way of life until I return to you, if God so wills. For these two abbots of ours who are present here, Tibba and Eabba, were sent by Ceolred, King of Mercia,[132] inviting me to come speak with him. And they have persuaded me to accept, for the sake of our monasteries in his kingdom. He has, in fact, promised to put the entire regulation of his life under my direction. And when I come back to you again, if God wills that I should live, I will bring with me the man whom I have found worthy to govern you. But if because of my repeated attacks of illness it should fall out otherwise in the providence of God, then whomever these witnesses of mine seated here beside me—the abbots Tibba and Eabba, the priests Tatberht and Hathufrith and the teacher Aluhfrith—whomever these shall come and announce to you, that is the man you must receive and install as your abbot. It is my order that you render to him that obedience which you have promised to God and to me and which hitherto you have fulfilled." Kneeling and bowing their heads to the ground, they promised with tears to carry out all his behests, and while they prayed there, bowed to the ground, our holy bishop blessed them and commended them to the Lord. From that day, as a community, they never saw his face again.

131. It is poetically appropriate that one of "Roman" Wilfrid's last acts was this bestowing of his blessing on the "Celtic" anchorite-calling of one of his monks.

132. In Chapter 57 Cenred had been the new king of Mercia, but now in the spring of 709 (or 710) he had resigned his crown and made the ultimate pilgrimage to Rome (see note 115). His successor did not live up to the high hopes that Wilfrid probably expected of him here (see note 119).

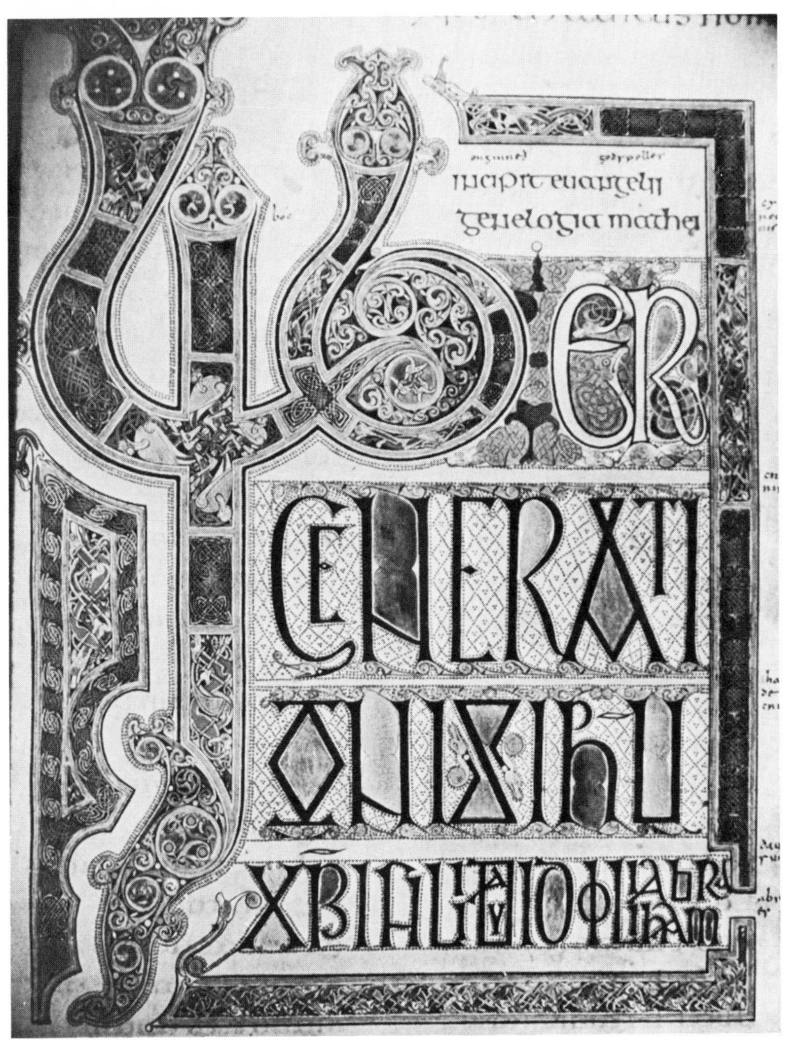

Plate I *The Lindisfarne Gospels*
(Opening page of St. Matthew's gospel)

Plate II *The Lindisfarne Gospels*
(Picture of St. Matthew writing his gospel)

Plate III *Lindisfarne Priory*

Plate IV *Melrose Abbey*

Plate V *Bamburgh Castle*

Plate VI *Cuthbert and the Angel*

Plate VII *Burgh Castle*

Plate VIII *Gravestones in the museum at Lindisfarne Priory*

Chapter LXV

So our holy bishop went on his way in peace with the blessing of all the Northumbrians, rulers and subjects alike, and journeyed to the kingdoms of the south where he found all his abbots delighted at his coming. There to some of them he explained the points of his last testament, mentioned above, and to each of them in due proportion he either made gifts of land to augment the livelihood of their monks, or he delighted their hearts with money. It was as though with an insight into the future he were distributing his inheritance to his heirs before his death.

At length they arrived at a monastery of his situated at Oundle where he had once dedicated a church to the Apostle Andrew. There all of a sudden he fell so ill that he realized the end of his life was near at hand. Mustering a few words he urged them to be mindful of all he had told them previously for their spiritual good. For one day on an earlier journey as they were riding along together he had told the priest Tatberht, his kinsman, the whole story of his life, from memory. It was as though he had foreseen his death. And he had gone over again the list of those properties in different places which he had already granted to abbots and those which he then gave orders for the granting of, such as the monastery of Hexham which he declared should be handed over to the priest Acca, who after him by the grace of God was bishop of blessed memory.

Now after he had spoken a little he blessed all the brethren, just as Jacob blessed his sons, and then quietly, without a sign or a murmur, he laid his head back upon the pillow and rested. The brethren meanwhile were chanting the psalms in choir day and night without pause, and mingling their tears with their singing,[133] until finally they came to the verse in the 103rd Psalm which reads, "Thou shalt send forth thy spirit, and they shall be created: and thou shalt renew the face of the

133. Giotto's fresco (in Santa Croce in Florence) of the funeral service for St. Francis is the perfect illustration for this scene—the tender grief in the faces of the friars as they chant the last prayers for their father.

earth." At that moment our holy bishop sent forth his spirit.[134] All were seized with wonder, for at this same moment they heard a sound like that of birds flying toward them. . . .

Chapters LXVI — LXVIII

[When many abbots had assembled to bring Wilfrid's body in a chariot to Ripon, a sound like that of flying birds was heard again over the monastery. Wise men said this was the sound of Michael and his angel bands carrying off Wilfrid's soul to heaven. After his body was borne in procession to Ripon and placed in the church that he had dedicated to St. Peter, signs and miracles began to occur. A nun was healed of a withered hand by touching a monk's cloak on which Wilfrid's body had been placed when it was being prepared for burial. When "some exiled noblemen with their soldiers plundered and burned the monastery at Oundle because of some wrong done them" they were unable to burn the building in which Wilfrid had died, and they were finally turned away by a young man in white with a golden cross. And the flames were also unable to burn one section of a thorn hedge that surrounded the monastery, the section nearest a wooden cross which had been erected where the bath water had been poured out after Wilfrid's body was washed for burial. Some time later "certain of the most noble of these men and their soldiers were surprised by their enemies, completely surrounded, and quickly overwhelmed and slain, except for some few of their companions who protected themselves with the sign of the cross and escaped."

Wilfrid's abbots and monks were fearful of what his old enemies might do now that their lord was not there to protect them. But on two nights during the first celebration of Wilfrid's anniversary a marvelous white arc appeared in the sky over Ripon as a sign that he was now as powerful an intercessor as his beloved Apostles Peter and Andrew and would guard his monks forever.]

134. Disagreeing with Bede's date of 709, Levison puts Wilfrid's death on Thursday, April 24, 710 (*England and the Continent*, pp. 278-79).

THE LIFE OF ST. GUTHLAC

---

by Felix

Preface to the LIFE OF ST. GUTHLAC

As far as we can tell, Felix was an Anglo-Saxon monk and wrote this Life in East Anglia sometime between 730 (sixteen years after Guthlac's death) and 740 (see Colgrave, *Felix's Life of St. Guthlac*, pp. 15-19). As its Prologue reveals, this hagiography is, interestingly enough, one of the first "literary" works that we know to have been "commissioned" by any Anglo-Saxon king (R. Girvan has remarked on the scarcity of instances of patronage in early England. See his "The Medieval Poet and His Public," *English Studies Today*, edited by C. L. Wrenn and G. Bullough [Oxford, 1951], p. 90). The same king might possibly have been the patron of the *Beowulf* poet (see Whitelock, *The Audience of Beowulf*, p. 29). The fact that Felix's book was intended for a royal audience instead of a monastic one may help to explain why its style is so unusually elaborate with epic formality and rhetorical adornment, especially alliteration. In the schoolboy manner of the eager Germanic Latinist, Felix decorates his prose with the curious poetic vocabulary and grandiloquent cadence derived from Aldhelm and the Celtic Latinists, from Vergil and the Christian Latin epic poets, and from late Latin rhetoric and rhythmic prose (see note 52 to Introduction. For the probable influence of late Latin Gallic rhetoricians, like Virgilius Maro, on Celtic Latin, see J. Kenney, *The Sources for the Early History of Ireland*, vol. I [New York, 1929] pp. 142-45. But see also R. Bolgar, *The Classical Heritage and its Beneficiaries* [Cambridge University Press, 1954] p. 404). Felix's is perhaps the most "heroic" of our seven Lives. It was much influenced too by the popular biography of St. Antony of Egypt (see note 2; and Kurtz, "From St. Antony to St. Guthlac.")

Colgrave's edition (*Felix's Life of Saint Guthlac*, Cambridge, 1956) improves on all previous editions, and is the one used for the present translation. It contains full critical apparatus (as do all Colgrave's editions), notes, and translation. There is a very free translation in Jones, *Saints' Lives and Chronicles*, and a translation of extracts in Whitelock, *English Historical Documents*, pp. 708-713. There are two Anglo-Saxon poems on Guthlac, the second of which seems based on Felix's biography (*The Exeter Book*, edited by G. Krapp and E. Dobbie [Columbia University Press, 1936] pp. 49-88). There is an Anglo-Saxon prose translation of Felix edited by P. Gonser in *Das angelsächsische Prosa-Leben des hl. Guthlac* (Heidelberg, 1909).

THE LIFE OF ST. GUTHLAC

HERE BEGINS the prologue to the Life of Saint Guthlac.

To my lord in the Lord of Lords, King Aelfwald,[1] rightfully reigning in the realm of the East Angles, dear to me beyond all the rest in the ranks of royal rulers, Felix, a servant of the catholic community, sends best wishes for good fortune forever in Christ. Obedient to your behest, but still not without some audacity on my part, I have undertaken this little book which you bade me compose about the life of our father Guthlac of blessed memory, and I have woven it of quite unpretentious fabric. In that confidence I have presented it to you with this request, that if any faulty word of mine therein should in any way offend the ears of the learned reader, as I imagine will happen, he should please note my apology at the beginning of the book.[2]

1. The fact that King Aelfwald of East Anglia (and not King Aethelbald of Mercia, as some have mistakenly supposed) commissioned this Life of a Mercian saint, and the fact that the Mercian King Aethelbald plays such a favorable part in its final chapters, suggests that the two kingdoms were on the best of terms during this period of eighth-century Mercian supremacy (Colgrave, *Felix's Life of St. Guthlac*, pp. 15-16). In the previous century King Penda of Mercia had killed two of East Anglia's most Christian kings—Sigbert and Anna. Aelfwald, who has been proposed as the possible patron of the *Beowulf*-poet (Whitelock, *Audience of Beowulf*, p. 29), seems to have been the last in the direct line of the East Anglian royal family of the Wuffings, who traced their descent through Woden (Stenton, "The East Anglian Kings of the Seventh Century," p. 48, in Clemoes, *The Anglo-Saxons*). One of these Wuffing kings must be the man commemorated by the Sutton Hoo ship-burial. Some scholars hold for Anna (Bruce-Mitford in Hodgkin, *History of the Anglo-Saxons*, 3rd ed., II, 718), others for his brother, Aethelhere (Stenton, *op. cit.*, p. 51; Green, *Sutton Hoo*, pp. 97 ff.). See note 23.

2. Felix's "apology" follows the usual medieval topos of "affected modesty" (see note 3 to *Life of St. Cuthbert*) and borrows from the usual hagiographical sources: Bede's prose *Life of St. Cuthbert*, Sulpicius Severus' *Life of St. Martin*, Evagrius' translation of Athanasius' *Life of St. Antony*.

Let him also keep in mind, I earnestly beg, that the Kingdom of God endures not by means of fluent words but by firm faith. Let him realize, in fact, that salvation was not preached to the world by orators but by fishermen. And let him not forget the words of St. Gregory who deemed it a ridiculous thing to tie down the words of heavenly inspiration by the rules of Donatus the grammarian.[3] And perhaps someone else may complain that I presumptuously and arrogantly snapped up this commission for myself while there were available very many other English scribes who could compose more splendidly than I, fountains of genius who send forth their pure and brilliant streams among the flowers of rhetoric and throughout the green meadows of literature. But let him understand that we took up this little work more out of obedience than out of our own choosing. Therefore, O reader, whoever you are, may you look kindly on the intention of my labors.

But if, as usual, you approach in the role of a disparager, take care lest, when you think you see the light, you be blinded by darkness; that is, lest when you find fault with confirmed facts, you be enveloped in the shadows of ignorance. Thus it happens with the blind that when they walk in the light they think they are lost in the dark. For, always wandering in darkness, they have no experience of light. And in the Bible blindness stands for ignorance, as the Apostle says, "Blindness has fallen upon a part of Israel, but only until the tale of the Gentile nations is complete" [Rom. 11:25]. Indeed, every evil has its origin in ignorance. Therefore let me advise you, dear reader, not to criticize things that seem strange to you, lest you yourself be criticized as strange by others. But I fear that these prolonged arguments of my apologia may annoy my readers and dull their understanding, so we shall close our ears to the carping complaints of our critics and, as if

3. Migne, *Patrologia Latina*, 75,516. Such remarks by the great Pope Gregory, who sent Augustine to England, are often cited as examples of the early Christian hostility toward the pagan classics (see Raby, *Christian Latin Poetry*, pp. 121 ff.). But perhaps they should also be seen as manifestations of the perennial "baroque" reaction to classical formalism. See Curtius, *European Literature and the Latin Middle Ages*, pp. 273 ff. and Marrou, *Saint Augustin et la fin de la culture antique* (Paris, 4th edition, 1958) pp. 663 ff. Pascal gets remarkably to the point—and to the point about the nature of hagiography as well—in no. 283 of his *Pensées.*

sailing across the surface of a vast whirlpool,[4] we shall steer our pen toward the life of St. Guthlac as though we were making our way toward the port of all life.

Since you have insisted that I write something for you about St. Guthlac's manner of life, I have therefore described how it began, what it was like before he made his holy vow, and in what manner of death it ended. This I have related just as I heard it, from reliable witnesses whom you know; and with the same proper craftsmanship I have avoided any inclination to add to or subtract from their account. I decided that this little book should be written for the useful purpose either of recalling the memory of so great a man to those who knew him, or of serving as a guide to this now widespread way of life for these who did not know him.[5] Writing about so great a man, I was careful to set down nothing without first of all inquiring most diligently into the actual facts. And what I finally wrote I did not presume to pass on to anyone for transcribing in book form till it had survived the most minute scrutiny of incontestable witnesses.[6] I made most careful investigations and asked advice on everything I wrote, from a most reverend Abbot Wilfrid and from the priest Cissa, a man I believe to be of a pure conscience,[7] and from others too who had been acquainted

4. Felix's Latin here contains one of his many echoes of Vergil (for this frequent Vergilian sea-image, note especially *Aeneid*, Bk. III, 197). See note 29 to *Life of St. Cuthbert.*

5. Even one of Wilfrid's monks at "Roman" Ripon felt this call to a hermit's life (Eddius, *Life of Wilfrid*, Ch. 64).). It was a strong sentiment in the Celtic North (witness Cuthbert) and expresses itself, for instance, in the preoccupation with the desert shown by the carver of the north face of the Ruthwell Cross (see note 21 to *Life of St. Cuthbert*).

6. Other hagiographers too explain how they presented a preliminary version for correction before they wrote their final copy. Willibald wrote the first draft of his *Life of Boniface* on waxed tablets, and transcribed it to parchment only after Bishops Lull and Megingoz had had the opportunity to examine it for any changes they might have wanted to make (Levison, ed. *Vitae Sancti Bonifatii* in Monumenta Germaniae Historica: *Scriptores Rerum Germanicarum in usum scholarum* [Hanover, 1905] pp. 104-05).

7. Felix's proposal of this ethical guarantee for his witness has been suggested as revealing how hagiographers intend not to present history but to praise and teach spiritual truths and heroic virtue. Miracles constituted the accepted language of this teaching, miracles considered not so much as separately identi-

with the man of God for some time and knew his life, at least to some extent.

So no matter how much of his life my pen may have captured, you must understand that you will have heard only the least among great matters, and few among many. For I am under no illusion that those authorities of mine could have known all of the facts, nor do I even boast that I have related all that information which they gave me. But in order to complete the story of so famous a man you should make inquiries wherever his miracles have shone forth, so that when everyone has reported what he knows, the matter of the following little book may be filled out. And so it is that in obedience to the command of your exceeding great love I have put the text of this little manuscript in as good order as I could, leaving the greater part of the tale for authors of greater talent to tell. I placed the beginning at the beginning and the end at the end.[8]

Here begins the Life.

Chapter I: *Concerning the times of his parents and their names.*

Now in the days of Aethelred,[9] the illustrious king of the English, there was a certain man of distinguished Mercian descent, named Pen-

fiable historical facts but as universal signs expressive of sanctity. The reader was less interested in seeing evidence that these particular events had actually happened than he was in seeing evidence that they were the kind of thing consistent with true sanctity. To provide this assurance the holy life of the witness himself would often be sufficient (see Jones, *Saints' Lives and Chronicles in Early England*, pp. 75 ff.).

8. For laconic wisdom this remark of Felix surely rivals Aristotle's famous dictum that every good drama has a beginning, a middle, and an end.

9. Aethelred was the king who became such a faithful friend of Wilfrid. See note 28 to the Introduction, and Chapters 43 ff. in Eddius' *Life of Wilfrid*, and note 96 to the *Life of Wilfrid*. The Mercian king, as overlord of the Middle Angles, had perhaps sent Penwalh to that kingdom as one of its ealdormen—perhaps also to remove this royal family from the temptation to claim Mercian succession.

walh, whose mansion stood in the territory of the Middle Angles and was furnished with all manner of good things.

Chapter II: *Concerning the origin and dwelling place of his father.*

Moreover this man's ancestral line ran back in regular order through the most noble names of illustrious kings to Icles,[10] in whom it had its beginning long ago.

Chapter III: *Concerning the lawful marriage of his parents.*

And so when he was flourishing in all the full vigor of the bloom of youth he took to himself a wife with all the seemly ceremonies of marriage. She was a maid of his own age, named Tette, chosen from among all the eligible young damsels of noble blood. From the very earliest days of her childhood she had been careful to cultivate maidenly modesty.

10. Icel (possessive case: *Icles*) was the great grandson of legendary King Offa of the continental Angles and was the first king of the Mercians, presumably in the fifth century (Chadwick, *Origin of the English Nation*, pp. 14 ff.). His father, Eomer, is mentioned in *Beowulf*, v. 1960. Perhaps it was Guthlac's royal blood that prompted his exile (referred to in Ch. 34) at the command of an apprehensive king. Bold young Guthlac, with his royal blood and his army-size *comitatus* of adventurers (Ch. 17), would have given any nervous king sleepless nights, even though this army was being employed against the king's enemies. We think of another royal exile and his band of men—Caedwalla (Eddius, *Life of Wilfrid*, Ch. 42). Felix even seems to indicate that Guthlac had at least given some thought to the kingship which might possibly have been his (Ch. 18, fifth sentence).

Chapter IV : *Concerning his conception and the course of the days of pregnancy.*

Then after some cycles of seasons had duly run their course, and the couple had complied with the conditions of the marriage right, it happened, in the normal pattern of nature, that she conceived and was pregnant. When the months of her carrying had tolled their count and the time of birth drew near, and her womb was troubled with the mystery of the new-felt violence of labor, then of a sudden a divine marvel, heralding a heavenly prophecy, appeared to those who were standing near and to the crowds who flocked in from everywhere. For the Almighty Holy One, who sees the future in the present, and for whom now is forever, sent a sign to make his soldier known, a token that he was already loved in God's heart.

Chapter V : *Concerning the prodigy manifested at the time of his birth.*

And when the hour of his birth had come, behold a hand appeared[11] (marvelous to tell!) shining and gleaming in golden-red splendor and reaching from the clouds of heavenly Olympus[12] to the arms of a cross in front of the house wherein the holy woman was giving birth to an infant destined for greatness.[13]

11. We see this great hand of God stretching down from the heavens in many an early medieval illuminated manuscript. In at least one instance, moreover, the scene is a golden one—on the exquisite Crucifixion page of the eleventh-century Anglo-Saxon Gospel of Judith of Flanders (M. 709 in the Pierpont Morgan Library in New York).

12. A similar literary fusion of the classical and the Christian is frequent in a later humanistic age, not only in such a poet as Milton but even in revised hymns of the Roman liturgy, for instance in the Hymn for Lauds in the Common Office of the Dedication of a Church (*Alto ex Olympi vertice Summi Parentis Filius . . .*).

13. In hagiographies such heavenly signs frequently attend the birth of saints (e.g., Eddius, *Life of Wilfrid*, Ch. 1).

Chapter VI: *Concerning the crowds who saw and a marvelled at the sign.*

But when people, seized with uncommon amazement, were rushing up from all sides to see the miracle,

Chapter VII: *Concerning the hand sent from the sky which marked the door of the house in which he was born.*

suddenly, after it had blessed the door of this house, the hand drew back and disappeared into the depths of heaven. Astounded anew by this second wonder, all who were present fell prone on the ground at the scene of the holy apparition and, not without some trepidation, humbly praised the Lord of glory.

Chapter VIII: *Concerning the various opinions of the amazed crowds.*

When they finished their prayers and supplications they gathered together and discussed among themselves what this strange thing could be which had stirred up uneasiness in many. And while with immense amazement and much argument they thus talked it over among themselves, a woman came running with astonishing speed from the room nearby where the child was being born, and she cried out, "Listen! A man has been born into our world for a great glory to come." Hearing this, some now interpreted that marvel in the sky as a divine presage announcing the glory of the infant. But others, conjecturing in shrewder fashion, did maintain that this child was predestined by divine dispensation for the reward of eternal happiness.

Chapter IX : *Concerning the widespread report of that prodigy.*

Now it happened that the multitude of those who witnessed this wonder was so immense that, before the lambent glory of the radiant sun had sunk beneath the verge of the western world, the wandering rumor of the miracle had reached almost all the borderlands of the Middle Angles.

Chapter X : *Concerning his baptism and his name derived from the name of his country.*

And so after eight circling days had traced their course through the heavens, the child was brought to the holy waters of the healing font and he was given as his own the name Guthlac, after the name of that tribe known as the Guthlacingas. It was as though he were named by heavenly inspiration, for the quality contained in his name appropriately matched his virtues. As those acquainted with that race attest, this word in the language of the English seems to consist of two parts, i. e., *Guth* and *lac*, which in the splendid Roman language means "war's reward."[14] And certainly he did battle against sin and win the reward of eternal bliss and the victory crown of life everlasting according to the Apostle's words, "Blessed is he who endures under trials. When he has proved his worth, he will win that crown of life, which God has promised to those who love Him" [James, 1:12].

14. But *lāc* at this time more probably still meant "play," so that Guthlac (like *beadu-lāc* in *Beowulf*) would mean "battle-play." (Perhaps Felix was not a native Anglo-Saxon.) It may be that Guthlac was descended from a great hero of that name, famous in the ancient songs of the people (see Colgrave, *Felix's Life of St. Guthlac*, p. 3).

Chapter XI: *Concerning his education and upbringing in his father's hall.*

Then, under the guidance of the divine will, after he had cleansed himself of the sins of his parents in the holy waters of the hallowed font, this child of marvelous promise was, in his father's halls, trained in the noble traditions of his ancestors.[15]

Chapter XII: *Concerning the sobriety of his infancy and his childish simplicity.*

While he was passing through the period of his infancy and making his first childish attempts to talk, he was never any trouble to his parents or nurses or to the troops of playmates he had. He refrained from imitating those things which usually give bad habits to children of his age: the impudence of boys, the silly chatter of housewives, the foolish tale-telling of the people, the vulgar bawling of country clowns, the paltry lies of parasites, the raucous cries of various kinds of birds.

Chapter XIII: *Concerning his docility and wise disposition of mind in learning the arts.*

He was possessed of extraordinary keenness of mind, to which he added a cheerful, frank countenance, a pure heart, and a gentle disposition.

Chapter XIV: *Concerning his obedience to his seniors and the love of his fellows for him.*

He was not found wanting in the proper reverence for his parents, nor in obedience to his elders, nor in love for his relatives; he was never

15. See note 51 to the Introduction, and note 6 to the *Life of St. Cuthbert.*

a bad influence on anyone, never vented his anger on anyone, never scandalized anyone, never "rendered anyone evil for evil" [Rom. 12:17], but he was ever the mildest of men.

Chapter XV: *Concerning the witness all bore to him and the divine grace shining in his face.*

He was refulgent with the radiance of a spiritual light so that everything he did revealed to all men what the future held for him.

Chapter XVI: *Concerning his sudden change of disposition.*

Then when his youthful strength had grown greater and a noble passion for power and greatness flamed up in his young heart, he called to mind the mighty deeds of heroes of old and, like one roused from slumber he put aside his former disposition, gathered about him troops of followers, and took to a life of war.[16]

Chapter XVII: *How he tried to restore a third part of the pillaged treasure to the owners.*

But always after he had laid waste with fire and sword the towns, palaces, villages, and fortresses of those who took the field against him, and after he had amassed immense booty for the comrades he had collected from all quarters and from different races, then as if inspired by heavenly counsel, he would restore to the owners a third of the accumulated treasure-hoard.

16. See note 14.

Chapter XVIII: *How, urged by spiritual impulses, he vowed that he would become a servant of God.*

So while the circling years traced almost nine orbits through the heavens, he hammered away unremittingly and devastatingly until he accomplished the celebrated overthrow of the hosts of foes who were harassing his land.[17] Their strength was so sapped at length, after suffering so much pillage and plunder and slaughter at his hands, that they were exhausted and kept the peace perforce. At this time Guthlac, the hero of blessed memory, was being whirled about on the tempest-tossed seas of the present world in the uncertain fortune of the passing years, amid the murky clouds of a half-discovered life.

Then one night it happened that after he had relaxed his tired body for its wonted rest and was, as always, trying intently and anxiously to fix his vagabond thoughts on the troublesome business of mortality, suddenly (marvelous to tell!) as though he were struck on the breast, a spiritual flame began to kindle the heart of this man. There as he thought upon the miserable deaths that had concluded the shameful lives of ancient kings of his race in ages past, and as he lay awake and considered the perishable wealth of the world and the pitiful glory of doomed life, then the vision of his own very death took form in his imaginings. Trembling in his watching heart at this inevitable conclusion of short life, he thought how day by day its course tended toward that end. He further remembered how he heard, "Let not your flight be in winter nor on the Sabbath" [Mat. 24:20]. As he was musing over these and similar things, suddenly moved by divine inspiration he vowed that if he lived to the morrow he would become Christ's man.

17. Guthlac's fighting was probably against the Welsh, whose raids later broke out again in King Cenred's reign (see Ch. 34), and against whom King Offa finally erected his great Dyke.

Chapter XIX: *How, having left his comrades, he made his way alone to Repton.*

So when the somber glooms of night had scattered and the fiery sun had risen over "the wretched race of men" [*Aeneid*, II:268] and the birds of morning were chirping from eager throats, Guthlac rose from his rude field-bed already dressed, made the saving Sign of the Cross over his heart, and then announced to his companions that they would have to choose another leader for their expedition since he resolved to devote himself to the service of God. When his followers heard this they were struck with immense amazement; they begged and implored him not to embark on this course he had announced. But he spurned their pleas and persisted, unmoved, in what he had undertaken. For the fire of divine grace so flamed in him that not only did he disregard the deference due his royal blood but he turned his back on his parents, his country, and the companions of his youth. From the time he reached the age of twenty-four and renounced the "pride, pomp and circumstance" of this world he held the hope of his sure faith fixed in Christ.

Chapter XX: *How, after receiving the apostolic tonsure, he abstained from all intoxicating liquor.*

Then he took to the road, forsaking all that was his, and journeyed to the monastery of Repton where, under an abbess named Aelfthryth,[18] he received the mystic tonsure of St. Peter, leader of the Apostles.[19] Then he donned monk's robes and began the battle of penance to atone for his sins. And from the time that he received the mark of the Apos-

18. Repton was another of the Anglo-Saxon double monasteries. See note 18 to *Life of St. Cuthbert.*

19. See note 17 to *Life of St. Cuthbert*, and Plummer, *Baedae Opera Historica*, II,150.

tolic tonsure he never tasted any intoxicating liquor, except at Communion time,[20] nor any kind of pleasant drink whatever.

Chapter XXI: *How he was intensely hated by all his fellows on account of this and afterwards, when they recognized his gentleness, how he turned the hearts of them all to an affection for him.*

Because of this he was bitterly disliked by all the brethren living with him there. But as soon as they had had the opportunity to prove the sincerity of his manner of life and the unassuming nature of his cheerful personality, he won all[21] hearts to return his love. He was of distinguished appearance, chaste in body, of a handsome face, and devout at heart. He was endowed with wisdom and gifted with prudence. His face was full of life; he was pleasant in conversation, exceptionally discreet, strong in his own inner manliness, unwavering in his judgment of what was right, big-hearted and tolerant, gentle and humble, strong in patience, and possessing a love that involved him in the cares of others. And indeed his wisdom so enhanced the grace of all his virtues that, in the Apostle's words, "his speech was ever brilliant, seasoned with the salt of divine grace" [cf. Col. 4:6].

Chapter XXII: *How he was instructed in the psalms and in the monastic discipline while grace illuminated him.*

When he showed a preference for learning the chanting of the psalms, after he had been taught his letters,[22] then divine grace bountifully

20. It was at this time still the custom to receive Holy Communion under both species.

21. One group of manuscripts (Colgrave, *Felix's Life of St. Guthlac*, p. 85, n. 21) states that Guthlac succeeded in winning over only "some" (*aliquorum*) of the nettled brethren.

22. And so had every young Anglo-Saxon to go either to a Celtic or Anglo-

nourished the fruitful soil of the hero's heart with gentle showers of heavenly dew. Under the tutelage of the very best masters he was, with the help of divine grace, instructed in Scripture and monastic discipline.

Chapter XXIII : *How he strove to imitate the individual virtues of all.*

So for two years he received his first training in the canticles, psalms, hymns, prayers and customs of the Church, and he set himself to imitating the particular virtues of each one of those who were living with him—the obedience of that one, the humility of this one, the patience of another, the forbearance of yet another, and the purity, temperance and agreeableness of each and all. To put it briefly, he imitated the virtues of all of them in all things.

Chapter XXIV : *How after two years of life as a cleric he sought the desert.*

After these four and twenty months had each wheeled by in the circling dance of the planets, while he in his monk's robes had lived a life of the greatest moderation, then with all that uncommon earnestness of his eager soul his thoughts turned to the desert. For whenever he read about the solitary life of the monks of olden times then his heart burned with a hungry longing to seek solitude in the wilderness.[23] To make

Saxon monastery to learn to read and write Latin—and even to learn to write his own language. On the Psalms in monastic education see note 34 to *Life of St. Cuthbert.*

23. The spell of the *Life of St. Antony* and the Egyptian desert lays a strong hold on Celtic and Anglo-Saxon monasticism (see note 16 to *Life of St. Cuthbert*, and note 5 to Felix). We see it mirrored in the life of St. Cuthbert too, and quoted by Cuthbert's biographer, as it is by Felix. Of all the Dark Age saints' Lives up till this time, Felix's comes closest to achieving the same logical and dramatic

a long story short, in the course of a few days he received the required consent of his superiors and, beginning that long journey which was to end in eternal bliss, set out to find his place of retreat.

There lies in the midland district of Britain a most dismal fen of enormous extent. It begins at the banks of the river Granta, not far from the fortified town they call Cambridge, and stretches from the south all the way to the sea in the north, in one vast tract. It consists mostly of swamps and bogs and an occasional black pool, exuding dank miasmal mists, and it is sprinkled with islands of marshy heaths crisscrossed with tortuous mazes of winding waterways.[24] And so

unity of construction as the *Life of St. Antony* (see Kurtz, "From St. Antony to St. Guthlac"). Felix, an East Anglian or at least writing in East Anglia, also quotes frequently from a Life (see Colgrave, *Felix's Life of St. Guthlac*, pp. 179-80) of the famous Irish hermit of East Anglia, St. Fursey (Fursa), whom King Sigbert the Learned (see Introduction, p. 18) had invited to establish a monastery inside the old Roman coastal fort of Burgh Castle (see note 65 to Introduction). This holy Irish visionary and his monastery in the Roman fort in Anglo-Saxon Britian have lately become linked with the fascinating puzzle of the royal East Anglian burial treasure found at Sutton Hoo. It has been suggested that Fursey and his brethren brought with them to England the decorated hanging bowl of Sutton Hoo (see Green, *Sutton Hoo*, p. 90), and further that the Sutton Hoo hoard of Merovingian gold coins was ransom money sent by friends in Gaul to buy freedom for some monks of Fursey's monastery who had been captured in Penda's invasion (Paul Grosjean, "Le tresor merovingien de Sutton Hoo, S. Feuillen et S. Éloi," *Analecta Bollandiana*, 78 [1960] pp. 364 ff.). Father Grosjean further suggests that the money was paid to Penda's ally, Aethelhere, pagan brother of Christian King Anna, who led the attack on this part of his brother's realm (and see Green, *Sutton Hoo*, pp. 98-99). In 655, having been King of East Anglia for less than a year, Aethelhere was killed, along with Penda, at the Battle of the Winwaed by King Oswy of Northumbria. He was very likely drowned and his body never found (see Bede, *Ecclesiastical History*, Bk. III, ch. 24). The ransom hoard, still among his possessions, was then placed—according to this theory—in his cenotaph at Sutton Hoo.

24. We hardly have to wait for the disclosure of the next chapter to know that this eerie marshland is possessed by monsters. Its description sounds for all the world like the forbidding mere of fiendish Grendel (*Beowulf*, vv. 1357 ff.), suggesting the haunted, twisted forest-imagery of Germanic painters like Grünewald or Max Ernst (see K. Clark, *Landscape into Art* [Penguin Books, 1956] pp. 50 ff.), and recalling more ancient sea-images of hell (see K. Malone, "Grendel and His Abode," in *Studia Philologica et Litteraria In Honorem L. Spitzer*, edited by A. G. Hatcher and K. L. Selig [Bern, 1958], pp. 297-308; and M. McNamee,

when Guthlac, this hero of blessed memory, learned of the wild places in that most desolate of wastelands he made his way there with the help of heaven by the most direct roads.

Chapter XXV : *How he was guided to Crowland by those who lived closest to the desert, on the feast of St. Bartholomew.*

And there it happened that when he was asking for information about the fenland from those who dwelt in its vicinity, and they were telling him many wild tales about the various sectors of this wild land, a certain one of the bystanders named Tatwine spoke up and boasted that he knew of yet another spot, an island hidden away even further back in the depths of the wasteland. He said that many had already made attempts to dwell there but had given up because of mysterious unheard-of monsters and other strange terrors that had haunted the fen. Elated at this news, the saintly hero entreated the man to show him the place.

Seeing that Guthlac was not going to brook "no" for an answer, the man consented and in a fishing skiff, with Christ as a companion, they made their way through trackless marshes far into the interior of the gloomy swamp and arrived at the aforesaid spot. It is an island called Crowland, situated in the heart of this morass and until a short time ago had remained uncultivated and practically unknown because of the lonely isolation of the wild place. Before Christ's servant, Guthlac, no settler had been stouthearted enough to live alone here on account of the phantom-demons that infested the site.[25] But God's hero despised the foe, and, with the help of heaven, took up his life here all alone amid the eerie shadows of the forlorn heath.

"*Beowulf*—An Allegory of Salvation?" *Journal of English and Germanic Philology*, 59 [1960] pp. 190-207). For the early history and description of this fenland, see H. C. Darby, *The Medieval Fenland* (Cambridge, 1940) ch. 1.

25. And the same was said of Cuthbert's retreat on Farne (*Life of St. Cuthbert*, Bk. III, ch. 1). One of the ancient sayings of Anglo-Saxon gnomic poetry states that the lonely fen is where the demon dwells (*Anglo-Saxon Poetry*, translated by Gordon, Everyman's Library [revised edition] 1954, p. 314).

Now it happened, through the dispensation of divine grace, that the summer day on which the blessed Guthlac arrived at the island of Crowland was the very day appointed for the celebration of the Mass of St. Bartholomew, so that Guthlac entered upon his life in the fenland with all confidence in the help of St. Bartholomew. Accordingly he dearly loved the inaccessible solitude of this retreat, looking on it as a gift presented him by God, and he vowed with all the strength of his soul to pass all the days of his life there.

Chapter XXVI: *How he returned to Repton to salute his brethren again.*

After he had remained there for some days and had explored painstakingly every last inch of the place, he began to consider going back for a talk with the companions whom that uncommon bond of fraternal love had linked to him in the bosom of the catholic family. For he had gone off from them before with no words of farewell, so he determined now to offer them counsel directed to helping them fare well.[26] Meanwhile the morrow's light had risen over "wretched mortals" [*Aeneid*, II:268] when he set forth on his return journey to the monastery. After a most friendly visit of ninety days with the brethren, he returned to his hermitage as though to the seat of his paternal inheritance, and two boys accompanied him on the trip.

Chapter XXVII: *How he returned again to Crowland on 25 August, the feast of St. Bartholomew.*

The return journey to Crowland was completed on the 25th of August, the day on which the solemnity of St. Bartholomew is celebrated,

26. My "farewell . . . fare well" is the best I could do to approximate the pun in Felix's Latin: *quos ante insalutatos dimittebat, iterum salutaribus praeceptis commendare disposuit.*

the saint under whose aegis Guthlac's whole adventure of life in the wilderness had been launched so providentially. He was now about twenty-six years of age as he entered in earnest with the help of heaven upon the life of a soldier of the true God amid the dreary mists of this lonely wasteland. Then girding himself with the arms of the spirit against the cunning strategy of the most terrible of foes, he grasped the "shield of faith, the breastplate of hope" [Eph. 6:11-17], the helmet of chastity, the bow of patience, the arrows of psalmody, and took his stand stoutheartedly in the shieldwall.[27] So strong was his trust that he hurled himself into the very midst of the raging ranks of hell with utter contempt for his foe.

O, how marvelous is the graciousness of the divine mercy, what a glorious thing is the watchfulness of the Father's love, how much to be praised is the predestination of the eternal Deity, how inscrutable are the decisions of the everlasting Judge, as the Apostle avows, "How incomprehensible are his judgments, and how unsearchable his ways" [Rom. 11:33]. For just as the illustrious Apostle of the Gentiles, who before time began had been predestined by God to preach the Gospel of His Son, was led forth from the dark mists of Jewish error while he was on his way to Damascus, so Guthlac, of saintly memory, was guided away from the seething whirlpool of the storm-tossed times, from the tortuously tangled ways of mortal life, from the black jaws of a falling world, to the warfare for eternal happiness, to the straight and narrow path, to the vision of the true light. And not only did God bless him with fame and veneration in the present life but He also established him in the joy of eternal glory and everlasting beatitude, just as the Apostle truly declared, "Whom he predestined, them he also called. And whom he called, them he glorified" [cf. Rom. 8:30].

27. As the battle imagery increases here, so does the characteristic Germanic alliteration of the old heroic poetry. And on the Pauline concept in the passage see note 25 to *Life of St. Cuthbert.*

Chapter XXVIII : *How he dwelt in a hut that he built in the side of a barrow which had been broken open, and what his rule of life was as a hermit.*

And so to begin my story of the solitary life of St. Guthlac, as I proposed to do, I shall be careful to tell exactly what I heard from Wilfrid and Cissa, his frequent visitors, and I shall repeat it in the same order in which it was told to me. Now on Guthlac's island there happened to be a tumulus, or grave-mound, built up of clods of earth, which had been dug into and laid open by treasure-hunters.[28] Through the aperture in its side a cistern of some sort could be seen and in this our holy hero, Guthlac, began to live after building a hut on top of it.[29] It was a fixed rule of his life, from the time when he first took up his abode in the fens, not to wear any woolen or linen garments, nor any clothing of any soft material whatsoever; but he passed all the days of his solitary life clad in garments of animal skins. So great was the abstinence of his daily life that from the time he first began to live at Crowland, he took no nourishment of any kind except for a small piece of barley bread and a small cup of muddy water, which he con-

28. See note 47 to Eddius' *Life of Wilfrid.*

29. It is very richly symbolic that Guthlac should have chosen a tomb for his hermitage, the place where he determined to bury all worldly desires and prepare for the death which was to lead to eternal life, and where he actually arranged that his dead body would be buried (Ch. 50). The intention of spiritual death surely helped dictate the burial-vault design of Coptic cells in early Egyptian monastic communities (H. Torp, "Aspects of Early Coptic Monastic Architecture," *Byzantion*, 25-27 [1955-57] pp. 513-538) which in turn was reflected in the plan of Celtic hermitages, like Cuthbert's (Chadwick, *Age of the Saints in the Early Celtic Church*, pp. 90 ff. See also notes 16, 26, 27 to *Life of St. Cuthbert*). It is often remarked too how much the stone tombs and beehive cells of the early Celtic monks resemble the Mycenaean tombs of the Homeric world (Brown, *Arts in Early England*, II, 18 ff.). For an interesting study of Guthlac's tumulus as it appears in the Anglo-Saxon poem known as *Guthlac A*, see Laurence Shook's article, "The Burial Mound in *Guthlac A*," in *Modern Philology*, 58 (1960), pp. 1-10.

sumed after sundown. At the hour when the sun dipped to the western edge of the world, then it was that he gratefully tasted the meager sustenance needed for his mortal life.

Chapter XXIX : *How he suffered his first temptation from Satan, namely the temptation to despair.*

Shortly after our hero of blessed memory had begun his hermit's life, as he was engaged one day in his usual custom of singing the psalms and canticles, that ancient foe of the human race like a roaring lion was setting the vast reaches of the sky reverberating with his horrid power and was plotting new wiles. Putting to the test all the wicked strength of his crafty mind, he shot a poisoned arrow of despair with all his strength, as from a drawn bow, and it stuck fast right in the center of the mind of Christ's soldier. Then while the poisoned barb poured in its dose of virulent venom, the soldier of Christ became confused and dulled in all his senses and began to despair about the life he had undertaken. He turned this way and that in his troubled mind but found no ground where he could stand secure. For as the enormous sins of his past life paraded ponderously through his thoughts, then it seemed to him that he could never be cleansed of them. He began to grow so utterly despondent that the life he had undertaken appeared as an infinite and insupportable burden.

Tortured thus for three days, Christ's servant did not know where to turn. But on the night of the third day, while the most valiant soldier of Christ was still stoutheartedly giving battle to these deadly thoughts, he suddenly began to chant, as though seized with the spirit of prophecy, "In affliction I called upon the Lord," etc. [Ps. 17:7]. And behold, in the morning watches his faithful helper, the blessed Bartholomew, presented himself to Guthlac's gaze. Nor was it a dream, but he plainly recognized the features of this resplendent visitor from heaven. So the hero—like a soldier who has been fighting desperately amid the swarming front ranks of the foe—when he realized of a sudden that help had reached him and was aware of the heavenly radiance of an angel comrade at his side, then on the instant the dark clouds of baleful thoughts dispersed, and his heavy heart grew light and he sang out triumphantly, "With the Lord at my side to aid me, I shall yet see my enemies baffled" [Ps. 117:7].

Then St. Bartholomew, remaining in Guthlac's presence, began to comfort him with spiritual counsel, and promised that he would evermore come to his aid in all of his trials. When Guthlac heard this from the friend he trusted most faithfully, joy overflowed his spirit and he fixed his faith forever, with all the uncommon strength of his soul, in the Lord Jesus. For the triumphant outcome of this first battle confirmed in his brave heart the hope of final glorious victory to come. And from that time on the devil never again used the weapons of despair against Guthlac, because once the saint had shattered them they could nevermore be of any avail.

Chapter XXX : *How in feigned friendship the devil tried to teach him to fast.*

On another day, while he happened to be thinking over the schedule of his daily life, all of a sudden, as though dropped from the sky, two devils presented themselves before him in human shape but with ferocious faces.[30] As though they were old friends of his, the two commenced to speak. "We know all about you. We certainly have no doubts about the strength of your faith, and we have used various varieties of weapons against you to test your perseverance and your invincible patience. Therefore we propose to leave off abusing you any further, and not only do we not wish to break up this rule of life you have resolved on, but we will even teach you the way of life of the ancient hermits. For Moses and Elias and the very Savior of the human race himself made it their first endeavor to scale the heights of fasting. And those renowned monks who dwelt in Egypt slew the vices of human weakness with the sword of abstinence. Therefore

30. Throughout this chapter Felix gives the devilish visitors a comic treatment often seen in medieval hagiography (see Curtius, *European Literature and the Latin Middle Ages*, pp. 425 ff.).

if you desire to wash away the sins of the past and to destroy the threatening sins of the future, you must afflict your flesh with the lash of fasting, and break the pride of your spirit with the scourge of abstinence.

"For, as much as you are broken down in this life, so much will you be made whole and strong in the next, and as much as you are afflicted in the present world, so much will you rejoice in the one to come. When you shall have absolutely prostrated yourself by fasting then you will be exalted all the more eminently in the presence of God. So let your fasting not be a thing of two or three days duration, nor let it be a daily abstinence from gluttony. No, a really effective chastisement is a seven-days fast. For just as God fashioned the form of the world in six days and rested on the seventh, so also is it fitting that man should refashion his spirit for six days by the form of fasting, and on the seventh day give rest to the flesh by partaking of food."

After he had listened to all this the blessed Guthlac rose up and sang out the words of the psalm, "Then shall my enemies be turned back," and so forth [Ps. 55:10]. As soon as Guthlac did this his crafty old foe vanished from his presence like smoke into the empty air.[31] Then to show his scorn of the devilish counsel, and to avoid seeming to agree with the pair of them in any degree, he picked up a piece of barley bread and began on the spot to eat his daily ration. Seeing themselves held so in contempt, the malignant spirits filled the land for far around with "a drear and dying sound," and there was "a voice of weeping heard, and loud lament" as they sobbed and made much moan.

From that time on, after he won the prize so overwhelmingly in the contest, the hero of God had nothing but contempt for apparitions of the foul spirits.

31. Without irreverence we can recognize in the Dark Age Christian mentality lingering remnants of the primitive and the pagan. Ageless instinct looked to prayerful incantation as a more potent spell against evil. There was much of magic in the power that even Constantine saw in the Cross (A. Alföldi, *The Conversion of Constantine and Pagan Rome* [Oxford, 1948] pp. 16 ff.). Anglo-Saxon charms and blessings often have little to distinguish between them (G. Storms, *Anglo-Saxon Magic* [The Hague, 1948]). In *Njal's Saga* the cross at times serves literally as a more powerful substitute for shield and sword (Chs. 101, 103).

Chapter XXXI : *How the evil spirits transported him bodily to the gates of hell.*[32]

Once in the dead of night, after an interval of a few days during this same period; Guthlac was keeping his accustomed prayerful vigil when all of a sudden he saw his small cell fill up completely with hideous hordes of foul spirits. Swarming in from all sides they met nothing that could block their entrance. They crept up through the floor and down through the matted roof. Neither the cracks between door panels nor the holes in the walls were tiny enough to keep them out. Bursting forth from heaven and earth swart clouds of them cloaked the whole sweep of the sky. They were horrible to see, in terrifying shapes with monstrous heads, long necks and pinched, ghastly faces, filthy beards, hairy ears, threatening brows, savage eyes, stinking mouths, horses' teeth. Flames vomited from their throats and they had twisted jaws, thick lips and dreadful voices. Their hair was charred, and they had gross mouths, pigeon breasts, scabby thighs, knobby knees, crooked shins, bulging ankles, and splay feet.[33] And from all their gaping mouths came a raucous clamor. So exceedingly horrible to hear was this strident caterwauling, that it seemed to swell and reverberate till the whole cavernous space between heaven and earth was a roaring bedlam of bellowing.

32. Felix's visit of Guthlac to hell has no parallel in the *Life of St. Antony*, but has many antecedents in other ancient and medieval literature from the *Odyssey* and the *Aeneid* to Gregory's *Dialogues* and the *Life of St. Fursey* (see note 23). Bede repeats Fursey's story of his vision and tells how the Irishman was seen to perspire profusely as he talked, though he was thinly clothed on a wintry day (*Ecclesiastical History*, Bk. III, ch. 19). Bede also fascinatedly retells the vision of hell seen by a Northumbrian, Drythelm, who often described it for King Aldfrith (*Ecclesiastical History*, Bk. V, ch. 12). And Boniface in his letters relates more visions of the other-world (Letters No. 2 and 92 in Emerton, *Letters of Saint Boniface*). See also H. R. Patch, *The Other World* (Harvard, 1950) and St. John Seymour, *Irish Visions of the Other World* (London, 1930).

33. The typical medieval literary device of cataloguing details (see Curtius, *European Literature and the Latin Middle Ages*, p. 92).

Without any delay they attacked. Sweeping into his house as into a fortification they tied up God's hero quicker than words can tell, dragged him out of his cell, and plunged him into the foul mire of the murky swamp. Then they took him through the wildest parts of the fen, dragging him through the most tangled thickets of thorn-bushes, lacerating all the parts of his body. After they had spent a large part of the gloomy night in such tortures, they made him stand for a little while, and they demanded that he give up his fenland hermitage. Finally in answer he began stoutheartedly to sing, as though in prophecy, the words of the psalm, "The Lord is at my right hand, that I be not moved" [Ps. 15:8].

Then they took hold of him again and began to beat him with whips that seemed made of iron. But when, after this whipping and innumerable kinds of other torments, they saw that he was still unshaken in heart and that he persisted with firm confidence in the stand he had taken, then they started to drag him aloft, with a frightful whirring of wings, up into the icy reaches of the sky where clouds are born. When he had been brought all the way up to the staggering summit of the dome of space, then (fearful to relate!) there in the north the stretches of the sky seemed to turn black in a darkling gloom of lowering clouds. From there he could descry winging to meet them countless squadrons of evil spirits. As soon as the bands had merged in one they wheeled their flight with an incredible uproar into the unsubstantial air and swept off with Christ's servant to the cursed jaws of hell itself.

And as he stared into the smoky caverns of the seething, roaring inferno of fire, he forgot all the torments he had up till now endured at the hands of the wicked spirits, as though he had never suffered them. For here he watched raging volcanoes of fire swelling up to belch out surges of flame, and there were sulphurous tornadoes of liquid fire and icy hail which seemed almost to splash the stars with their incandescent spray. Here and there among the fire-blackened pits and the burning gulfs, devils could be discerned running about and torturing in various agonizing ways those souls damned to a miserable fate. Then when God's hero, Guthlac, shuddered at the sight of such torments, the throngs of attendant demons shouted out as with one voice, "Look now, we have been given the power to thrust you into these torments, and there amid the pains of the most frightful depths of hell we have been commissioned to rack you with all manner of suffering. Here is the fire, enkindled by your sins, and it is ready now to consume you. Look how the portals of Erebus gape open for you, spewing fire from yawning fissures. See how the bowels of Styx churn with desire to devour you, and how the swirling gulfs of simmering Acheron stretch wide their dreadful jaws."

Such threats they made, and many others like to these, but the hero of God despised them all. With his nerves yet unshaken, his soul firm and his mind clear, he made answer to them, "Woe to you, sons of darkness, seed of Cain, you are but dying cinders among the ashes. If it is in your power to put me to these tortures, then look, here I stand, ready.[34] Why vomit out these idle threats from your lying hearts?"

Chapter XXXII: *How Bartholomew appeared to him there and ordered him to be carried back.*

But just when they were readying themselves as if to hurl him into the waiting torments of hell, suddenly St. Bartholomew presented himself before them clothed in golden glory from the heavenly seat of shining Olympus.[35] With the overpowering brilliance of celestial splendor he sundered the deepest darkness of the murky night with a flash of light. The evil spirits, of course, could not bear the splendor of this heavenly radiance, and so began to rage and to roar, to fear and falter and flee.[36] But St. Guthlac, as soon as he realized that his most faithful ally had arrived, was glad and fairly overflowed with joy.

34. Guthlac is quite unaware that he is anticipating a more famous *Hier stehe ich.*

35. Another of Felix's quaint and charming weddings of the classical and the Christian. It is a three-party wedding though, and includes the heroic Germanic alliteration. But see also note 52 to Introduction.

36. Felix's Latin alliterates even more in this passage than my translation indicates.

Chapter XXXIII: *How he was carried back by the foul spirits with the utmost quiet to his dwelling.*

Then St. Bartholomew ordered the mobs of minions to take Guthlac back to his own dwelling in all quietness, without vexing him or harming him in any way. Without delay they submitted to the Apostolic commands and quicker than words can tell they performed what he ordered. They carried Guthlac back with the utmost gentleness, bearing him so softly upon the rowing of their wings that he could not have been conveyed more smoothly in any chariot or ship. When they arrived at the region of mid-air the sound of voices was heard singing a psalm, most suitably chosen, "The saints shall go from virtue to virtue," and so forth [Ps. 83:8].

Then as day was about to dawn, and the sun had swept "the heavens free of the shades of night" [*Aeneid*, 11:210], Christ's champion, having won the victory over his foe,[37] stood once more on the island of Crowland and there offered his thanks to Christ. While he was making the customary offering of morning Lauds[38] to the Lord Jesus, he glanced aside for a moment and saw standing at his left, and weeping, two of the attendant spirits. They were the pair he had taken note of above all the others, and when he inquired why they lamented, they answered, "We mourn for our power which you have shattered everywhere, and we bewail our helplessness in the face of your strength. We dare not touch you or even come near you." And with this they fled "like smoke" from before his face [Cf. Ps. 67:2].

37. Felix's Latin is especially epic here, full of heroic and military expressions: *Christi athleta, adepto de hostibus triumpho* [or *tropheo*]. See notes 61 and 64; and see note 22 to Eddius' *Life of Wilfrid.*

38. Felix, doubtless a monk himself, seems to be deliberately careful that Guthlac follow the exact Benedictine order of the day. One of the especially fixed rules of the Benedictine horarium was that the morning prayer of the Office, lauds, should always begin at *aurora*, the first light of day (Butler, *Benedictine Monachism*, pp. 279 ff.).

Chapter XXXIV : *How he put whole phantom troops of devils to flight by singing the first verse of the 67th psalm.*

Now in the days of Cenred,[39] King of the Mercians, it happened that the Britons, inveterate enemies of the Saxon race, were harassing the English people with raiding and pillaging and even with oraganized, large-scale devastation.[40] One night about the time of cockcrow, while Guthlac was engaged in his customary prayerful vigil, all of a sudden a dream-filled sleep appeared to come over him and he seemed to hear the uproar of a rioting crowd. Then in less time than it takes to tell it, he started up out of his dozing and hurried from the cell where he had been sitting. Standing outside, his ears straining to catch every sound, he could make out the words spoken by a crowd and realized that a mass of Britons was advancing on his dwelling. For in years gone by he had lived in exile among them, so that he was able to understand their barbarous speech.

But back to my story—the Britons were struggling through the swampy land to reach his dwelling, and at almost the same moment he saw all his buildings ablaze, flames leaping high above them. Then the crowd closed in on Guthlac himself and began to toss him in the air on the sharp points of their spears. But finally God's hero recognized the thousand-fold forms of his old foe of the thousand-fold tricks and sang out, as if prophetically, the first verse of the 67th psalm, "Let God arise," and so forth.[41] The instant that they heard this the whole demon host vanished like smoke from before his face, swifter than speech.

39. On Aethelred's nephew, Cenred, who succeeded to the throne in 704, see Eddius' *Life of Wilfrid*, Ch. 57, and note 115.

40. But Felix does not mean to imply, as has been supposed, that it was actual British warriors whom he goes on to describe as Guthlac's tormentors. The concluding sentence of the chapter should make it clear that the Celtic-speaking invaders were merely his regular demon enemies under another appropriate disguise.

41. This same verse (2) of Psalm 67 was used by St. Antony to rout his demon tormentors (Athanasius [and Evagrius' translation], *Vita S. Antonii*, in *Patrologia Graeca*, 26, 863-64).

Chapter XXXV : *How his spirit of prophecy revealed the murderous purpose of a cleric who had come with the intention of slaying him.*

Not long subsequent to this, after Guthlac, our hero of worshipful life, had been winning frequent battles against the plots of his slippery foe, the devil took stock of his own broken power, and plotted in his poisonous heart new stratagems against the saint. Now there happened to be a cleric named Beccel who voluntarily offered himself to the hero as a servant and proposed to live religiously for God under Guthlac's direction. But an evil spirit crept into his heart and began to puff him up with the pernicious arrogance of vainglory. Next, after he had seduced him with the inflated pretentiousness of hollow pride, he also set about implanting in his mind the idea of getting a sharp sword and murdering the master under whose direction he had begun his life in God's service. The devil dangled before Beccel's mind the thought that if he were able to slay Guthlac, then afterwards he would have the saint's place and enjoy the highest respect of kings and princes.

So one day when this cleric had come to tonsure Guthlac, as he was acustomed to do every twenty days, he was suddenly seized with a mighty madness. Athirst with an uncontrollable lust for the blood of the man of God, he went right up to him to kill him. But the Lord was in the habit of granting the saint foreknowledge of the future, and so now Guthlac became aware of this new guilty sin and started to question the cleric. "O my dear Beccel, why do you harbor the old enemy in your foolish heart? Why don't you vomit out the deadly dose of bitter poison? For I know that you have been deceived by the evil spirit, so turn away from those disgraceful thoughts which the hateful calumniator of the human race has insinuated into your mind, and confess them."

Then the cleric, as soon as he understood that he had been seduced by the evil spirit, threw himself at the feet of the mighty hero, tearfully confessed his crime, and humbly prayed for pardon. Then Guthlac thereupon not only graciously granted forgiveness for the fault, but even promised to come to his aid in future tribulations too.

Chapter XXXVI: *How evil spirits terrified him one night in the shapes of various beasts.*

Since we have explained above how much the venerable Guthlac prevailed against those diabolic snares which were real and visible, now we shall go on to show how he overcame also the feigned frauds of the evil spirits. About this same time, one night when Guthlac was earnestly occupied with his accustomed prayers, he thought the whole island where he lived trembled all over with an enormous rumbling. Then after a short interval, suddenly he heard a noise like herds of cattle thundering together and bearing down on his house with a great shaking of the earth. Almost at the same instant he beheld a nightmare horde of many monstrous beasts come crashing through into his house from all directions. A roaring lion lunged at him savagely trying to tear him with bloodsmeared teeth. A bull bellowed in his face, as it tore up the earth with its hoofs and dug its gory horn into the ground. Then a bear, gnashing its teeth horribly, threatened to bash him as it swung either paw through the air with terrible power. And a serpent reached out its scaly neck and bared the deadly venom of its fangs.

To conclude in brief—a grunting boar, a howling wolf, a whinnying horse, a bellowing stag, a hissing snake, a lowing ox, a croaking raven, all raised an ear-splitting din of horrible noises to craze the true soldier of the true God. But Christ's servant had only contempt for spectres of this sort, and after arming his heart with the sign of salvation, spoke thus. "O most wretched Satan, it is so obvious how powerful you are. Are you now imitating the whinnying and grunting and croaking of miserable beasts, you who once attempted to liken yourself to the eternal God? Therefore I command you, in the name of Jesus Christ who banished you from heaven, to desist from this tumult." And on the instant the whole apparition vanished into the empty air, in less time than it takes to tell.[42]

42. St. Antony too was threatened by such a devilish menagerie (Athanasius [and Evagrius] *Vita S. Antonii*, *Ibid.*, 855-858). For the modern reader, C. S. Lewis has created the monstrous horror of a similar scene in *That Hideous Strength*, Ch. 16.

Chapter XXXVII : *How a raven dropped a written document into the midst of the swamp, and how the waters could not damage it.*

Another time it happened that a certain servant of God who had come to talk with Guthlac stayed as a guest on the island for some days. During this visit he was writing on some leaves of parchment one day, and when he came to the end of what he was writing he left the house and betook himself to his prayers in one of the oratories. Thereupon a certain raven who lived nearby hopped into the house of this guest, and as soon as he spied the manuscript he snapped it up at once in his beak. When the guest happened to glance outdoors he saw a bird flying off carrying a manuscript in his mouth. Then as soon as he discovered that his parchment was missing he realized that it was his own manuscript that had been carried off by the raven.

Now it chanced that at the same moment St. Guthlac was just coming out of his oratory, and noticing the dejection that had so suddenly descended on this brother, he tried to console him and promised that his document could be recovered for him with the help of Almighty God, without whose power no leaf is blown down from a tree and not a single sparrow falls to the ground. In the meantime they watched the bird fly off some distance to the south, and then dip down into the marshy scrub of the swamp where suddenly it disappeared from their sight as though it had vanished into oblivion. But St. Guthlac, his stout heart full of firm faith, bade the monk get into a skiff lying at the landing-place nearby and make his way in among the thick tangle of reeds where a passageway would disclose itself to him.

So the man followed out the saint's instructions and proceeded where the path led him. Then when he had arrived at one of the ponds that lay not far from the island, his gaze was caught by a reed close at hand sticking up above the surface in the very center of the pool. Its top was bent down and it was swaying from side to side with the rippling of the swamp water. And there, hanging perfectly balanced on the tip of the reed as though placed there by a human hand, were the parchment leaves. Marvelous to tell, it appeared that they were being touched by the lapping water and yet they were perfectly dry. So the monk snatched the document from the reed in a state of great astonishment and gave thanks to God. Then he returned to the house and paid his respectful thanks to the revered man of God for what had happened. But Guthlac insisted that what had transpired was due not to his merit but to God's tenderness of heart.

Chapter XXXVIII : *How he put up with the crows' mischief and how the birds and fishes of the swampy fenland came at his call.*

Now on this same island there were two crows who were so annoying and troublesome by nature that they would destroy anything which could be broken or dropped in the water, or torn in bits, or stolen, or soiled. Their urge to damage knew no respect for anything. For they would go into houses with the most brazen boldness like lawless looters and steal everything that they could find inside and out. Even the servant of God was subjected to their various annoyances and bore them with patience and piety, so that the example of his long-suffering was manifested not only among men but was displayed among birds and beasts as well. For the grace of his surpassing love for all creatures so abounded that the birds of the wild wasteland and the roving fishes of the swampy fen came swimming and flying at the sound of his voice as to a shepherd. They were even accustomed to take food from his hand, each the kind of food his nature required. However, not only did the creatures of earth and air obey his commands, but even the very air and water themselves obeyed this true servant of the true God. For it is no wonder that every creature should be obedient to the commands and wishes of him who faithfully and wholeheartedly served the Creator of them all. But too often we lose dominion over the creation which is subject to us, precisely because we neglect to serve the Lord of all creation, as it is written, "If you be willing, and will hearken to me, you shall eat the good things of the land," and so forth [Is. 1:19]. Likewise is it written, "If you have faith like a grain of mustard seed," and so forth [Mt. 17:19].

Chapter XXXIX : *How the swallows obeyed his behests.*[43]

There is also another spiritual miracle of Guthlac's which I would like to tell. It happened one day, that while he was talking with a very worthy man named Wilfrid, who had long been linked to Guthlac in the bonds of spiritual friendship and was a frequent visitor of his, quite unexpectedly two swallows suddenly flew into the house and without any hesitation perched on Guthlac's shoulders as though they had simply returned home. With wide-open beaks and throbbing throats, and every sign of great joy, they sang songs. Then as they chirruped and chattered along in their tuneful little voices they hopped about on his arms and knees and chest. Wilfrid of course was amazed, and bursting with curiosity, begged Guthlac's leave to speak about the matter. He asked how it was that these birds were so trusting as to come near him, since they were from the wild swampland and not at all used to being around human beings. But St. Guthlac answered and said, "Have you not read that with him who is united with God in a pure spirit all things are joined together in God? And that he who forsakes the companionship of men, seeks the companionship of animals and the friendship of angels. For while a man is enjoying the companionship of men he can hardly expect the companionship of angels."

Then he took a little basket and placed a straw in it. Reacting to this as though to a sign they had been trained to recognize, the birds straightway set about building a nest there. In the space of about an hour they had collected odd bits of rubbish and finished the nest. Then St. Guthlac stood up and fixed the basket in the arch of the roof and the birds began to live there as though they had acquired their own proper place of residence. Nor did they ever presume to select a place for their nesting without first consulting Guthlac's wishes. Each year they would come to the man of God and beg him to point out a place for their home. "Let no one consider it absurd to learn the nature of obedience from birds, for as Solomon says, 'Go to the ant, O sluggard, and consider her ways, and learn wisdom'"[44] [Prov. 6:6].

43. See note 21 to *Life of St. Cuthbert*.

44. Most of this sentence, including the quotation from Proverbs 6:6, comes from Bede's prose *Life of St. Cuthbert*, at the conclusion of Chapter 20.

Chapter XL: *How, while he was seated indoors, it was revealed to him in some mysterious manner that outside, some distance away, two gloves were being carried off by crows; and how he predicted that they would be returned within the hour.*

And there is the story of another particular miracle which I feel must be told, a miracle of Guthlac's foreknowledge. Now at that time there happened to be in exile a certain Aethelbald, of celebrated Mercian stock.[45] One day, in the company of the aforesaid Wilfrid, he came by boat to the island for a visit with the man of God, as he often did. But when Wilfrid went to the prow of the boat to jump ashore it seems that he left his gloves in the stern. They then went on to call on the holy man of God and after they had greeted each other and were conversing about various things, suddenly Guthlac, as though filled with the spirit of prophecy, inquired whether they had left anything in the boat. For though he was sitting inside the house and could see outside no further than the entrance, yet the Lord often revealed distant things to him. When Wilfrid answered that he had forgotten his two gloves and left them there, Guthlac announced that his crows now had possession of the gloves—as proved to be the case.

For they went outside at once, and there on the summit of the roof of one of the houses was a black robber of the raven race busily tearing at a glove with his impudent beak. After St. Guthlac reproved the bird in a gentle tone of voice, it abandoned the glove on top of the house and, like a fleeing fugitive ashamed of his crime, flew off into the west. Wilfrid managed to get the glove down from the rooftop on the tip of a pole, and then he began to worry about the loss of the other glove, realizing full well that so great a man had the power to

45. Chased into exile by the profligate young King Ceolred (see Ch. 49), Aethelbald could expect comfort from Guthlac not only as his kinsman in the blood royal but also as from one who himself had been an exile (Chs. 2 and 34). So did Wilfrid, exiled more than once himself, comfort two royal exiles (Eddius, *Life of Wilfrid*, Chs. 28, 42). And see note 21 to Introduction.

recover the second one for him just as he had the first. But Guthlac, perceiving that Wilfrid was taking the loss of the glove rather hard and that he was troubling his mind over it, set about cheering him with playful banter and assured him that God had the power to recover the lost article for him in no time at all if only their faith did not falter.

But to make a long story short, before Guthlac had even finished what he was saying, the signal for announcing visitors was sounded and three of the brethren were seen standing at the island landing place. Quicker than speech, Guthlac went to meet them, his face beaming cheerily as usual. For the grace of his exceeding love was always reflected in his speech and in his face. As soon as he had greeted the monks, one of them with a bow of his head begged pardon for their intrusion and explained that along the way he had chanced to find a glove which had been dropped from the claws of a crow, and then he showed the glove to the saint. Guthlac took it from the man's hand and smiled for a moment as he paid grateful homage in spirit to the graciousness and considerateness of God. Then he bade the brethren farewell and returned the glove to Wilfrid as he had promised.

Chapter XLI : *How he restored to health a man who had been tormented by an evil spirit for four years.*

About this same time, in the borderland of the East Angles, there happened to be a young man named Hwaetred who was—so the story goes—of illustrious lineage. Though he was living a life of daily dutifulness and respect for his parents, nevertheless, one day while he was at home, suddenly without any sign of warning, an evil spirit began to attack him with great violence. So terrible was the madness which afflicted him that he tore his own limbs with anything he could lay hands on—wood and iron, and with his own teeth and nails. Nor was it only himself who was wounded by his savage insanity, but everyone he could possibly reach was lacerated by his fierce teeth. He began to rage so violently that no attempts by anyone to restrain him or to bind him were successful. In fact, on one occasion when a crowd had gathered and a group of men attempted to bind him, he snatched up a well-filed double-bladed axe and with murderous blows stretched the dead bodies of three men on the ground.[46]

But after he had been ravaged for four full years by this dreaded scourge of madness, and the strength had been drained from his wasted and horribly emaciated body, finally he was taken by his parents to the sacred shrines of the saints to be bathed in the holy and healing waters by priests and bishops. But when none of them availed to extirpate the virulent venom of the deadly spirit, and after every sort of remedy had been tried and rejected, then at last they returned home.

But one day, when the grief-stricken parents had come to the point of wishing more for the death of their son than for his life, a report reached them of a hermit who dwelt on the isle of Crowland in the midst of the fen. His fame for miracles of many kinds was supposed to have spread far and wide through almost the whole of Britain. As soon as they learned this they definitely made up their minds and prepared to take the stricken youth thither at daybreak. So when the dull mists of night had been driven away and the sun had brought forth a golden dawn in the sky, they took their possessed son, with his limbs bound, and started out on their journey. When evening fell they turned aside to an island not far from Crowland and spent the night there. Then when day dawned they came to the landing place on Guthlac's island, sounded the signal, and begged to speak with the famous man.

He at once made himself available to them, radiating warmth as he always did from the glow of his great love. Then after they had told him their sad tale from its beginning, God's hero was filled with compassion for the parents' anxiety and for the miseries of all troubled humanity, and he straightway offered them the gracious love of his fatherly heart. Without delay he took the hand of the afflicted boy and led him inside the oratory, and there for three straight days Guth-

46. Felix gives us a terrifying glimpse of those axes that flashed so murderously on many an Anglo-Saxon and foreign battlefield. Like the figures on Keats' Grecian urn they can be seen on the Bayeux Tapestry, caught forever in the spell of this marvelous web of linen, threatening terrible blows that will never fall. See the superb color plates in *The Bayeux Tapestry*, edited by F. Stenton, *et. al.* (London, 1957).

lac prayed on his knees and fasted. On the third day at sunrise he washed the invalid with water from the sacred font, and then breathing into his face the breath of health he drove out all the power of the evil spirit from the boy. The young man, like one who has been brought safely into port out of the waves of a raging sea, drew long, shuddering sighs from deep in his heart, and he realized that lost health and strength were his again. Now from that time till the day of his death he suffered no further molestation or perturbation by the unclean spirit.

Chapter XLII : *How, quicker than a word is spoken, he freed a warrior from the torment of a foul fiend by giving him the cord he wore about his waist.*

On another occasion one of the exiled Aethelbald's warrior-companions, named Ecga, was so violently assailed by the terrible assaults of an evil spirit that he was no longer aware of who he was or where he lived or what it ever was that he was on the point of doing. The strength of his body and of his limbs remained unimpaired, but his power of speech, of discussion, and of understanding failed him completely. His relatives feared that he would become incurably insane; so one day they brought him to the hermitage of the heroic Guthlac. There, no sooner had he girded himself with the saint's waistband than he felt all the madness reft from him and his mind restored to him whole and sound. And he wore that belt ever after so that to the last day of his life he was nevermore molested by Satan.

Chapter XLIII : *How he discovered and made known a fault committed by a certain abbot's servants even though they were far away.*

Among other things God's hero, Guthlac, began to grow strong in the spirit of prophecy—predicting future events, and recounting to persons around him things happening at a distance. For example, one time a certain abbot decided to come and talk with Guthlac, as he often did. After he had set out on the trip, two of his servants, pleading some feigned reason as an excuse, asked the abbot's leave to turn off and go by another route dictated by the reason they had alleged. Granting them permission, the abbot continued on his way.

But after he had arrived for his conversation with Guthlac, and they were refreshing each other with deep draughts of Holy Scripture, St. Guthlac began to question him in the midst of their conversation. "Why did those two clerics (whom he mentioned by name) not wish to accompany you hither as they have been in the custom of doing?" The abbot explained that they had obtained his permission to go by another way because of something else they needed to do. But St. Guthlac, for whom the Lord made distant things present by divine inspiration, bent his head for a moment and turned his face away, smiling. Now since the abbot perceived that obviously a different story had been revealed to the man of God, he humbly asked him, and even besought him in Jesus' name, to disclose clearly what had been shown him about the pair.

Then Guthlac gave in to the humble entreaties of this friend who was joined to him by a spiritual bond in Christ, and began to trace out for him each step of his men's journey. He said that the pair of them had turned aside to the house of a certain widow, and though it was not yet the third hour of the day, had proceeded to get drunk at her sumptuous table.[47] Not only did Guthlac recount their journey from its beginning but he even described their food and conversation in detail. For this had been shown him by divine power, just as the knowledge of the theft by Giezi had been granted to Eliseus by divine disclosure [cf. IV (II) Kings, 5:25]. So strong was the spirit of divine grace in him that he perceived distant and future things as though they were present. The abbot, therefore, after he had received some

47. A typical bluff and hearty English touch which we meet again at the Tabard Inn, and at the Boar's Head in Eastcheap. A proper Antonine temptation would have involved some seductive siren. The "third hour of the day" is a humorous reference to Acts, 2:15. In one of his letters St. Boniface complains that drunkenness seems to be a vice peculiarly Germanic (Emerton, *Letters of St. Boniface*, p. 141).

salutary instruction from the worshipful Guthlac, wended his way home again.

But when the two clerics in question next met up with the abbot, as they often did in the course of their household duties, he had them sit down in his office, and ordered everyone else to leave. Then he asked them where they had delayed so long the day before. "False face hiding what false heart did know," they said that they had lingered in the house of a friend of theirs. But the abbot answered that someone had informed him that they had been in the widow's house, and he mentioned her by name. But the pair contradicted him with the utmost insolence and denied everything he said. Checking their impudence, the abbot presented them with clear evidence of their guilt and ordered them to confess. Finally, since they were unable to "kick against the goad" [Acts, 9:5] of this known evidence, the two threw themselves on the floor and confessed to every detail of their journey, exactly as Guthlac had already described it.

Chapter XLIV : *How to two clerics who had come visiting him he disclosed their hiding of a pair of flasks along the way.*

About this same time two of the brethren from a certain monastery came one day to hear St. Guthlac's teaching, for by then the remarkable reputation of so great a man had spread everywhere. Now when they had arrived at the island they had with them two full flasks of beer, and after talking the matter over between themselves they hid the flasks by the wayside in some gravel in the marsh so that when they set out for home again this supply would serve to lighten their journey. Meantime they proceeded to enjoy the verbal refreshment offered by the holy hermit.

After he had instructed them awhile in salutary spiritual doctrine, his cheerful face broke out into an easy smile and he asked them banteringly in passing, "My dear sons, why didn't you wish to bring those two flasks here which you have hidden away in the ground under some marsh underbrush?" At this the astonished pair were thunderstruck and bowed down on the ground, praying pardon for the offense committed. But St. Guthlac, putting his hands under their chins and lifting up their faces, granted them pardon, assured them of his friendship, and blessed them for the journey.

Chapter XLV: *How the report of his miracles spread to the borders of Britain, and how a warrior was healed by the touch of his garment.*

It was also during these same times that many different people of various ranks of society flocked to see God's hero—abbots, lay brothers, warriors, the wealthy, the afflicted, the poor—not just from the land of the Mercians nearby but even from the more distant districts of Britain, one and all, drawn thither by the fame of his miracles. Everyone, no matter what the need that drove him, hoped for comfort from this man of such great holiness: those who were tormented by sickness of body, or by the possession of evil spirits, or by the need of acknowledging mistakes committed, or by reason of other punishments of whatever nature from which the human race needs freeing. Nor did the hopes of any of these people prove illusory. For from Guthlac no sick man went away without relief; no one distressed, without assistance; no one sad, without joy; no one weary, without encouragement; no one sorrowing, without comfort; no one worried, without counsel. So strong was Guthlac in real love that he bore the burdens of one and all alike.

Now it happened that among all these multitudes who for different reasons were flocking in from every part of the land to speak with the saint, there came for that same purpose one of the followers of the above-mentioned exile, Aethelbald. This retainer, whose name was Ofa,[48] had been wandering through the country fields of a boon companion of his one day, and as he was walking through some thorny

48. Ofa was rewarded for staying with his lord in exile because shortly after Aethelbald became king we see Ofa signing himself to a charter as the king's *minister* (see note 24 to Introduction) and later as ealdorman (Whitelock, *English Historical Documents*, pp. 449–50). For further examples of such Anglo-Saxon loyalty see D. Whitelock, *Beginnings of English Society* (Pelican History of England, Vol. II, 1952) pp. 31 ff.

places he trod heavily on a thorn lying hidden under the weeds of some uncultivated ground. The thorn drove into the center of his sole and pierced right through the whole structure of his foot, tearing its way in as far as the ankle. However, despite his failing strength, he continued on with the journey he had begun, and with the most extreme difficulty reached the island in which God's hero waged his warfare for the Lord. After he had passed one night there, a good half of his body, from the loins to the soles of his feet, puffed up with an inflamed swelling. He was so racked with the torture of this fresh pain that he could neither sit nor stand nor lie. All his joints were inflamed, and excruciating burning seared the very marrow of his bones, till he seemed more like a dying man than a sick man.

When Guthlac was told of this he ordered the sufferer brought to him. Then as soon as he had heard the cause of the affliction explained from its beginning, the man of God took off the sheepskin coat that he was accustomed to wear at prayer and wrapped it around the sick man. At once, quicker than a word is spoken, at the very moment when he felt himself wrapped in the saint's garment the thorn was dislodged from his foot like an arrow shot from a bow, and landed as far away as if it had been thrown. At the same time all the violently inflamed swelling quitted the joints of all his limbs, and he stood up forthwith and began to walk on his healed foot.

The next day, after speaking with Guthlac, he went on his way with a happy heart and without any impairment of his health, he who had bid fair to lose his whole body because of the sickness of one member. Then all who had been present to witness this miracle marveled at the strong faith of God's hero and gave glory to the Lord.

Chapter XLVI : *How by the gift of foreknowledge he repeated to Wigfrith words which the latter had uttered while absent from him.*

There is another particular miracle of Guthlac's prophetic prescience which I would not like to leave out. With divine largesse he had been granted the gift of seeing the words of those absent as though they were written down before his eyes, and of understanding the thoughts of those present as though they had been spoken aloud. Now when a certain bishop named Headda came, as though inspired by divine counsel, to converse with Guthlac, he had with him in his retinue a bookish man named Wigfrith, who was riding along in the company of the other servants of the bishop. Some of those around him began talking of the marvelous virtues and miracles of the heroic Guthlac, others discussed the saint's unflagging austerity of life and miracles worked by him which no one else had yet heard of;[49] others broke into argument questioning whose power it was in which he worked those miracles.

But Wigfrith assured them all that if he could just see the man, he would be able to determine definitely whether he were a true priest of the divine religion or a fake pretender of sham sanctity. He declared that he himself had lived amongst the Irish[50] and that there he had seen counterfeit anchorites, posing to be of various religions, who he found out could really predict the future and work other miracles, but by what power he knew not. He said that there were also priests of the true religion among the Irish and that they too were powerful workers of signs and miracles. And since he had been in the habit of visiting them frequently and talking with them, he assured the company that what he had learned from these holy men would enable him to detect the religion of imposters.

And so this bishop Headda arrived for his visit with the worshipful man of God and, after exchanging fraternal greetings, they began to pour out for each other most liberal libations of Scriptural nectar. And indeed the splendor of divine grace in God's hero was so brilliant that whatever he said in sermons or instructions seemed expressed by the mouth of an angel. There was in him such a wealth of wisdom that whatever he said he confirmed by examples from the divine Scriptures.

49. In some way like this were the traditional heroic poems created. One such is composed on Beowulf's deeds by a skillful thegn while a group of warriors are riding back from the fen pool into which the monster has slunk, mortally wounded by Beowulf (vv. 867 ff.).

50. And so had many Anglo-Saxon students, noble and commoner alike (Bede, *Ecclesiastical History*, Bk. III, ch. 27). Willibrord spent twelve years there (Alcuin, *Life of Willibrord*, Ch. 4).

Chapter XLVII: *How he received the order of priesthood from Bishop Headda.*[51]

After the aforesaid bishop then had partaken of Guthlac's conversation and had savored the lessons of his wisdom, sweeter than honey, all of a sudden in the midst of their talk he humbly bowed his head and begged Guthlac to receive priestly orders at his hands. Guthlac, naturally unwilling to refuse such a plea by the bishop, fell prostrate before him forthwith and promised to obey the bishop's wishes. The bishop then rose up with joy in his heart and, after first hallowing the little church, consecrated Guthlac to the most high God as a faithful priest.

After the ordination ceremonies were completed, God's hero was prevailed upon at the bishop's request to come to a special dinner that day, contrary to his custom. Then when the dishes were served and the company was about to begin the meal, St. Guthlac looked at the above-mentioned Wigfrith, seated some distance away, and said to him, "O brother Wigfrith, now what do you think of that cleric whom yesterday you promised to judge?" Utterly astonished at this, Wigfrith got up from his place and impulsively threw himself at full length on the floor before Guthlac, and humbly prayed for pardon, confessing that he had sinned. All present were astounded and began to look at each other in stunned amazement. Then St. Guthlac said, "Verify this for yourselves by asking one another whether any of you has told me about this matter." This consecration of the island of Crowland and the ordination of the blessed Guthlac to the priestly office took place in the autumn, five days before the day when the Mass of St. Bartholomew is customarily celebrated.[52]

51. Since Headda was Bishop of Lichfield, historians point to this ordination as an indication of the subordination of Lindsey (old kingdom in which Crowland lay) to Mercia at this period (Stenton, *Anglo-Saxon England*, p. 49).

52. August 21. See Chapters 25, 27.

Chapter XLVIII : *How to Ecgburh's question about his successor he is supposed to have answered that the heir who would come after him was at the moment still a pagan.*

On another occasion in the course of the passing years, the most reverend virgin of the virgins and spouses of Christ, the Abbess Ecgburh, daughter of King Aldwulf,[53] sent to the worshipful hero Guthlac, most exalted in merit, a leaden coffin and a linen cloth folded up in it and asked that it be kept for the burial of the man of God. In fact she begged him by the revered and awful name of the heavenly King. Stretching herself out in the shape of the gallows tree of the cross, with arms extended in token of humble petition, she begged him to accept the gift for the purpose indicated. She sent another faithful brother as messenger, bidding him make this same sign of humble entreaty in the presence of Guthlac. She likewise instructed him to ask the man of God who would inherit the hermitage after his death.

Guthlac, after gratefully accepting the substantial gift of the holy nun, is said to have replied to her question by saying that the heir of his hermitage was still among a pagan people and had not yet approached the baptisimal font, but that it would shortly come to pass. And that he had spoken in the spirit of prophecy was proved by the outcome of the future affair. For the very Cissa who in our day holds the hermitage of God's hero Guthlac, received baptism some years later in Britain, as he himself often tells it.

Chapter XLIX : *How he cheered an exile who came to him, and foretold that the kingdom would soon be his.*

It is pleasant to recount also a particular case of spiritual prescience by the prophetic heart of Guthlac the hero. It happened at the time

53. King Aldwulf was the father of the King Aelfwald for whom Felix wrote this *Life of St. Guthlac* (see note 1).

while Aethelbald, that exile whom we mentioned above, was being harried from place to place, nation to nation, King Ceolred[54] ever in pursuit. One day when his endurance and that of his followers had been worn thin by the anxious strain of many perils, and their strength had come to an end, he went for one of his frequent talks with St. Guthlac, hoping that divine counsel might appear now that human counsel had failed. Then while he was talking with Guthlac, that blessed hero of God began to unfold the future to him in detail, speaking as though divinely inspired.

"My dear son, your sufferings I know full well, and all those tribulations of yours from the very beginning of your life are only too familiar to me. And because your misfortune has touched my heart I have entreated the Lord in his graciousness to come to your aid. Now he has heard me and has granted you the rulership of your race and has made you lord of your land, and the necks of your enemies he will bow down beneath your heel, and you shall win their wealth and you shall look on the backs of those who hate you fleeing from your face, and your sword shall fell your foes.[55] Therefore take heart, because the Lord is your helper. But be patient, lest you fall into a course which cannot be supported. For your kingdom is not to be given you by rapine and plunder, but you shall receive it from the hand of God. Wait for him whose days have run out because the hand of the Lord lies heavy on him, whose hope was placed in wickedness, and whose days shall pass away like a shadow."[56]

From the time that Guthlac spoke thus to him, Aethelbald placed his hope in the Lord. And that hope proved not to be vain, for every single thing that the man of God foretold happened in exactly that same order and detail, as is proved by the way things have turned out up to the present.

54. See Eddius, *Life of Wilfrid*, Ch. 64, and notes 132, 119.

55. The extent to which this prophecy came true is indicated by the grand titles given Aethelbald in Charters (see Whitelock, *English Historical Documents*, p. 453).

56. Ceolred, son of King Aethelred, despite the high hopes he raised in Wilfrid at the beginning of his short reign (Eddius, *Life of Wilfrid*, Ch. 64), was a dissolute ruler (see note 119 to *Life of Wilfrid*). Boniface wrote of a visionary who saw Ceolred in hell (Emerton, *Letters of St. Boniface*, p. 30).

Chapter L : *How he endured many temptations in his last illness and what instructions he gave for his burial; how he committed his last wishes to his sister, and how he breathed forth his spirit mingled with the words of prayer.*[57]

But since mankind from the very beginning of its tragic mortality "creeps in this petty pace from day to day" toward death, and with the departing years generations and kingdoms also pass away, thus it is that though we all differ in our merits and punishments and rewards yet the same end waits for all of us alike, master and servant, learned and unlearned, young and old.[58] For as death was bequeathed us in Adam, so will it have dominion over us all. For whoever has tasted the sweetness of our life, cannot escape the bitterness of death.

And so it happened in the course of things that after the beloved Guthlac, God's man, had lived as an anchorite for thrice-five cycles of years in devoted service to the King of heaven, then the Lord Jesus decided to take up his servant out of the wearisome vassalage of this life into the repose of eternal blessedness. One day when he had remained in his oratory wholly occupied with his prayers, he was suddenly gripped by a spasm inside his body, and then as soon as God's hero felt a sudden seizure of deathly faintness came over him, he realized

57. Felix took much of the following description of Guthlac's death from Bede's account of Cuthbert's death (prose *Life of St. Cuthbert*, Chs. 37-39). See note 70 to Introduction.

58. Elegiac laments such as this have a long literary history. But somehow Anglo-Saxon poetry seems to be charged with this *lacrimae rerum* theme in a special way, perhaps because of the prevalence of exile as an emotional factor in this aristocratic Heroic Age world (see note 21 to Introduction), perhaps because everywhere on the island were the Roman ruins of a dead empire (which contributed a good deal even to Thomas Hardy's elegiac mood—e. g., Ch. 11 in *The Mayor of Casterbridge*), and perhaps because out of the now-vanished extent of pagan poetry it would have been sentiments like these which would have marked some poems for preservation in monastic libraries. There is a deep similarity between the plaintive note of the Anglo-Saxon elegies and that of the Hebrew Psalms. And see Kennedy, *The Earliest English Poetry*, Ch. 4.

at once that the Lord had laid his hand upon him. Thereupon, singing in his heart, he set about getting ready for the happiness of the eternal kingdom. For seven days the deadly illness ravaged him, and on the eighth day he reached his end.

Now it was on the Wednesday before Easter that he had taken ill, and eight days later it was again on a Wednesday, the fourth day of the Easter festival, that his illness ran its course and he departed to go to the Lord. One monk, named Beccel, was living with him at this time and it is from his account that we have recorded our description of the death of God's hero. He had come to Guthlac on that very day when the illness had first struck him, and when he had begun to ask the saint about various things, as he always did, Guthlac was slow to answer and finally dragged the words out with a sigh. The monk said to him, "My lord, has anything happened to you? Did some attack of illness strike you this past night?" "Yes," Guthlac answered, "some attack of illness did strike me this night." Then the brother asked, "My father, do you know the reason for your illness? What do you think will be the end of this spell of sickness?" The man of God replied, "My son, the reason for my sickness is so that the spirit may be separated from this body, and the end of my illness will be on the eighth day, on which day I shall have completed the course of this life and must 'be dissolved and be with Christ' [Phil. 1:23]. For one must cast off the burden of the flesh to follow the Lamb of God." When he heard this the brother wept and sighed and watered his sad cheeks with streams of tears. To console him, God's hero said, "My son, do not be at all sad. It is not painful for me to go to eternal rest with my Lord whom I have served." For so great was his faith that death, which to all other mortals seems a fearful and terrible thing, he thought of as repose or as reward for toil.

Meanwhile the slow hours had grown into four days, and Easter Sunday arrived. Despite his failing strength God's hero arose, and after offering the Sacrifice of the Lord's body and drinking the libation of Christ's blood, he proceeded to explain the Gospels to this same brother who testifies that never before or since has he heard such profound wisdom from the mouth of any one. Finally when the seventh day of his illness had arrived the brother visited him about the sixth hour and found him lying in a corner of his oratory facing the altar.

But Guthlac did not speak with him because the gravity of his illness had robbed him of the power of speech. After a while, to the brother's entreaty that he leave some last words with him before he died, God's hero straightened up his wasted body for a moment away from the wall against which he was lying, and said with a sigh, "My son, the time is now at hand, so listen to my last wishes. After the spirit has abandoned this poor body of mine go to my sister Pega and tell her that the reason I saw so little of her in this life was so that we could see each other forever in the everlasting happiness of Our Father. Tell her also to place my body in the coffin and wrap it in the linen which Ecgburh sent me. It is true that I didn't want to clothe my body in any linen while I was alive, but for the love of this dear daughter of Christ I have carefully saved the gifts she sent me to wrap my dead body in."

In reply to these words of Guthlac, the brother said, "My father I know how very ill you are, and that you are even dying as I listen to you speaking, so I beg you to tell me one thing which has disturbed me for a long time and which I have never dared to ask you about. For from the time that I first began to live with you I have heard you talking morning and evening with someone, I know not who. So I beseech you not to leave me worried about this thing after your death."

Then, after a short while, God's man breathed heavily and said, "My son, do not be troubled about this thing. For I shall reveal to you what I did not want any man to know while I was alive. From the second year that I began to dwell in this hermitage the Lord has sent an angel to be my consolation and to speak with me every morning and evening. He has revealed mysteries to me which it is not lawful for man to tell, he has softened the harshness of my life with messages from heaven, and he has revealed distant things to me, putting them before me as though done in my presence. O son, guard these words of mine and tell them to no one else except Pega, or Ecgberht the anchorite if you should ever have occasion to speak with him, for he alone will understand that these things so happened." He finished speaking[59] and, leaning his head back against the wall, drew a long sigh from the very depths of his being. But after he had breathed

59. Felix's *Dixerat* here is one of many contributions to the epic formality of the passage's Latin.

very heavily for a short while, his spirit revived again, and it seemed as though the perfume of honey-laden blossoms issued from his mouth and filled the whole house with the scent of nectar.

Then, in the course of that night, while the brother was attending to his nocturnal prayers, he saw the whole house aglow with a fiery radiance that lasted from midnight until dawn. Then when the sun rose, God's hero raised himself up for a short while almost as though he intended to get on his feet, and began to speak with the brother. "My son, get ready to go on your journey, for time is now pressing me to be loosed from this body; my spirit has run the course in the race of this life and is impatient to be borne to those joys whose course has no ending." As he finished speaking, he reached his hand over to the altar and fortified himself with the Communion of Christ's body and blood, then raising his eyes to heaven and lifting his hands on high, he released his soul to the joys of perpetual bliss.

Meanwhile the brother had watched the house inundated with a sudden splendor of heavenly light, and had seen something like a tower of fire reaching from earth to the sky, and compared with whose brilliance the sun, now in mid-heaven, seemed pale as a lamp in daylight. And he heard angels sing till the whole vault of the sky reverberated as with thunder, while he perceived the island to be laden with the fragant breath of different spices. Then the brother, shaken by a formless fear and unable to bear the brilliance of the incredible shining, took a skiff and pulling away from the landing place set out on that journey whither God's hero had bade him go.

Coming therefore to the holy virgin of Christ, Pega, he recounted to her in order all the behests of her brother. But when she had heard them she collapsed as though fallen headlong from a height, and as she lay on the ground she was consumed to the very marrow of her bones by the great violence of her grief; her tongue was still, her lips were mute, and all her life force ebbed away as though she were dead. After a little space of time, as though awakened out of a dream she drew long sighs from the depths of her heart, and gave thanks for the will of the Almighty. The following day they came to the island according to the injunctions of the blessed man, and found the whole place and all the buildings full of fragrance like that of ambrosia. For the space of three days that handmaid of God commended the soul of her brother to heaven in prayers and hymns, and on the third day she buried that blessed body in his oratory according to his wish and covered it with earth.

Chapter LI : *How after twelve months his body was found to be incorrupt.*

But then God in his graciousness desired to make more widely known the greatness of the glory in which the holy hero dwelt after his death, and so in the same way that He had previously manifested the splendor of his life far and wide among peoples, tribes and nations by means of numerous extraordinary miracles, so now He provided a similar proof of His continuing eternal regard for the saint. For after a period of twelve months had gone by since his burial, God put it into the mind of Guthlac's sister to rebury her brother's body in another grave. So on the anniversary of his burial, before a number of brothers and priests and other ecclesiastics of various ranks, his coffin was opened and his whole body found to be intact. It was as though he were still alive. The joints of his limbs were so pliant and flexible that he seemed much more like one asleep than dead. And all the garments he was clothed in were not only untainted but still shone with their first newness and original brightness. As soon as all present caught sight of this they shook in their shoes and were so astonished they scarcely could speak; they hardly dared look upon the miracle and knew not what to do.

When Christ's handmaid, Pega, perceived all this her soul was stirred with joy and, while the hymns and prayers of the Church were chanted in his honor, she wrapped the sacred body again in the cloth which the anchorite Ecgberht had sent for this purpose while Guthlac was still living.[60] However, she did not put the coffin in the earth but rather in a special tomb which today we see built up and decorated by King Aethelbald with marvelous ornamented work in reverence for the divine power. There in blessedness the triumphant body of the

60. In Ch. 48 the burial cloth was presented by Abbess Ecgburh. Perhaps there was a copyist's mistake in an early unrecorded manuscript.

great hero rests to this very day,[61] and by his intercession anyone who pleads in honest faith will experience the graciousness of divine compassion.

O hero of blessed memory, O master of divine grace, O vessel of honor, O physician of salvation, O herald of truth, O treasure of wisdom! O what richness and grandeur in word and speech was his! How prompt and proficient he was in settling disputes! How quickly and capably he solved problems in Scripture! With how unremitting a service he attended on God, so that naught was found in his heart but loyalty, nothing in his soul but love, peace, mercy, and compassion. No one ever saw him angry, nor arrogant, nor proud, nor disturbed, nor depressed; but he was always the same, cheerful of face, gracious in speech, of a pleasant mind, of a prudent disposition, humble of heart, so that to friends and strangers alike his nature seemed more than human.

Chapter LII : *How after his death he appeared to Aethelbald and by signs revealed to him things that were to come.*

When the aforementioned Aethelbald, the exile, dwelling in distant districts, heard of the death of the blessed father Guthlac who had been the sole refuge and consolation of his tribulations he was seized straightway with grief and made his way to the saint's corpse, hoping to be granted in the Lord some easing of his burden by the intercession of so great a hero as Guthlac. When he approached the sepulchre he said through his tears, "My father, you know my afflictions, you have always helped me. While you were alive I never despaired in my distress; you were by my side through many dangers. Through you I called on the Lord and he set me free. But now whither shall I turn my face, and whence will there be help for me? Who will offer me counsel, most excellent father, if you abandon me? Who will console me? In you have I hoped, nor has the hope played me false."

61. The Latin word Felix uses here (*triumphale*—"triumphant"; and see ch. 10) to describe the body of his hero (*tanti viri*) is a special term referring to the victory celebration staged for a victorious Roman general, and hence adds a further epic quality to the passage. See Introduction, pp. 23 ff. and note 64.

With these words and others like them he cast himself full length on the ground and humbly prayed as he bathed all his face in a flood of tears. Then when the shades of evening had fallen and his mind tossed and turned in a "restless ecstasy" of gloom, he went to spend the night in the hut where Guthlac had always put him up as a guest. A little while after he had finished his evening prayers and when his heavy eyes had had their way and he was dozing, suddenly he was shocked awake by a burst of extraordinarily brilliant light which lit up all the cell where he was lying. But even as he trembled with the first shock of this mysterious vision he perceived that the blessed Guthlac was standing before him robed in angel glory, and that he was speaking to him.

"Have no fear, be of stout heart, for God is your helper. I have come to you because the Lord, at my request, has heard your prayers. Be not sad, for the days of your sorrow are past, and the end of your troubles is at hand. For before the sun has completed twelve of its yearly revolutions around the globe, you shall be handed the scepter of your kingdom." They say, moreover, that Guthlac not only foretold his kingship, but revealed the course of his life in detail and the manner of its ending.[62] Then Aethelbald replied to him, "My lord, what sign will there be to assure me that everything is going to happen this way?" Guthlac answered, "Your sign will be this: This morning before the third hour of the day those who live in this place will receive a timely gift of food from an unlooked-for source."

As the holy man said this, the light which had appeared before Aethelbald vanished from his sight. And with no delay the deed followed hard upon the word, for before the third hour of the day arrived the sound of the signal at the landing-stage was heard and men could be seen there carrying the unlooked-for supplies. From that time on, Aethelbald kept in his heart all that Guthlac had said to him, and believed "with a most absolute trust" that all those things would come to pass. He anchored an immovable faith in the prophecies of God's hero, and that faith did not deceive him. For from then until the present

62. It is hard to believe Guthlac revealed to Aethelbald that he would actually be murdered by his own bodyguard (see account of the year 757 in Simeon of Durham, *Historia Regum*, translated in Whitelock, *English Historical Documents*, p. 241). And see note 63.

day the sceptered fortune of his reign has grown from day to day through the succeeding years.[63]

Chapter LIII : *How after Guthlac's death a blind man was healed with salt that the saint had blessed.*

Nor with Guthlac's death and burial have the signs of miracles and wondrous healings ceased to shine forth everywhere to the present day, those same signs which the Lord had granted to men while the saint was yet living. While living he was reluctant to glorify himself with a pretentious reputation for miracles, but after his death the greatness of his merits and of his power was revealed by the monuments of his many miracles.[64]

For instance, there was the case of a father of a family in the province of Wissa whose eyes had lost the power of sight and after a period of twelve months had become so coated with a cloudy yellowish film that he could no longer distinguish the bright light of day from the black darkness of night. After trying applications of ointments to no avail, he despaired of finding a remedy and finally learned that he was threatened with permanent loss of sight. Then he thought of a happy plan, and asked to be taken to the most blessed body of God's hero, Guthlac. "I know for certain and am confident that if any object which he has blessed touches my eyes I shall straightway be healed and sight shall return to my eyes."

His friends thereupon did as he had asked; they brought him by boat to the landing-place on the island of Crowland and asked to speak

63. Aethelbald's long reign saw him become one of the most powerful of Anglo-Saxon kings but not without a touch of tyranny (Stenton, *Anglo-Saxon England*, pp. 202 ff.). This latter, plus the open scandal of his private life for which St. Boniface rebuked him (see Whitelock, *English Historical Documents*, pp. 751 ff.), may very possibly account for his eventual murder in 757.

64. In likening Guthlac's miracles to "monuments" Felix uses again a special Latin term to extend a final epic tone to his story and intensify the hero-saint fusion (a *tropheum* was a Roman trophy or monument awarded for a military victory). See note 61.

with the revered virgin of Christ, Pega. She recognized his fervent faith and unwavering hope and permitted him to be led into the oratory where the body of the blessed Guthlac lay. She also took a lump of glutinous salt which had previously been blessed by Guthlac and scraped off a little of it into some water. Then when they let this water trickle, drop by drop, between the eyelids of the blind man, marvelous to tell, at the touch of the first drop the clouds of blindness were forced away and light poured back into his eyes. In fact even before they had poured the healing water between the eyelids of the second eye he had described in detail everything in the house and announced that sight had been given him in that very same moment. Then, after grace had graciously opened the long-closed windows of his face, and he realized that the light he once had lost had been found again, he became the leader of those who had led him, and returned home. After drawing light from the fountain of light he returned whence he came but he did not return just as he had been, and he saw those who saw him whom previously he had been unable to see. And to God he paid that fitting thanks which all know how to give.

LIVES
OF THE ABBOTS

---

by Bede

Preface to Bede's LIVES OF THE ABBOTS

Bede, who spent most of his life quietly at Jarrow (the story of whose founding he tells in his *Lives of the Abbots*), is one of the outstanding figures of the whole medieval period . . . "a man not only unique in himself, but the most important forerunner of the Carolingian Revival" (Laistner, *Intellectual Heritage of the Early Middle Ages*, p. 94). In his Northumbrian monastery on the North Sea (and we think back 200 years to Cassiodorus, in his monastery on the Ionian Sea, directing the transcribing of vital western manuscripts, of which at least one famous copy was to make its way to Bede's monastery—see note 44 to *Life of Ceolfrith*) he studied the precious books that Benedict Biscop, the main "hero" of this biography, had brought back from all over the battered seventh-century West, and then in clear, fluent Latin, sometimes eloquent and always remarkably sane, he poured back into the depleted bloodstream of Europe the basic elements of her Roman cultural heritage. His sanity is still relevant. "There is no period in the history of Britain in which Bede is antiquated. . . . No author in the Dark Ages has so little of the 'Gothic' qualities that offended the enlightenment of the Renaissance" (W. P. Ker, *The Dark Ages* [London, 1904] p. 141).

Good studies of Bede are available in Duckett, *Anglo-Saxon Saints and Scholars*, Ch. 3; R. W. Chambers, *Man's Unconquerable Mind* (London, 1939), Ch. 1; *Bede: His Life, Times, and Writings*, edited by A. H. Thompson (Oxford, 1935), whose essay by M. Laistner on Bede's library is reprinted in Laistner's *The Intellectual Heritage of the Early Middle Ages* (Cornell University, 1957), pp. 117-149, along with another important study by Laistner, "Bede as a Classical and a Patristic Scholar" (pp. 93-116).

He finished his greatest book, the *Ecclesiastical History of the English People* (still our major source for the history of England before 732) within a few months of the battle in which Charlemagne's grandfather turned back the Saracen flood from France. It has survived in many manuscripts (see M. Laistner, *A Hand-list of Bede Manuscripts* [Cornell, 1943]). Two of the best of them, including the Leningrad Ms., which some scholars believe to have a note in Bede's own hand (see Dekkers and Gaar, *Clavis Patrum Latinorum*, p. 309; and see objections by David Wright in *Revue Bénédictine*, 71 [1961], pp. 265-73), have recently been published in facsimile (*Early English Manuscripts in Facsimile*, Copenhagen. Vol. II, 1952, the Leningrad Ms.; Vol. IX, 1959, the Moore Ms.). The best available edition of the book, though it did not make use of the Leningrad Ms., is in Charles Plummer's *Venerabilis Baedae Opera Historica* (Oxford, 1896. Reprinted in 1946 as two vols. in one). It also contains (I, 364-387) the text of Bede's *Lives of the Abbots* from which I made the present translation. Bertram Colgrave and R. A. B. Mynors are preparing a much needed new edition and translation of the *Ecclesiastical History*. P. H. Blair has an interesting lecture, *Bede's Ecclesiastical History of the English Nation and its Importance Today*, published at Newcastle, 1959.

A useful companion to Bede's *History* is P. F. Jones' *A Concordance to the Historia Ecclesiastica of Bede* (Mediaeval Academy of America, 1929). New editions of Bede's various works are currently appearing among the *Corpus Christianorum* series published by Brepols in Turnhout. Bertram Colgrave is preparing a new edition of Bede's *Life of St. Felix* (see *Patrologia Latina*, 94,789-798). Convenient translations of Bede's *History* are available in the Everyman's Library (No. 479) and in the Penguin Classics (L 42). A good portion of it is translated in Whitelock, *English Historical Documents*, pp. 587-686. The Everyman's Library volume also contains a translation of Bede's *Lives of the Abbots* and his prose *Life of St. Cuthbert*.

BEDE: LIVES OF THE ABBOTS

Chapter I

THE DEVOUT servant of Christ, Biscop, named Benedict,[1] was inspired by divine grace to build a monastery in honor of the most blessed Peter, Prince of the Apostles, near the mouth of the River Wear on the north side. The land was contributed by Ecgfrith,[2] the respected and very religious king of that nation, who also assisted in other ways with the construction. Benedict then, with diligence and with the same piety which had prompted him to build the monastery, ruled it for sixteen years that were filled with the tribulations of travel and of illness. If I may use the words with which the blessed Pope Gregory praised the life of the abbot of this same name [i. e., Benedict of Nursia], "Both in grace and in name Benedict was a man of worshipful life. From the very days of his boyhood he thought like a man, his manners and habits were older than his years, he gave himself over to no idle pleasure-seeking."[3]

He was descended from a noble family among the Angles, but by no less a nobility of mind he was found worthy to be forever raised into the society of angels.[4] In fact though he served as a soldier in the personal *comitatus*[5] of King Oswy[6] and was rewarded with a landed estate befitting his rank, yet at about the age of twenty-five [i. e., about

1. For his Anglo-Saxon patronymic, Baducing, see Eddius, *Life of Wilfrid*, Ch. 3.
2. See note 37 to *Life of St. Cuthbert.*
3. Gregory, *Dialogues*, Bk. II, ch. 1.
4. Bede's pun on "angels" and "Angles" echoes Pope Gregory's famous play on these words (see Bede, *Ecclesiastical History*, Bk. II, ch. 1; and see note 12 to Introduction).
5. See notes 2 and 24 to Introduction, and note 35 to *Life of St. Cuthbert.*
6. See notes 14 and 24 to *Life of St. Cuthbert.*

653] he abandoned property bounded by time in order to acquire an eternal estate.[7] He turned his back on earthly military service with its reward of gifts tainted with time in order that he might serve as a soldier of the true King and thus win an everlasting kingdom in the heavenly city. He left home and kindred and country for the sake of Christ and the Gospel, that he might receive the hundredfold and possess eternal life. He refused to pay court to marriage of the flesh so as to have the power to follow the Lamb, robed in the white glory of virginity in the Kingdom of Heaven. He declined to father mortal children in the flesh, predestined as he was by Christ to raise immortal sons for Him in heaven by his spiritual teaching.

Chapter II

So he left his country behind him and went to Rome[8] where he took pains to do what he had long burned with desire to do—see with his bodily eyes the shrines of the bodies of the blessed apostles and pray in their presence. Then from the moment he returned home he never passed up an occasion of speaking enthusiastically, to all who would listen, about the various forms of religious life which he had seen and which he so loved and reverenced.

At this time Alchfrith,[9] son of the aforesaid King Oswy, was preparing to go to Rome to worship at the tombs of the apostles as Benedict had done, and he accepted Benedict as his companion for the journey. And though his father cancelled Alchfrith's proposed trip and made him stay home within the kingdom, Benedict nonetheless, being the high-spirited young nobleman that he was, went ahead with the journey he had undertaken and hurried on to Rome for the second time [665], in the reign of Pope Vitalian of blessed memory.

After he had drunk in not a little of the sweet wisdom of salvation, just as he had before, then after some months he departed for the Isle

7. See note 49 to Introduction.

8. He left in the company of another noble young pilgrim, Wilfrid, whom he later impatiently left behind at Lyons (see Eddius, *Life of Wilfrid*, Ch. 3)

9. See note 24 to *Life of St. Cuthbert*, and note 24 to *Life of Wilfrid*.

of Lérins[10] where he joined the community of monks, received the tonsure, took the distinguishing vow of a monk, and followed the regular discipline with all due earnestness. After two years of instruction in the proper principles of monastic life, he was overcome once again by his love for Peter, Prince of the Apostles, and determined to return to the city which was hallowed by his remains.

Chapter III

Nor was it long before the arrival of a merchant ship allowed him to satisfy his wish [i. e., about 668]. At that time Egbert,[11] King of Kent, had sent from Britain a man named Wighard who had been selected for the office of bishop after having been sufficiently instructed in all ecclesiastical discipline by the Roman disciples of the blessed Pope Gregory in Kent.[12] The king wished to have him consecrated bishop at Rome so as to have a man of his own race and language for his bishop. Thereby the king and his people might be so much the more perfectly instructed in the Scriptures and the rites of the Christian religion inasmuch as they would receive these things not through an interpreter but from the tongue of a fellow countryman and at the hands of a kinsman. But when this Wighard came to Rome he and those who

10. On one of the Isles of Lérins (on another was the prison of the mysterious Man in the Iron Mask) in the Mediterranean just off Cannes is this monastery of St. Honoratus. Founded in the fifth century it became one of the focal points of early western monasticism. See Chadwick, *Poetry and Letters in Early Christian Gaul*, pp. 147 ff. Eastern elements in Northumbrian monastic culture may in part trace to Benedict's connection with Lérins and its monastic relationships with Syria and Egypt. And see note 16 to *Life of St. Cuthbert.*

11. See note 55 to *Life of Wilfrid.*

12. Bede (*Ecclesiastical History*, Bk. III, ch. 29) mentions that Wighard was selected by Kings Oswy and Egbert acting in agreement "with the decision and consent of the holy church of the English people." Plummer points to the incident as an important step in the development of a conscious unity among the Anglo-Saxons (*Baedae Opera Historica*, II,200). It is significant too that Oswy's initiative in this matter comes but a few years after his decision for Rome at the Synod of Whitby in 664 (see Eddius, *Life of Wilfrid*, Ch. 10).

had accompanied him on the journey fell victims to a violent pestilence and all died, before he could receive the honor of episcopal rank.

But the Apostolic Father did not wish this devoted mission of the faithful to fail of its deserved success by reason of the death of the envoys, so after consultation he appointed one of his own clergy to be sent as archbishop into Britain. This was Theodore, a man accomplished in both secular and ecclesiastical learning, and this in both languages, that is, Greek and Latin.[13] For his colleague and adviser he was given the Abbot Hadrian, a man who was very energetic and very prudent, in equal measure. And since the pope saw that the revered Benedict would prove to be a man of wisdom, industry, piety and nobility of soul, he put the newly consecrated bishop and his attendants in his hands. He bade him in the interest of a greater good give up the pilgrimage for Christ that he had undertaken and return to his country so that he could bring with him the master of truth whom he had been so diligently seeking, and for whom he could serve as both interpreter and guide not only on the journey to Britain but after he had settled down there and begun to teach. So Benedict did as the pope ordered, and in due time they arrived in Kent [i. e., 669] and were most thankfully received. Theodore ascended the episcopal throne, and Benedict was given the monastery of blessed Peter the Apostle to rule, where later the aforesaid Hadrian was made abbot.

Chapter IV

After ruling this monastery for two years, Benedict set out on his third trip from Britain to Rome[14] and completed it with his usual good fortune. He brought back with him a good number of books pertaining to all branches of sacred literature, some of which he had purchased at a favorable price and some of which had been given him as gifts by friends. On the way home he stopped at Vienne to pick up books he had bought there and left in the keeping of friends.

13. See note 32 to *Life of St. Cuthbert.*

14. But, counting the trip from Lérins, this was really his fourth Roman trip.

Then when he arrived back in Britain he took a notion to visit King Cenwalh[15] of the West Saxons whose friendship he had enjoyed for some time and whose kindness had come to his assistance more than once. But the king had been carried off by a premature death just at this time [i. e., 672], so turning his steps finally toward his own people and the land where he was born, Benedict came to King Ecgfrith of Northumbria. He told him the story of all that he had done from the time he forsook his country in voluntary exile as a young man. He did not conceal the religious zeal which consumed him; he disclosed all that he had learned about ecclesiastical and monastic usage in Rome and elsewhere; he displayed how many sacred volumes, how many relics of the blessed apostles and martyrs of Christ he had brought back. And so he found such great favor with the king and became so intimate a friend that Ecgfrith straightway made him a gift of seventy hides of his own land and directed him to build a monastery on it to the First Pastor of the Church. And this monastery was built, as we recalled in the Preface, at the mouth of the River Wear on the left bank, in the year 674 from the Incarnation of the Lord, in the second indiction, [16] and the fourth year of the reign of King Ecgfrith.

Chapter V

Before more than a year had gone by after the foundation of the monastery, Benedict crossed the sea to Gaul in search of masons to construct a stone church for him in the Roman manner which he had ever loved so well.[17] He asked for them, he received them, and he brought

15. See note 25 to *Life of Wilfrid.*

16. Indictions were ancient Roman dating units, consisting of fifteen-year cycles (Plummer, *Baedae Opera Historica*, II,38-9). The preservation of this old Roman computational system in Anglo-Saxon charters and other official documents is another manifestation of that strange fascination Rome held for the Anglo-Saxon mind. See notes 8 and 39 to *Life of St. Cuthbert.*

17. At York several years before, Wilfrid had restored Paulinus' stone church (Eddius, *Life of Wilfrid*, Ch. 16). The Anglo-Saxons traditionally built in wood (their word for "build" and "timber" had the same root) and possessed an awe of Roman stone work (see note 39 to *Life of St. Cuthbert*), which was perhaps

them back.[18] Out of love for St. Peter in whose honor he was building he showed so much enthusiasm in the work of construction that, within the space of one year from the time the foundations were laid, the roof was put on and you might have witnessed the solemn rites of Mass being celebrated inside. When the work was drawing to completion he sent messengers to Gaul to obtain glassmakers (artificers till then unknown in Britain)[19] who could glaze the windows of the church and of the minor chapels and of the dining rooms. The men were found and came, and not only did they complete the work asked of them, but by its means they also enabled the Anglian people to become acquainted with this particular craft and learn it, truly a handicraft admirably suited for making church lamps or other vessels called for by so many different needs. But all these other things pertaining to the service of the altar and of the Church—sacred vessels, vestments—he took pains like a merchant monk to import from abroad, since they were not to be found at home.

Chapter VI

And as for yet other items—ornaments for his church and protective charters—which would not be found even in Gaul, he resolved, like

not fully laid to rest till the construction of these early stone churches. The pilgrim to Monkwearmouth today is often shocked to find the little church and its tall, square tower black with the grime of this northeastern coal region. But then he takes comfort in fancifully tracing back some of the sooty stain on the stones to the Viking burning in the ninth century and the Norman burning in the eleventh. He can be reasonably certain that parts of the present church actually do date all the way back to Benedict Biscop's day. Long-snouted interwined animals carved in the remains of the western porch are so remarkably like the beasts that decorate some of the Sutton Hoo jewelry (see note 47 to *Life of Wilfrid*) and the Book of Durrow that it would be difficult to date them later than this last quarter of the seventh century (see Fisher, *The Greater Anglo-Saxon Churches*, pp. 99-100). See Plummer, *Baedae Opera Historica*, II, 101-02.

18. The marked rhetorical pattern of this Latin sentence suggests a playfully ostentatious echo of Caesar's *veni, vidi, vici* ("I came, I saw, I conquered.")

19. But Wilfrid's windows at York, built by artisans from Kent, seem to have antedated Benedict's at Monkwearmouth by a few years (see Eddius, *Life of Wilfrid*, Chs. 14, 16; and note 62 to *Life of Wilfrid*).

the indefatigable provider that he was, to bring them from Rome. So, as soon as he had his monastery organized in the pattern of the rule, he made his fourth[20] trip to Rome [in 678] and returned laden with a much more profitable freight of spiritual merchandise than before. First of all, he brought back a vast number of books of every kind. Secondly, he brought a rich treasury of relics of the apostles and martyrs of Christ for the benefit of many a church yet-to-be built in the land of the Angles. Thirdly, he introduced in his monastery the manner of singing and chanting and conducting the church ceremonies in accord with the Roman usage by obtaining from Pope Agatho the arch-chanter of the Church of the blessed Apostle Peter and abbot of the Monastery of St. Martin, named John. Benedict brought this man of Rome to the Angles to teach in his monastery in Britain. After his arrival he not only taught his pupils *viva voce* what knowledge of things ecclesiastical he had acquired at Rome, but he also left behind him a good number of instructions that he had committed to writing, and which are still preserved in the library of the same monastery in memory of him. Fourthly, Benedict brought back as a gift of no mean value a letter of privilege which he had received from the venerable Pope Agatho with the permission, consent, desire, and even the urging of King Ecgfrith,[21] and which guaranteed that the monastery he had founded should be absolutely and forever secure and free from all outside intrusion. Fifthly, to adorn the church of St. Peter the Apostle which he had built, he brought back painted representations of the saints. A likeness of the Mother of God, blessed Mary ever virgin, with the twelve apostles, he placed for ornament in the vaulting of the central nave of the church, fixed to boarding that reached from wall to wall. The south wall he decorated with scenes from the Gospel story. He adorned the north wall the same way with pictures of the

20. This was his fourth trip from Britain, but his fifth trip in all because he had made one from Lérins (see Chapters 2, 3). It was on this fourth journey that Ceolfrith accompanied Benedict to Rome (*Life of Ceolfrith*, Chs. 9, 10).

21. At the very time Benedict was in Rome with Ecgfrith's blessing, Wilfrid too was there appealing to Pope Agatho against King Ecgfrith's and Archbishop Theodore's decision to deprive him of his bishopric (Eddius, *Life of Wilfrid*, Chs. 29 ff.).

visions of the Apocalypse of St. John.[22] This he did so that all those entering his church, even those unable to read, could gaze on the dear face of Christ and his saints wherever they looked, albeit only in representation; or so that they could call more vividly to mind the grace of the Lord's Incarnation; or so that having that perilous moment of the Last Judgment as though it were happening before their eyes, they might remember to keep a stricter watch over themselves.

Chapter VII

Now King Ecgfrith took no little delight in this virtue and industry and devotion of the venerable Benedict, and he saw that the land he had given him for the building of a monastery had been well and profitably given, so he thoughtfully augmented the gift with a grant of forty more hides of land. In a year [*i. e.*, in 681 or 682], after sending just seventeen monks there with the priest Ceolfrith as their appointed abbot, Benedict built the monastery of St. Paul the Apostle [at Jarrow] with the advice of, in fact at the order of, the same King Ecgfrith. The king merely made one condition, that there always be preserved between the two monasteries a common peace and harmony, a common family spirit and love, so that, for example, just as the body cannot be separated from the head, through which it breathes, and the head cannot disregard the body, without which it cannot live, so no one should dare make any attempt to set at odds with each other these monasteries which are united in the fraternal companionship of the first two apostles.

This Ceolfrith, whom Benedict appointed as abbot, had been at his side through thick and thin from the first beginnings of the previously founded monastery and had taken advantage of the opportunity to go with him to Rome to further his education and to satisfy his devotion.

22. On the important place of the Apocalypse in medieval art see M. R. James, *The Apocalypse in Art*, British Academy (London, 1931). On the positioning of mural paintings in medieval English churches see K. Kendon, *Mural Paintings in English Churches During the Middle Ages* (London, 1923), pp. 123 ff.; and M. D. Anderson, *The Imagery of British Churches* (London, 1955), pp. 64 ff.

At this same time Benedict made an abbot of the priest Eastorwine from the monastery of St. Peter, and put him in charge of that same monastery with full power of rule. Thereby, with this added strength of a most dear comrade, Benedict would be enabled to bear more easily the burden which he had not been able to sustain alone. Nor should anyone think it out of place for one monastery to have had two abbots at the same time. It was demanded by Benedict's frequent absence on the business of the monastery, his constant setting out across the sea and the uncertainty of his return. History tells us that even the most blessed Peter the Apostle, because of a pressing need, appointed two bishops in turn to rule the Church of Rome under him. And that great Abbot Benedict himself [of Nursia], as the blessed Pope Gregory writes of him, appointed twelve abbots over his disciples, according as he deemed useful, and this without any detriment to charity, in fact with an increase of charity.

Chapter VIII

This man Eastorwine, therefore, as we mentioned, undertook the task of governing the monastery in the ninth year after its foundation, and he remained at that post till his death four years later. In the eyes of the world he was a nobleman, but he transmuted the nobility of his blood into a greater nobility of soul[23] as befits a servant of God, instead of making it a matter for snobbery and contempt of others, as some do. He was, in fact, a cousin of his abbot, Benedict, but so genuine was the noblemindedness of both of them, so absolute was their contempt for mere worldly nobility, that Eastorwine after he entered the monastery never even thought of asking for any special regard to be shown him in consideration of his relationship or his nobility, nor did Benedict think of proffering any. Instead, this young man of high purpose found his honor in subjecting himself to the rule in all things, on an equal footing with the rest of the brethren.

23. Bede is fond of this Heroic-Age transmutation and points it out in the case of a number of the noble Anglo-Saxon monks and nuns (see Plummer, *Baedae Opera Historica*, II, 90-91).

And even h hthouge had been a soldier in the personal retinue[24] of King Ecgfrith, yet from the time he left behind him the things of this world and laid down his arms to take up soldiering of the spirit[25] he remained so unassuming and so very much like the rest of the brethren that he found his joy in winnowing and threshing grain with them, in milking the ewes and cows, in working in the bakery, the garden, the kitchen, and in all the occupations of the monastery, cheerfully and obediently. Even after he had assumed the name and the office of abbot, his attitude toward others remained unchanged, in accord with what a wise man once counseled, "If they will make thee master of the feast, do not give thyself airs; bear thyself as an equal" [Eccl. 32:1], gentle, affable, and kind to all. Yet, when he considered it opportune, he restrained the erring by the discipline of the rule, more often however by simply admonishing them in such an earnest, naturally lovable manner that no one had any wish to offend and draw a troubled frown over the bright joy of his abbot's face. Often when he came upon any of the brothers at their work, in the course of his rounds as he tended to the business of the monastery, he would join right with them in their chores, whether it meant trying his hand at controlling the course of the plow, or beating out iron with a hammer, or waving the winnowing fan, or doing anything else of that kind. For besides being a young man of gentle speech and a cheerful, generous nature, and of an appearance that commanded respect, he also possessed great physical strength.

He ate of the same food as the rest of the brethren in the house, and he slept in the same common room where he had slept before he was abbot, so that even when he was taken ill and already foresaw his death by certain signs, he continued to lie for two more days in this common dormitory. Then for the five last days up to the hour of his death he was placed in a private room. One day he left it to sit outside in the open air where he called all the brethren around him, and, then prompted to the last by his loving heart, he gave each of them the kiss of peace, while they wept in their grief at the loss of such a father and shepherd. He died during the night of the seventh of March

24. Bede calls him a *minister* of the king. See note 24 to Introduction.

25. See note 6 to *Life of St. Cuthbert.*

while the brethren were chanting the morning psalms of Lauds.[26] He had entered the monastery when he was twenty-four years old and lived in it twelve years. Seven of these years he spent in the priesthood, and for four of them he directed the government of the monastery. And so, "abandoning his earthbound and death-doomed body,"[27] he went to seek the Kingdom of Heaven [*ca.* 686].

Chapter IX

But now that we have looked ahead a little into the life of the much-revered Eastorwine, let us return to the point we had reached in our story. Not long after he had appointed Eastorwine abbot of the monastery of St. Peter the Apostle, and Ceolfrith abbot of the monastery of St. Paul, Benedict went to Rome for the fifth time[28] from Britain and returned [probably in 686] richly laden as always with a huge treasure of ecclesiastical goods. Again there was a great wealth of sacred books, and no less rich a collection than before of holy paintings. He showed them pictures of the life of Our Lord which were to be hung for decoration all the way round the inside of the church of the Blessed Mother of God which he had built in the principal monastery. And then he displayed pictures meant to adorn the monastery and the church of St. Paul the Apostle, representations of the correspondence between the Old and New Testaments, devised with the greatest exactitude. For instance, one picture coupled Isaac carrying the wood on which he was to be sacrificed, and Christ in like manner carrying the cross on which He was to suffer, both next to each other, one above the other. Another compared the Son of Man raised aloft on the cross,

26. In the Benedictine order of the day the *matutina psalmodia* would be Lauds of the Divine Office, chanted at the first light, about 5 o'clock in the morning (see Butler, *Benedictine Monachism*, p. 279).

27. Bede's *terrenos artus moribundaque membra relinquens* sounds very much like a quote from some Latin Christian heroic poem. It is very close to verse 732 of Book VI in Vergil's *Aeneid*.

28. But this was his sixth trip in all. See note 18.

to the serpent raised up by Moses in the desert.[29] Among other things he also brought two mantles all of silk and of incomparable workmanship, for which he later received three hides of land on the south bank of the Wear River, near its mouth, from King Aldfrith[30] and his counselors—for on his return he found that King Ecgfrith had been killed while he was away.[31]

Chapter X

But in the midst of the joy which his coming brought with it, he discovered the sorrow there was at home. In a plague which had ravaged the land the revered priest Eastorwine, whom he had made abbot before he left for Rome, had departed this life, together with a large number of the brethren committed to his care.[32] Yet there was also some consolation, for he learned that in Eastorwine's place another most respected and most kindly man from the same monastery, Sigefrith the deacon, had soon been substituted by the choice of his brethren and of his fellow-abbot, Ceolfrith. He was a man well-trained in the knowledge of Scripture, graced with the finest qualities of character

29. These pictures interestingly reflect the patristic tradition of Scriptural exegesis which interpreted the Old Testament as prefiguring the New. This tradition throws much light on the interpretation of the Anglo-Saxon Christian poems (see B. F. Huppé, *Doctrine and Poetry: Augustine's Influence on Old English Poetry* [State University of New York, 1959] especially Chapter 5). Benedict Biscop's picture that couples Isaac with Christ suggests, for instance, that the Anglo-Saxon poem, *Genesis*, need not be considered poetically incomplete even though it concludes with the sacrifice of Isaac. For Isaac always prefigured Christ and the subsequent drama of the redemption.

30. See note 30 to *Life of St. Cuthbert.*

31. Ecgfrith and his army were slaughtered by the Picts in the ill-fated Battle of Nechtansmere in 685, less than a month after the dedication of St. Paul's Church at Jarrow for which Ecgfrith had given the land and had even marked out the spot for the altar (*Life of Ceolfrith*, Ch. 12; and see note 37 to *Life of St. Cuthbert*).

32. And in Ceolfrith's monastery all were carried off by the plague except for the abbot and one young boy who was probably Bede himself (see *Life of Ceolfrith*, Ch. 14, and note 18).

and possessed of a wonderful power of self-control. But for the better protection of the virtues of his soul an infirmity of the body weighed heavily upon him, and to help preserve the innocence of his heart he suffered from a damaging and incurable disease of the lungs.[33]

Chapter XI

Not long afterward, Benedict himself was taken seriously ill and soon began to fail. And in order that the devoted ardor of such great love might be tested by the sister virtue of patience, the divine goodness stretched both men on the bed of mortal sickness. Thus after their infirmity had lost utterly its battle with death, he could bring them to life again with the balm of ease unending and of peace and light beyond that of earth. Sigefrith, too, as was said, was wasted away by the slow deterioration of his lungs and brought to the edge of death. Benedict's malady crept over him slowly and inexorably for three years and then struck him with a paralysis so shattering that in all his lower extremities he was left dead before his time; only the upper parts of his body—without whose life what is left cannot be called a man—were saved to do their service to the virtue of patience. In the midst of their suffering the two of them never ceased to give thanks to God, and spent much time in prayer and in counseling the brethren. Benedict took advantage of the brothers' frequent visits to encourage them in their observance of the rule he had laid down. "You must not think" he said, "that this institute which I drew up for you was simply the impulsive voice of my heart, without any study having gone into it. What I have passed on to you, to be observed to your own benefit, is nothing but a compilation of all the practices I learned from the seventeen monasteries, that, in the course of my frequent travel abroad, I found out were the best."[34]

33. In his Latin, Bede pairs *corporis* ("of the body") with *animi* ("of the soul") and then goes on to play *NOCivo vitio pulmonum* ("damaging disease of the lungs") off against *inNOCentiam cordis* ("innocence of heart"). Lest his pun be missed he follows *innocentiam* immediately with *nocivo.*

34. Benedict's words afford us an insight into the special individualistic

He gave orders that the excellent and most extensive library which he had brought from Rome, and which is so necessary for the education of the Church, should be jealously preserved intact, and should not be allowed to fall into disrepair through neglect, or be dispersed. And another injunction which he carefully made a point of repeating to them again and again was that in the selection of an abbot no one was to suppose that the thing to be sought for was family descent and not rather probity of life and doctrine.[35] "And I tell you truly," he said, "in comparing two evils, if God should decide that all this property on which I have built this monastery should be turned back into a wilderness forever, I would find it much easier to bear than if my brother in the flesh, who we know walks not in the way of truth, should succeed me as abbot and rule this monastery. Therefore always be very careful, my brothers, never to seek a father for yourselves on the principle of who his family is, and never to seek an outsider. But according to the prescriptions of the rule of that great Abbot Benedict of former days, and according to the prescriptions of our own privilege, look for whoever shall be approved by common consent at a meeting of your community as the most capable and worthy by his virtuous life and wise teaching to fill such an office, and for whomever all shall unanimously and knowingly have selected as the best in an election

nature of Golden Age Anglo-Saxon monasticism. At heart there was something typically "Heroic Age" about it, a diversion or redirection of the Germanic *comitatus*-loyalty of sworn men for an outstanding leader. There was an individuality about the monasteries answering to the personality of their founders; monasteries grew with the renown of their leaders. Ceolfrith left the monastery of Ripon to live under famous abbots in Kent and East Anglia (see Chs. 3, 4). The monastic rule in Northumbria did not seem to run counter to this phenomenal Golden Age monastic "individuality." Personal loyalty counted most. The tearful parting of Ceolfrith from his monks is perhaps the most moving example of such devotion. It reminds us of the groans for the lost leader in *The Wanderer*. As prior of Lindisfarne, Cuthbert ran into a stubborn wall of resistance when he tried to impose on the monks some customs contrary to those handed down by their father Aidan (see note 24 to *Life of St. Cuthbert*). Ironically enough, this same Heroic-Age individuality which inspired early English monasticism worked also for its downfall. Monasteries proliferated out of all measure and too often became mere family affairs (see note 33 to Introduction).

35. See Introduction, p. 20; and note 129 to *Life of Wilfrid*.

conducted in all charity. Then you will summon the bishop and ask that this man be confirmed as your abbot by the usual blessing. "For," he said, "those who bear children of the flesh in the manner of the flesh must seek in earth and flesh for heirs to this inheritance of earth and flesh. But those who bear spiritual sons for God by the spiritual seed of the Word, should take care that everything they do be spiritual. Among their spiritual children let them esteem him as the greatest who is endowed most generously with the grace of the Spirit, just as earthly parents always recognize their first-born as taking precedence over the rest of their children and always give him the preference over the rest when they portion out their inheritance."

Chapter XII

And I most certainly should tell how the holy abbot Benedict, to break up the interminable boredom of the many sleepless nights he passed in the restless grip of his sickness, used to call for someone to read to him about Job, the model of patience, or about anything in Scripture which could cheer a sick man, stir up the failing life in him, and raise him out of the depths of depression to thoughts of things beyond the world. Of course he could not get out of bed to pray and he even found it very taxing to try to chant all the usual prayers of the psalter where he was. But, practical as always, he hit upon a way to satisfy his religious devotion by having some of the brethren come to him at each of the various canonical hours of daily and nightly prayer and chant the regular psalms in two choirs. Then he would sing along with them insofar as he was able, and so what he had not been able to do by himself he made good with their assistance.

Chapter XIII

At last when both the abbots, exhausted by their long illness, realized that they were near death and would never again be fit enough to govern their monasteries (surely such a terrible infirmity of the flesh afflicted them only so that the virtue of Christ might be made perfect in them), they took a desire one day to see and talk with each other again before they died. So Sigefrith was carried in a litter to the little room where Benedict was lying on his bed, and with the help of those who were caring for them they were laid right next to each other. But though they were lying with their heads on the same pillow, it was pitiful to see how neither could muster enough strength to turn his face near enough to the other to kiss him farewell, so even in this they had to be assisted by the brethren.

Then after Benedict had consulted to very good effect with Sigefrith and with all the brethren together, he summoned the Abbot Ceolfrith whom he had put in charge of the monastery of St. Paul—a man related to him not as much by the kinship of blood as by the fellowship of virtue—and with everyone approving and judging this to be the very best thing, he appointed him abbot of both monasteries. For Benedict believed that in every respect it would be a help toward preserving the peace, unity, and concord of the two places if they were always to have but one abbot and ruler. He often cited the example of the kingdom of Israel, how it always remained secure from foreign invasion as long as it was ruled by one of its own people, the same ruler for all. But after the nation was torn apart by internecine strife as a result of the sins of these kings, then it began to die a little at a time, till at length it was shattered to its foundations and disappeared from history. And he counseled them to keep in mind always that saying of the Gospel, "every kingdom divided against itself will be made desolate" [Lk. 11:17; Mt. 12:25].

Chapter XIV

Then at length, two months after these events, the venerable Abbot Sigefrith, dear to God, having passed through the fire and water of the trials of time, was conducted into the paradise of everlasting rest and entered the place of the Kingdom of Heaven [on August 22, 688 or 689], offering to the Lord in the sacrifice of perpetual praise those vows which he had most carefully promised to God with pure lips. And then, four months later, Benedict, the conqueror of vices and the noble doer of virtuous deeds, was conquered by the feebleness of the flesh and arrived at the door of death.[36] "The night drew on, chilly with winter winds," soon to give birth to a holy day of everlasting joy and serenity and light. The brethren gather in the church and pass the sad and sleepless night chanting psalms and praying. The melody of divine praise eases their heavy weight of sorrow at the passing of their father. Others never move from the chamber in which the sick man was courageously awaiting the departure of death and the arrival of life. As had become customary on other nights, the Gospel is read aloud by a priest through the night to console him in his suffering, and when the moment of death finally threatens he is given the Sacrament of the Lord's Body and Blood as food for the journey.

And thus that holy soul, so long purified and tested by the scourging flames of fruitful suffering, abandoned the red furnace of the flesh and flew in freedom to the glory of heavenly bliss. Even the psalm which was being sung for him at that moment gives testimony to the glorious triumph of his flight that brooked no interfering or delaying by evil spirits. For the brethren who had gathered in the church at the beginning of the night and were singing through the psalter in order, had at that moment just come to the 82nd psalm, which begins, "O God, who shall be like to thee?" [Ps. 82:1]. The whole text of this psalm reechoes with the thought that although both the earthly and spiritual enemies of Christ's Name may ever strive to overthrow and destroy the Church of Christ and every individual faithful soul, yet on the contrary it is they who will be confounded and routed and who will perish forever after the Lord has terrified them, He who has no equal and reigns alone, the most exalted One, over all the earth. Hence it was rightly interpreted as a disposition of heaven that that particular psalm was being recited at the moment when that soul which, with the Lord's help, no enemy would have the power to overcome, was taking flight from its body. It was the sixteenth year after he founded the monastery that this holy witness of the faith went to his repose in the Lord, on the

36. Death is the saint's "moment of truth," as it was the hero's; and almost instinctively Bede's sentences now intensify their epic cadence, shift rhetorically into the historical-present, and also increase their alliteration in the manner of late Latin and Germanic heroic poetry.

12th of January [689 or 690], and he was buried in the Church of St. Peter the Apostle so that after death he would be even physically near to the relics and the altar of him whom he ever loved in life and who opened the gate of the Kingdom of Heaven to receive him.

[We omit Bede's concluding nine chapters, which are devoted to Ceolfrith. What they tell is said more fully in the *Life of Ceolfrith* that follows.]

THE ANONYMOUS LIFE OF CEOLFRITH ABBOT OF JARROW

Preface To LIFE OF CEOLFRITH

This biography of the Northumbrian monk who taught Bede at Jarrow is one of the finest pieces in England's early literature. Its Latin is clear and competent and its writer has the craftsman's good sense to tell a story straightforward and let his hero's deeds speak for themselves in their own noble way. His account of old Ceolfrith's parting from his weeping monks is grand and unforgettable. It stays in the memory like Arthur's taking his last farewell of Sir Bedivere and sailing away to the Isle of Avalon. Bede's grief at Ceolfrith's departure interrupted his work (see his introduction to Book IV of his commentary on Samuel [*Corpus Christianorum*, Series Latina, Vol. 119 (1962) p. 212]).

The biography was written sometime between Ceolfrith's death (in late 716) and 725 (Colgrave, *Proceedings of the British Academy*, 1958, p. 58). The author's firsthand knowledge of events, and some first-person remarks in the account (e. g., in Ch. 5), argue that he was a monk at Wearmouth. Hwaetbert, Ceolfrith's successor as abbot, has been suggested as the author, but some remarks in the text make this doubtful (see my note 34 to *Life of Ceolfrith*). Bede made use of this biography when he wrote his *Lives of the Abbots* (see Plummer, *Baedae Opera Historica*, I, xlvi-xlvii).

The best text is by C. Plummer in his *Baedae Opera Historica* (Oxford, one-volume reprint of 1946) I,388-404. It is from this text that I made the present translation. Another translation is available in Whitelock, *English Historical Documents*, pp. 697-708.

In this biography, and in Bede's *Lives of the Abbots*, I have numbered Plummer's paragraphs as chapters, for uniformity with the other biographies and for corresponding ease of reference.

THE LIFE OF CEOLFRITH

HERE BEGINS the life of the most holy abbot, Ceolfrith, from whom the blessed Bede received the habit of holy religion and who after his death merited to receive the palm of eternal happiness.

Chapter I

In his letter, Paul, the apostle, advises the Hebrews, "Do not forget those who have had charge of you, and preached God's word to you; contemplate the happy issue of the life they lived, and imitate their faith" [Heb. 13:7]. Hence it is perfectly clear, my dearest brethren, that you do very well in deciding to have set down for you in writing the memory of our most reverend father and superior, Ceolfrith, who explained God's word to us. For he was most assuredly that kind of man whose life of devotion to God should fitly be followed, not only in its ending but also in its beginning and its whole intervening course, and whose unfeigned faith should be copied for its constancy.

Chapter II

For, to begin with, his parents were noble[1] and were religious people and he himself from the very first years of his boyhood was intent on leading a virtuous life. When he was almost eighteen [i. e., about the year 660], he elected to put aside his secular garb and become a monk; so he entered the monastery that is situated in the place called

1. His father, like Benedict Biscop, served in the *comitatus* of King Oswy (see Ch. 34). And see Introduction, p. 10.

Gilling.[2] His brother, Cynefrith[3] a devout man dear to God, had ruled this monastery, but now shortly before this time he had entrusted the rule to their relative, Tunberht, who was later to be consecrated bishop of the church of Hexham. Cynefrith himself was lured away to Ireland,[4] partly by his strong attraction to the study of Scripture and partly by his desire to serve the Lord in a freer manner with more opportunity for prayer and affectionate devotion.

Chapter III

And so after Ceolfrith was devotedly received by his kinsman, he set about even more devotedly living the life of the monastery, giving himself with enthusiasm to the reading and the working and the regular discipline in all things. It was not long after this that his brother Cynefrith and others of the Anglian nobility who had gone to Ireland to study Scripture departed for eternal life by the brief passageway of death. At this same time Tunberht, along with Ceolfrith and some other brethren of his monastery, accepted Bishop Wilfred's invitation to remove to the monastery of Ripon.[5] There Ceolfrith settled into the regular life of the rule, and after the proper time had passed was chosen

2. King Oswy, to the great horror of Bede, had had the much-loved King Oswine of Deira murdered at Gilling in 651 (Bede, *Ecclesiastical History*, Bk. III, ch. 14). Oswy's Queen Eanfled, daughter of King Edwin and friend of Wilfrid (Eddius, *Life of Wilfrid*, Ch. 2, etc.), was instrumental in getting Oswy repentantly to found a monastery there in charge of the Celtic-trained Anglian monk Trumhere, a relative of Oswine (Bede, *Ecclesiastical History*, Bk. III, ch. 24). So it happened that both Cynefrith and Ceolfrith, sons of one of King Oswy's most respected nobles, entered the monastery which had been newly founded in atonement for Oswy's foul crime. We wonder what complex of motives may have been involved in the brothers' decisions.

3. About these quaint Anglo-Saxon names (Cynefrith, Ceolfrith, Tunberht, Tohrthelm, Sigefrith, etc.) there is always something hard and bright, like the bite of swords and the gleam of armor. While in their women's names there is often a lilt of birdsong (Ethelthryth, Hereswith, Osthryth, etc).

4. See note 21 to Introduction.

5. See Eddius, *Life of Wilfrid*, Ch. 8 and note 28.

for the priesthood by this same bishop[6] and ordained at about the age of twenty-seven (i. e., about the year 669). Shortly thereafter he traveled to Kent[7] to help satisfy his desire for the fullest possible understanding of the rules of monastic life and of the priesthood which he had undertaken.

Chapter IV

He came also to East Anglia to observe the monastic practices of Abbot Botulf,[8] who enjoyed a widespread reputation as a man of exceptional life and teaching and a man filled with the grace of the Holy Spirit. Ceolfrith was instructed so thoroughly, insofar as the brief visit would permit, that when he returned [to Ripon] there was no one of that day more learned in either the ecclesiastical or the monastic rule. However, unlike certain others, he could not be enticed away from his humble attitude of mind either by consideration of his state of life, or of his learning, or of his noble name.[9] On the contrary, he endeavored to subject himself in everything to the observance of the rule. In fact, for no little while he held the office of baker, yet despite the flour to be sifted, the oven to be fired up and cleaned, and the loaves to be baked in it, he was very careful not to omit either the study or the performance of his priestly duties. At this same time he was also put in charge of the instruction of the brothers in the observance of the rule, in which office he was expected, to the best of his acquired learning and his zealous religious fervor, to instruct the ignorant and to correct the contumacious.

6. See Note 6 to *Life of Wilfrid.*

7. After training under Wilfrid with his strong Roman preferences it is not surprising that Ceolfrith should wish to visit Kent, where lay Canterbury, the center of the Roman mission. The learned Theodore had but lately arrived there as the new archbishop.

8. Botulf (Botolf, Botwulf), after whom the Boston in Lincolnshire (and hence the one in Massachusetts too) is named (i. e., Botulf's stone, or Botulf's stone cross, or stone church. See Ekwall, *Concise Oxford Dictionary of English Place-Names*, 4th ed), seems to have followed the Benedictine Rule in his monastery. And see note 34 to Bede, *Lives of the Abbots.*

9. A wry anticipatory comment on the events of Chapter 8.

Chapter V

Then the time came which the heavenly Master had appointed for giving him a higher position of authority over the souls of the faithful. Benedict, our shepherd and abbot of blessed memory, had become well aware of Ceolfrith's gifts of learning, piety and devoted application to work, so when he prepared to found this monastery,[10] where the graciousness of God has brought us together, he succeeded in getting Bishop Wilfred to appoint Ceolfrith as his helper and assistant in establishing the monastery. And this was not at all because there was any real need to learn from Ceolfrith's teaching on the part of a man as experienced as Benedict, who had so often crossed the sea to travel through Gaul and Italy and among the Islands [of Lérins][11] and was already very well acquainted with the rules of life of the famous monasteries.

Chapter VI

Hence he was accustomed to say that the rule which he taught he had learned in seventeen of the most ancient monasteries, and that wherever he had observed anything that was very good he had tucked it away in the purse of his memory and brought it back to Britain for us to follow. But even though the Apostle Barnabas, for instance, was a good man, filled with the Holy Spirit, and with faith, still when he was about to teach at Antioch he came first to Tarsus where he knew he would find Saul. For he remembered that the latter had given indications of remarkable spiritual gifts even in the course of his novice days in the newly-embraced faith, and Barnabas desired to take advantage of his help in carrying out the ministry of the word that he was ready

10. The monastery of Monkwearmouth or Wearmouth. See Bede, *Lives of the Abbots*, Chs. 1, 4.

11. See Bede, *Lives of the Abbots*, Ch. 2, and note 10.

to embark on. And though Moses was chosen and trained by the Lord himself to lead the people of Israel, he was also provided with the help of his brother Aaron, so that with the assistance of this priest-prophet he could accomplish a task' whose enormous weight of responsibility he might well have feared to bear alone. So also in like fashion the great Abbot Benedict, even though he was most learned in all matters of monastic discipline, yet in establishing his monastery he sought the help of Ceolfrith who could strengthen the observance of the monastic life by a devotion to the study of religious teaching equal to Benedict's own, and could help with the service of the altar since he was in priestly orders.

Chapter VII

So they began to build the monastery near the mouth of the River Wear in the year of the Lord's incarnation 674, the second indiction, and the fourth year of the reign of King Ecgfrith from whom they received the land. At first they were given fifty hides of land but later this was greatly augmented by the liberality of the same king and of other kings and nobles. The second year after the monastery was founded, Benedict crossed the sea to ask Abbot Torhthelm, with whom he had been close friends in former years, for builders who could direct and assist him in his building of a stone church.[12] After he had obtained some, he brought them from Gaul to Britain.

Chapter VIII

Meanwhile the office of prior was becoming a burden for Ceolfrith, and the freedom of the quiet monastic life began to appeal to him far more than the responsibility of ruling others. For he became subjected to the bitterest and most spiteful persecution by certain nobles who

12. See Bede, *Lives of the Abbots*, Ch. 5, and note 17.

were unable to bear his regular discipline.[13] So he returned to his monastery [at Ripon] and eagerly dropped back into the familiar life of obedient service. But when Benedict followed and pleaded with him to come back, Ceolfrith gave in to his loving entreaties and returned to carry out sedulously the duties which he had undertaken with Benedict, of establishing the monastery and putting it in order.

Chapter IX

The church, an exceptional piece of work, was completed in a very short time and was dedicated in honor of blessed Peter the Apostle.[14] Then the most reverend Abbot Benedict prepared to go to Rome for the purpose of bringing home a supply of sacred books, some dear memorial of the remains of the blessed martyrs, a painting of the Bible story that would be worthy of veneration,[15] and other gifts such as he was accustomed to bring back from his travels through many lands. But most of all he wanted instructors in the liturgical usage of the Roman rite who could teach the proper methods of chanting and of conducting services in the church he had just founded.

Chapter X

Ceolfrith accompanied him, eager for the opportunity in Rome to learn more about the duties of his monk's life than he had been able to

13. Heroic-Age individuality and wanderlust, especially in Celtic spirits, found Roman discipline irksome. Bede tells (*Ecclesiastical History*, Bk. IV, ch. 4) how Colman's attempt to found a joint Anglo-Celtic monastery on Inishbofin failed because the Irish monks insisted on heading for far places in the summertime while their outraged Anglo-Saxon brethren were left to harvest the crops, which the Irish insisted on sharing when they returned in the winter.

14. See note 130 to *Life of Wilfrid*.

15. See Bede, *Lives of the Abbots*, Ch. 6.

learn in Britain. Meanwhile the priest Eastorwine, a kinsman of Abbot Benedict, was left in charge of the monastery until their return. Then, with the help of the Lord, things turned out as they had planned. They learned much in Rome about the discipline of the Church, and they brought back with them to Britain the archchanter of the Roman Church, John, abbot of the monastery of the blessed Martin, who instructed us fully, both orally and by his writings, in the method of chanting according to the proper rite.[16]

Chapter XI

Then eight years after they had begun the etablishment of the aforesaid monastery [of Monkwearmouth], King Ecgfrith was pleased to present [i. e., in the year 681 or 682], for the ransom[17] of his soul, another forty hides of land to the most reverend Abbot Benedict. On this property [at Jarrow], there was to be a church and monastery dedicated to the blessed Paul; however, the latter was not to be separated from the community of the former monastery but joined to it in all things in brotherly harmony. The task of accomplishing this was laid on Ceolfrith and was performed most energetically. For, after all the buildings that were most in demand for the monastery's needs had been constructed, then he came to the place with twenty-two brothers—ten tonsured and twelve still awaiting the grace of tonsure. There he undertook to observe the very same discipline of the regular rule, and all the same canonical procedures of chanting and reading which they followed in the first monastery, even though at the moment not all of those by any

16. I have translated *per ordinem* as "according to the proper rite." It might also mean "antiphonally." On the Gregorian method of "ordered" (*ordinatus*, says Du Cange's *Glossarium mediae et infimae Latinitatis*, under "cantus") chant, introduced by Gregory's first missionaries to Britain and differing apparently from whatever was the Celtic style of chant, see Plummer's note in *Baedae Opera Historica*, II, 118-19.

17. Our author's word is *redemptio*, for which Niermeyer (*Mediae Latinitatis Lexicon Minus*) gives "ransom money" and *wergeld* as the first meanings. It is this radical significance of Christian *redemptio* ("redemption") which C. S. Lewis intended when he named the hero of his planetary novels Ransom.

means who had come with him knew how to sing psalms, or much less how to read in the church, or how to say either the antiphons or the responsories. But they were aided by their love of the religious life and by the example and wise persistency of their earnest superior. For while he was in the process of planting the deep root of monastic observance he made it a practice to visit the church while the brothers were there, often during all the canonical hours, and to take his meals and his rest with them, so that if there was anything that needed correction, or if anything had to be taught to the novices, he could do it personally.

Chapter XII

Then the third year after the foundation of the monastery he began to build the church that was to be consecrated in the name of the blessed Apostle Paul, on the site where Ecgfrith himself had marked out the location of the altar. The building rose so quickly day by day that, even though the workers were few, by the second year after it was begun it had progressed far enough to be dedicated. Now at the same time that the most reverend Abbot Benedict had made Ceolfrith abbot there, he had appointed his kinsman and priest, Eastorwine, whom I have mentioned already, as ruler of the earlier monastery. This was not indeed because one and the same monastery can or even should have two abbots, but because he himself was constantly being called away by the King, who wished to consult his good sense and mature judgment. Hence he lacked the time to be involved in the everyday matters of government and administration within the monastery and so he sought for an associate in his office with whose help he could more easily and satisfactorily bear the requisite burden of authority. Moreover he was in a hurry to go to Rome again in order to bring home from abroad the things needed for the monasteries he had founded.

Chapter XIII

But while he was away in foreign parts a sudden blast of the plague struck Britain and cut a wide swath of slaughter. Very many from both his monasteries were snatched off to the Lord, among them the revered Eastorwine himself, dear to God, in the fourth year since he had become abbot. In his place the brethren appointed as abbot, after they had consulted with Abbot Ceolfrith, the deacon Sigefrith of the same monastery, a man of marvelous holiness, thoroughly trained in the study of Scripture and especially interested in it.

Chapter XIV

Furthermore, in the monastery over which Ceolfrith had charge, all who were able to read or preach or recite the antiphons and responses were carried off by the plague, except for the abbot himself and one young boy who had been raised and educated by him and who today, as a priest in the same monastery, dutifully relates Ceolfrith's laudable deeds by pen and by word to all who wish to know them.[18] Now he, that is the abbot, exceedingly sad at heart over the aforesaid plague, directed that the former manner of their service be suspended, and that instead they should recite all their psalms without antiphons, except at vespers and matins. After this had been done for the space of one week, to the accompaniment of many tearful regrets on his part, he could not bear to have it go on any longer, so he ordained again that the sequence of psalms with their antiphons be restored in accord with the regular custom of the monastery.

With all the brethren[19] doing their best to follow the lead of himself and the boy, he was able to carry out with no little labor what he had prescribed, until such time as he had enough men to take part in the

18. The boy was undoubtedly Bede who tells us himself, in the autobiographical note at the end of his *Ecclesiastical History* (Bk. V, ch. 24), that his parents brought him to Monkwearmouth to be educated when he was seven years old. Willibrord too (Alcuin, *Life of Willibrord*, Ch. 3) and Boniface (Willibald, *Life of Boniface*, Ch. 1) were put into monasteries at a similar early age. Eddius tells how the nobles gave their sons (as did Willibrord's parents, for instance) into Wilfrid's charge at Ripon to be educated either for the Church or for the king's *comitatus* (*Life of Wilfrid*, Ch. 21).

19. That is, the survivors among those monks who had not yet been trained to read and chant.

divine service with him, either trained by himself or brought in from elsewhere.

Chapter XV

So when Benedict came home from Rome, laden down as always with wares from foreign lands, he was heartsick indeed over the disaster that had happened, but very happy that Sigefrith, a man dear to God, had been elected abbot to fill Eastorwine's place. And he exhorted him to be diligent in attending to the charge committed to him, while he himself assisted him in teaching and with prayers. But not long after this they both fell ill, and as time went on the sickness grew till both were confined to bed. They were not even able to raise themselves to a sitting position.[20]

Chapter XVI

Consequently, after he had consulted with the brethren, Benedict called Ceolfrith and appointed him abbot of both monasteries. And he decreed that there should be but one monastery in all things, even though situated in two places, and that it be governed always by one abbot, and guarded by the protection of the same privilege. Furthermore, as is stipulated both by the wording of this privilege which he had received from Pope Agatho[21] and by the rule of our holy father Benedict [of Nursia], an abbot was never to be sought for this monastery on the grounds of family descent but on the grounds of his manner of life and his devotedness to teaching.[22] It was in accord with this principle that Benedict himself had just appointed Ceolfrith, who was joined to him more by a spiritual relationship than by a natural one,

20. Bede tells us that Sigefrith had always been afflicted with a serious disease of the lungs (*Lives of the Abbots*, Ch. 10).
21. See Bede, *Lives of the Abbots*, Ch. 6.
22. See Bede, *op. cit.*, Ch. 11, and note 35.

Plate IX *Franks Casket*
(Germanic battle scene)

Plate X *Franks Casket* (Gifts of the Magi)

Plate XI *Ruthwell Cross*

Plate XII *Ruthwell Cross* (north face)

Plate XIII *Ruthwell Cross* (Center of north face)

though indeed he did have a brother near to him in the consanguinity of the flesh but most distant from him by the poverty of his love.[23]

Chapter XVII

And so Ceolfrith was appointed abbot there in the third year of King Aldfrith, in the first indiction, the twelfth of May [688 or 689], which was the eighth year after the foundation of the monastery of the blessed Paul. And the same year the venerable abbot and deacon, Sigefrith, purified by a long illness, departed for the heavenly kingdom on August 22, in the third year after he had become abbot. Moreover, at the beginning of the following year, on January 12, the Abbot Benedict, dear to God, entered into the rest and glory of the heavenly life, having spent sixteen years in monastic government. He too died after enduring the crucible of a long sickness, in the course of which he continued always to give thanks to God.

Chapter XVIII

Benedict had ruled by himself over the monastery of the blessed Apostle Peter for eight years; and for another eight years he had devoted his concern also to the monastery of the blessed Paul through the person of Ceolfrith. During the first four of these last years, as was explained above, he governed the monastery of the blessed Peter with Eastorwine as assistant; and for the following three years he had Sigefrith as his partner in authority, and for the last year, Ceolfrith. Benedict was buried in St. Peter's in a side-chapel[24] to the east of the altar, where the bones also of the most reverend abbots Eastorwine and Sigefrith were later translated.

23. *Ibid.*

24. Our author's word, *porticus*, seems best translated as "side-chapel." See note 65 to *Life of Wilfrid.*

Chapter XIX

Now that Benedict had passed from death to life, Ceolfrith took over the management of each monastery, or rather of one monastery situated in two places, and devoted himself to it adeptly and diligently for twenty-seven years. For he was a man of penetrating intelligence, vigorous in action, ardent in his zeal for justice, passionately in love with God and fearful of Him at the same time. Stern in correcting sinners, he was gentle in encouraging the penitent, diligent in preserving and teaching the precepts of monastic life,[25] gracious at putting heart in the poor and giving them alms. He was also generous with money, whether in giving it when it was asked of him or in making recompense for it when it was given to him. And he devoted himself conscientiously and with religious regularity to prayer and the singing of the psalms.

Chapter XX

Therefore, the monasteries he ruled were enriched abundantly both with external wealth and no less with internal.[26] To make them more secure against looting by the impious, he sent legates to Rome to ask Pope Sergius[27] of blessed memory for a letter of privilege, which he

25. For a charming revelation of his disarmingly zealous personality see his account, in the last part of his long letter to Pictish King Nechtan (Bede, *Ecclesiastical History*, Bk. V, ch. 21), of how he told off the Irish Abbot Adamnan in the matter of the Celtic tonsure.

26. See Bede, *Lives of the Abbots*, Ch. 15; and see note 29 to Introduction.

27. Among these monks Ceolfrith sent must have been Hwaetbert, who was to succeed him as abbot (Ch. 29). Bede says that Hwaetbert spent some little time at Rome in Pope Sergius I's reign (*Lives of the Abbots*, Ch. 18) and implies that he was there as late as 701, the last year of the pope's life and the year in which he discovered a relic of the True Cross (*De Temporum Ratione*, Ch. 47). Dickins and Ross (*The Dream of the Rood* [London, 4th ed., 1954] p. 19) follow Brandl's mistake (*Scottish Historical Review*, 9 [1911-12] p. 145) in assuming it was Ceolfrith himself who was in Rome on this occasion.

received, like the one Benedict had received from his predecessor, Agatho. He enriched the monasteries most lavishly with the vessels used for the service of the church and the altar. He made princely additions to the library which he and Benedict had brought from Rome; among other things he had copies made of three Bibles, and then placed two of these in the churches of his two monasteries, so that it would be easy for any one who wished to read any chapter of either Testament to find what he wanted. As for the third copy—being about to set out for Rome, he decided to offer it as a gift to the blessed Peter, Prince of the Apostles.[28]

Chapter XXI

For when he realized he was so tired out in his old age that he could no longer guide his pupils by the example of his youthful enthusiasm, he hit upon the happy solution of handing over the government of the monastery to younger men while he himself went to live as a pilgrim in the home of the Apostles. There he would be relieved of earthly responsibilities and free to devote himself to prayer while he waited for his last day, following the example of his brother Cynefrith who, as we related above,[29] resigned the charge of his monastery out of a desire for contemplative life, and exchanged his homeland for voluntary exile for the Lord's sake.

Chapter XXII

Therefore he readied a ship, decided on who he would pick as envoys for Rome, arranged for the gifts which would be brought to the blessed Peter, and procured a sufficient supply of the things necessary for so

28. The famous Codex Amiatinus, one of the best manuscripts of the Vulgate. See note 44. See M. Rickert, *Painting in Britain in the Middle Ages*, Baltimore, 1954, p. 29 (notes 30, 31, 32).

29. See Ch. 2.

great a journey. But the fact that he himself was going to go with them he advisedly kept secret for the time being, for fear that if his plans were made public he either would be prevented or delayed by his friends or would surely be given generous gifts of money by many people whom he would have neither the time nor the ability to remunerate in person. For this hallmark of a bountiful spirit he ever retained, that whenever any gift was given him by anyone, whether of high rank or low, he would never for any reason let the person go away unrecompensed, but would oftentimes bestow a more generous favor on his benefactor.

Chapter XXIII

At last when everything was ready and the day of departure was at hand he summoned to the church all the monks who were in the monastery of St. Peter and explained what he was about to do. They all broke into tears and falling prone on the ground they grasped his feet and implored him with floods of tears not to go away so precipitately but to stay with them for a day at least. So he gave in to their pleas and remained with them that day and night, which was the Tuesday before Pentecost Sunday. Then in the morning, accompanied by many of the brethren, he set out to speak with the brethren stationed in the monastery of St. Paul and to tell them that he had now resolved to go away. And as they wept openly, greatly upset by this totally unexpected departure of his, he spoke gently and fondly to the whole assembly, asking them to keep the rule he had taught, to remain in the fear of the Lord, and not to put their pleas and tears in the way of this journey which he had decided on. And he begged them to pardon him if he had ever let his zeal overbalance his sense of justice, for he himself had already forgiven from the bottom of his heart all who had offended him in any way, and he prayed that the Lord would be gentle with them all then and forever.

Chapter XXIV

But not for some little time did he finally succeed, over their protestations and with he himself in tears, in gaining their leave for his departure, granted duly with a good grace and with their blessing. They then earnestly implored him to commend them often to the Lord in his prayers if he should arrive at the sacred shrines of the Apostles, or, if he should die on the way, to remember always to intercede for their salvation.

Chapter XXV

He left [St. Paul's at Jarrow] the same day, either urged on by the desire for traveling, or driven by weariness at the wailing of the brethren.[30] But first he ordained that, with the approval of his blessing according to the rule of holy Father Benedict and the statutes of their privilege, they should appoint as their abbot whomever they considered to be the most worthy among them. Then he returned to the monastery of St. Peter.

As soon as morning came and Mass had been sung in the Church of St. Peter and the Church of St. Mary, with those present receiving Communion, Ceolfrith got ready for the journey without delay and called all the brethren into the Church of St. Peter. He asked them to pray for him, and he himself said a prayer; then he kindled the incense and with the thurible in his hand took his stand on the altar steps where he had so often read during services, and then gave the kiss of peace to many of the brethren—for his grief and theirs prevented him from giving it to all of them. Then he went out with the thurible to the oratory of St. Lawrence Martyr, which is in the brothers' dormitory, while they followed singing the antiphon of the prophet,

30. Our author, in the monastery of Monkwearmouth, directs some brotherly banter at the monks of Jarrow.

"The way of the just is made straight, and the road of the saints is prepared" [Is. 26:7]. And "going from virtue to virtue" [Ps. 83:8], they added the 66th Psalm, "May God have mercy on us, and bless us: may he cause the light of his countenance to shine upon us, and may he have mercy on us" [Ps. 66:2].

Then, after he had incensed, he came out of the oratory and exhorted all of them again to keep peace with one another, to beware of quarrels, detractions, and all occasions of scandal, to correct sinners singly at first, according to the Gospel precept, then two or three together, and to strive to recall them to the way of Truth, rejoicing if their efforts prove fruitful, otherwise bringing forth their offenses finally in public. He exhorted them to preserve concord and brotherly unity with the brethren who were at St. Paul's, and to remember that both are one monastery and must always be ruled by the same abbot lest the inner bond of brotherhood should be sundered and the door thrown open to harmful invasion from without, as in the example of the Hebrew people who never enjoyed any rest from external calamity once the folly of the son of Solomon had divided them against themselves.

Chapter XXVI

When he finished his talk they all went down to the river,[31] taking up again the antiphon and psalm mentioned before, escorting their father with so sad a song for they knew he was about to leave them. Then once more he gave to each of them the kiss of peace, while again and again their chant was choked off by their tears. At the riverside a prayer was said; then he went aboard the ship and took his seat in the prow, and deacons sat beside him, one holding a golden cross which he had made, the other holding lighted candles.

Chapter XXVII

As the ship sped across the river and he looked on the brethren lamenting his departure and listened to the throbbing strains of their chant

31. The Wear River.

so charged with sorrow, he was quite unable to hold back his own sobs and tears. All he could find words for, over and over again, was "My Christ, be gracious to that company! O Lord Almighty, watch over that band of men! For my part I am most certain that never have I known any better than they or more eager to obey. My Christ, my God, take care of them!" And so [on the far bank] he left the ship, knelt before the cross, then mounted a horse and rode away, leaving behind him the cares of this world, but also hastening away from his own blood and kind, the people of the Angles,[32] in order to live as a pilgrim in foreign lands where with a freer and less divided spirit he might devote himself to contemplating the fellowship of the angels[32] in heaven.

Chapter XXVIII

Returning to the monastery the brethren prayed and then entered into council about what they should do, and they decided that in prayer and fasting they should seek to learn from the Lord whom they ought to appoint as their abbot. But their venerable father as he was leaving had ordered that none of them was to fast on the day of his departure but rather that all of them were to have a great feast, and for that reason he had even enjoined certain members of his party to remain with them till the dinner was over—now it was the Thursday before Pentecost Sunday. So it seemed to the brethren that the best they could do would be to keep a fast the following day and night and not break it till the ninth hour[33] on Saturday, for the vigil of this Sunday's solemn feast prevented them from prolonging the fast any further than that. But they would also add more psalms to their regular prayer, distributing them properly throughout the various canonical hours, and everyone would implore the Divine Goodness that on that day when he had so graciously hallowed the beginnings of his Church with the coming of the Holy Spirit, he would now by the grace of the same Spirit point

32. The same play on the words "angels" and "Angles" that Pope Gregory the Great had made famous (Bede, *Ecclesiastical History*, Bk. II, ch. 1).

33. That is, about 3 P. M.

out to those, who were also a portion of that same Church, a worthy superior.

Chapter XXIX

So after all these things had been done as planned, on Pentecost Sunday a good number of the brethren came over from the monastery of St. Paul, and by the common decision of both monasteries Hwaetbert[34] was selected as the one to be installed in the office of abbot. He had lived in this monastery from his youth, was well versed in both ecclesiastical and monastic knowledge, and was already highly esteemed as a priest. As soon as he was elected abbot he composed a letter in which he commended his father and predecessor to the Apostolic Father, and at the same time he prepared gifts to send along with it, then he followed after Ceolfrith with some of the brethren. Having found him in Aelfberht's monastery, which is situated in the place called Cornu Vallis,[35] he read the letter to him and handed over the gifts which he was to present.

Chapter XXX

Ceolfrith gladly accepted the brothers' election and confirmed it with his blessing, then he instructed Hwaetbert at some length in many matters having to do with the manner in which he should conduct the government of the monastery.

This letter begins as follows:

34. Hwaetbert has been suggested as the author of this *Life of Ceolfrith* (Dekkers and Gaar, *Clavis Patrum Latinorum*, item 1342, p. 301) but, in that case, it would be difficult to see how he could have written the very next sentence in the text. See note 27 also on Hwaetbert.

35. Ceolfrith and his party had ridden south to the mouth of the Humber River where they were waiting for a ship to the continent. Levision suggests that the "Aelfberht's monastery" may refer to the monastery of Willibrord's father, Wilgils (*England and the Continent in the Eighth Century*, p. 55, note 1). See Alcuin, *Life of Willibrord*, Ch. 1.

"To my most dear lord in the Lord of lords, the thrice-blessed Pope Gregory,[36] Hwaetbert your humble servant, abbot of the monastery of the most blessed Peter, prince of the Apostles, in Saxony,[37] sends greetings forever in the Lord.

I, together with the holy brothers in these lands who desire with me to bear the most sweet yoke of Christ in order to find rest for their souls, do not cease to give thanks to the dispensation of the divine judgment which has deigned in our day to place you as a glorious vessel of election at the head of the government of the whole Church, so that by means of this light of truth and faith with which you are so liberally endowed by heaven, it may shed a goodly share of the radiance of its goodness even over lesser folk. And we thus commend to your gracious holiness, most beloved father and lord in Christ, the venerable gray hairs of our most dear father and abbot, Ceolfrith, who raised us and kept watch over our spiritual liberty and peace in the quiet of our monastery.

And first of all we give thanks to the holy and undivided Trinity for the fact that he has reached the holy happiness of the rest he has so long desired, even though it was not without the greatest pain, grief, and sorrow on our part that he left us, accompanied by our tears.

Weary though he is in his old age, he has devoutly sought out once again those shrines of the blessed apostles which have never failed through the years to rejoice his heart whenever he recalled how as a young man he had visited them to marvel and to worship.[38] After the more than forty long years of labor and continuous responsibility during which, in the office of abbot, he presided over the government of monasteries with unmatched love of virtue, now as though newly called to the life of heaven, at the extreme limit of his years on the very edge of death, he has ventured once again to become a pilgrim-exile for Christ so that the fervent flame of devotion may more freely consume the ancient thornbushes of worldly cares in the furnace of his spirit.

Hence we also beseech your Paternity that you will carefully perform for him that final office of love which we have not been found worthy to render. And we know for certain that though you have his body, yet both we and you have his spirit—that spirit devoted to God,

36. Pope Gregory II, who three years later was to change Winfrith's name to Boniface and commission him as his missionary to the Germans (Willibald, *Life of Boniface*, Ch. 5).

37. Rarely used by Anglo-Saxon writers as a name for Britain (see Plummer, *Baedae Opera Historica*, II,368).

38. See Ch. 10.

whether it be still in the body or set free from bodily chains—as a great patron and intercessor with the heavenly Goodness for our sins."

Chapter XXXI

Now Ceolfrith set forth from his monastery on June 4 [716], the fifth day of the week; and on July 4th, a Saturday, he boarded a ship preparing to put to sea from the mouth of the Humber River. Before touching the shore of Gaul the ship made landings in three provinces, in each of which Ceolfrith was received with honor and held in veneration by all as one who had determined to crown the grace of venerable perfection with an incomparable example of virtue.

Chapter XXXII

The voyage completed, he arrived at the land of Gaul on August 12, a Saturday, and here too he was honored magnificently by everyone, most of all by King Chilperic[39] himself, who besides the gifts which he offered, gave him letters-of-passage through all the provinces of his realm so that he would be received in peace everywhere and no one would dare to cause him any delay on his journey. Moreover, when Ceolfrith was about to leave, Chilperic graciously commended him and all his company to Liutprand, king of the Lombards.[40]

On the 25th day of September, the sixth day of the week, he arrived at Langres, a city in Burgundy, and there, exhausted by old age and illness alike—in fact exactly as the Scripture puts it— "his strength failing in a good old age, he was gathered unto his fathers" [Gen. 25:8]. He was 74 years old, had exercised the functions of a priest for 47 years, and had governed by himself in the office of abbot for 35 years.

39. King Chilperic II of Neustria, one of the unhappy "long-haired" Merovingian kings (Wallace-Hadrill, *The Long-Haired Kings*, pp. 240, 246).

40. Boniface was to enjoy the king's welcome hospitality more than once in the course of his journeys to Rome (Willibald, *Life of Boniface*, Chs. 5, 7).

Chapter XXXIII

He left behind in the monasteries [of St. Peter and St. Paul] a company of Christ's soldiers more than 600 in number, and almost 150 hides of land, according to the way of reckoning customary with the Angles.

From the time he departed from his monastery until he closed the account of his last day, he sang the psalter of David right through thrice daily, besides the regular singing of the canonical hours; and this he did as an addition to a very old custom of his whereby for many years he had been in the habit of singing the psalter through twice daily. And he offered the Holy Sacrifice to the Lord for himself and those dear to him every single day without fail, even on the occasions when he was too exhausted to ride horseback and was being conveyed in a horse-drawn litter, except for that one day at sea when the ship was tossed about by storms and he was in great distress the whole time, and except for the four days immediately preceding his death.

Chapter XXXIV

Traveling with him had been a company of nearly eighty men drawn from various places, all of whom followed and revered him like a father.[41] And he had given orders to his attendants that if they should learn of any of these followers who had no provisions they were at once to give him either food or the money to buy it. For he was kind-hearted by nature and was a remarkable patron of the poor. So it was that the destitute and the homeless made common cause of their grief as Ceolfrith passed through his last agony to death, and they thus bore witness that they had lost one who stood in place of father and guardian to them.

He had taken great pains and great care to live according to this particular courtesy of the spirit not only because it was called for by

41. See note 34 to Bede, *Lives of the Abbots.*

the fear and love of God, but also because it had been handed down to him from his father as though by right of inheritance.[42] Indeed his father, who happened to hold a very noble office in the royal *comitatus*,[43] always took the greatest delight in those works of mercy done for the poor. In fact on one occasion when he had prepared to receive the king with a most sumptuous banquet, and some unexpected wartime emergency had arisen and prevented his coming, Ceolfrith's father gave thanks to divine providence and straightway decided that all the poor, the pilgrims, and the enfeebled be called in from all round to the feast. What was to have been offered to the earthly king and his young followers, he offered now to the supreme King in the person of his lowly ones for the sake of his eternal reward. Moreover he himself in person tended to all the wants of the male guests and he directed his wife to offer the women personally all the services of the most lowly housemaid.

Chapter XXXV

Now Ceolfrith arrived at Langres on September 25, at the beginning of the fifteenth indiction, as we have said, about the third hour of the day. Halting his company in the meadows outside this city he was gladly received by Gangulf, the lord of that district, who in fact had met Ceolfrith before en route and had kindly assured him that his home would be open to him even if he himself should happen to be away. Now he anxiously implored Ceolfrith not to depart from there unless he were quite well, but, if God should so will it, to await his entrance into heavenly life there rather than at the shrines of the holy martyrs [in Rome].

42. Another example of this Heroic-Age continuity of spirit between the noble household and the monastery. See, for instance, note 51 to the Introduction and note 6 to the *Life of St. Cuthbert.*

43. See note 24 to the Introduction.

Chapter XXXVI

So it happened that at about the tenth hour of the very day on which he had arrived, he went to the Lord. In the morning, with a great procession of his own company and of the citizens of that city, his body was borne for about three miles to Gangulf's monastery, located in the southern quarter of the city at a distance of about a mile and a half, and was buried in the church of the holy martyr-brothers, Speusippus, Eleosippus, and Meliosippus. They were sons of the same mother born at one birth, and were crowned with martyrdom there long ago and were buried in the same place. There too lies their grandmother named Leonella, who also was released from the prison of the body by her martyr's profession of faith.

Chapter XXXVII

Then after their father was buried, some of the brethren who had escorted him from Britain returned home again anxious to tell in his own monastery the story of where and when he had died. But some others were determined to complete the journey to Rome and present the gifts that Ceolfrith had sent, among which was that Bible we have mentioned, transmitted from the Greek and Hebrew sources in the translation of the blessed priest Jerome, and which in its beginning had some verses inscribed thus:[44]

> To the justly worshipful body of the renowned Peter,
> Crowned by august tradition as head of the Church,
> I, Ceolfrith, abbot in the ultimate land of the Angles,

44. It was by these verses that the Codex Amiatinus (see note 28) in the Laurentian Library in Florence was finally identified as the book Ceolfrith had destined for the pope (see Dekkers and Gaar, *Clavis Patrum Latinorum*, p. 309, no. 1377). It seems to derive from a manuscript in the library of Cassiodorus (Brown and Bruce-Mitford, *Evangeliorum Quattuor Codex Lindisfarnensis*, II, 13 ff.).

Do send these pledges of my devoted affection,
Desiring that amid the heavenly joys of so great a father
There may ever be a place for the memory of me and mine.

Chapter XXXVIII

Still others preferred to remain in that same city of Langres, prompted by the love for their father buried there. Later on, however, they carried out their prior resolve and desire to visit Rome. Meanwhile the most reverend abbot's companions found such favor with Gangulf that after Ceolfrith's burial he entertained them all at a splendid feast, and afterwards for those who were setting out in their various directions he provided provisions and guides for the journey. And for those remaining there he appointed daily rations for as long as they wished to stay.

Chapter XXXIX

As for how the Apostolic Father felt about Ceolfrith and his gifts, we have the witness of the letter which he sent back, and which reads as follows:[45]

> Gregory the bishop, servant of the servants of God, to the religious abbot Hwaetbert. Having read with care and pondered over the tenor of your reverence's letter, it is clear that you rejoice with us at the truth by whose grace are called even 'those things that are not, just as those that are' [Rom. 4,17]. By your allusion to our election you show that you profess most prompt obedience to the authority of the apostolic right whose office we administer, though unworthy. Wherefore know that you should the more earnestly pray for him whose reign you welcome, laboring by his side with your continual prayers, so that he may be of use to himself, to you, and to many. Pray, furthermore, for him whose venerable gray hairs, dedicated to God, you devotedly commended, and who, before he was re-

45. The text of this letter is corrupt and my translation does the best it can with the jumbled Latin.

ceived by us, was translated by God's summons from time to eternity, but not before he had sent on a gift—for which he shall be forever remembered—to my lord and our common patron, the blessed Peter, supreme lord of the Apostles. Approving of his faith in the offering of this gift, we have deemed him worthy of constant commemoration in our prayers.

In conclusion we pray that this most successful instructor in the holy monastic rule may lead his worthy pupils to stand before God, and that the divine grace which took him up into heaven will make him the equal in honor with Aaron and Moses, who were elected as leaders of God's people as they made their way to the land of promise, and with that holy Elias who was suddenly snatched up into heaven, all of them to be honored for their merits. And we pray that the divine grace may adorn the disciple who survives him and has been given followers to be governed, with a generous supply of the divine gifts of worthiness in office such as were received by Joshua, a most capable leader, and by Phineas and Elisha. Farewell.

Chapter XL

Those companions of our father so dear to God who returned to us related how on the next night after his venerable body had been consigned to the tomb, while three custodians of the same church were occupied with their regular nightly worship, suddenly a scent of most marvelous fragrance flooded the whole church. Then a light appeared, and after remaining fixed for some little time finally moved up to the roof of the church. Running outdoors at once, the men saw the same light rising swiftly into the sky and making everything in the vicinity visible, lighting it up as though it were daytime. Thus it was openly made known that ministers of eternal light and everlasting joy had been present, and had hallowed the resting place of the holy body by their visitation. Hence a custom grew up among the inhabitants of that place that each day during the times for daily and nightly prayer, after the psalms had been sung in the canonical manner, then all the men would kneel at Ceolfrith's tomb and pray. Moreover, there were widely known reports of other signs and of cures performed there by the grace of Him who is wont to aid his saints battling in the present life, and to crown them as victors in the next. Amen.

THE LIFE OF ST. WILLIBRORD

---

by Alcuin

Preface to Alcuin's LIFE OF WILLIBRORD

It is appropriate that the Northumbrian Alcuin, who was taught the cultural heritage of the Roman West by Bede's disciples, and who in turn conveyed it to Charlemagne's rebuilding world, should have written a biography of his relative, Willibrord, who inaugurated this Anglo-Saxon mission to the continent (of course it was incomparable Wilfrid who had made the first beachhead, but he left it to Willibrord, and finally Boniface, to exploit—see Ch. 26 in *Life of Wilfrid*). Like Willibrord, and Boniface after him, Alcuin too considered himself a *peregrinus*, a voluntary-exile on the continent (see Haddan and Stubbs, *Councils and Ecclesiastical Documents*, III, 499 [top], 470 [middle]. In rhetorical Latin (midway between Aldhelm's and Bede's) meant for public religious reading in a monastery, Alcuin wrote this hagiography some fifty years after its hero's death. Thus distanced from his subject, his account is far more formal, epic, and "romanesque" than the warmer, more informative *Life of Ceolfrith* and *Life of Wilfrid* and Bede's *Lives of the Abbots*.

The best text, from which I have made this new translation, is that edited by W. Levison in Monumenta Germaniae Historica, *Scriptores Rerum Merovingicarum* (Hanover and Leipzig, 1920) VII, 116-127. There is a translation by A. Grieve (*Willibrord, Missionary in the Netherlands, 670-739*. Westminster, 1923), and one by Talbot in *The Anglo-Saxon Missionaries in Germany*, pp. 2-22. Whitelock translates a few extracts in *English Historical Documents*, pp. 713-715.

There is a scholarly biography of Willibrord in French by Gabriel Verbist (*Saint-Willibrord*. Louvain and Paris, 1939). W. Levison has a fine short account in *England and the Continent*, pp. 53-69. On Alcuin see my note 33 to the Introduction.

THE LIFE OF ST. WILLIBRORD

Chapter I[1]

IN THE province of Northumbria on the island of Britain there was a family man named Wilgils, Saxon by race, who with his wife and whole household lived a devout life in Christ—as subsequent events were to reveal. For he renounced the world and chose to live a monastic life. But his passion for the spiritual life grew even stronger so a short while later with an even more demanding enthusiasm he gave himself up to the punishing life of a solitary. For many years he dwelt on a promontory that juts out from the mouth of the River Humber into the North Sea. There in a little oratory dedicated to St. Andrew, the Apostle of Christ, he served God so zealously with fasts, prayers, and vigils that he became famous for miracles and his name was on everyone's lips. To the crowds who flocked to him he always addressed the same heartening appeal and the gentle corrective of the Word of God.

1. In a traditional Preface, not translated here, Alcuin dedicates the book to Beornred, who was Archbishop of Sens and Abbot of Echternach. Some of Alcuin's remarks afford an interesting insight into the purposes behind the composition of these hagiographies. "I have composed two little books," he writes. "One walks along in the language of prose and could be read publicly to the brethren in the community, if this should seem fitting in your judgment. The other runs on poetic feet and is meant only to be mused over by your scholars in the privacy of their cells" (Monumenta Germaniae Historica, *Scriptorum Rerum Merovingicarum*, VII,113). He concludes by saying that it is up to the archbishop to decide whether the prose Life and the verse Life are worth being recorded or whether they should be summarily erased (*an pumice radenda feroci*). See note 6 to *Life of St. Guthlac.* Bede, too, had written both a prose and verse version of his *Life of St. Cuthbert.* It was a common medieval exercise to write the same work in both forms (see Curtius, *European Literature and the Latin Middle Ages*, pp. 461-62).

He was so highly respected by the king and nobles of the nation that they bestowed on him in perpetuity some small grants of land adjacent to his headland hermitage for the building of a church to God. Within its walls the devoted father brought together a community of servants of God that was small indeed but sincere.[2] Here his body rests while he wears heaven's crown after the long trial of his holy labors, and to this present day his descendants have possession of the place in the tradition of his holiness. Of whom I am the last in merit and in time to have succeeded in rightful sequence to the rule of this little monastery, and now I have written, at your behest, Most Blessed Bishop Beornred, this record of the most holy father and most excellent of teachers, Willibrord. With the grace God has given you, you have been a most worthy heir to so great a father in the dignity of his high priesthood and in the tradition of his family and in the care of the sanctuaries which, as we know, he built in God's honor.[3]

Chapter II

But let me get back to where I began and tell the full story of Willibrord's birth, and of the signs there were that he was specially chosen by God while he was still in his mother's womb. For like the most holy precursor of Our Lord Jesus Christ, blessed John the Baptist, who was sanctified in his mother's womb and who, like the morning star ushering in Christ the sun, was born of devout parents—as the Gospel says— for the future salvation of many, so St. Willibrord, destined also for the salvation of many, was born of parents who were manifestly devout. For that holy man Wilgils, about whom we were just speaking, was led by the predestination of God to enter into marriage for the sole purpose of begetting this son who would be a blessing to many peoples.

2. Here perhaps is where Ceolfrith waited in 716 for the ship that was to carry him off on his last pilgrimage (see note 35 to the *Life of Ceolfrith*).

3. Beornred was now the abbot of Willibrord's famous Monastery of Echternach (see note 29).

Now it happened that his wife, Willibrord's mother, saw a vision in her sleep during the dead of night. It seemed to her as though she were looking at a new moon in the sky, which grew before her eyes until it became full. Then, as she gazed spellbound, suddenly it fell from its course and dropped into her mouth. She swallowed it, and her body glowed with the splendor of the moon. Then she awoke, terribly frightened. When she told the dream to a certain devout priest he asked her if she had had her customary relations with her husband on the night that the vision had come to her. She said that she had, and then he told her: "The moon which you saw grow from small to large is a son whom you conceived that very night and who will dispel the gloomy darkness of error with the light of truth. And wherever he goes he will walk in the splendor of heaven's light and reflect it in the full moon of his holiness, and by the dazzling lustre of his fame and the beauty of his life he will draw the gaze of many to himself." The truth of events followed out closely this interpretation of the dream.

Chapter III

So it happened, after the requisite cycle of time had passed, that the woman gave birth to a son [about 658]; and when he was born a second time at the sacred baptismal font his father gave him the name of Willibrord. As soon as he grew out of his infancy[4] his father handed him over to the church at Ripon[5] to be instructed by the brethren in religious learning and in sacred letters, so that his tender age might grow strong with sound training in a place where he would see nothing but what was noble, hear nothing but what was holy. Even in his

4. This perhaps means that Willibrord was six or seven years old at the time (see Verbist, *Saint Willibrord*, pp. 27-30). And see note 18 to the *Life of Ceolfrith*, for similar cases.

5. Willibrord thus became a spiritual "son" of Wilfrid (see Eddius, *Life of Wilfrid*, Ch. 26) and may have been received into Ripon by the victor of Whitby before the latter, in the full flush of his triumph, went to Gaul to be consecrated bishop (see *Life of Wilfrid*, Chs. 11 ff.).

early boyhood divine grace bestowed on him such power of understanding and strength of character, as much as could be suited to his years, that you might have thought our times had seen the birth of a new Samuel, of whom it was said: "But the child Samuel advanced and grew and pleased both God and men" [1 Kings (1 Samuel) 2,26]. There in the monastery this boy who was destined to help so many people received the clerical tonsure and made his devout profession as a monk.[6] There among the rest of the young men of the same most holy monastery he received his education. He was second to none in his eager enthusiasm, in his practice of humility and in his application to study. In fact so marked was this talented boy's progress from day to day that he attained to a maturity of character and of understanding that far belied his boyish years and his slight, frail body.

Chapter IV

And so the young man reached his twentieth year, distinguished alike for his sacred learning, his prudence, and his goodness. But then his soul flared up with the passionate desire for a more rigorous life, and his heart stirred with the longing to go on pilgrimage.[7] Now he had heard tell that in Ireland there was a great springtime of scholars and of learning, and his spirit was roused by the stories he heard about the lives of certain holy men, especially of the blessed bishop Egbert,[8]

6. Verbist suggests that this would have been about 673, when Willibrord was fifteen (*Saint Willibrord*, p. 30).

7. This restlessness of spirit, with its hint of a divine gallantry, stirred Wilfrid too, and Benedict Biscop, and Ceolfrith and Boniface, and the author of *The Seafarer*, and so many other kings and nobles and monks of the Celtic and Anglo-Saxon Golden Age (see note 46 to the Introduction). It seems almost to draw this northern monastic world into some deep brotherhood with an older world of "pilgrim"-heroes, the world of Gilgamesh and of Jason and of the Odysseus of the 26th Canto of the *Inferno*.

8. Bede tells us of this holy visionary who as a young Anglo-Saxon noble had, like Willibrord, gone to study in Ireland, and then had vowed to remain "in exile" there. Till his death at ninety he labored to bring the Celtic Christians in line with the practices of Rome (*Ecclesiastical History*, Bk. III, ch. 27).

called "the Saint," and of the revered priest Wictbert. Both of them were driven by their yearning for the heavenly fatherland to leave their home and country and kindred and go away to Ireland. There they lived alone as hermits, free of the world and full of God, feasting every day on the sweetest fare of heavenly contemplation. It was their holy life that young Willibrord was so eager to emulate, so with the approval of his abbot and of the brethren he set out for Ireland by the quickest route and joined the company of those men.[9] Like a very provident bee he fed on the honey-filled blossoms of their friendship and built sweet honeycombs of virtue in the apiary of his heart. There for twelve years the future teacher of many peoples was instructed by these remarkable masters both in holy piety and in sacred learning until he reached the maturity of manhood, the full age of Christ.

Chapter V

At the age of thirty-three, therefore, the flame of an even greater faith blazed so high in the heart of this extraordinary man that it suddenly seemed to him a paltry thing to toil so for his own sanctity alone if it were not going to avail other people too through his preaching of the truth. He heard that in the northern regions of the world the harvest was great indeed but the laborers few. And so—by the arrangement of God— it was in fulfilment of the dream his mother once had had of him, that Willibrord now took it into his head to sail to those foreign parts. He was conscious only of his own decision, unaware as yet of the divine hand in the matter, when he made up his mind to bring the dazzling light of the Gospel, *Deo volente*, to those peoples long languishing in a dull world of no faith. Taking eleven brethren with him,[10] all armed with the same enthusiastic faith as himself, he

9. His decision to leave Ripon may also have been influenced by the expulsion from York of his spiritual father, Bishop Wilfrid, which happened about this same time (Eddius, *Life of Wilfrid*, Ch. 24).

10. The number of the entire band was most likely fixed at twelve because of the symbolic association with Christ's twelve apostles. Aidan had chosen twelve English boys to be instructed at Lindisfarne (Bede, *Ecclesiastical History*, Bk. III, ch. 26).

went aboard ship. Some of these afterwards were to be crowned with martyrdom for their intransigence in preaching the Gospel, while others were to receive the rank of bishop and rest in peace after the labors of their holy preaching

So the hero of God sailed with his companions [in the year 690], as we said, and after a very favorable voyage lowered sail at the mouth of the Rhine River. Stepping onto the land of their desire filled them all with new life and they hurried on to the old fortified Roman town of Utrecht, which is situated on the bank of the same river. It was inside this fortress[11] some time later, after the faith had grown with God's help, that St. Willibrord established his episcopal see. But now the Frisians who dwelt with their king, Radbod, in that same region where the fort was situated, were still defiling themselves with pagan rites. Willibrord, therefore, thought it better to make his way into Francia to see Pippin,[12] the ruler of the Franks, a man of great energy, famous for his victories and the probity of his character. Pippin received Willibrord with all honor, and unwilling to deprive himself or his people of such a teacher he provided him with various properties within the boundaries of the kingdom. They were conveniently located so that from them Willibrord could sally forth to uproot the thorns of idolatry and more abundantly sow the seed of the most pure

11. The Latin *castellum* Alcuin uses here should not remind us of a later medieval castle with its towering clustered battlements, but rather of a large rectangular enclosure (on the order of log forts in the American Wild West) with Roman brick and mortar walls, like Pevensey Castle in Sussex or Burgh Castle in Suffolk. See Plate VII.

12. Like Ebroin (see Eddius, *Life of Wilfrid*, Ch. 25, and note 85) who had been murdered in 681, Pippin II was one of the powerful Carolingian Mayors of the Palace in a turbulent land of figurehead Merovingian kings (see Einhard's vivid picture in the first chapter of his *Life of Charlemagne*). Pippin had managed to gain control of both Austrasia and Neustria by his victory at Tertry three years before Willibrord arrived, but Radbod would be a thorn in everyone's side for almost thirty more years (see note 25; and *Life of St. Boniface*, Ch. 9 and note 9). He was evidently responsible also for the failure of an earlier mission to Frisia by another of Egbert's Anglo-Saxon disciples, Wictbert (see this *Life of Willibrord*, Ch. 4; and Bede, *Ecclesiastical History*, Bk. V, ch. 9). Willibrord would thus have heard the whole story from Wictbert after the latter returned to Ireland. He then probably expected the worst even before he met the testy Frisian.

word of God in new-ploughed land, in fulfillment of the prophet's command: "Break up anew your fallow ground, and sow not upon thorns" [Jer. 4:3].

Chapter VI

So Willibrord made his way most zealously here and there through all the region giving himself up to that work of evangelization he had so hungered for. Far and wide in the fields of many hearts, moistened by the dew of grace from heaven, the seed of life flowered into most bountiful harvest at the sound of his preaching. The ruler of the Franks was delighted with his most saintly devotedness and with this remarkable increase of the faith. Accordingly, with the help of sensible advice, he concluded that to promote a still greater growth he would send Willibrord to Rome[13] to be raised to the honor of archbishop by Pope Sergius, the most saintly man of that time.[14] For once he had received the apostolic benediction and the mandate he would be armed with greater confidence and authority and could return to the work of the Gospel as the official emissary of the Pope. "And how shall they preach unless they be sent?" the Apostle had said [Rom. 10:15].

But when Pippin attempted to persuade the man of God to this he refused at first, replying that he was not worthy of the honor of such great authority. He cited the requirements established by the apostles, and protested that he fell far short of the list of virtues which the great preacher to the Gentiles, instructing his son Timothy, had decreed a

13. Bede states (*Ecclesiastical History*, Bk. V, ch. 11) that Willibrord had already made a prior trip to Rome, very shortly after his arrival at Utrecht, to obtain the Pope's blessing on his new ministry.

14. Pope Sergius I had many contacts with Anglo-Saxon England. In 689 he had baptized dying King Caedwalla in Rome (see note 102 to *Life of Wilfrid*). He ratified the decrees of his predecessors granting privileges to Wilfrid's Ripon and Hexham (see Eddius, *Life of Wilfrid*, Chs. 43, 46, 53), and in 700 he received Ceolfrith's envoys and sent privileges to Monkwearmouth and Jarrow (*Life of Ceolfrith*, Ch. 20). About 693 Pope Sergius entertained Aldhelm most graciously and sent him home with letters of privilege for his monastery at Malmesbury (Duckett, *Anglo-Saxon Saints and Scholars*, pp. 71-72).

bishop must have [1 Tim. 3; 2 Tim. 2,4]. Pippin then respectfully urged the contrary, which Willibrord as modestly denied. But at last he bowed to the unanimous opinion of everyone concerned and gave his consent, or rather, which is a greater thing, he was forced to it by the direction of God. He preferred humbly to obey the opinion of many, rather than stubbornly hold out for his own. And thus Willibrord found himself put at the head of a quite distinguished embassy, provided with presents worthy of the apostolic dignity, and set on the road to Rome.[15]

Chapter VII

Now four days before he arrived there, it happened that an angel appeared to the Apostolic Father in a dream and told him that Willibrord should be received with every possible honor as a man selected by God to bring the light to multitudes of souls, that he was coming to Rome for the purpose of receiving the archiepiscopal dignity, and that he should be granted anything he requested. Well informed therefore by this admonition, the Apostolic Father received Willibrord with great joy and with every possible mark of respect. And after he had had the opportunity to see for himself Willibrord's ardent faith, his devout piety, and the plenitude of his wisdom, then he announced to the public a suitable day for the consecration and invited the venerable clergy to take part in the service. Thereupon in the Church of St.

15. With these "presents" starting off on the long road from Pippin II to Pope Sergius went the first real link in the Carolingian policy of close relationship with Rome. Till now Rome had figured little in the life of the Frankish Church, and it is significant that the man who thus bridged the distance between them should be an Anglo-Saxon. For from its inception the Anglo-Saxon Church had been close to Rome (see Levison, *England and the Continent*, pp. 57 ff. and R. R. Darlington, "The Anglo-Saxon Period," in *The English Church and the Continent* [London, 1959] pp. 9 ff.). In 752 another Anglo-Saxon monk, Boniface (acting also as papal delegate), was to anoint the first Carolingian king, Pippin III (see Levison, *op. cit.*, pp. 116 ff.). Still another Anglo-Saxon monk, Alcuin, the author of our present Life, was to play a large role in the relations of Pippin's son, Charlemagne, with Rome.

Peter,[16] Prince of the Apostles, he publicly consecrated him as archbishop with all the splendid ceremony called for by apostolic tradition. Then he bestowed the name "Clement" upon him, robed him in his episcopal vestments, and confirmed him in the high honor of his office with the bestowal of the sacred pallium, like the mantle of Aaron. Moreover with the utmost graciousness he made him a present of whatever saints' relics or church furnishings he asked for or even manifested any desire for. And finally, with some helpful instructions, he sent Willibrord back to the work of the Gospel, fortified with the papal blessing and enriched with gifts.

Chapter VIII

Having received the blessing of the Apostolic See, it was with greater confidence now that this devoted preacher of God's word returned to the ruler of the Franks. Pippin welcomed him back with the greatest display of honor, and then under the aegis of his authority sent him forth to preach the Gospel, especially in the northern districts of the kingdom where hitherto the fire of faith had cast less light either because of the paucity of teachers or the dull insensibility of the inhabitants. The more God's man saw the necessity of doing away with the age-old famine of ignorance in those regions, the more urgently he gave himself up to planting the seeds of life there. How great his harvest was in those places, with the help of divine grace, there are people alive today who can testify, the people throughout the cities, towns, and forts whom he led by his holy chiding to the knowledge of truth and the worship of the one Almighty God. Witnesses too are the churches which he built in every district, and the communities of servants of God which he founded in various localities.

16. Levison points out, however, that he was actually consecrated in the church of Santa Cecilia in Trastevere, on November 21, 695 (*England and the Continent* p. 59).

Chapter IX

The hero of God even made an attempt to send the rivers of heavenly truth coursing beyond the borders of the kingdom of the Franks. He was not afraid, for instance, to face the King of the Frisians, Radbod, who was a pagan along with his people—and of course wherever he ventured he always announced the word of God most fearlessly. Nonetheless this king of the Frisians received the man of God kindly, with a certain lowly grace. But Willibrord was unable to get him to open the gates of his stubborn heart to the appeal of eternal life.

And when he saw that he could hope for no success with Radbod he diverted the line of march in his missionary campaign towards those most fierce of peoples, the Danes.[17] But their king at that time, so we are told, was Ongendus,[18] a man more savage than any wild beast and harder than any stone. Nevertheless, he did treat the herald of the truth with respect—through the intervention of God.[19] But when

17. This remark may be an indication that Alcuin wrote our *Life of Willibrord* after the "most fierce Danes" had descended in their dragon ships on the England he had left. In a letter of 797 to the clergy and nobility of Kent he is indignant that "a pagan people is ravaging our shores at will, plundering like pirates" (Haddan and Stubbs, *Councils and Ecclesiastical Documents*, III, 510).

18. Ongendus is sometimes mistakenly confused with the Swedish King Ongentheow who is mentioned once in *Widsith* (v. 31), and often in *Beowulf* where his death at the hand of King Hygelac's warrior, Eofor, is recounted (vv. 2486 ff. and 2961 ff.). His death occurred in the early years of the sixth century (see Kemp Malone's note in his revised edition of *Widsith* [Copenhagen, 1962] pp. 188-190)

19. We can hardly resist a smile at Alcuin's mystification over the deportment of Radbod and Ongendus. They are perfidious pagans, the "other," as Samaritans were to the Israelites, as Saracens to Roland, and as everybody to Sartre. Yet somehow they seem to have treated Willibrord decently and even with respect. In his puzzlement Alcuin can only resort to the miraculous for an explanation— "through the intervention of God." It is hard for our sophisticated tolerance to be sympathetic with this embattled early-medieval Christian mind and its youthful gargantuan appetite for contradictions and its impetuous disregard for the complicated spectral range between black and white. "The Christians are right and the pagans are wrong," chants the *Song of Roland* (laisse

Willibrord realized that he had bumped up against a stone wall in the case of this people which was so obdurately set in its ways, wholly given over to idolatry, and unresponsive to the possibility of a better life, then he took thirty boys which they offered him and hurried back to God's chosen people, the Franks. But in the course of the journey he was careful to instruct the boys in the faith and to baptize them, just in case he should lose any of them to the perils of the long voyage or in attacks by the ferocious inhabitants of that land. He determined to anticipate any trickery by the devil and arm these newly acquired souls of his with the Sacraments of the Lord.

Chapter X

In the course of his journey the holy preacher of God's word arrived at a certain island on the border between the Frisians and the Danes. The people who live in the vicinity call it Fositeland[20] after a god of theirs named Fosite, because some sanctuaries of this god had been built on the island. The pagans stood in such great awe of this place that not one of them would dare lay his hand on any of the animals that fed there or on anything else there, no matter what. No one would even be so bold as to drink from the spring that rose there, except in deathly silence.

Now God's hero was driven ashore on this island by a storm and remained there several days waiting for the winds to die down and the weather to become fit for sailing. But he had slight regard for the foolish superstition about the place and for the fierce anger of the king who was supposed to condemn violators of these shrines to a horrible death. So Willibrord baptized three men in the spring pool with the prescribed invocation of the Holy Trinity, and he ordered

93). In a letter of 790 Alcuin reports with satisfaction that all is at peace for the moment on the continent. King Charles has finally converted the recalcitrant Old Saxons and Frisians to the faith, "some by rewards and others by threats" (Whitelock, *English Historical Documents*, p. 774). And see note 42 to Introduction.

20. Present-day Heligoland.

the animals grazing on the land to be slaughtered to feed his company.[21] As the pagans watched this they expected the violators to be seized with madness or struck dead on the spot. But when they observed that they suffered no harm they themselves were struck dumb with terror. Later they reported to King Radbod what they had seen done.

Chapter XI

The king exploded into a terrible rage and determined to take vengeance on the priest of the living God for the insults done to their gods. Thrice a day for three days he drew lots according to his custom, but the true God defended his own and the fatal lot was never able to fall on the servant of God or any of his party—except for one in the group, who was finally singled out by lot and crowned with martyrdom.

Then the holy hero was called before the king who violently upbraided him and demanded to know why he had violated their sacred places and insulted their god. The herald of truth answered him with steady courage:[22] "He whom you adore, O King, is not God but the devil. He has fooled you with a most foul delusion so that he can thrust your soul into everlasting fire. For there is no God but one, who created sky and earth and sea, and everything that is in them. Whoever worships him with true faith will have life forever. As the servant of that God I here today bear witness to you of the truth, calling on you to renounce at long last that foolishness of an ageless delusion which your ancestors have perpetuated, and to believe in the one Almighty God and Our Lord Jesus Christ. I call on you to be baptized in the font of life and wash away all your sins, so that with all wickedness and wrongdoing cast away from you you may live henceforth as a new man in all reasonableness, righteousness, and holiness. If you do this you will win an eternal life of glory with God and his saints. But if instead you spurn me when I point out to you the path of salvation,

21. And we think of Odysseus and his mariners trespassing on another sacred island.

22. An expression typical of heroic epic again, as in so much of this Life.

then be most certainly assured that you will suffer eternal tortures and hellish flames along with the devil to whom you pay court."[23]

Astounded at all this, the king replied: "I see that you truly had no fear of our threats, and that your words match your deeds." And although he refused to believe in the truth that Willibrord preached, still he sent him on his way with every show of respect back to Pippin, the ruler of the Franks.[24]

Chapter XII

The king was most happy to see him back again and asked him now to devote all his energies to that particular work of evangelization which God had destined for him, to uproot the thorns of idolatry there and

23. This amazing performance Alcuin has given to Willibrord seems to reflect not only the defiant courage of the Germanic hero and the Christian martyr but even something of the high-handed haughtiness of the Roman Empire. The Roman inheritance of the Christian Anglo-Saxon was far older than St. Peter's and involved the *Aeneid* along with the New Testament. The shade of Aeneas' father had told him: "Remember, Roman, your destiny is to rule the world with law. This is to be your art—to force all men to live in peace, to spare the conquered and overthrow the tyrant" (*Aeneid*, VI, 851-53). As Odysseus had despised the uncivilized Cyclops, the proud Roman looked down on the lawless barbarians—Caesar on the Gauls, Tacitus on the Britons and the Germans. And the northern barbarians accepted the Roman superiority. They feared and admired this El Dorado in the distant south where wine flowed and gold and silver abounded, where speech was charmed into parchment scrolls, where men lived in stone citadels built by giants and from out whose gates marched the matchless legions without number. Even in the Empire's old age when they conquered her they did it with a certain respect. In their turn they were proud to be Romans (see note 8 to *Life of St. Cuthbert*).

24. It is said that Radbod never quite got Willibrord's words out of his head, and that the year before he died he actually consented to be baptized by St. Wulframm, Archbishop of Sens. But at the last moment the Archbishop made the mistake of telling him that his heathen ancestors were in hell. The rugged old king drew back from the font, declaring that he could not possibly turn his back on all his ancestors and go live with the few people in heaven (see Plummer, *Baedae Opera Historica*, II, 289).

plant the word of God in each and every locality with all urgency; which request was enough to set Willibrord off into a foment of activity. He covered every district of that land, working his way through each city, village, and fort. In the places where he had already brought the Gospel he exhorted the people to hold fast in true faith to the good resolves of their heart. And as the number of the faithful grew from day to day and those who were united in the knowledge of the word of God became an ever greater multitude of believers, many began to be moved by their fervent piety to offer their estates to God's hero. As soon as he received them he had churches built on them and priests and other fellow-workers of the Gospel appointed for each, so that this new people of God's would have places where they might gather on feast days either to listen to helpful instructions or to be taught the precepts of the Christian faith by those from whom they had received the gift of holy Baptism. And so, with the help of divine grace, the hero of God made more and more progress day by day.

Chapter XIII

Finally Pippin, the ruler of the Franks, died and his son Charles took over the rule of his father's kingdom.[25] He brought many nations under the power of the Franks, among them that of the Frisians which he added to his father's domain by a glorious victory over Radbod. St. Willibrord was then appointed missionary to the Frisians and his episcopal see was established in the fortress-town of Utrecht. Seizing upon this opportunity for further evangelization he bent every effort to lead to the baptismal font this people which had just been won by Pippin's sword. He would not rest as long as the least shadow of their old delusion and ignorance still lurked in the land, so he proceeded

25. Pippin II died in 714. After several years of strife among several claimants to power, Charles Martel, a natural son of Pippin, emerged as the victorious Mayor of the Palace. He defeated Radbod about 718. In 732, the year after Bede finished his *Ecclesiastical History*, Martel turned back from France the Arab tidal wave that had already engulfed a great part of the rest of the old Roman Empire.

as quickly as possible to flood the whole country with the light of the Gospel. So that shortly the testimony of the prophet was fulfilled in the case of that people: "In the very place where once the doom was uttered, 'You are but strangers to me,' they shall be welcomed as sons of the living God" [Os. 1:10].

Chapter XIV

The divine power also worked very many miracles through the medium of his servant. Although the ministry of preaching the Gospel must take precedence over any working of miracles or any display of supernatural powers, yet for the glory of God who granted them I feel that I must not pass over certain happenings which are reported. I feel that they should be brought into my story lest things which are known to have happened in former times should be lost for future generations.

So let us begin with the time when the holy man had set out on one of his regular missionary journeys and came to a village called Walichrum,[26] in which there was one of the few remaining idols of the old superstition. Now God's hero with his impetuous zeal smashed the idol to pieces before the eyes of its custodian.[27] The man flared into a towering rage and with his sword struck the priest of God on the head with all the force of his furious wrath in vengeance for this insult to his god. But God protected his servant and he received no injury from this murderous blow. When Willibrord's companions saw it, however, they rushed up to kill the impious wretch for his wicked audacity. But though the man of God out of the goodness of heart had them release the culprit and let him go, that same day the man was seized by a demon spirit and three days later unhappily put an end

26. Today's Walcheren Island in Zeeland. During the Roman occupation it possessed a shrine to the goddess of navigation, and during the Nazi occupation it was put to the service of a more terrible god. V-bomb launching sites were established on it.

27. Pope Gregory's instructions to his first Roman missionaries in Willibrord's own homeland had advised destroying idols, but preserving their shrines (Bede, *Ecclesiastical History*, Bk. I, ch.30).

to his miserable life. Because Willibrord had followed the Lord's command and refused to take vengeance for his injuries, the more quickly was he avenged by the Lord— just as He said of those injuries which the wicked do not fear to inflict on his saints: "'Revenge is mine, I will repay,' saith the Lord" [Rom. 12,19].

[Chapters 15 to 22 recount other miracles that Willibrord was said to have worked.]

Chapter XXIII

This hero who was dear to God had also foretold certain things by his prophetic spirit which the subsequent outcome of events has proved were true. For instance, he baptized Pippin [III], the son of that most valiant leader of the Franks, Charles [Martel], and the father of this most noble Charles [the Great] who at present rules right gloriously the empire[28] of the Franks, honored with the greatest triumphs and with every dignity. Concerning his father, Pippin, St. Willibrord uttered this prophecy in the presence of his disciples: "Take note, all of you, that this infant will be renowned and exalted beyond measure, and will be greater than all the leaders of the Franks who have gone before him." Now the truth of this prediction is proved in our own day, and there is no need to procure witnesses for something that the judgment of the whole kingdom acknowledges. For all his people know for what victories this most noble conqueror is celebrated, and how far he has stretched the borders of our empire, and how devotedly he has fostered the Christian religion in his kingdom, and how he has labored in defence of the Church of God in foreign lands. All of which things can much better be seen by eyes than they can be set forth in words.

28. In a note to his edition of the text (Monumenta Germaniae Historica, *Scriptorum Rerum Merovingicarum*, VII, 133, n. 2) Levison remarks on the significance of Alcuin's choice of this word. Thus even before Charlemagne's famous coronation as emperor, Alcuin refers to his "empire" in terms that relate it to the former Roman Empire. And see Levison, *England and the Continent*, pp. 121-23.

[Chapters 24 to 31 deal with more miracles, and the final chapter, 32, is a homily for St. Willibrord's feast day. Chapter 24 tells us briefly that "on the seventh of November [739] he departed from this pilgrimage for the eternal fatherland and was buried in the monastery of Echternach which he had built."][29]

29. He died at the grand old age of 81 after spending the final years of his busy life in the quiet seclusion of his beloved Echternach, with his memories and his prayers. Pippin had given him the land for this monastery, almost forty years earlier, in the pleasant countryside of eastern Luxembourg, near Trier (see Verbist, *Saint Willibrord*, pp. 146 ff. and photograph facing p. 160). Echternach was to Willibrord what Fulda was to Boniface, what Ripon was to Wilfrid, and what Monkwearmouth and Jarrow were to Benedict Biscop. (On the beautifully illuminated *Echternach Gospels*, now in the Bibliothèque Nationale in Paris, see note 46 to *Life of St. Cuthbert*). In the eighth-century Calendar of Saints called "Willibrord's Calendar," now in the Bibliothèque Nationale, there is a somewhat jumbled marginal entry, seemingly in the old missioner's own hand, recording two milestones of his life: his arrival on the continent, and his consecration by Pope Sergius (see Levison, *England and the Continent*, p. 65). A facsimile of this November page of the Calendar can be seen facing p. 97, in Verbist, *Saint Willibrord*; and in Cabrol and Leclercq, *Dictionnaire d'archéologie chrétienne et de liturgie*, Vol. III, Pt. 2, following columns 2603-4. It has been well said that Willibrord was to England what Columbanus was to Ireland, and that his work inaugurated a century of personal, spiritual, Anglo-Saxon influence on the continent (Levison, *op. cit.*, p. 60).

THE LIFE
OF ST. BONIFACE

---

by Willibald

Preface to Willibald's Life of Boniface

Of Winfrith from Wessex, known to history by his Roman name, Boniface, it has been said that he "had a deeper influence on the history of Europe than any Englishman who has ever lived" (Dawson, *The Making of Europe*, p. 185). He was important as a missionary *peregrinus* (pilgrim-exile), from the Rome-oriented Anglo-Saxon Church, working in the ancient Germanic land of his fathers, and as an ecclesiastical statesman helping the Frankish rulers reorganize Merovingian chaos (see Levison, *England and the Continent*, pp. 70-93; and George Greenaway, *Saint Boniface* [London, 1955], pp. 38-59). It has even been said that "it was the Anglo-Saxon monks and, above all, St. Boniface who first realized that union of Teutonic initiative and Latin order which is the source of the whole mediaeval development of culture" Dawson, *op. cit.*, p. 186).

Willibald, an Anglo-Saxon volunteer on Boniface's German mission, was a monk stationed at Fulda. He is not to be confused with the other Willibald, an adventurous relative of Boniface, who toured the Holy Land (see the story of his pilgrimage, written down by an Anglo-Saxon nun on the German mission, and translated in Talbot, *The Anglo-Saxon Missionaries in Germany*, pp. 152-177), became a monk at Monte Cassino, and was finally made Bishop of Eichstätt by Boniface. Our *Life of Boniface* was written about fifteen years after the saint's death, and though the Latin is rather tortuous, the story has an impressive epic tone, and it also gives us some valuable contemporary information about Boniface. An 11th-century biography of Boniface tells us that Willibald wrote at a time when "there were many people still alive who had been present at Boniface's martyrdom" (see Levison, *Vitae Bonifatii*, pp. 104-05).

There is an edition of Willibald's biography in Monumenta Germaniae Historica, *Scriptorum* II, 331-353 (1829), but there is a much better one by Levison in his *Vitae Sancti Bonifatii Archiepiscopi Moguntini*, in *Scriptores Rerum Germanicarum* in usum scholarum ex Monumentis Germaniae Historicis separatim editi (Hannover and Leipzig, 1905), pp. 1-57 (which I refer to in this book as Levison, *Vitae Bonifatii*). It is from this edition that I made my translation.

Besides the short studies on Boniface by Levison and by Greenaway, mentioned above, there are available good accounts in Duckett, *Anglo-*

Saxon Saints and Scholars, Ch. 4; and in Godfrey, *The Church in Anglo-Saxon England*, pp. 230-253. The best edition of Boniface's correspondence is by M. Tangl, *S. Bonifacii et Lulli Epistolae*, in Monumenta Germaniae Historica, *Epistolae Selectae*, Tomus I (Berlin, 1955). In translation, many of his letters are available in E. Emerton's edition, *The Letters of Saint Boniface* (Columbia University Press, 1940), and some in Whitelock, *English Historical Documents*, and in Talbot, *The Anglo-Saxon Missionaries in Germany*. The latter also contains complete translations of Willibald's *Life of Boniface* and of a 9th-century biography of Sturm, Boniface's first abbot of Fulda. An older translation of Willibald, still available in some libraries, is by G. W. Robinson, *The Life of Saint Boniface* (Cambridge, Mass., 1916). A biography of Boniface in French by G. Kurth (*Saint Boniface*, 680-755, 2^e^ edition, Paris, 1902) is still available in a translation (from the 4th French edition) by V. Day (*Saint Boniface*, 680-755, Milwaukee, 1935); and there is a good study in German by Theodor Schieffer: *Winfrid-Bonifatius und die Christliche Grundlegung Europas* (Freiburg, 1954).

THE LIFE OF ST. BONIFACE

[Boniface's original name was Winfrith and he was born in the Anglo-Saxon kingdom of Wessex[1] about 675. The first three chapters[2] of this Life tell of Winfrith's entering the monastery of Exeter as a strong-willed young boy, and how later on, after outgrowing the educational possibilities of this monastery, he transferred to another one at Nursling, between Southampton and Winchester in Hampshire, which appears to have offered opportunities for more advanced learning. There he achieved something of a reputation for his knowledge and piety and was ordained priest at about the age of thirty.]

Chapter IV: *How he was sent to Kent by the unanimous choice of the Church prelates, and how afterwards he went to Friesland.*

So HE spent some little time laboring to tame his heart to the rule of the virtues I have mentioned, and in his priestly life from day to day he presented ever greater evidence of fine qualities. Then, during the reign of Ine,[3] king of the West Saxons, a situation of some ur-

1. It is interesting that our final hero-saint in this chronicle of a Golden Age that has been largely Northumbrian, should be from the southern kingdom of Wessex, whose age of glory was yet to come.

2. There is also a Preface, in the traditional hagiographical pattern, which borrows generously from the fifth-century letter of Victorinus of Aquitaine (see text of Preface in Levison, with notes, *Vitae Sancti Bonifatii*, pp. 1-4). Willibald addresses the Life to Megingoz, bishop of Würzburg, and to Boniface's close friend and successor in the see of Mainz, Bishop Lull. And see note 6 to *Life of Guthlac.*

3. Ine, a great warrior-king of Wessex, was one of the many Anglo-Saxon rulers who abdicated their thrones to die in pilgrim-exile in Rome (see Introduction, pp. 18 ff., and note 46). He is most famous for his code of laws which has survived in a copy from King Alfred's day and affords a valuable insight

gency suddenly developed from a new dissension that had broken out, and at the king's suggestion a synodal council of the clergy was called at once by the leading prelates. As soon as all had gathered, the priests present launched into an intelligent and most useful discussion on the question of this recent dispute. After some consultation it was sensibly decided that responsible envoys should be dispatched to the archbishop of Canterbury, Berhtwald[4] by name, lest their acting in any way without consulting so important a bishop should label them either with presumption or temerity. When this very reasonable deliberation had been concluded and the whole council and the entire body of the clergy had reached an agreement, the king straightway addressed the assemblage and inquired who was going to be appointed spokesman of this embassy. Without any delay Winfrith was called for and was led up to the king by Winberht, the abbot highest in honor who was in charge of the monastery spoken of already, and by Wintra who presided over the monastery called Tisbury, and by Beorwold who governed in a godly manner the monastery called by the old word Glastonbury,[5] and by many other fathers—all holy monks. The king thereupon appointed him spokesman of the legation, gave him his instructions and provided him with a retinue, and sent him off under his royal protection.[6]

into the social life of seventh-century Wessex (most handily available in Whitelock, *English Historical Documents*, pp. 364-72).

4. This is the same Berhtwald (successor to the great Theodore) who figured so often in the stormy life of Wilfrid (see Eddius, *Life of Wilfrid*, Chs. 46, 50, 60, etc.).

5. Glastonbury in Somerset, whose famous abbey is now but a romantic ruin, is a magic name in England's legendary past. As one of the ancient foci of continental merchant traffic (see C. and J. Hawkes, *Prehistoric Britain* [London, 1947] pp. 114 ff.) it was naturally one of the points at which Christianity first touched Early Britain. A primitive church and shrine made it a hallowed spot. Joseph of Arimathea and the Holy Grail became part of its story and drew it into the Arthurian legend (see J. A. Robinson, *Two Glastonbury Legends: King Arthur and St. Joseph of Arimathea* [Cambridge University Press, 1926]; L. S. Smithett, *St. Joseph of Arimathea at Glastonbury*, 7th edition [London, 1955]; G. Ashe, *King Arthur's Avalon* [London, 1957]; R. S. Loomis (ed.), *Arthurian Literature in the Middle Ages* [Oxford, 1959]). In Boniface's own day Aldhelm prevailed upon his good friend, King Ine, to put up new buildings for the abbey at Glastonbury (see Duckett, *Anglo-Saxon Saints and Scholars*, pp. 45-46).

6. This incident, besides its interest as our oldest account of a West Saxon synod, gives us our first picture of Boniface in his role of an ecclesiastical states-

Thus entrusted with the embassy by order of his superiors, Winfrith reached Kent after an uneventful journey. To the archbishop there who bore the episcopacy's highest honor, he delivered the king's message in its entirety, and did a masterful job of presenting it all in orderly fashion. Then, after receiving a favorable response, he returned to his own country a few days later and made to the king, sitting in session with the same prelates as before, a very creditable presentation of the reverend archbishop's favorable reply—to the great satisfaction of all concerned. And so from that time on, by the gracious dispensation of God, his name became known and was held in high esteem among lay and ecclesiastical dignitaries alike. So much did his reputation continue to grow that he was invited to their synods time after time.

But a heart that is dedicated also to God is not overly affected by tenders of esteem nor puffed up by men's praise. So it was that Winfrith gradually became more intently absorbed in many thoughts of quite another nature. He began to draw away from the company of his parents and his kinsfolk, and his heart was more often away in pilgrim places in some far country[7] than in the land of his fathers. After he had thought it over most carefully in his own mind for a long time—this forsaking of his family and his country—finally he took his spiritual father [Abbot Winberht], of blessed memory, into his counsel, and disclosing frankly all these secret plans that he had kept hidden within his own thoughts, he appealed to the holy man with great urgency for his consent. At first the abbot was much surprised and astounded, and forbade the desired journey for the time being, though Winfrith begged and pleaded. The abbot hoped that delay might cool the ardor of Winfrith's desire. But in the end, as the providence of Almighty God made itself felt, the petition of the suppliant prevailed. And he entered upon the journey of his desire with the sincere affection of his abbot and of all the brethren, who were part of his monastic life. And by the dispensation of the Lord their great affection also helped him to complete the journey, for they generously supplied him with the money he needed

man. In the best Roman traditions of the Empire he moves about capably in the courts of kings—as Wilfrid had done.

7. Note the marvelous correspondence with verses 58-61 in the Anglo-Saxon poem, *The Seafarer*. And see *Life of Willibrord*, Ch. 4, and note 7; and note 46 to Introduction.

and also with a great fund of tears and prayers offered from their hearts to the Lord for him.

So now that he was fitted out with the armor of the spirit and well supplied with the necessary goods of this world, he took two or three of the monks with him, whose physical and spiritual support he needed, and set forth on his way. In due course, after traversing immense stretches of land in the happy company of the brethren, he arrived at a place where there was a market with merchandise offered for sale and which is still called today by the old word of the Angles and Saxons—Lundenwich [i. e., London]. After a short while some sailors were ready to make a return voyage so the new passenger went on board ship with great eagerness, by leave of the shipmaster, and paid his fare. Favoring winds brought them to Dorstet[8] where he tarried awhile, offering due praise to God day and night. But the pagans had launched a serious invasion and the resultant hostilities between Charles, Mayor of the Palace and renowned leader of the Franks, and Radbod, King of the Frisians, had caused turmoil among the populations of both sides.[9] Most of the churches of Christ in Friesland, which before had been subject to Frankish authority, were now despoiled and destroyed under Radbod, and the clergy were expelled. Moreover, the pagan shrines and temples were rebuilt and the cult of idols, sad to say, was restored.

So when the man of God saw all this wicked perversity he went to Utrecht and waited there a few days, and when King Radbod arrived he went to speak to him. Then he made a tour of inspection through many districts of the land to find out whether he could find anywhere a place for preaching in the future. And he made up his mind that if an opportunity for preaching the Gospel should ever come to light in any part of this land, there he would bring the seed of the word of God. And indeed, after the passage of many years, the glorious witness of his martyrdom confirmed this resolution.

8. A place near present-day Utrecht.

9. This was the second year of the insurrection (mentioned in *Life of Willibrord*, Ch. 13) which had broken out after Pippin II's death in 714. "Charles" (Charles Martel), Pippin's son, finally emerged victorious. Radbod died in 719. See note 25 to *Life of Willibrord.*

But it is a singular gift of the holiness of the saints that when they see their labor is of practically no avail for a time and without any green signs of spiritual sprouting, then they just pick up and move to some other locality that is rich with the fruit of their labor. For it is futile to dwell in a place where there is no harvest of holiness to be gathered in. Now the holy man had been living for some time in this sterile land of the Frisians. Summer had passed and autumn was all but gone. So he abandoned the parched land that lacked the dew of heavenly fruitfulness and, taking with him the companions of his travels, he returned to his native soil.[10] He went back to the solitude of his monastery and after being welcomed home by the loving brethren, who fairly danced with delight, he passed the winter there, and the next winter as well. Thus he followed out the saying of the Apostle of the Gentiles: "For there I have determined to winter" [Tit. 3:12].

ChapterV-VII: *How he stayed on with the brethren for a little while after the death of his abbot, and how afterwards he went to Rome with letters of recommendation from his bishop.*

[Declining the abbotship of Nursling, which was offered to him after Winberht's death, Winfrith set out for Rome in the summer of 718 with letters of recommendation from Bishop Daniel of Winchester.[11] Sailing from London again he landed this time at Quen-

10. Radbod, the villain in our story, thus achieved the dubious distinction of having worn out the patience of three very holy Anglo-Saxons: Wictbert (note 12 to *Life of Willibrord*), Willibrord (*Life of Willibrord*, Ch. 5), and now Winfrith.

11. Bishop Daniel later sent Boniface a letter with his well-meant but rather impractical suggestions for converting the heathen (in *The Ethos of the Song of Roland* [Johns Hopkins, 1963, p. 138] G. F. Jones unhappily attributes this letter to Boniface himself). The original text of the letter can be read in Tangl, *S. Bonifatii et Lulli Epistolae*, pp. 38-41, and in Haddan and Stubbs, *Councils and Ecclesiastical Documents*, III, 304-06. Translations are conveniently available in Emerton, *The Letters of St. Boniface*, pp. 48-50, and in Whitelock, *English Historical Documents*, pp. 731-33.

tavic[12] where he waited till a large company could be gathered.[13] They made their way across the Alps, enjoyed the hospitality of the Lombards (*Langobardorumque erga illos humanitatem*),[14] evaded the arrogant savagery of the Byzantine soldiers of Ravenna (*militumque malitiosam superbiae ferocitatem*), and arrived safely in Rome. Winfrith was kindly received in audience by Pope Gregory II in the spring of 719 and sent to make a report on the missionary possibilities among the German people, and commissioned as their missionary.[15] (At the same time the Pope changed Winfrith's name to "Boniface.") On his way back he stopped for a friendly visit with Liutprand,[16] King of the Lombards, then passed on over the Alps, through Bavaria, and made his official inspection of the churches in Thuringia. In the same year he learned of the death of Radbod and seized the occasion to further the evangelization of Friesland. He helped the aging Willibrord for several years but, with some difficulty, refused Willibrord's offer to make him a bishop and his assistant. He finally told Willibrord: "I received a mandate from Pope Gregory to work among the German people. In my function as legate of the Apostolic See to the Western lands of the barbarians I voluntarily joined myself to this mission of yours which is under your authority. This I did of my own free will, but without the knowledge of my exalted lord to whose service I am still to this day subject and bound by vow. Therefore I do not dare receive this office of such surpassing excellence (i. e., the bishopric) without consulting the Apostolic See and

12. The old Roman port where Ebroin had, by a fortunate mistake, expected Wilfrid to land in 678 (see Eddius, *Life of Wilfrid*, Ch. 25).

13. Testimony to the perils which lay in wait for the Dark-Age traveler. There was at least relatively more safety in numbers.

14. Boniface was to break more than one journey to Rome by a pleasant visit with King Liutprand of the Lombards. Wilfrid earlier on his way to Rome in 679, had been received by a Lombard king, Perctarit (Eddius, *Life of Wilfrid*, Ch. 28); and Caedwalla of Wessex, on his way to Rome in 688 (see note 102, *Life of St. Wilfrid*), was entertained by Perctarit's successor, King Cunincpert, whose wife was an Anglo-Saxon (Levison, *England and the Continent*, p. 14). Perhaps Cunincpert's wife had herself been a pilgrim to Rome and had chanced on a happier interruption to her journey than the many Anglo-Saxon women-pilgrims whom Boniface once complained about in a letter (see translation in Emerton, *The Letters of Saint Boniface*, p. 140).

15. Boniface's mandate is the oldest example of such a document that we possess (see translation in Emerton, *op. cit.*, pp. 32-33).

16. Just three years before this, Chilperic II had given Ceolfrith letters of recommendation to Liutprand, letters which he never delivered (see *Life of Ceolfrith*, Ch. 32).

getting the mandate of an express command." So, with Willibrord's blessing, Boniface went off to his mission work among the Germans of Hesse and Thuringia.]

We have touched rather briefly on each step of his career from the beginning with a documented picture of the holy man's strength of character and the fearless energy with which he labored for the Lord, with the intention of recalling now in more detail the remaining incidents that we have collected from his sainted life. After he had won a host of Frisian people for the Lord, and multitudes had been led by his teaching of the spirit to the point where they could see the truth illumined unmistakably in a radiance of light, only then did he move on under God's protection to preach in other parts of Germany. He came to the place we mentioned before [i. e., Amanburch in Hesse], ruled by the twin brothers, Dettic and Deorulf. There, with God's help, he turned the people away from a sacrilegious worship of idols which they had been wickedly practicing under a kind of pretense of Christianity. For a great number of people he was able to lay open the path of right reason, tear away the horrible mask of their ignorance, and pull them back from the deadly superstitution of heathendom. He formed a community of religious sizable enough for a small monastery he built. And he did all these same things for the people of Hesse who dwelt near the borders of the Saxons and were still wandering in the dark, practicing pagan rites. He taught them the precepts of the Gospel and freed them from the thralldom of demons.

After he had thus washed away in Baptism the pagan past of thousands of people, then he sent off to Rome a willing messenger and faithful bearer of his letters, Bynnan by name.

[Boniface reported all that he had accomplished so far and asked for instruction with regard to certain problems of the mission work. The pope's reply, brought back by Bynnan, included an invitation to come to Rome again.]

Quickly he gathered a large force of retainers, surrounded himself with a goodly retinue of the brethren, and made his way through the lands of the Burgundians and the Franks and across the Alps. Then he traversed the marches of Italy and the boundaries guarded by the soldiers [of the Byzantine Exarchate of Ravenna] and when at last he caught sight of the walls of Rome he broke into hymns of due thanksgiving to the King of Heaven.[17] Boniface went at once to the Church of St. Peter and refreshed himself with heartfelt prayer. After giving his tired limbs a little rest he sent a message to the Blessed Pope Gregory to announce that the servant of God had arrived. Thereupon he was kindly received and conducted to the pilgrims' lodge.[18]

As soon as there was a convenient day for their visit the glorious bishop of the Apostolic See came to the basilica of St. Peter the Apostle and the servant of God was at once ushered into his presence. After they had exchanged a few words of greeting the Apostolic Pontiff at once proceeded to question him about the Creed and the traditional Christian truths. Before very long Boniface respectfully replied: "My Apostolic Lord, I realize that as a stranger I am unskilled in this language with which you are so familiar,[19] so I beg you to grant me a little time in which to write down my testimony of faith. Thus the mute letters may be able to give an intelligent account of my faith, which my spoken words cannot." The Pontiff consented at once and asked him to present this document soon. Before very long Boniface had produced an account of his faith in the Holy Trinity written in a learned, polished style, and sent it to the Pope. Nonetheless he had to wait a few days longer.

Then he was called back again and shown into the Lateran Palace, where he humbly cast himself face down at the feet of the Apostolic Pontiff and asked for his blessing. The Pope as quickly raised him from the ground, and handing him back his document in which the complete and pure truth of the Christian faith was clearly revealed, he asked him to be seated at his side. Then he gave him very helpful

17. Perhaps he and his company broke into something like the exultant ninth-century marching hymn, O *Roma nobilis, orbis et domina*, with which later pilgrims greeted the sight of the Eternal City (see, for example, *The Penguin Book of Latin Verse*, ed. F. Brittain [1962], p. 155).

18. This account of Boniface's second Roman visit (722) has a certain charm. It gives us a vivid picture of the machinery of the old Empire still moving in its stately yet efficient way. Here is the official from the barbarian provinces reporting at Rome, being duly impressed by its splendid pageantry and reassured by its awareness of his periphery of the world, and at length returning with fresh loyalty to his portion of the grand task of Empire.

19. Pope Gregory II was speaking the "popular language" (*lingua vulgarica*) of the Romans (Levison, *Vitae Bonifatii*, p. 28, note 1).

instruction and advice with regard to the teaching of the Church, exhorting Boniface to preserve intact the bulwark of the faith and to preach it seriously to others to the best of his ability. He brought up many other questions too concerning holiness of life and the truths of the faith and asked Boniface's opinion about them. And so they spent almost the whole day talking back and forth between themselves. And at last the Pope inquired how the people, who formerly had wandered along the crooked paths of evil, reacted to the proofs of the faith he preached to them. And when he was satisfied from Boniface's reply that he had actually separated a vast multitude of people from the sacrilegious worship of demons and joined them to the communion of the holy Church, only then did he let Boniface know that he wished to confer the dignity of the episcopate upon him and present him as their leader to those peoples who till now had not known the loving care of a pastor and who, in the words of Our Lord God, were neglected as sheep who have no shepherd. And because Boniface dared not contradict this great bishop who governed the Apostolic See, he gave his consent and obeyed. So then the Supreme Pontiff fixed a day for the consecration, the thirtieth day of November [722].

When the holy day dawned, which was both the sacred feast of St. Andrew and the day of Boniface's consecration, the Holy Pontiff made him a bishop and conferred on him the honor of the name of Boniface[20] and presented him with a little book in which the sacred laws of ecclesiastical discipline had been compiled from episcopal synods. The Pope then charged him henceforth to preserve inviolate this episcopal codification of established laws and to base on these laws the instruction he gave to his people. He offered him too the friendship of the holy Apostolic See for himself and all those subject to him, henceforth and forever.[21] And he sent letters in his own holy name

20. Willibald has confused this visit with Boniface's previous one in 719. It was on the prior occasion that Pope Gregory gave him the name "Boniface." He is called by that name for the first time in the papal letter of commission given him at that time (see translation in Emerton, *The Letters of Saint Boniface*, p. 32; text in Tangl, *S. Bonifatii et Lulli Epistolae*, p. 17, and see note 1). On the reasons for Willibrord's being given the name "Clement," and Winfrith's being given the name "Boniface," see Levison, *England and the Continent*, pp. 59-60, and note 1 on p. 60.

21. Boniface's swearing personal allegiance to the Pope, and the Pope's

placing this saintly man, newly graced with the honor of bishop, under the powerful protection and care of the illustrious Duke Charles.[22]

Boniface thereupon made his way by long and winding roads to the borders of the mighty peoples of the Franks and then presented himself to their ruler, whom we mentioned. Respectfully received by him, he delivered to Duke Charles the letters of the Roman Pontiff. Afterwards, subject now to Charles' authority and protection, he returned, with the Duke's consent, to the confines of the Hessians among whom he had already lived for awhile.

Many of the Hessians now were brought into the Catholic faith and received the sevenfold gift of the Holy Spirit and the laying on of hands. Others, however, whose spirit was still too feeble, refused to accept the unalloyed truths of the faith in their entirety. And there were also those who offered clandestine sacrifice to trees and springs, and even those who did it openly.[23] There were occult, and even public, soothsayers who read the future in animals' entrails and in the flight of birds, and carried on all kinds of divining and spellbinding and sacrificial rites.

promising favor and protection in return might be a scene between any Anglo-Saxon thegn and his king. Such *comitatus*-loyalty, so important in all medieval society, was especially the hallmark of the Anglo-Saxon Golden Age, both in the court and the monastery (see Godfrey, *The Church in Anglo-Saxon England*, p. 62; and see Introduction to the present book, p. 2 ff. and p. 15). Boniface's oath, couched in the solemn formality of the old Empire, can be read in translation in Emerton, *The Letters of Saint Boniface*, p. 41; text in Tangl, *S. Bonifatii et Lulli Epistolae*, pp. 28-29.

22. This letter to Charles Martel can be read in translation in Emerton, *op. cit.*, p. 45. Other interesting letters in which Pope Gregory commends Boniface officially to all the German Christians, to Thuringian leaders, and to the people of Old Saxony, can be read in Emerton, *op. cit.*, pp. 42 ff. In a letter to Bishop Daniel of Winchester, some twenty years later, Boniface remarks on how necessary the support of the Frankish secular power is for the continuance of his mission among the Germans (Emerton, *op. cit.*, pp. 115-16). The proximity of Frankish military force made his show of strength possible at Geismar, while the lack of it beyond the Zuyder Zee was to cost him his life.

23. Even at home in Boniface's own England such pagan practices were still being explicitly legislated against as late as the eleventh century. Church laws in Northumbria, dating perhaps from the episcopate of Wulfstan of York, prohibit anyone's having on his land a shrine around a stone or a tree or a well (Whitelock, *English Historical Documents*, p. 438, no. 54).

But there were also pagans with more sense who abhorred all this heathen impiety and would have nothing to do with it. With the advice of these latter he took a stand against all this by daring to cut down an immense oak tree which the pagans, in their own ancient language, called the Oak of Thunor [Donar], and which stood in a place called Geismar.[24] While some of the brethren stood by, Boniface collected all his courage—for a great mob of pagans stood there, cursing bitterly in their hearts against this enemy of their gods—and cut into the tree. But though he had made only a small notch in the tree, suddenly its whole mighty mass, shaken by a divine blast from on high, which splintered its topmost branches, came crashing down and split asunder into four parts, as though by the avenging judgment of God. There for all to see were four giant sections of the trunk, all of equal length, though none of the brethren had laid a hand on it. At the sight of all this the pagans abruptly changed sides, left off their cursing of the moment before, and began to believe in the Lord and to bless Him. Afterwards the holy bishop talked the matter over with the brethren and decided to use the timber from this tree to build a wooden oratory which he dedicated in honor of St. Peter the Apostle.

[Boniface then went into Thuringia and succeeded in putting down some heretical sects which had crept in under rulers who weren't friendly to Christianity. Gradually the number of the faithful grew and even a monastery was built.]

So the fame of his holy preaching traveled far and such a number of stories grew up around him that the sound of his name was heard through the greater part of Europe. From the land of Britain a great host of monks came to him—readers, and writers, and men trained in other skills.[25] Of these by far the greater number put themselves under

24. A typical instance of the Heroic Age ἀγών ("contest") (see note 22 to *Life of Wilfrid*), the trial of strength between the Christian God and the pagan god, which so often settled the issue in these warrior-minded times. See, for instance, Chs. 100, 101, 102 in *Njal's Saga* and Ch. 13 in *Life of Wilfrid*.

25. Here we have the Germanic Invasions in reverse, some 300 years after the orignal ones. Now Rome comes to Germany, from the north. For more details on Boniface's new recruits see Levison, *England and the Continent*, pp. 76 ff.

his authority for this high task of rescuing people in many places from the blind depravity of paganism. They fanned out widely through the populace, some in the land of the Hessians, some in Thuringia, and preached the word of God in the countryside and in the villages. The number of those who received the sacraments of the faith among each of the two peoples was enormous.[26]

[On the death of Pope Gregory II (731), his successor, Gregory III, renewed the papal pledge of friendship with Boniface and his people. After a sally into Bavaria to inspect the Churches and expel a schismatic, he returned to Hesse and Thuringia and built more churches. Now in his old age, Boniface made a third journey to Rome (738) where he was lionized not only by the Romans but as well by pilgrim Franks, Bavarians and Saxons.[27] On the way home he stopped for a last visit with his old friend Liutprand, King of the Lombards. In Bavaria he stopped with Duke Odilo long enough to reform morals among the Christians and to divide the country into four dioceses, for each of which he consecrated a bishop. With the close cooperation of Carloman and Pippin, who succeeded Charles Martel (in 741), Boniface instituted a revival and reform of the German churches, including the establishment of annual synodal councils and the formation of new dioceses. Pippin continued the close support of the Church after he became sole ruler (in 747),[28] and with his

26. Boniface's extensive correspondence during these years makes fascinating reading. It reveals a warmly human yet very strong-willed, genuinely holy, intelligent, sensible, great man. The best letters are easily available in Emerton, *The Letters of St. Boniface*, and there is a smaller selection in Whitelock, *English Historical Documents*. He wrote tender letters (see note 31), stern letters (see note 32 to Introduction), letters begging the Anglo-Saxons to help him convert the Saxons (Emerton, p. 74). Significantly, he often writes Anglo-Saxon monasteries to ask for copies of manuscripts, especially of Bede's works, while Anglo-Saxon kings ask him for hawks and falcons. He sends lances and shields to Guthlac's friend, King Aethelbald of Mercia (Emerton, *op. cit.*, p. 123). He even sends gifts of wine and spices to England (Emerton, *op. cit.*, pp. 78, 169, etc). Ten years after Boniface's death, Abbot Cuthbert of Monkwearmouth wrote to Boniface's successor in Germany, Archbishop Lull, to request glassmakers and a skilled harpist (Whitelock, *English Historical Documents*, pp. 765-66).

27. Perhaps it was on this occasion that he first won Lull for the German mission (Levison, *England and the Continent*, p. 78).

28. In 747 Carloman resigned to enter a monastery in Rome, but he was so bothered with constant visits by distinguished Franks on pilgrimage that he finally withdrew to the greater seclusion of Monte Cassino (Einhard, *Life*

permission the now ailing Boniface consecrated his dear friend, Lull, to succeed him at Mainz.[29] Then, in the last months of his life, Providence ineluctably drew him (in the summer of 753) back north to the watery lowlands of intransigent Friesland, that he might complete the heroic saga of his missionary life where he had begun it many years before.]

Chapter VIII

. . . By some mysterious presentiment he was able to foretell the approaching day of his death to Bishop Lull and tell him even in what fashion death now at long last would come to him.[30] He discussed with him detailed plans for the building of churches and the teaching of the people.[31] And he said to him: "For I long to finish the journey which

of Charlemagne, Ch. 2). Boniface, significantly, took part in King Pippin III's anointing (see note 15 to *Life of Willibrord*).

29. In 745 Cologne had become Boniface's see for a few years, but about 748 he transferred it to Mainz (Levison, *op. cit.*, pp. 86-87).

30. There is a tone of Germanic epic or saga about the whole concluding chapter of Boniface's life. In this farewell conversation with Lull we can almost hear Beowulf again talking with Wiglaf as he looks back over his career and forward to the doom he senses awaiting him. Then as Beowulf strides into the dragon's lair, Boniface sails resolutely toward threatening Frisia. And as there is some symbolism of demonic primeval darkness about Beowulf's dragon and about monstrous Grendel stalking outside Heorot's circle of light, so Boniface is heading toward a lost region beyond the Zuyder Zee, in the outer barbarian darkness beyond the Roman pale. (One of the latest studies to develop J. R. R. Tolkien's brilliant insight into the symbolism of *Beowulf's* monsters (*Proceedings of the British Academy*, XXII [1936] 245-295) is Nora Chadwick's "The Monsters and Beowulf," in Clemoes, *The Anglo-Saxons*, pp. 171-203) About Boniface's death, and Beowulf's, there is a feel of the heroic dramatic gesture and larger-than-life patterning. In their concentrated focusing, the Age of Heroes and the Age of Saints reach beyond the realism of epic to drama. The *Beowulf*-poet and Willibald both to some extent make their heroes set the stage for their deaths. Roland later will do so even more dramatically. He dies on a gesture, raising his battle-glove heavenward.

31. See the beautifully tender letter Boniface wrote two years before his death to Fulrad, Abbot of St. Denis (Whitelock, *English Historical Documents*, pp. 759-60). With the loving concern of a dying Anglo-Saxon king for his

yet lies ahead of me. I am powerless to draw back from this pilgrimage of my heart. Even now the day of my departure is at hand and the hour of my death draws nearer. Shortly I shall escape from the prison of the body and return in freedom to claim my prize of immortality. Yours is the destiny, my dearest son, of completing the building of these churches in Thuringia which I have only begun. Yours is the most urgent task of leading this people out of the wasteland of their blind wandering. And I ask you to finish that church at Fulda[32] which I started to build, and bring my old body there, worn out with its many years." After a pause he added: "And now, my son, prepare carefully all those things which must be packed up for our use on our journey. And do not forget to put a linen cloth in my chest of books to wrap my poor old body in."

[Boniface and his party sailed down the Rhine[33] and made theit way through the mazy waterways of Friesland across the Zuyder Zee. In the thoroughly pagan land just beyond it he baptized "many thousands of men, woman and children" with the help of Bishop Eoba from Utrecht. After waiting out the winter he and his company resumed operations in the summer of 754. On the night of June 4th he and a band of picked followers pitched their tents on the banks of the Boorne River (near Dokkum in the modern Dutch province of Friesland) intending to administer Confirmation on the morrow to many newly baptized Christians.]

But when the day grew light and the morning sunrise broke upon the world, it was a world turned upside down, for there advancing

devoted *comitatus* he begs the abbot to see that Pippin, after Boniface's death, takes care of the great numbers of English disciples and helpers who had flocked to his side in the German mission. And see Wilfrid's final arrangements for his own faithful followers (*Life of Wilfrid*, Ch. 63).

32. The monastery begun by Boniface in 744, and to which he looked forward as the dear retreat of his old age and as his final resting place (see his letter of 751 to Pope Zacharias, in Emerton, *The Letters of Saint Boniface*, pp. 157-59). And see note 29 to *Life of Willibrord.*

33. And every traveler of the Rhineland will recognize the tragic appropriateness in Boniface's sailing to his death by way of the most beautiful stretch of the Rhine, from Mainz northward. His flotilla headed down river between the towering slopes already charged with the legendary gloom of doomed Siegfried, and of Drachenfels, and of Götterdämmerung.

on them were not friends but enemies, not new Christian worshippers but new executioners. Brandishing spears and shields, a vast throng of the pagans burst into the camp. At once Boniface's escort rushed to arms on all sides and ran out against them. They stood poised to defend the saints—later martyrs—against this mindless mob of raging people, when the hero of God suddenly stepped out of his tent. At the first sound of the crowd's furious onslaught he had called the band of clergy to his side and had taken up the saints' relics which he always had with him. Now he immediately scolded his followers and forbade any fighting. "Do not fight them, lads. Lay down your weapons. What we are taught by the Gospel is true, and we must not give back evil for evil, but good for evil. This now is that very day we have long dreamed of. That moment of freedom we have yearned for is right here. So be heroic in the Lord and suffer this royal grace of his will gladly. Keep your trust in him and he will set your souls free."[34]

Then he turned to the priests and deacons and other clerics standing beside him, God's sworn men all of them, and spoke to them like a father: "My hero brothers, be bold of heart. Have no terror of these slayers of the body, for they have no power to kill the soul, which lives forever. Take cheer in the Lord and fix the anchor of your hope in God, because in another instant he will give you your eternal reward and lead you to your rightful seat in the great hall of heaven among the fellowship of the angels noble beyond earthly measure.[35] Do not surrender yourselves to the doomed love of this life. Snare not your

34. Here we have the Germanic *comitatus*-loyalty in stupendous reverse, the superb Christian tour de force. What a sameness and a difference there is between Boniface's words and the exhortations to final resistance in *The Battle of Maldon* and *The Song of Roland*. Boniface's heroism is the "absurd" new heroism of the Sermon on the Mount, but its language is still that of the Heroic Age. Boniface exhorts his *comitatus* to a more reckless and "hopeless" courage than Byrhtnoth does; and Boniface's men, as Byrhtnoth's, fall about their lord to a man. Contrast Boniface's encounter here in the late Golden Age with Wilfrid's similar one in the young Heroic Age (*Life of Wilfrid*, Ch. 13).

35. Willibald's language here is that of Germanic heroic poetry. Just as in poems like *Andreas* and *Genesis* so here the angelic court is envisioned in terms of a royal hall, like Heorot, with the *comitatus* attendant upon its king. In the interlinear Anglo-Saxon of the *Durham Ritual*, "thegn" is often the gloss for "angel," especially where the context is an heroic one (*Publications of the Surtees Society*, 140 [1927] 70, etc.).

heart with the base and hollow blandishments the heathen do. But submit courageously to this brief instant of death so that you may reign with Christ forever."

While he was lovingly urging his disciples on to the martyr's crown with these heartening words, suddenly the raging storm of pagans overwhelmed them with swords and every sort of weapon, and stained the bodies of the saints with the blood of a happy death.

[The bodies were brought to Utrecht, from where Boniface's body was eventually conveyed to Fulda.[36] Miracles took place at his tomb there. The last chapter (IX) tells of a spring of fresh water—so scarce in Friesland—which miraculously welled up at the site of the martyrdom while Pippin was erecting a mound there on which to build a memorial church.]

36. Another medieval biographer of Boniface gives a final epic touch to his description of the funeral-ship procession back up the Rhine. After the cortege disembarked and continued its sad journey on land, at each spot where a midday or overnight halt was made they erected a cross "to give due honor to this greatest of victors in his triumph" (Levison, *Vitae Bonifatii*, p. 103). The Latin terms are those used for the official "triumph" celebration accorded victorious Roman generals, and victorious athletes (*ac triumphatorem omnium in suo agonitheta triumphantes*). See note 22 to *Life of Wilfrid*, and notes 61 and 64 to *Life of St. Guthlac*. As a final note I should point out that Levison gives 754 as the year of Boniface's death (*England and the Continent*, p. 90, n. 2) but it is disputed.

BIBLIOGRAPHICAL NOTE

The following is a selective list of works more frequently made use of in the writing of this book.

Acta Sanctorum. ed. J. Bollandus, et al. Antwerp, Brussels, 1643 ff.

Analecta Bollandiana. Brussels, 1882 ff. [periodical supplement to *Acta Sanctorum*].

Anderson, A. O. & M. O., eds. & trs. *Adomnan's Life of Columba.* London & New York: Nelson, 1961.

Athanasius, *Vita S. Antonii.* (Migne, *Patrologia Graeca,* 26, 838-978). Translations available in Schaff, P. and Wace, H., eds., *A Select Library of Nicene and Post-Nicene Fathers of the Christian Church,* Second Series (New York, Oxford, London, 1892) Vol. IV, pp. 195-221; Deferrari, R. J., ed. *Early Christian Biographies* (The Fathers of the Church, Vol. 15), New York, 1952, pp. 127-216.

Baldwin, C. S. *Medieval Rhetoric and Poetic.* New York, 1928.

Battiscombe, C. F., ed. *The Relics of Saint Cuthbert,* Oxford Univ. Press, 1956 [invaluable scholarly studies of Cuthbert's world].

Bede, (see Plummer).

Bishop, E. *Liturgica Historica,* Papers on the Liturgy and Religious Life of the Western Church. Oxford, 1918.

Blair, P. H. *An Introduction to Anglo-Saxon England.* Cambridge, 1956 [Available in paperback].

—. *Roman Britain and Early England,* 55 B. C.—A. D. 871. A History of England, eds. C. Brooke and D. M. Smith; Vol. I. Edinburgh, 1963.

Bright, W. *Chapters of Early English Church History,* 3rd ed. Oxford, 1897. [A mine of interesting information, though later research qualifies some of its facts.]

Brown, G. B. *The Arts in Early England.* 6 vols. in 7. London, 1903-37.

Brown, T. J. *Evangeliorum Quattuor Codex Lindisfarnensis* [Lindisfarne Gospels]. See Kendrick, T. D.

Bruce-Mitford, R. L. S. *Evangeliorum Quattuor Codex Lindisfarnensis* [Lindisfarne Gospels]. See Kendrick, T. D.

Butler, E. C. *Benedictine Monachism*, Studies in Benedictine Life and Rule. New York, 1961, reprint.

Chadwick, H. M. *The Origin of the English Nation.* Cambridge, 1924.

—. *Studies on Anglo-Saxon Institutions.* New York: Russell & Russell, reprint, 1963.

— *et al. Studies in Early British History.* Cambridge, 1959.

Chadwick, N. *The Age of the Saints in the Early Celtic Church.* Oxford Univ. Press, 1961.

—. *Poetry and Letters in Early Christian Gaul.* London, 1955.

—, Jackson, K., *et. al. Celt and Saxon*, Studies in the Early British Border. Cambridge, 1963.

—, *et. al. Studies in the Early British Church.* Cambridge, 1958.

Clapham, A. W. *English Romanesque Architecture Before the Conquest.* Oxford, 1930.

Clavis Patrum Latinorum. See Dekkers.

Clemoes, P., ed. *The Anglo-Saxons*: Studies in some Aspects of their History and Culture Presented to Bruce Dickins. London, 1959.

Colgrave, B. "The Earliest Saints' Lives Written in England," *Proceedings of the British Academy*, 44 (1958) 35-60. [A classic on the subject, it is also published separately by Oxford University Press, 1959.]

—, ed. and tr. *The Life of Bishop Wilfrid by Eddius Stephanus.* Cambridge, 1927.

—, ed. and tr. *Two Lives of Saint Cuthbert*, a life by an anonymous monk of Lindisfarne and Bede's prose life. Cambridge, 1940.

—, ed. and tr. *Felix's Life of Saint Guthlac.* Cambridge, 1956.

Collingwood, R. G., and Myres, J. N. L. *Roman Britain and the English Settlements.* Oxford, 2nd edition, 1945.

Corpus Christianorum. Series Latina. Turnhout, 1953 ff. [Meant eventually to replace Migne, *Patrologia Latina.*]

Curtius, E. R. *European Literature and the Latin Middle Ages.* New York, 1953. [An invaluable work, available in paperback.]

Davis, N. & Wrenn, C. L., eds. *English and Medieval Studies*, presented to J. R. R. Tolkien. London, 1962.

Dawson, C. *The Making of Europe*, An Introduction to the History of European Unity. New York, 1934. [Available in paperback.]

Deanesly, M. *The Pre-Conquest Church in England.* London, 1961. [A stimulating survey, but disappointingly documented.]

Dekkers, E. and Gaar, E. *Clavis Patrum Latinorum*, 2nd ed. (*Sacris Erudiri*, Vol. III) Bruges, 1961. [Critical catalogue or prospectus for the *Corpus Christianorum*].

Delehaye, H. *The Legends of the Saints.* New York 1962. [A basic study, available now in paperback.]

Dolley, R. H., ed. *Anglo-Saxon Coins*; studies presented to F. M. Stenton. London, 1961.

Duckett, E. S. *Anglo-Saxon Saints and Scholars.* New York, Macmillan, 1947.

—. *The Wandering Saints of the Early Middle Ages.* New York: Norton, 1959.

Early English Text Society Publications. London: Original Series, 1864—date; Extra Series, 1867-1935.

Emerton, E., ed. and tr. *The Letters of St. Boniface.* Columbia University Press, 1940.

England and the Mediterranean Tradition; studies in art, history, and literature; edited by the Warburg and Courtauld Institutes, University of London.· Oxford Univ. Press, 1945.

Evagrius, *Vita S. Antonii* [Latin translation of Athanasius' Greek]. Migne, *Patrologia Graeca*, 26, 838-978.

Finberg, H. P. *The Early Charters of the West Midlands.* Leicester, 1961.

Fisher, E. R.. *The Greater Anglo-Saxon Churches*, An Architectural-historical Study. London, 1962.

Fox, C. F., ed. *The Early Cultures of North-West Europe* (H. M. Chadwick Memorial studies). Cambridge, 1950.

Girvan, R. *Beowulf and the Seventh Century.* London, 1935.

Godfrey, J. *The Church in Anglo-Saxon England.* Cambridge, 1962. [An excellent survey incorporating modern research.]

Green, C. *Sutton Hoo*; The Excavation of a Royal Ship-burial. London, 1963.

Haddan, A. W. and Stubbs, W., eds. *Councils and Ecclesiastical Documents Relating to Great Britain and Ireland.* Oxford, 1869-78. 3 vols. in 4. [original texts] [Far more use was made of this work than my Index has attempted to indicate].

Harden, D., ed. *Dark-Age Britain*; studies presented to E. T. Leeds. London, 1956.

Hessels, J. H., ed. *An Eighth Century Latin-Anglo-Saxon Glossary*. Cambridge, 1890. [Corpus Glossary].

—ed. *A Late-Eighth Century Latin-Anglo-Saxon Glossary*. Cambridge, 1906. [Leiden Glossary].

Hoare, F. R., ed. and tr. *The Western Fathers*; being the lives of SS. Martin of Tours, Ambrose, Augustine of Hippo, Honoratus of Arles, and Germanus of Auxerre. New York, 1954. [In translation.]

Hodgkin, R. H. *A History of the Anglo-Saxons*, Oxford Univ. Press, 3rd ed., 1952. [It is this edition, vol. II, which contains an Appendix, "The Sutton Hoo Ship-Burial," by Bruce-Mitford.]

Howorth, H. *The Golden Days of the Early English Church*, From the Arrival of Theodore to the Death of Bede. London, 1917. 3 vols. [Very interesting but facts need checking with later works].

Jones, C. W. *Saints' Lives and Chronicles in Early England*; together with the first English translation of *The oldest life of Pope St. Gregory the Great* by a monk of Whitby, and *The life of St. Guthlac of Crowland* by Felix. Cornell Univ. Press, 1947.

Jones, P. F., *A Concordance of the Historia Ecclesiastica of Bede*. Medieval Academy of America, 1929.

Kendrick, T. D., Brown, T. J., Bruce-Mitford, R. L. S., *et al.*, eds. *Evangeliorum Quattuor Codex Lindisfarnensis*: Musei Britannici Codex Cottonianus Nero D. iv [Lindisfarne Gospels]. Olten, Switzerland, Vol. I (facsimile), 1956; Vol. II (notes), 1960.

Kennedy, C. W. *The Earliest English Poetry*, A Critical Survey of the Poetry Written before the Norman Conquest. Oxford Univ. Press, 1943. [Many of his translations of Anglo-Saxon poetry are now available in paperback.]

Knowles, D. *The Monastic Order in England*; A History of its Development from the Times of St. Dunstan to the Fourth Lateran Council, 940-1216. Cambridge, 2nd ed., 1963.

Kramer, S. N. *Mythologies of the Ancient World*. New York, 1961. [Available in paperback].

Kurtz, B. P. "From St. Antony to St. Guthlac," *Univ. of Calif. Publications in Modern Philology*, XII (1926), 103-46.

Laistner, M. L. W. *Thought and Letters in Western Europe, A. D. 500 to 900*. rev. ed. Ithaca, 1957.

Leclercq, Jean. *The Love of Learning and the Desire for God*; a study of monastic culture. New York, 1961 [available in paperback].

Levison, W. *England and the Continent in the Eighth Century*. Oxford, 1946. [It would have been impossible for my Index to indicate the extent to which I used this book.]

—, ed. *Vitae Sancti Bonifatii Archiepiscopi Moguntini*. (Scriptores Rerum Germanicarum in usum scholarum ex Monumentis Germaniae Historicis separatim editi) Hannover and Leipzig, 1905, pp. 1-57.

—, ed. *Vita Willibrordi Archiepiscopi Traiectensis*. (MGH, *Script. Rer. Merov*. Hannover and Leipzig, 1920) VII, 81-141.

Lindsay, W. M., ed. *The Corpus Glossary*. Cambridge, 1921

Lloyd, J. E. *A History of Wales*, From the Earliest Times to the Edwardian Conquest. London and New York, 3rd ed., 1948.

Loomis, R. S., ed. *Arthurian Literature in the Middle Ages*. Oxford, 1959.

—. *Wales and the Arthurian Legend*. Cardiff, 1956.

Meissner, J. L. *The Celtic Church in England after the Synod of Whitby*. London, 1929.

Migne, J. P., ed. *Patrologiae cursus completus*. *Patrologia Latina*, Paris, 1844-80; *Patrologia Graeca*, Paris, 1857-1912. [But see *Corpus Christianorum*.]

Monumenta Germaniae Historica, ed. G. H. Pertz. Hannover and Berlin, 1826, ff.

Nennius. *Historia Brittonum*. See Wade-Evans, A. W.

Parry, T. *A History of Welsh Literature*. Oxford, 1955.

Plummer, C., ed. *Venerabilis Baedae Opera Historica*. Oxford, 1896; reprinted as two volumes in one, 1946. [Invaluable, though needs updating.]

Raby, F. J. *A History of Christian Latin Poetry from the Beginnings to the Close of the Middle Ages*. Oxford, 2nd ed., 1953.

Rolls Series (*Rerum Britannicarum Medii Aevi Scriptores*, or, Chronicles and Memorials of Great Britain and Ireland during the Middle Ages). London, 1858-1911.

Ryan, J. *Irish Monasticism; Origins and Early Development*. London and New York, 1931.

Sawyer, P. H. *The Age of the Vikings*. London, 1962.

Sisam, K. *Studies in the History of Old English Literature*. Oxford, 1953.

Stenton, F. M. *Anglo-Saxon England*. Oxford, 2nd ed., 1947. [My Index gives no indication of the extensive use I made of this book.]

Sulpicius Severus. *Life of St. Martin* (Migne, *Patrologia Latina*, 20,

159-175). Translation in Hoare, *The Western Fathers* [q.v.], pp. 10-44.

Surtees Society, Publications of the, Durham, 1835 ff.

Talbot, C. H., ed. and tr. *The Anglo-Saxon Missionaries in Germany*; Being the Lives of SS. Willibrord, Boniface, Sturm, Leoba, and Lebuin, together with the Hodoeporicon of St. Willibald and a Selection from the Correspondence of St. Boniface. New York, 1954 [In translation].

Tangl., M., ed. *S. Bonifatii et Lulli Epistolae.* (MGH, *Epp. Selectae*, Tomus I) Berlin, 2nd ed., 1955.

Vleeskruyer, R., ed. *The Life of St. Chad*; an old English homily. Amsterdam, 1953.

Vries, Jan de. *Heroic Song and Heroic Legend.* Oxford Univ. Press., 1963. [survey-study, available in paperback.]

Wade-Evans, A. W., tr. *Nennius's "History of the Britons," together with "The Annals of the Britons" and "Court pedigrees of Hywel the Good" also "The Story of the loss of Britain."* London, 1938.

Walker, G. S., ed. and tr. *Sancti Columbani Opera* (Scriptores Latini Hiberniae, Vol. 2). Dublin Institute for Advanced Studies, 1957.

Wallace-Hadrill, J. M. *The Long-Haired Kings*, and other studies in Frankish history. New York, 1962.

Whitelock, D. *The Audience of Beowulf.* Oxford, 1951.

—, ed. *English Historical Documents, c. 500-1042* (English Historical Documents, ed. D. C. Douglas. Vol. I) Oxford Univ. Press, 1955 [Invaluable collection of sources, in translation].

Williams, G. *An Introduction to Welsh Poetry*, From the Beginnings to the Sixteenth Century. Philadelphia, 1952.

Williams, I. *Lectures on Early Welsh Poetry.* Dublin Institute for Advanced Studies, 1954.

Wilson, R. M. *The Lost Literature of Medieval England.* London, 1952.

Wrenn, C. L., ed. *Beowulf*, with the Finnesburg fragment. London, 1958. [All my translations are made from this edition of the text.]

Wright, C. E. *The Cultivation of Saga in Anglo-Saxon England.* Edinburgh, 1939.

INDEX

For major biographical entries, e. g., Aidan, Benedict Biscop, Cuthbert, etc., the items have been arranged in chronological rather than paginal order.

An asterisk indicates that the work mentioned is fully identified in the Bibliographical Note.

INDEX

INDEX

INDEX

INDEX

INDEX